Modernist Wastes

Historicizing Modernism

Series Editors
Matthew Feldman, Professorial Fellow, Norwegian Study Centre, University of York; and Erik Tonning, Professor of British Literature and Culture, University of Bergen, Norway
Assistant Editor: David Tucker, Associate Lecturer, Goldsmiths College, University of London, UK

Editorial Board

Professor Chris Ackerley, Department of English, University of Otago, New Zealand; Professor Ron Bush, St. John's College, University of Oxford, UK; Dr Finn Fordham, Department of English, Royal Holloway, UK; Professor Steven Matthews, Department of English, University of Reading, UK; Dr Mark Nixon, Department of English, University of Reading, UK; Professor Shane Weller, Reader in Comparative Literature, University of Kent, UK; and Professor Janet Wilson, University of Northampton, UK.

Historicizing Modernism challenges traditional literary interpretations by taking an empirical approach to modernist writing: a direct response to new documentary sources made available over the last decade.
Informed by archival research, and working beyond the usual European/American avant-garde 1900–45 parameters, this series reassesses established readings of modernist writers by developing fresh views of intellectual contexts and working methods.

Series Titles

Arun Kolatkar and Literary Modernism in India, Laetitia Zecchini
British Literature and Classical Music, David Deutsch
Broadcasting in the Modernist Era, Matthew Feldman, Henry Mead and Erik Tonning
Charles Henri Ford, Alexander Howard

Chicago and the Making of American Modernism, Michelle E. Moore
Ezra Pound's Adams Cantos, David Ten Eyck
Ezra Pound's Eriugena, Mark Byron
Great War Modernisms and The New Age *Magazine,* Paul Jackson
James Joyce and Absolute Music, Michelle Witen
James Joyce and Catholicism, Chrissie van Mierlo
John Kasper and Ezra Pound, Alec Marsh
Katherine Mansfield and Literary Modernism, ed. by Janet Wilson, Gerri Kimber and Susan Reid
Late Modernism and the English Intelligencer, Alex Latter
The Life and Work of Thomas MacGreevy, Susan Schreibman
Literary Impressionism, Rebecca Bowler
Modern Manuscripts, Dirk Van Hulle
Modernism at the Microphone, Melissa Dinsman
Modernist Lives, Claire Battershill
The Politics of 1930s British Literature, Natasha Periyan
Reading Mina Loy's Autobiographies, Sandeep Parmar
Reframing Yeats, Charles Ivan Armstrong
Samuel Beckett and Arnold Geulincx, David Tucker
Samuel Beckett and the Bible, Iain Bailey
Samuel Beckett and Cinema, Anthony Paraskeva
Samuel Beckett's 'More Pricks than Kicks', John Pilling
Samuel Beckett's German Diaries 1936–1937, Mark Nixon
T. E. Hulme and the Ideological Politics of Early Modernism, Henry Mead
Virginia Woolf's Late Cultural Criticism, Alice Wood
Christian Modernism in an Age of Totalitarianism, Jonas Kurlberg
Samuel Beckett and Experimental Psychology, Joshua Powell
Samuel Beckett in Confinement, James Little
Katherine Mansfield: New Directions, ed. by Aimée Gasston, Gerri Kimber and Janet Wilson

Upcoming titles

Samuel Beckett and Science, Chris Ackerley

Modernist Wastes

Recovery, Re-Use and the Autobiographic in Elsa von-Freytag-Lorighoven and Djuna Barnes

Caroline Knighton

BLOOMSBURY ACADEMIC
LONDON • NEW YORK • OXFORD • NEW DELHI • SYDNEY

BLOOMSBURY ACADEMIC
Bloomsbury Publishing Plc
50 Bedford Square, London, WC1B 3DP, UK
1385 Broadway, New York, NY 10018, USA
29 Earlsfort Terrace, Dublin 2, Ireland

BLOOMSBURY, BLOOMSBURY ACADEMIC and the Diana logo
are trademarks of Bloomsbury Publishing Plc

First published in Great Britain 2020
This paperback edition first published in 2022

Copyright © Caroline Knighton, 2020

Caroline Knighton has asserted their right under the Copyright,
Designs and Patents Act, 1988, to be identified as Authors of this work.

For legal purposes the Acknowledgements on p. xv–xvi constitute
an extension of this copyright page.

Cover design: Eleanor Rose

All rights reserved. No part of this publication may be reproduced or transmitted
in any form or by any means, electronic or mechanical, including photocopying,
recording, or any information storage or retrieval system, without prior
permission in writing from the publishers.

The third party copyrighted material displayed in the pages of this book are done so on
the basis of fair use for the purposes of teaching, criticism, scholarship or research in
accordance with international copyright laws, and is not intended to infringe upon the
ownership rights of the original owners. Please contact the Publisher if you own
any of the work contained within the book as some copyright was difficult to
trace though every attempt was made to try and clear these for use.

Bloomsbury Publishing Plc does not have any control over, or responsibility for,
any third-party websites referred to or in this book. All internet addresses given
in this book were correct at the time of going to press. The author and publisher
regret any inconvenience caused if addresses have changed or sites have
ceased to exist, but can accept no responsibility for any such changes.

A catalogue record for this book is available from the British Library.

Library of Congress Control Number: 2020934293

ISBN:	HB:	978-1-3501-2902-3
	PB:	978-1-3502-4930-1
	ePDF:	978-1-3501-2903-0
	eBook:	978-1-3501-2904-7

Series: Historicizing Modernism

Typeset by Integra Software services Pvt. Ltd.

To find out more about our authors and books visit www.bloomsbury.com
and sign up for our newsletters.

To Margot and Kit,
And to James

Contents

List of figures	xi
Editorial preface to historicizing modernism	xiv
Acknowledgements	xv
List of abbreviations	xvii

Introduction: Textual mess and modernism's gendered wastes		1
	i. Modernism and Barnesean wastes	9
	ii. What is waste? Bodies, cities, texts	16
1	Stunning subjects and disruptive body practices	31
	i. Marginality and modernity: Critical histories of exclusion and the case of Baroness Elsa von Freytag-Loringhoven	37
	ii. Gods, mutts and Readymades: 'America's comfort – sanitation!'	49
	iii. Calculated containment: New Women and the New York Dada mecanamorphic portraits	67
	iv. 'Not me. Not that': The Baroness Elsa von Freytag-Loringhoven and the grotesque protrusions of modernism's marginalia	84
2	Art dazzle: Modelling, performance and the Baroness's self-representational practices	99
	i. Self-Representational practices, collage and the Baroness's Dada portraits	105
	ii. Making mischief, or looking through a glass dynamically	116
	iii. Chimera in the croquis class: Spectacle, performance and the Baroness's body-work	131
	iv. Übermarionettes and living statues	145
3	'Not dead': Djuna Barnes's mature autobiographic poetics	157
	i. 'This generations vulgarity': Djuna Barnes and the 'biographic impulse'	161

| | ii. Textual waste and the structural patterns of Djuna Barnes's re-made modernism | 172 |
| | iii. 'Circulation in the theme': Repetition, refrain and variation across the Patchin Place cycles | 179 |

4	Troubling structures: Inner time and the 'Baroness Elsa' manuscript	195
	i. The Baroness's interruptive poetics	196
	ii. Cutting, stitching, weaving: Ida-Marie's 'strange handiwork'	205
	iii. Alexis Carrel and *Nightwood*'s troubling structures	213
	iv. Denying the called response: Mothers, daughters and *The Antiphon*	228

Coda: Modernism recovered	239
Notes	245
Bibliography	280
Index	292

List of figures

1. Djuna Barnes and Elsa von Freytag-Loringhoven on the beach at Le Crotay *c.* 1926. Elsa von Freytag-Loringhoven Papers. Special Collections, University of Maryland at College Park Libraries — xviii
2. Man Ray, letter to Tristan Tzara with film still of Elsa von Freytag-Loringhoven posing. Postmarked 8 June 1921. Bibliotèque litéraire Jacques Doucet, Paris, Man Ray Trust/ADAGP, Paris and DACS, London, 2019 — 45
3. Alfred Stieglitz, *Fountain* by R. Mutt. The Blind Man (No. 2), May 1917. Philadelphia Museum of Art: The Louise and Walter Arensberg Collection, 1950. (1950-134-1053) © 2019. Photo The Philadelphia Museum of Art/Art Resource/Scala, Florence — 55
4. Elsa von Freytag-Loringhoven and Morton Schamberg, *God,* 1917. Philadelphia Museum of Art: The Louise and Walter Arensberg Collection, 1950. (1950-134-182) — 63
5. Elsa von Freytag-Loringhoven, *Forgotten – Like this Parapluie – I am by you, Faithless Bernice, c.* 1924. Gouache and ink. Elsa von Freytag-Loringhoven Papers. Special Collections, University of Maryland at College Park Libraries — 66
6. Francis Picabia, *Les Saint des saints.* From *291,* No. 5–6, July–August 1915. © RMN-Grand Palais/Francis Picabia — 71
7. Francis Picabia, *Portriat d'une jeune fille Américaine dans l'état de nudité.* From *291,* No. 5–6, July–August 1915 © RMN-Grand Palais/Francis Picabia — 73
8. Francis Picabia, *La Fille Née sans Mère c.* 1914–15 ink on paper, 10 ½ × 8 ½ in. Alfred Steiglitz Collection, 1949 (59.70.18). New York Metropolitan Museum of Art. © 2019. Image copyright The Metropolitan Museum of Art/Art Resource/Scala, Florence — 77
9. Marius de Zayas, *ELLE*; From 291, No. 9, 1915. © RMN-Grand Palais/Marius de Zayas — 80
10. Francis Picabia *Voilà Elle.* From 291, No. 9, 1915. © RMN-Grand Palais/Francis Picabia — 81

11 International News Photography, *Baroness von Freytag-Loringhoven working as a model.* 7 December 1915. Bettman/Corbis photo agency   83
12 Elsa von Freytag-Loringhoven, *Portrait of Berenice Abbot c.* 1923. Mixed media collage of synthetic materials, cellophane, metal foils, paper, stones, metal objects, cloth, paint, etc., 8 ⅝ × 9 ¼ in. New York, Museum of Modern Art (MoMA). From the collection of Mary Louise Reynolds. 336.19 © 2019. Digital image, The Museum of Modern Art, New York/Scala, Florence   108
13 International News Photography, *Baroness von Freytag-Loringhoven working as a model.* 7 December 1915. Bettman/Corbis photo agency   114
14 Elsa von Freytag-Loringhoven, *Portrait of Marcel Duchamp, c.* 1920. Photograph by Charles Sheeler. Bluff Collection, photograph courtesy Francis M. Naumann Fine Art, New York   118
15 Man Ray and Marcel Duchamp, *Rrose Sélavy*, 1921. © Man Ray 2015 Trust/ADAGP, Paris and DACS, London 2019   119
16 Man Ray, *Marcel Duchamp*, 1916. © Succession Marcel Duchamp/ADAGP, Paris and DACS, London 2019/© Man Ray Trust/ADAGP   120
17 Elsa von Freytag-Loringhoven, letter to Sarah Freedman, undated. Black ink on paper. Previously unpublished. Elsa von Freytag-Loringhoven Papers. Special Collections, University of Maryland at College Park Libraries   137
18 Elsa von Freytag-Loringhoven, Advertisement for 'Baroness Croquis' Modelling School, 1927. Elsa von Freytag-Loringhoven Papers. Special Collections, University of Maryland at College Park Libraries   138
19 Theresa Bernstein, *Woman with a Parrot c.* 1917. Oil on canvas, 40 × 25 inches. Formally of the Martin and Edith Stein Collection   140
20 Theresa Bernstein, *Elsa von Freytag-Loringhoven* (*c.* 1917). Oil. 12 × 9 inches. Photograph courtesy Francis M. Naumann Fine Art, New York   142
21 Djuna Barnes 'Work in Progress: Rite of Spring'. Typescript, undated. Special Collections, The University of Maryland at College Park Libraries   183
22 Elsa von Freytag-Loringhoven, 'Memory Stench', handwritten draft. Ink on paper. Previously unpublished. Elsa von Freytag-Loroinghoven Papers. Special Collections, University of Maryland at College Park Libraries   194

23 Djuna Barnes, 'Baroness Elsa' Preface. Typed and annotated page dated 7 December 1924. Elsa von Freytag-Loroinghoven Papers. Special Collections, University of Maryland at College Park Libraries 198

24 Elsa von Freytag-Loringhoven handwritten letter to Djuna Barnes, *c.* 1924. Elsa von Freytag-Loroinghoven Papers. Special Collections, University of Maryland at College Park Libraries 204

25 Elsa von Freytag-Loringhoven handwritten letter to Djuna Barnes, 12 July 1924. Elsa von Freytag-Loroinghoven Papers. Special Collections, University of Maryland at College Park Libraries 211

Editorial preface to historicizing modernism

This book series is devoted to the analysis of late nineteenth- to twentieth-century literary modernism within its historical contexts. *Historicizing Modernism* therefore stresses empirical accuracy and the value of primary sources (such as letters, diaries, notes, drafts, marginalia or other archival materials) in developing monographs and edited collections on modernist literature. This may take a number of forms, such as manuscript study and genetic criticism, documenting interrelated historical contexts and ideas, and exploring biographical information. To date, no book series has fully laid claim to this interdisciplinary, source-based territory for modern literature. While the series addresses itself to a range of key authors, it also highlights the importance of non-canonical writers with a view to establishing broader intellectual genealogies of modernism. Furthermore, while the series is weighted towards the English-speaking world, studies of non-Anglophone modernists whose writings are open to fresh historical exploration are also included.

The key aim of the series is to reach beyond the familiar rhetoric of intellectual and artistic 'autonomy' employed by many modernists and their critical commentators. Such rhetorical moves can and should themselves be historically situated and reintegrated into the complex continuum of individual literary practices. It is our intent that the series' emphasis upon the contested self-definitions of modernist writers, thinkers and critics may, in turn, prompt various reconsiderations of the boundaries delimiting the concept 'modernism' itself. Indeed, the concept of 'historicizing' is itself debated across its volumes, and the series by no means discourages more theoretically informed approaches. On the contrary, the editors hope that the historical specificity encouraged by *Historicizing Modernism* may inspire a range of fundamental critiques along the way.

Matthew Feldman
Erik Tonning

Acknowledgements

This book was a project in three parts, and at each stage I have been incredibly fortunate to have had the support and insight of a great many wonderful people. Special thanks go to my PhD supervisor Jo Winning, who taught me to love my own messy working practices, and was so generous with her time and wisdom over the course of my doctoral research. Thanks also to my examiners, Tim Armstrong and Alex Goody, who not only encouraged me to consider developing my thesis into a book project, but also reached out and offered advice and support in the intervening years.

Completion of this project would not have been possible without the Arts and Humanities Research Council, which funded my three years of doctoral study and enabled my research trip to the Djuna Barnes and Elsa von Freytag-Loringhoven archives held at the University of Maryland. I was particularly touched by the enthusiasm and interest demonstrated by Beth Alvarez, then curator of Literary Manuscripts in Special Collections, University of Maryland Libraries in assisting me with my research. My thanks also to her successor, Amber Kohl, for all her help with the final stages of the project. I would also like to express my gratitude to the Author's League Fund and St Brides Church, London, for granting me permission to cite from the unpublished manuscripts and correspondence of Djuna Barnes, and to Francis Naumann for permission to reproduce images from his collection. Thanks are also due to the editorial team at Bloomsbury, especially to Lucy Brown, Ben Doyle and David Avital; to the enthusiasm and encouragement expressed by the Historicizing Modernism editorial board; and especially to series editors, Matthew Feldman and Erik Tonning.

To all of my friends and family who listened, counselled and cajoled, I am grateful to you all. To Sam and Michael in particular, thank you for turning up at all the right moments to remind me to get on with it, and to Becky, who was there every day. I owe a debt of gratitude to my wonderful siblings Anna-Marie and William, and to my parents Moira and Chris whose love, support and belief in me and this project have been humbling. Finally, I would like to acknowledge the patience and grace with which my children Margot and Kit accepted this intrusion into their young lives, and to express my love and deepest thanks to my partner James, who has championed me through each stage of this project, and without whom it would never have been possible.

List of abbreviations

Djuna Barnes

A	*The Antiphon*
CP	*Collected Poems with Notes toward the Memoirs*
DB Papers	*The Papers of Djuna Barnes*
N	*Nightwood*
R	*Ryder*

Elsa von Freytag-Loringhoven

BS	*Body Sweats: The Uncensored Writings of Elsa von Freytag-Loringhoven*
EvFL Papers	*The Papers of Elsa von Freytag-Loringhoven*

Figure 1 Djuna Barnes and Elsa von Freytag-Loringhoven on the beach at Le Crotay *c.* 1926. Elsa von Freytag-Loringhoven Papers. Special Collections, University of Maryland at College Park Libraries.

Introduction: Textual mess and modernism's gendered wastes

Wearing the lip of a burnished coal scuttle for a helmet strapped to her head with a scarlet belt which buckled under the chin, Christmas tree baubles of yellow and red as earrings, a tea strainer about her neck, a short yellow skirt barely covering her legs, and over the precision of her breasts a single length of black lace she would walk the city.

Djuna Barnes, 'Baroness Elsa' c. 1933

She does have a tendency to save everything that is on a piece of paper, and to compound the problem she is forever making notations on anything in sight, and it then must be saved for future reference. Poems on grocery lists. All these papers are just piled up on her desk in no apparent order. She said there are many good poems buried under the heaps and scraps, but a mine-detector will be needed to find anything.

Hank O'Neal, The Barnes Diaries

It is a sunny afternoon in Normandy in May 1926. Two women stand on a beach, their shadows hitting the sand at a sharp angle. Their bodies inclined towards one another, hips cocked, their open poses mirror one another as they turn, squinting in the sun, to face the camera. The taller woman is more immediately recognizable as the recalcitrant modernist Djuna Barnes (1892–1982), her smart tweeds and silk blouse conforming to the enduring image of her as a figure of supreme Left Bank expatriate elegance in the 1920s and '30s. In a fashionable drop-waist dress and boxy cloche hat, her smiling and smartly dressed companion is, in fact, the iconoclastic and ultra-provocative avant-garde visual artist, poet and performer the Baroness Elsa von Freytag-Loringhoven (1874–1927), rather more conventionally attired than we might expect to find her.

Taken in 1926, just a year before the Baroness's untimely death and ten years before the publication of Barnes's landmark novel, *Nightwood*, the photograph lacks some of the more sensational elements of the Baroness's costume described by Barnes above and reiterated across the accounts of William Carlos Williams, Margaret Anderson and Claude McKay, amongst others. Nevertheless, in the handmade earrings, bangles, rings and unusual purse on a beaded string we can certainly trace the patterns of recovery and re-use that informed the Baroness's waste-based art practice and sensational modes of self-display, of the objects that she gleaned from unexpected places and recombined in startling new forms.

In this respect the beach is a rather appropriate place to find the Baroness. We might easily imagine her combing the shoreline for odd bits of flotsam and jetsam just as she had earlier performed her own form of urban mudlarking, finding treasures where others only saw trash. Tellingly, in trying to recapture a sense of the Baroness some years later, Barnes would return to this seaside excursion, recreating a particularly macabre scene to hone in on the older woman's capacity for excess, her tendency to tip past the point of 'proper' aesthetic contemplation into the more grotesquely visceral:

> Where appreciation should stop, she carried it grossly over into appreciation for the decay in a dog dead on the beach of La Crotois [*sic*]. She examined that body with the eye of the connoisseur which in her father had stopped at plumbing and in her mother had stopped at Goethe, to see what was exact and perfect and complete in decay. It made her horrible as a consequence to the person accompanying her [...] she, gifted with the generosity of the curious, brought back, to people who did not want to hear, the most "gruesome" details of her wanderings by the beach or in the undergrowth, so that her excess of "culture" estranged her, just as her excess of disease, inborn and running about her inner structure, brought her to a suppuration that she considered a visitation as important and as noteworthy of study, as the problem which makes men dedicate their lives to surgery.[1]

Slipping between a description of the Baroness's aesthetic interest in the forms and processes of decay and of an identification of the Baroness herself as an excessive and contaminating force, Barnes draws attention not only to the fundamental role of waste in shaping the Baroness's art practice, but also to certain anxieties provoked by the material and metaphorical functioning of waste or excess, anxieties that this book positions as of central importance in crystallizing definitions of literary modernism, techno-industrial modernity and early twentieth-century commodity capitalism.

The vivid depiction of the Baroness bringing herself to a suppuration as she transgressed the boundaries of propriety, of the body and of the historical avant-garde is a wonderfully evocative way of visualizing the Baroness's embodied art practice, of her mode of discharging material from herself in her art and writing. It also points to a kind of excessive over-production that has characterized responses to Barnes's own writing practices. From the extensive correspondence between Djuna Barnes and attentive reader Emily Holmes Coleman chronicling the gestation of Barnes's 1936 novel *Nightwood*, to the frequently referenced editorial interventions of T.S. Eliot and the introduction of Hank O'Neal into Barnes's Patchin Place apartment in 1978, tensions between notions of waste and efficiency, obfuscation and communication, structure and disintegration, have played a persistent role in organizing Barnes's texts, framing responses to her *oeuvre*, and of positioning Barnes in relation to modernist histories. Critical engagements with Barnes's texts in this respect have, until recently, treated waste in almost exclusively negative terms, as something messy, unproductive and in need of clearing up.

In its material contexts, anxieties over waste in relation to the Barnes corpus have frequently fallen under an editorial or authorial concern with questions of *textual mess*. As O'Neal's recollections suggest, Barnes's writing practice was densely accumulative and retentive, her own personal archive system of collecting everything, in no particular order, frustrating attempts to immediately distinguish the textually valuable – such as a lost draft of a late poem – from the 'heaps and scraps' that a more efficient system would have quickly identified *as waste* and disposed of accordingly. O'Neal's recovery of these grocery lists, often interrupted by lines of poetry or recurring images from the *Creatures in an Alphabet* series, somewhat undermines his own frustrated identification of them as rubbish, and his inclusion of photographic reproductions of these most quotidian and ephemeral of items in his memoir is telling.[2]

Similarly, the correspondence between Barnes, Coleman and Eliot regarding the 'pulling together' of the manuscripts for both *Nightwood* and the later verse tragedy *The Antiphon* reiterates the difficulties presented by these 'excessive' manuscripts: the unfocused nature of their narrative structure and plotting, the sometimes-insurmountable obscurity of Barnes's language, and the sheer volume of unfiltered material presented in these successive drafts. As Eliot put it in one of the several exasperated letters exchanged during the fraught period of *The Antiphon*'s production:

> It seems to me what is needed is much more drastic cutting, twelve to fifteen pages. […] I know it is painful to sacrifice what one feels to be good lines, but you had to cut a good deal, you will remember, out of "Nightwood", stuff which

was quite good enough to stay in, except that there was *too much of it*, and with a play, still more than with prose fiction form, it is undesirable far to overstep the limits of the essential. Will you have another shot at it?[3]

Eliot's concern for Barnes's somewhat excessive textual production and her apparent reluctance to dispose of extraneous material is supported by the sheer volume of Barnes's papers, now collected at the Special Collections, University of Maryland.[4] Rather than streamlining, having 'another shot' at polishing a manuscript invariably generated more of this textual mess, as is well documented through the archived drafts and lengthy correspondence with editors and early readers in relation to *Nightwood* (1936), *The Antiphon* (1958), the posthumously published Patchin Place poetry and *Creatures in an Alphabet* (1982).

In addition to the extensive revisions of individual passages, poems, poetic cycles or whole manuscripts undertaken by Barnes in the production of her texts, the archived textual material also draws attention to the author's tendency to mess up the printed page – to intervene, interrupt and rupture her own texts and the letters she received through dense and detailed annotation. Concurrent with broader shifts in critical and archival practice brought about by a rapid expansion of digital technologies in the twenty-first century charted recently by J. Matthew Huculak, recent scholarship of Barnes and her contemporaries has demonstrated a renewed interest in this textual waste, turning increasingly to manuscripts, marginalia, correspondence and other ephemera in developing critical examinations of the contexts and processes involved in twentieth-century literary production and the historicization of modernism.[5]

In this respect, as our definitions of modernist literary modes and methods of analysis have expanded, we have perhaps come to accommodate mess, to embrace it even as a sign of the discontinuities, fragmentation and rupture so closely tied to the experience of techno-industrial modernity, and to formal and stylistic elements of high modernist aesthetics. As the recent rise of critical interest in modernist periodical culture suggests, much of what the mid-century anthologized as modernism was worked out in the pages of little magazines and journals, itself a vast and messy terrain mixing high and low, canonical and forgotten in a way that somewhat belies the notion of a coherent modernist paradigm insulated from the process and mechanisms of modernity and mass-culture.[6] Expanding our sense of which textual objects are included in our definitions of modernism, and introducing more collaborative forms of scholarship, the vast range of material introduced by periodical studies and the expansion of media and digital technologies to process these complex topographies have ushered in new methodologies and analytic tools which have certainly shifted our relationship to textual mess in recent decades.

Intersecting with interdisciplinary research being undertaken in the emergent field of discard studies, this book aims to reconsider certain forms and functions of waste within the material and cultural contexts of early twentieth-century modernity, literary modernism and the historical avant-garde. In dialogue with work that has identified the prescient need to ask questions about the economic, environmental and cultural factors involved in determining what and how we throw out, *Modernist Wastes* breaks new ground in identifying some of the ways in which waste in its broadest sense was instrumental in shaping aesthetic or ideational categories of the early twentieth century, and of its recurrence as a disruptive textual strategy in relation to them. A grounding proposition in my thinking throughout this project has been that critical claims for modernism's 'newness' are worked out in relation to waste, to the critical processes of its identification, regulation and removal.

Waste, I want to suggest in the first instance, offers feminist scholars in particular a useful structural model for addressing the processes of containment and exclusion that shaped (early, male-centred) modernist canons, and of organizing projects of critical recovery now. Secondly, while the action involved in the identification, regulation and repudiation of waste illuminates issues relating to modernism, gender and canonicity, attention to its structural functioning also allows us to consider the disruptive potential of such recuperative gestures, illuminating both the work done by current feminist scholarship, and of deliberate textual strategies that self-consciously staged recovery and re-use as a way of complicating early critical formulations of modernism as a closed or internally coherent system.

Such work has introduced compelling points of departure for a discussion of textual mess as a generative and illuminating aspect of Barnes's writing practices and of the somewhat vexing relationship between modernism and literary history that is staged in her stylistic recovery and re-use of the outmoded and archaic, the used and devalued, and in the formal patterns of return and repetition structuring her autobiographic poetics. Writing to Coleman towards the end of 1937 Barnes makes explicit connections between the messy textuality of her writing practices and the tensions between disclosure and more complex narrative structures, cautioning that 'One must not betray that place, or it will heal up, and you'll know nothing more of it clearly'.[7] Paradoxically, the healed wound, and by extension the 'sealed' text under Barnes's treatment, produces a kind of finality that interferes with more complex processes of comprehension, ones that instead require modes of narrative and textual openness analogous to the open wound.

More recently, Julie Taylor and Daniella Caselli have both identified this passage as offering compelling insights into the complex relationships between personal testimony, modernist art and the unsettling patterns of repetition and return at work across the Barnes corpus. While Taylor uses trauma theory to read these patterns as offering 'fascinating insights into the affective complexities of childhood trauma [and] a playful and pleasurable "witnessing" of the literary past', Caselli positions this openness as an essential feature of Barnes's 'illegitimate poetics', facilitating the recovery and re-use of material which are 'never treated as a way of reshaping tradition [...] but as a form of collusion with a past which, far from nostalgically pure, is tainting and compromising'.[8] Intersecting with these readings, I want to suggest that attention to the structural forms and functions of waste provides a useful basis for reading Barnes's messy (inter)textuality, of the patterns of her autobiographic poetics and of anxieties bound up with modernism's relationship to the past and to its own historic moment.

Whether manifesting in Coleman's repeated criticisms of *Nightwood*'s lack of an 'essential unity' or the extensive editorial streamlining and re-structuring of her major texts, such notions of textual mess or excess were invariably viewed negatively by her contemporaries, even as they celebrated her work. In these critical contexts, waste is consistently classified as inefficient, mess as confusing: both should be eliminated.[9] In one particularly direct letter from 1935 Coleman writes 'you have pulled the book together, and made it more of a constructional unity; it was nothing before (from the point of view of a work of art); it was a mess'.[10] While her editors worked to minimize instances of excessive textual production, in terms of both suggesting cuts to 'bloated' manuscripts and expressing concern for Barnes's seemingly chaotic writing practice, Coleman's comments also point to broader correlations between notions of 'mess' and definitions of 'art' itself. Emphasizing a rhetoric of efficiency, clarity and order, art under Coleman's treatment is 'constructional unity'; it must communicate, and it will not accommodate mess.

Certainly, such concerns were not lost on the author herself. Describing her juvenilia as 'utterly wasteful', lamenting the time wasted not working on 'serious' literary projects, and making frequent reference to the messy materiality of her writing practice, Barnes's letters are acutely conscious of questions of efficiency and waste.[11] In a letter accompanying an early completed draft of *The Antiphon* sent to Eliot at Faber and Faber, Barnes's apologies for the 'state of the manuscript' take into account the 'shape' of the text and the appearance of a script peppered with spelling and grammatical errors, as well as the author's concerns over the inefficiency of her working practice.[12] However, alongside a clearly articulated sense of this material messiness, Barnes's letters also direct us to a consideration of waste in its more symbolic contexts, as that which has been cast out or rejected. Writing to Natalie Barney in 1963, Barnes wryly highlights an awareness of her own increasingly peripheral position in relation to crystallizing definitions of literary modernism. She writes:

> My remarks about my writing may have misled you. I haven't the faintest idea of being a "best seller" (wouldn't you know, Ryder was!) [...] There is not a person in the literary world who has not heard of, read and some stolen form NIGHTWOOD. The paradox that is [sic] in spite of all the critical work flooding the press since 1963, not three or four have mentioned my name. I am the "most famous unknown of the century!" I cannot account for it, unless it is that my talent is my character, my character my talent, and both an estrangement.[13]

While acknowledging the digestion and incorporation of her work into twentieth-century literary culture, Barnes suggests that her identity as a named author can thus only operate as a form of estrangement, cut off and cast out from the sanctioned roll-call of approved (and, in 1963, predominately male) representatives of high modernist aesthetics.

Barnes's reputation as an infamous unknown persists despite the considerable amount of critical attention that her work now receives from a robust community of international Barnes scholars within the expanding and intersecting fields of literary modernism and cultural histories of modernity.[14] Part of what is so compelling about this particular mode of identifying her as one of many significant 'forgotten female modernists' is the short-hand through which the gendered dimension of decades of critical neglect is brought to bear on current discussions. In terms set out by Bridget Elliott and Jo-Ann Wallace in their broad study of women in modernism, such a formulation evokes both the discourse of modernism, and a feminist strategy of recovery, which is to say it identifies the processes of exclusion as it challenges and expands such canonical formations through its recuperative gestures.[15]

If Barnes's 'estranged' position here can be interpreted on one level as the regulation or removal of a set of literary practices somewhat compromised by their proximity to the tainted or corrupting from crystallizing formations of literary modernism that is some way analogous to the exclusion of 'mess' from Coleman's definition of Art, then the systematically marginalized condition of the Baroness Elsa von Freytag-Loringhoven certainly raises pertinent questions regarding the role played by notions of efficiency, unity, coherence and a rejection of waste in both its material and symbolic forms in the definition, regulation and digestion of modernist and avant-garde practices.[16]

Almost entirely absent from early critical histories of twentieth-century avant-garde activity, the Baroness developed a corporeal, performative visual art practice in which pilfered commodity goods and used trash items or objects gleaned from the gutters of New York city were combined alongside organic material in multi-media collages, complex Readymade sculptural assemblages and a uniquely provocative mode of hand-made costuming and display. Directly relating her modes of self-display and her collage practices Barnes recalls the Baroness as:

> One of the most astonishing figures of early Greenwich Village life. She had a head like a Roman emperor's, short, sometimes razored, once shellacked, red hair. She batiqued her tailored suites, made earrings from grave-flowers and Christmas tree decorations, and had a voice and a constitution of iron. She kept a skeleton by her bed and did portraits of her past in feathers, paint, and glass beads. She did a 'portrait' of Marcel Duchamp, a champagne glass out of which arose tufts of flowing feathers. She was very difficult to know. She thought nothing of breaking your front window with a brick if you would not answer the door, but after you answered, it was worth to hear her recite, in beautiful periods, Hamlet and Goethe. She would have been the most sought after woman in Paris had she been wealthy. She knew it, for Paris is a city that makes lions of other nations *détraqués*, if they can do it in style; she could not.[17]

Applying the tin-cans, curtain rings and cutlery that she collected directly to her body in an elaborate and outlandish form of *couture d'ordures,* the Baroness reproduced her own body as a living, moving and resolutely handmade Dada assemblage, one that unpicked the elegant and the 'high' through the homespun and her own 'junk stitching'. As Barnes captures here, the Baroness's modes of self-display, her collecting practices and her collage aesthetic are absolutely interwoven within this waste-based production, and the 'difficulty' of her person and her work is experienced as similarly inseparable as she paraded through the private and public spaces of New York in the 1910s and early 1920s.[18] Her sexually explicit and formally challenging poetry was widely published across a range of little magazines including *Transition, The Little Review* and *Broom,* and yet until the re-processing of the archived materials, these original manuscripts and an experimental autobiography remained buried within the Djuna Barnes Papers, and access to the Baroness's writings was thus severely restricted.

While recent scholarship including a detailed biography, a collection of the Baroness's poetry and a range of art-historical and literary studies have certainly done much to ensure that the Baroness 'has moved from the peripheries of New York Dada to occupy a central position', her containment within the margins of modernist histories is, nevertheless, of central interest to this book.[19] Indeed, alongside the actual marginalization of the historical figure of the Baroness (and her lost, misattributed or forgotten work), the references to her as an entertaining and colourful footnote in the memoirs and letters of her contemporaries are often framed through a vocabulary fixated with images of filth, waste and mess. Demonstrating a telling slippage between a discussion of the materiality of her art practice – of the ways in which she worked *with* waste – and an over-identification of the Baroness *as* a polluting form of waste herself, these footnotes and anecdotes in the 'margins' of modernism are revealing as to the full spectrum of figurative or symbolic uses to which concepts of waste were put to work in the specifically American contexts of the early decades of the twentieth century. What might oppositions between efficiency, unity, coherence and mess have to do with the definition, regulation and digestion of modernist poetics and practices? What are the particular anxieties provoked by both Barnes's and the Baroness's work in this respect and do they in fact go considerably further than concern over textual or material messiness? Does modernism have a problem with waste?

i. Modernism and Barnesean wastes

"Why not rest? Why not put the pen away?
Doctor O'Conner, Nightwood

While the letters between Barnes and her various friends, readers and editors testify repeatedly to the messy materiality of a writing practice which compulsively produced textual waste in the form of multiple drafts, annotated manuscripts and handwritten sheets which she collected and kept, the relationship of the Barnes corpus and Barnesean aesthetics to ideas of 'waste' and 'mess' goes considerably further than her own excessive production.

On a figurative level, Barnes's poetry and fiction appear flooded with images of waste: Sophia Ryder's collaged walls, covered with 'multitudinous and multifarious crayons, lithographs and engravings' (*R*: 13); the decaying interiors and broken or abandoned objects that litter *Nightwood*, *The Antiphon* and the early poetry providing the colourful backdrop for a host of marginalized and underworld figures to move through.[20] Objects and character are intimately bound together in this respect. To just take *Nightwood* as an example, alongside the water-stained books, rusty forceps, broken scalpels, empty perfume bottles and 'swill-pail [...] brimming with abominations' (*N*: 116) cluttering the room of the excessively loquacious Doctor Matthew Mighty Grain of Salt Dante O'Connor, we have Nora, host of the strangest kind of '"pauper's" salon' tangled with weeds and ruined gardens where 'one felt that early American history was being re-enacted' (*N*: 77–78). Counterpointing Nora's deep connection to history and its ghostly recurrence coming forward in her, there is Felix – fixated by lineage, blood and his own fraudulent ancestry, someone so pained by his sense of absent history that he has created his own, not unlike 'the squatter' Jenny Petheridge, the faintly repellent collector of other people's lost objects.

Centrally, of course, we have Robin herself, 'the infected carrier of the past [...] we feel that we could eat her, she who is eaten death returning' (*N*: 60). Surrounded by a 'confusion of potted plants, exotic palms and cut flowers', our introduction to 'la Somnambule' in the *Hotel Récamier* significantly moves us from more figurative treatments of waste to a reflection on its structural patterns:

> The perfume that her body inhaled was of the quality of that earth-flesh, fungi, which smells of captured dampness and yet is so dry, overcast with the odour of oil of amber, which is an inner malady of the sea, making her seem as if she had invaded a sleep cautious and entire. Her flesh was the texture of plant life, and beneath it one sensed a frame, broad, porous and sleep-worn, as if sleep were a decay fishing her beneath the visible surface. About her head there was an effulgence as of phosphorous glowing about the circumference of a body of water – as if her life lay through her in ungainly luminous deteriorations – the troubling structure of the born somnambule, who lives in two worlds – meet of child and desperado. (*N*: 55–56)

The miasmic qualities of the passage are striking, especially in their emphasis on the olfactory and the liquid. Objects that were clearly defined and separate start to lose their shape here, their edges blurring and becoming indistinct as they become corrupted by this creeping 'inner malady'. Accumulating clauses, the structure of the sentence itself starts to disintegrate, swelling to accommodate these luminous deteriorations.

The 'troubling structure' that Barnes establishes in this passage forms the focus of my discussion of the recurrence of the 'failed' collaborative 'Baroness

Elsa' project in the final chapter. Nevertheless, its presence is felt across *Modernist Wastes* in the disruptive effect of one order's intrusion into another – the involuntary recurrence of the low in the high, the past in the present, of matter out of place that characterizes the Baroness's art practice and stands as a useful textual analogue for the patterns of return, refrain and variation structuring Barnes's writing.

Anachronistic, stylistically challenging and linguistically perverse, Barnes's texts not only repeat themselves in a series of intertextual echoes – like the 'telltale rings of the oak' that come forward in *Ryder*, *Nightwood* and the Patchin Place poetry, the late verse tragedy *The Antiphon* recuperates narrative material from the 1928 novel *Ryder* – but stage the 'illegitimate' return of antiquated language, estranged literary history and an aping of outmoded illustrative techniques, as Caselli has described. From the imitation woodcut illustrations and dripping Beardsleyesque ink drawings that Barnes produced as visual accompaniments to so much of her poetry and prose, through parodies of Chaucerian verse to the loosely Jacobean verse structures reanimated by *The Antiphon*, the Barnes corpus refuses to 'make it new' but returns to the used and devalued, to the wastes of literary tradition and history.

Intimately linked to the embodied and repetitive nature of her 'wounded' poetics, the Barnes corpus stages intertextual reverberations and returns textual waste as a means of 'troubling' notions of linearity, genealogy and tradition, and exposes such constructions as inauthentic, illegitimate and impure. Rejecting notions of a coherent or carefully contained text or self, waste figures in the Barnes corpus as a generative point of making and unmaking. The 'troubling structure' invoked in relation to Robin here is reconfigured across both Barnes's texts and the Baroness's waste-based practices in order to reintroduce the messy, irrational or anachronistic – the autobiographic itself – in a complicating proximity to modernist modes invested in a rhetoric of 'newness', and is revealing as to the kinds of anxieties underpinning such pronouncements. Given Becci Carver's succinct summation of the 'typically modernist' attitude towards the ordered and ordering structures of literature and an anxiously negotiated relationship to (classical) tradition and mythic structure as a means of escaping the perceived incoherence of modern life, the antagonistic operations of waste within and between Barnes and the Baroness's work become increasingly obvious.[21]

From the overtly masculine, misogynistic and heterosexist example of international avant-garde movements, including Italian Futurism, Vorticism, Dada and Surrealism, to the centralization of aesthetic ideals of objectivity, impersonality and classicism proposed and promoted in the influential criticism of Eliot and Hulme, and the insistence on the 'hard and clear' in poetry promoted by Ezra Pound's *Imagisme*, emergent definitions of modernist experiment centralized traditionally 'masculine' ideals and what it rejected was coded in strikingly corporeal and gendered terms: the sentimental, the bloated, the unformed.

If we are to accept the claim that certain dominant modes of and modernism and early twentieth-century avant-garde production are founded on the repudiation of the messy or compromising trappings of ornamental excess, we can also identify the formalization of this bias in the critical paradigm of New Criticism that was so influenced by Eliot's thought, and would dominate modernist scholarship through the mid-century. Adhering to the somewhat masculinist terms set out by Eliot, the emergence of modernism as a coherent field of academic study also privileged and rarefied a narrow selection of male writers.[22] As the first chapter will address, such formulations were also influential in shaping the visual thematics of the historical avant-garde, and Marcel Duchamp's extended citation from Eliot's 1919 essay 'Tradition and the Individual Talent' with regards to poetic impersonality in his 1957 lecture 'The Creative Act' and his earlier comments with regards to the Readymade as an object selected with 'visual indifference' are revealing in this respect.[23]

The significant impact of feminist literary and art historical criticism since the 1970s has consistently challenged the politics, aesthetics and canons associated with high modernism and the historical avant-garde. Within this vast body of broadly revisionist work, notable critical attention has been focused on the means through which such 'masculinist' aesthetics were promoted, alongside the outright misogynistic pronouncements at work in the formation of dominant modernist and avant-garde groupings. In more recent decades close attention has been given to the mechanisms through which women were systematically marginalized within these early critical histories.[24] Reflecting on this systematic neglect, Rita Felski has surmised that, despite a historical neglect of women contribution to modernist formations, 'emerging theories, histories and readings of modernism by feminist critics are helping to reconstitute the map of literary history, not only by offering gendered readings of the existing modernist canon, but by rediscovery a largely forgotten history of women's experimental art'.[25] This study engages with the rich body of scholarship developed through the 1980s and 90s that was invested in the 'recovery' of forgotten female practioners from the margins of a canonical modernism 'unconsciously gendered as masculine'.[26] Expanding on more contemporary dicsussions which seek to reframe monolithic definitions of modernism with more nuanced and interdisciplinary treatments of modernist cultures and networks, it also proposes a careful attention to the historical conditions through which such a marginalization is framed.[27]

In this respect, early formations of the modernist canon actualized what these literary programmes espoused in more metaphorical terms, the anxious rhetoric of casting out wastes coded as feminine – the 'pulp' of popular sentimental nineteenth-century literary, the 'baggy' and 'fleshy' excess of a decadent over-production – translating to the exclusion of women writers and artists.[28] That such rejected material was gendered explicitly as 'feminine' has been well documented, notably by Andreas Huyssen's 1986 examination of 'Mass Culture as Woman' in which he maintains that 'the political, psychological, and aesthetic discourse around the turn of the century consistently and obsessively genders mass culture and the masses as feminine, while high culture, whether traditional or modern, clearly remains the privileged realm of male activities'.[29] Taking such scholarship alongside the lines of inquiry opened up by critical approaches to masculinity in 'crisis' established by Elaine Showalter, it becomes apparent that anxieties over waste, anxious (re)definitions of modern(ist) masculinity and the gendering of modernist aesthetics are bound together in interesting and mutually illuminating ways. With Klaus Theweleit's influential study of fascist masculinity and the anxieties presented by the feminized 'floods' of modernity – manifested in its melting-pot metropoles, its teeming and 'hysterical' masses, and the dissolution of traditionally defined gender roles popularly represented by the voracious and sexually liberated New Woman – which threatened to engulf and subsume the autonomous masculine subject, these connections are made more explicit.

As one of the more infamous promoters of a set of distinctly 'modern(ist)' practices based upon principles of 'maximum efficiency', modernist impresario and orchestrator of the hyper-efficient Imagist movement Ezra Pound was critical of Barnes's work. Writing to T.S. Eliot just after the publication of *Nightwood*, Pound included a limerick which deftly encapsulates modernism's gendered resistance to the messy, formless or wasteful:

> There once wuzza lady named Djuna
> Who wrote rather like a baboon. Her
> Blubbery prose had no fingers or toes;
> And me wish whale had found this out sooner.[30]

While the opening line replicates a conventional trope of these short, humorous verses, the rendering of the 'young lady' and the active processes of her writing in the past tense work to separate and differentiate the speaker from both the

the subject and her grotesquely unformed prose. Anxiously shifting between the gendered body and the textual body, Pound's construction of Barnes's baboonish 'blubbery prose' absolutely relies in notions of female physically as similarly formless and inert. Within the rigidly metered and simply rhymed limerick, Pound restores stylistic order, and the hard, contained body of the poet-male producing it.

As Armstrong has detailed in relation to Eliot and Pound's correspondence during the gestation of *The Waste Land,* Pound cast himself as a purifier of texts; intervening in discussions of Vivien Eliot's health or taking the knife to Eliot's manuscript, Pound worked to disinfect wastes coded as feminine and to minimize excess.[31] Given Pound's conception of poetry as *phallic* and prose as *excremental,* this restructuring in verse reveals not only a desire to impose his own vision of form and structure, but an anxiety about modernism's proximity to the 'feminine', its imagined polluting or disintegrative qualities and the threatened fragmentation or dissolution of the male body.

This masculinist modernist attitude is highlighted in the unpleasant vehemence with which Pound and Eliot conflated Amy Lowell's body and her verse in their (private, but widely circulated) criticisms of both her poetry and adoption of the distinctly 'modern' methods of advertising and promotion. The unnecessary corporeality of such descriptors as 'flabby' and 'leaky' in the private discussions of her poetry, coupled with the delight taken in such cruel nicknames as the 'Hippopoetess' and 'Amy-just-selling-the-goods', reveals not only a barely disguised misogyny, homophobia and weight-hate at the heart of modernist histories, but a profound anxiety over the roots of modernity – and modernism – itself.[32] In denigrating and ridiculing the fat, female, lesbian body, these male modernists produced their own foil for defining and affirming the emergence of the modern textual/corporeal body as hard, disciplined and controlled and, in distinguishing themselves from her in such corporeal terms, successfully retrieved their poetic projects from contamination by both a nineteenth-century poetic sentimentality and a feminized, mass-produced modernity.[33]

Pound's phallic hardness, the ordering principles of Eliotian myth and tradition, and Hulme's revival of a firm, coherent and contained classicism all broadly shape the modernism whose relationship to material and metaphorical notions of waste I consider here, a 'high modernism' described by Jessica Feldman as:

> An object to be admired (or in some cases excoriated) for its self-sufficiency and self-involvement, [...] imagined, by artists and critics alike, as purely

sculpted, paradoxically spiritual or cerebral for all its hardness, and preferably not for sale. Its internal incoherencies are bounded by its autonomy, made whole by its separation, at times its rupture, from the familiar. It takes the long and impersonal view, turning away from the ordinary and the fleshy, the vulgarly emotional and the preachy.[34]

Neither Barnes nor the Baroness is absolutely opposed to the terms set out by Feldman here, and it is this troubling proximity that is revealing of the terms of modernism's relationship to waste.

Proceeding through structural patterns of return, revision, repetition and variation, Barnes's modernism is engaged with waste on several fronts: the anachronistic stances struck by an oeuvre which stages an 'illegitimate' return of antiquated language, literary history and an aping of technologically outmoded illustrative techniques; the internal reverberations of repeated and counterpointed histories – particularly apparent in *The Antiphon's* recuperation of narrative material from the earlier *Ryder*; the representations of the marginalized, decayed and illegitimate or transgressive that flood her fiction and poetry; the resistance to generic categorization enabled by the fluid combinations of journalism, prose, autobiography, poetry, drama and illustration, evident in both individual texts and across the oeuvre as a whole. I want to suggest that questions regarding the definition, conceptualization and treatment of waste and mess are, in fact, essential for developing discussions of Barnesean aesthetics, for pushing for a more comprehensive treatment of the structural role played by Barnes's autobiographic poetics (a treatment which seeks to move away from a critical language of 'evasion' and 'allusion' that is frequently invoked to support straightforwardly biographical readings); and for addressing Barnes's problematic relationship to modernism. At once cannibalizing itself and borrowing at will from other literary, biblical, mythological and historical sources, Barnes's corpus demonstrates what Caselli has aptly described as a 'poetics of impropriety', an 'improper modernism'. The notion of deviation, subversion or transgression attached to ideas of impropriety is founded upon the primary existence of clearly defined standards, codes or systems; if 'modernism' is the system here, Barnes's impropriety disrupts the principles of its operation and complicates its coding.

How then might an examination of the cultural work performed by waste inform a discussion of the methods and motivations for the (gendered) marginalization of certain authors and artists? Does critical attention to the forms and functions of waste allow us to embrace the generative potential of figurative and literal messes rather than banishing them? What might the messy materiality of Barnes and the Baroness's embodied practices, and the accumulative patterns of recovery, revision and repetition structuring their autobiographic modes have to say about modernism?

ii. What is waste? Bodies, cities, texts

> The dangerous and contaminating are those things which don't fit within the ordering structures.
>
> William I. Miller, *The Anatomy of Disgust*

From the intimate knowledge of the workings of our individual bodies to the systems implemented to ensure the flow of excreted matter away from the body, waste, at its most familiar, is defined as that which is thrown out or cast off – and which is ascribed an alterity in this process of expulsion becoming 'filthy', 'unclean' and 'polluting'. As William Cohen suggests, 'that which is filthy is so fundamentally alien that it must be rejected; labelling something filthy is a viscerally powerful means of excluding it'.[35] Dangerously unproductive, 'waste' also designates an excessive over-production, the surplus which modernized industrial management techniques worked to minimize or eliminate through careful regulation.

In the contexts of international early twentieth-century Anglo-American modernist and avant-garde movements including the hyper-efficient Imagist and Vorticist groupings, the techno-mechanical fantasies familiar to the visual thematics of New York Dada, and the clean, contained lines and pure functionality of Le Corbusian architectural design, such a concern over questions of efficiency or economy might seem purely aesthetic. However, given the persistent gendering of waste and its conceptual correlates 'filth', 'mess' and 'dirt' as a distinctly feminine threat in early twentieth-century aesthetic and cultural discourse alongside the actual marginalization of female modernists and avant-garde artists within subsequent critical histories, claims that 'to be modern meant to espouse and endorse efficiency' demand closer critical attention[36]. How does waste 'work' in relation to certain rationalist or masculinist modernist projects? What anxieties or concerns cohere around literal and symbolic notions of waste during this period? How do early twentieth-century discourses of efficiency, productivity and hygiene connect literary modernism to questions of gender, textuality, space and the body? Does attention to waste – what is designated as such, how it is treated, the cultural work that it performs – then reveal something about modernist ideologies, anxieties and practices?

As David Trotter has suggested in his excellent study of the idea of 'mess' in the nineteenth century, while mess is a phenomenon involving chance and accident, 'waste' by contrast 'is an effect that can be traced back to its cause. It bears the perceptible imprint of human agency, of human purpose, of system.'[37] In examining the connections between waste and its systems, we must first address the structural work performed by waste, that is, the way in which definitions of waste involve a process of identification, regulation and removal to maintain and monitor distinctions between clean and unclean, inside and outside, centre and periphery that work on both material and metaphorical levels.

Any formulation of the relationship between waste and system relies to a certain extent on the structural analysis of dirt as 'matter out of place' within cultural specific ordering frameworks proposed by Mary Douglas.[38] In her analysis of the role played by dirt and taboo across different cultures and historical periods, Douglas proposes that the taboos placed on certain 'unclean' objects, practices or peoples are not inherent to those items themselves, but the result of their location in relation to the system in which they operate:

> If we can abstract pathogenicity and hygiene from our notion of dirt, we are left with the old definition of dirt as matter out of place. This is a very suggestive approach. It implies two conditions: a set of ordered relations and a contravention to that order. Dirt then, is never a unique, isolated event. Where there is dirt there is system. Dirt is the byproduct of a systematic ordering and classification of matter, in so far as ordering involves rejecting inappropriate elements. The idea of dirt takes us straight into the field of symbolism and promises a link-up with more obviously symbolic systems of purity.[39]

Confrontation with filth and the horror and violence or revulsion that it inspires thus reveals, under Douglas's treatment, both the existence of a system and the codes and borders maintained by that particular cultural framework. What appears as unclean filthy is simply that which, by being 'out of place' within an ordering framework, 'violates a sense of the order of the world'.[40]

While waste and dirt are obviously connected in the manner in which they are cast out and repudiated, we could make a distinction here between the correct functioning of waste (as the identification and smooth removal of the excessive, surplus, or used to ensure maximum efficiency) as *complementary* to the structural regulation of the ordering system from which it passes, and the disruption or *challenge* presented to such structuring frameworks by the re-appearance of matter where it does not belong; while properly managed wastes respect systems and order, 'matter out of place' indicates a confusion of categories and a collapse of the ordering structure. To examine what is classified as 'matter out of place' is to address the categories of that system, the 'order' that it upholds.

Such a theoretical formulation of waste as existing within a symbolic system opens up interesting lines of inquiry for the positioning of waste, junk and mess in relation to theories of value. Discarded and forgotten waste, it might initially seem is useless, without value. However, in its properly regulated status, waste can retain a generative capability by accepting both its relocation within the ordering structure and the lowering of value that results from this newly defined status. A transitory object that has exhausted its value in one order (that of useful objects), it is cast down and out of that order and absorbed by another (that of junk, rubbish or waste). In proposing a framework of economic value which places considerations of 'rubbish' at its centre, Michael Thompson has identified two general categories of objects: transient (finite and decreasing in value) and durable (infinite and increasing in value). While the transition of durable objects to transient ones is easily conceivable within the contexts of damage, overuse or replacement, the reverse movement – from transient to durable – is, Thompson suggests, more explicitly tied to notions of value. As with the example of the objects discarded by one generation as rubbish and emerging as the antiques and collectables of another, Thompson suggests that a third category, that of rubbish itself, is essential for the re-evaluation of the transitory object to durable status. A 'covert category', rubbish 'is not subject to the control mechanism (which is concerned primarily with the *overt* part of the system, the valuable and socially significant objects) and so is able to provide a path for the seemingly impossible transfer of an object from transience to durability'.[41] Decreasing in value, the transitory object eventually passes into rubbish where it persists, discarded, out of time and seemingly valueless. Unregulated or undetected by the system it has been marginalized by, it is the *potential for value* contained in rubbish that enables the transition of transitory to durable objects.

Of course, the condition of rubbish as harbouring potential value is also intimately tied to its positioning within these ordering systems. As rubbish it persists, it has not been finally cast down and out as unassailably other. As Trotter suggests, unlike mess 'waste can often be recycled, or put to alternative uses; if the system which produced it cannot accommodate it, some other system will. Waste remains for ever potentially in circulation because circulation is its defining quality'.[42] Interestingly, the logic of maximum efficiency and the elimination of waste that drives this potentially unstable circulation of such matter is not limited to material objects, but also attached to potentially polluting corporeal wastes. As Laporte has proposed economic concerns become increasingly tied to corporeal ones through questions of value, with human faeces itself emerging at various historical moments as valuable both in itself, as a commodity, and in the utopian fantasies of closed, self-sustaining (agricultural) systems.[43]

Thus, with regards to questions of 'value', we could surmise that there is an internal conflict within our literal and metaphorical conceptions of waste, mess and filth – a conflict between that which is useable and that which is absolutely polluting, that which can be reused and retains value and that which only corrupts and must be excluded absolutely. So long as it remains in its 'proper' place within the system, carefully regulating a limited circulation and permitting re-use to maximize efficiency, waste – or, more explicitly waste management – serves to showcase the power of the system in which it is produced and that it maintains: 'Waste is the measure of an organism's ability to renew itself by excluding whatever it does not require for its own immediate purposes. However foul it may have become, it still gleams with efficiency. It testifies, in its very dereliction, to the power which cast it down and out.'[44]

As William Miller emphasizes in his 1997 study *Anatomy of Disgust*, the body is a particularly fraught and compromised site when it comes to tensions between the absolutely corrupting and the reusable, one that manifests most powerfully in the sensation of disgust. The inside of my body, Miller demonstrates, is more polluting than the outside of my body, the 'mess of gooey, oozy, slimy, smelly things' hidden away, out of my own sight, beneath a protective layer of skin.[45] My skin, like the sensation of disgust provoked at the thought of the exposure of the oozing innards beneath, is central to the process of the recognition and maintenance of difference through which I define myself, and is the point at which I visualize and attempt to make literal the solidity of my own body and my distinction from others. Thus, with reference to Bakhtin's corporeal topography of the grotesque, it becomes clear that the points at which those sealed boundaries are most vulnerable – particularly the anus, genitals or open mouth – are also the compromised and potentially polluting zones which demand closer policing.[46]

The disgust provoked by an open mouth, the unsolicited exposure of genitals or the excretion of others is thus described as the mechanism through which the illusion of the inviolability of the body is maintained, rejecting and turning away from 'the danger of unclarity and disorder' presented by those corporeal zones at which the boundaries between inside and outside are most dangerously blurred.[47] Pertinently, the proximity between the sensation of disgust and the perceived transgression of the boundaries between inside and outside, self and other threatened by such 'compromised' corporeal zones takes on a decidedly gendered aspect when we consider the binding of certain historical constructions of femininity, female sexuality and corporeality to notions of waste, filth and corruption.[48] Indeed, while all bodies seep, leak and excrete, there has been an overwhelming tendency in the history of Western thought to project any anxieties that might be associated with such a threat to the autonomous, self-contained and rational individual into a construction of the female body as leaky, unstable, un-contained and excessive, as absolute 'other' to the thinking, masculine subject.[49] As Elizabeth Grosz has convincingly argued in her combination of Douglas's structural analysis of dirt and Kristeva's theory of the abject, the female body is constructed in opposition to the thinking masculine subject as 'leaking, uncontrollable, seeping liquid; as formless flow, as viscosity, entrapping, secreting [...] a formlessness that engulfs all form, a disorder that threatens order'.[50]

Such a process of identity formation is, of course, deeply entrenched within psychoanalytic thought and theory. While I will go on to cover this terrain in more detail it usefully signposts my thinking here that the identification and repudiation of 'waste' is central to early twentieth-century negotiations with masculinity and contemporaneous attempts to define and regulate modernist aesthetics, particularly as worked out in the international centres of the modern(ist) metropolis.

Ideological or analytical in focus, a dense body of work invested in the examination of urban consciousness and its relationship to notions of waste has developed since the nineteenth century. From Freidrich Engels's conception of the modern industrial metropolis as the site of man's estrangement and of the disintegration of the working-class family, the various journalistic pieces, reform movements and planning reports emphasizing connections between squalid living conditions, physical disease and moral decay, to the work of sociologists Max Weber, Gustave Le Bon and Georg Simmel, the metropolis preoccupied contemporary commentators.[51] As the period of industrial modernity gathered steam, urban centres came under increasing focus as dangerous and disruptive spaces where previously rigid classed, raced and gendered boundaries or behavioural codes shaping the real and imaginary spaces of the city were blurred and contested. Anxieties surrounding the unregulated movement and activity of the urban poor, unchaperoned women and immigrant workers became increasingly centralized in popular discourse throughout the ninetieth century, and the extensive urban restructuring programmes imagined and actualized in the period seemed clearly aimed at the re-instatement of such boundaries through the organized exclusion of such 'disruptive elements' from the modern city.[52]

Fears of the urban masses were widespread throughout western centres, explained in part by the supplanting of late medieval feudal structures with new, democratic forms of political organization throughout the modern period which, by the nineteenth century, had become increasingly attached to the threat of revolution. As cities grew, fears of the revolutionary mob, the urban masses and the faceless crowd came into increasingly high relief against crystallizing notions of the bourgeois individual. Distinctions between the bourgeois individual and the masses were explicitly gendered as discussions of the seemingly unstable, amorphous and engulfing crowd increasingly evoked a language of dirt, disease and criminality associated with the urban poor and infused within a symbolic framework of traditionally 'feminine' characteristics – hysteria, messy corporeality, instability, excessive and threatening sexuality. On these gendered grounds, the modern metropolis has been theorized predominately as a site of flux, dynamism and alienation, the terrain upon which the battle for individual (bourgeois, white, masculine) subjectivity is waged against the engulfing forces of markedly feminized modernity. In this respect the 'intimate unity of the modern self and the modern environment' proposed by Marshal Berman's model of a dynamic and dialectic modernity must be critically re-considered to emphasize the strikingly gendered conception of both the modern subject and modern space that pre-figures such formulations.[53]

In chronicling a brief history of modern man's struggle for independence and individuality, early theorist of urban consciousness Georg Simmel famously proposed:

> The deepest problems of modern life flow from the attempt of the individual to maintain the independence and individuality of his existence against the sovereign powers of society [...] but in each of these the same fundamental motive was at work, namely the resistance of the individual to being levelled, swallowed up in the social-technological mechanism.[54]

The antagonism identified by Simmel between the individual and the socio-cultural structures of his epoch finds its most modern expression in the tensions between the 'inner life' of the individual and the constant demands made upon him as he moves through the metropolis. Under the 'intensification of emotional life due to the swift and continuous shift of external and internal stimuli', Simmel insists that the individual must preserve himself by creating a 'protective organ for itself against the profound disruption with which the fluctuations and discontinuities of the external milieu threaten it'.[55] This 'protective organ' is conceived of as a shield, not simply against the physical shocks and starts of life in a busy city, but as absolutely necessary to withstand the 'domination of the intellect' threatened by the sinister union of the modern metropolis and a mature money economy.

Given the familiar accounts of the metropolis as an unstable space in unequivocally gendered terms alongside the well-established connections between capitalist modes of consumption, leisure and the commodification of the female body in prostitution, Simmel's fears for the rational (masculinized) individual in the hyperemotional (feminized) city are particularly striking.[56] If the mature money economy as fully realized in the metropolis erodes individuality and difference, the expansion of an objective culture only concerned with 'the exchange value which reduces all quality and individuality to a purely quantitative level' clearly threatens the dissolution of the individual within this indistinct (and feminized) metropolitan mire.[57] Thus both the *blasé* attitude and the critical distance that it provides are, under Simmel's treatment, increasingly necessary strategies for the survival of modern urban consciousness.

Interestingly Simmel suggests elsewhere that this critical distance is also a pre-requisite for the continued production of art within the metropolis as the city 'becomes aesthetic only as a result of increasing distance, abstraction and sublimation'.[58] Certainly, objective distance, a hard-won impersonality and abstraction are all familiar modernist tropes and, given the outright misogyny of several prominent early twentieth-century avant-garde movements, Dorothy Rowe's suggestion that 'it is male avant-gardists and writers who signify most dramatically a sense of subjective instability in the face of the fragmentary experience of metropolitan modernity' certainly bears further attention.[59] While such aesthetic strategizing will be treated more comprehensively in following chapters, it is enough to emphasize here that this 'protective organ' was conceptualized to preserve the individual subject continually assaulted by the feminized floods and swamps of metropolitan modernity. Before examining early twentieth-century avant-garde aesthetic responses to these threats and anxieties in later chapters, it might be useful to briefly consider how conceptions of urban space and modern subjectivity were shaped in response to anxieties arising from the modern metropolis and the various strategies of managing and containing these threats.

Such sensitivity to issues regarding the relationships between the production of subjects, gendered subjectivity and space has been of central importance to developments in critical theory in recent decades. While Marxist geographers were among the first to define the dialectical relationship between society and space – elucidating the extent to which, while socially produced, it is nevertheless a condition for social production – other critical frameworks have considered and critiqued the production of space and society. A robust body of feminist criticism has developed around questions as to how and by whom space is produced and used, and to address the representations, performance or regulation of gender, sexuality and ethnicity within specific spaces. As Beatriz Colomina has suggested, 'space is, after all, a form of representation'; we can begin to identify the forces at work in the shaping of a geographically and temporally located site of modernity, what such a space *represents*, and the ways in which such representations are inscribed upon the bodies and regulated body practices within that space.[60]

While literature exploring early twentieth-century encounters with the metropolis seems, almost overwhelmingly, to address this 'subjective instability', in more recent decades feminist scholars from a variety of disciplines have demonstrated and interrogated the primacy of such overtly masculine models of subjectivity in critical histories of modernization, modernity and the metropolis. Keen to investigate the liberating aspects of women's encounters with the modern city, such studies focus increasingly on the active role of women in the metropolis, particularly in their contribution to social and cultural production as journalists, writers, editors, artists, patrons and political radicals.[61] As Elizabeth Wilson has emphasized, 'while the city might have been perceived as a place of growing threat and paranoia to men, [it] might a place of liberation for women'.[62]

In this respect, Barnes's journalistic practices – notably her satirizing of a nineteenth-century fascination with Baedekers and guide books, and her involvement with the pioneering genre of stunt journalism – are particularly interesting, although fall beyond the scope of this project. While the (conventionally male) *flâneur* could 'impose order upon the potentially disorientating diversity of the city' as a journalist, the (predominately female) stunt journalist places her body in deliberately disorientating situations.[63] Indeed, while articles like 'How It Feels to Be Forcibly Fed', 'My Adventures Being Rescued' and 'The Girl and the Gorilla' all engage with modes of performance and spectacularity in placing the disorientated body centre stage, Barnes's Greenwich Village series, her Coney Island pieces and her probing into the less-explored corners of Brooklyn and Chinatown all challenge the claims of any guide book to control, regulate and order the heterogenous experience of modern life in the city. At once animating and transgressing the spaces mapped by Barnes's early journalistic writings, the Baroness's urban promenades and her street-scavenging clearly take this disruption of the mapped metropolis off the page and onto the streets.

Modernist Wastes addresses modernism's relationship to waste, and its correlates mess, filth and dirt, from three interrelated positions. First, building on the scholarship that has emerged from the burgeoning and inter-disciplinary field of waste-theory, it identifies the ways in which 'waste' broadly defined functions as an essential component in the definition and maintenance of various systems of regulation, containment and expulsion that maintain and police boundaries, bodies and texts.[64] Indeed, as has been well established in the critical disciplines of anthropology and psychoanalysis, the proper functioning of waste (as clearly defined and efficiently repudiated) speaks for the smooth and successful working of the system it is produced within, serving 'critical functions in social management, psychological formation and cultural formation'.[65] In her discussion of the abject, Julie Kristeva privileges this process of waste-making as central to the identification and regulation of the subject; in violently rejecting the abject – that which sits uncomfortably between subject and object like faeces, the cadaver or the body of the mother – Kristeva maintains that the subject attempts to define itself through a continual regulation and re-affirming of its corporeal boundaries.[66] At once the space of contamination and the contaminating matter itself, the abject continually challenges the stability of these illusory boundaries; the violent sensation of abjection as a desire to expel is thus explained as a mechanism through which such divisions are policed and maintained.

Secondly, considering relationships to waste in their specific historical contexts, we can see that from such messy corporeal and psychological beginnings, this process of waste-making and repudiation becomes increasingly centralized in the various rationalizing projects associated with the birth of the modern industrial age. The identification of centre and periphery and the relegation of objects, bodies, matter and practices to the margins are constructional elements of such projects, systematically identifying, isolating and removing that which disrupts order. Locating reactions to excremental waste in its historical contexts, Domique Laporte's observation of the centrality of the repression or elimination of waste from cultural fields of production and consumption in the regulation of their proper functioning is highly instructive in this respect.[67] As such, distinctions between clean and unclean, order and mess, public and private, not only structure the 'domain of the disgusting' which have informed a range of cultural, religious and historical practices, but were augmented and put to new uses in the period of rapid industrial and technological expansion which spanned the mid-nineteenth to early twentieth centuries.[68] Through extensive urban rationalization and the mass dissemination of discourses on health, sanitation and morality, the topography of the modern metropolis and the composition and behaviour of its inhabitants were anxiously discussed, classified and managed throughout this period.

Intriguingly, as literary and cultural criticism has started to note, material waste – garbage, rubbish, junk – is a distinctly modern concern. Intimately connected to the rise of consumer culture in America, material waste in the form of trash and junk only emerged as a concept in the late nineteenth century with a marked shift away from the production and consumption of durable items to increasingly disposable ones, as Susan Strasser has described.[69] Within the contexts of industrial modernity, notions of 'progress' thus became increasingly wedded to the successful management of this waste, and while the nineteenth century reinforced structural distinctions between the centre and periphery, public and private, clean and unclean, the early twentieth- century perfected modes of maintaining and regulating such distinctions.[70]

Aimed specifically at maximizing economic efficiency through careful regulation and management of labour and productivity, the popularization of American scientific management principles in large-scale manufacture and mass-production developed by F.W. Taylor and Henry Ford provides a useful focalizing point in my treatment of the ideational functioning of waste during this period.[71] Implementing a system whereby waste could be identified, contained and, ideally, eliminated from the process of industrial production altogether, these models of scientific management attempted to rationalize production through the careful regulation and standardization of the space of the factory, the body of the worker and the potentially 'dangerous flows of labour and capital that were released by the new machine-age economies'.[72]

This emphasis on regulation and efficiency was certainly not limited to the spheres of production, but radiated out into a range of cultural, socio-political, psychological and aesthetic discourses throughout the period. Proliferating alongside anxieties surrounding the emergence of the modern metropolis and various urban restructuring programmes designed to address these concerns, discourses relating to the gendered body's relationship to consumer capitalism were increasingly popularized. In keeping with this renewed focus on problematic bodies, medical and reformist discourses on hygiene and public health and the emergence of various techniques for regulating the body through dietary and fitness regimes including Fletcherism and the Müller technique rose to prominence, a trend which can of course be traced through the explosion of popular discourse around the science of eugenics in the early decades of the twentieth century.[73] As James Scott has suggested in his study of the systems associated with 'high modernism':

> Every nook and cranny of the social order might be improved upon: personal hygiene, diet, child rearing, housing, posture, recreation, family structure, and, most infamously, the genetic inheritance of the population. The working poor were often the first subjects of scientific social planning. [...] Subpopulations found wanting in ways that were potentially threatening – such as indigents, vagabonds, the mentally ill, and criminals – might be made the objects of the most intensive social engineering.[74]

Clearly, these various rationalizing tendencies and theories were profoundly inscribed on the bodies and texts produced during the period and compelling connections can certainly be drawn between the regulation of bodily or social practices and the production of modernist texts.

Finally then, a core concern of this inquiry is to assess the extent to which discourses of efficiency and the logic of exclusion that regulates the processes of waste-making might provide an illuminating model for exposing the methods and motivations of gendered processes of marginalization, regulation and 'containment' imposed on the bodies, texts and subsequent critical histories of certain modernist authors and avant-garde practitioners. Addressing Shari Benstock's claim that 'fear of contamination is the founding premise of modernism',[75] this project examines the anxious gendering of early twentieth-century negotiations with modernity in order to consider the ways in which a masculinist rhetoric of efficiency and economy not only informed dominant strains of modernist and early- twentieth-century avant-garde aesthetics, but has structured subsequent critical histories of the period through a process of 'calculated containment'. Identifying the enthusiastic engagement with forms of waste in the plastic, autobiographic and performative practices developed by Barnes and the Baroness, this book examines the ways in which the *return* of material or metaphorical wastes in these somewhat disordered or disordering texts, performances and self-representational practices thus disrupts and challenges dominant modernist modes, the retrospective construction of neatly organized critical histories and the masculinist, rational discourses central to crystallizing concepts of modernity and early formulations of modernist projects. In this respect waste is compellingly malleable, functioning within modernist discourse as a strategy of containment *and* as a radical challenge to dominant aesthetic and cultural modes.

Thus, while *representations* of waste in modernism are of interest to this book (particularly considering the accumulation of images of waste and dissolution that become increasingly apparent in the work of 'late modernists' including Mina Loy, Samuel Beckett and the Joyce of *Finnegans Wake*),[76] closer examination will be given to work that, rather than simply describing waste, is in fact identified *with* or *as* waste in troubling ways. 'Troubling' takes on a dual aspect here in both the *negative* connotations generally ascribed to waste, filth and mess and, more pressingly, as something that 'troubles' definitions of canonical modernist aesthetics or early twentieth-century avant-garde practices. In this respect, I am particularly interested in the role played by material waste in the junk-assemblages, *couture d'ordures* and self-representational practices developed by Elsa von Freytag-Loringhoven, the frequent identification of the Baroness with, or even *as*, a polluting form of waste in the memoirs of her contemporaries, and Barnes's own distinctly disruptive, 'disordered' and accumulative autobiographic poetics and writing practices. The textual excess and intra-textual reverberations generated by the two women's correspondence and the 'failed' collaborative autobiographic project that they embarked upon in 1924 and would intermittently occupy Barnes until her death in 1982 mark it as a privileged example of 'modernist wastes' – accumulative, disruptive and subject to uncanny recurrences.

The first two chapters will focus on the erasure of the Baroness Elsa von Freytag-Loringhoven from critical histories of twentieth-century avant-garde activity, and develop a close analysis of the forms and functions of her disruptive self-representational and waste-based embodied art practices – or *body-work* – respectively. The first of these two chapters, 'Stunning Subjects and Disruptive Body Practices', will introduce the Baroness as a way of framing the examination of the relationships between modernity, literary modernism and gendered conceptions of 'waste' explored across this project. Identifying the absence of fleshy, messy bodies in conventional indexes of New York Dada, this chapter considers the extension of modernism's relationship to notions of efficiency, structure and a vexing 'newness' briefly outlined here into the historical avant-garde gathered in New York during the turbulent years of the First World War.

Importantly, in highlighting the discrepancies between the critical erasure of the Baroness from modernist or twentieth-century avant-garde histories, and the neurotic invocation of her grotesque body across the memoirs and short stories of her contemporaries, these chapters explore the relationship of Elsa's embodied waste-based aesthetics to modes of rational modernist practice, and the methods and motivations of her relegation and containment within its margins. Through various theoretical treatments and definitions of the grotesque and the abject, the first chapter examines the methods and motivations of this containment and considers the ways in which this reconstructed and decidedly grotesque body is re-appropriated and 'put to work' in definitions and clarifications of both avant-garde and modernist practices.

Developing the analysis of this body-work, the second of these Elsa chapters, 'Art Dazzle: Modelling, Performance and the Baroness's Self-Representational Practices', brings the Baroness's own self-representational practices to the fore. Looking closely at the autobiographic, performative and corporeal dimensions of her waste-based practices activated in her multi-media portraiture, her aggressive assertion of 'posing' as art and her elaborate costuming practices, this chapter considers some of the ways in which waste can be activated as a strategy for reading against models of containment or regulation traditionally organized in the female nude.

Taken together, these chapters aim to frame the second half of the book's discussion of the nuances between Barnes's 'messy' autobiographic poetics and the 'biographic impulse' at play in critical treatments of her work. While the third chapter '"Not Dead": Djuna Barnes's Mature Autobiographic Poetics' considers Barnes's own description of her writing as a bleeding wound as a way of connecting the messy materiality of her writing practices and the structures of repetition, return and refrain structuring her Patchin Place production, the final chapter, 'Troubling Structures: Inner Time and the "Baroness Elsa" manuscript', returns to the 1930s, introducing the collaborative 'Baroness Elsa' biography as an important and under-acknowledged intertext which illuminates the structural patterns and preoccupations of both *Nightwood* and Barnes's later work.

Through a close examination of Barnes's late production including the Patchin Place poetry cycles, *The Antiphon* and the 'Baroness Elsa' biography, I contend that, in contrast to biographic readings which attempt to contain and explain Barnes's challenging texts within easily navigable narrative frameworks, the individual and collaborative auto/biographic poetics developed by these women disrupt and rupture the official narratives imposed upon them. In turning to the biography, and in particular the figure of Elsa's mother, Ida-Marie and her own disruptive art practices, this chapter will reflect on the extent to which an autobiographic poetics interested in the return and revision of old, officially forgotten material might be productively read in light of Elsa's own, more explicit working with waste.

Writing to Coleman and enthusing about her recent discovery of Alexis Carrel's *Man, the Unknown,* Barnes claims to have found a philosophy to explain her own thinking about time and memory, that which she claimed to 'have been screaming about for years'; an 'inner time' founded in the 'crafting and fashioning things out of ourselves, in quiet places, Hardship, privation, ascetacism [*sic*] … past time, of which we are all compiled'.[77] In stark contrast to an Eliotian notion of 'historical sense' and 'tradition', James Joyce's mythic frameworks, or the repudiation of an immediate past and poetic origins identified by Michael Levenson as essential to stability and coherence of modernist poetic theory,[78] the disordering structures of 'past time' and the cluttered objects that collect there do not stabilize her texts but radically disrupt such organizing frameworks. Connecting authorial and autobiographic selves, troubling notions of authenticity, originality, propriety and impersonality these texts work to keep the wound open, recovering and reusing used and worn-out material like the Baroness's spectacular Readymade objects, collage-poems and elaborate costumes; or, indeed, like the Baroness herself who the younger journalist Barnes captured as 'an ancient human notebook on which has been written all the follies of a past generation'.[79]

1

Stunning subjects and disruptive body practices

> I hear New York has gone mad about "Dada", [...] What next! This is worse than the Baroness. By the way, I like the way the discovery has suddenly been made that she has all along been, unconsciously, a Dadaist. I cannot figure out just what Dadaism is beyond an insane jumble of the four winds, the six senses, and plum pudding. But if the Baroness is to be the keystone for it, – then I think I can possible know when it is coming and avoid it.
>
> Hart Crane, c. 1920

Writing in the *New Republic* in 1928 the sociologist and literary critic Lewis Mumford called for an incorporation of modernism into interior and urban design as a means of satisfying the 'desire to have our feet firmly planted in our own age'.[1] Analysing and defining these 'modern forms' as 'the emphasis of function and structure [...] simplicity and directness',[2] Mumford directly links modernism, in design and elsewhere, to the modernization of industrial production, placing the machine (and the material commodities it is able to reproduce) as central to both modernist aesthetics and modern life. This utopian symbiosis of modes of production and modes of representation is, perhaps, most strongly asserted in the subtle invocation of the re-imagined body as the formative principle beneath shifts in contemporary tastes towards the unequivocally 'modern'. Citing contemporary trends in fashion and architecture, Mumford locates the modern body as central in overcoming what he terms the 'period model' of design:

> Whereas the designs of women's clothing and skyscrapers had long been sloughing off ornamental excrescences, had reduced themselves steadily to the essential line and mass, in one case, the human body and its contours, and in the other, the steel skeleton and it planes, we clung to style and ornament of the past in every other department.[3]

Reciprocally mapped on to one another the body and the designs that it inspires are reconstructed here according to a logic of reduction, simplification and functionality. In a subtle but striking move, it is not only modern design which is reformulated and redefined per the rational logic of industrial production, but conceptions and representations of the body itself. With an emphasis on function and structure, the modernist canon of simplicity and directness identified by Mumford relies on the construction of a coherent 'modern' body 're-energized, re-formed, subject to new modes of production, representation, and commodification'.[4]

Such a re-imagining of corporeal form founded on the principles of structure and simplicity is particularly prevalent to a discussion of the visual thematics of New York Dada. Looking through the shiny and seductive pages of the various exhibition catalogues, art history books and academic studies that traditionally centred the retrospectively identified New York Dada movement around the tripartite pivot of Marcel Duchamp, Francis Picabia and Man Ray, 'bodies' do not seem to figure. Indeed, the organic, fleshy mess of bodies would be something of an incongruous embarrassment within the visual field of glass, mechanical arms, chocolate grinders and egg beaters that we might bring to mind. Endlessly reproducible and reduced to their most basic functioning, the Readymade objects and erotically charged mechanical fantasies typically associated with the movement offer a more ambivalent visual antecedent for Mumford's rational modernism, redrawing the lines between man and god, nature and machine, man and woman in their modes of machine-age representation.

In the specific contexts of New York Dada however, one defiantly messy body has persistently haunted the edges of this man-made world, disrupting the emphasis on reduction, simplicity and functionality prioritized as a sign of the modern in Mumford's account. As an artist's model, experimental poet, performer, autobiographer, Dada Queen and iconocalstic visual artist, the Baroness Elsa von Freytag-Loringhoven pioneered a diverse and challenging art practice. And yet, in their letters and memoirs, her contemporaries seem more preoccupied with reconstructing her as a stunning subject of their own narratives than developing serious discussions of her explosive Dada poetry or intriguing found-object constructions. Impossible to ignore and often unsettling to encounter, confrontations with the Baroness 'dressed in rags picked up here and there, decked out with impossible objects suspended from chains, swishing long trains, like an empress from another planet' galvanized the attempts of her contemporaries to identify, categorize and fix this recalcitrant body within their own accounts.[5]

Reflecting the common feeling of those who encountered the Baroness that she had 'all along been, unconsciously, a Dadaist', Hart Crane's dismissal of New York Dada reveals more than his fraught ambivalence towards the broader movement's absurdist tendencies, but highlights one of the ways in which the Baroness's body was readily appropriated, reconstructed and put to work in formulating contemporary definitions of modernist and avant-garde activity. What he describes elsewhere as the frustrating 'flamdoodle' of Dada might be hard to pin down, but once its energies have been contained in the figure of the Baroness, it is considerably easier to identify and to avoid. Given that Crane was also fond of burlesquing the Baroness with a confused blend of admiration and disgust, such attempts to 'contain' her unruly production and disruptive energy also pose pressing questions regarding the sublimation of her work within modernist production.[6]

In considering the treatment of this body as modernist anecdote and artist's model, I want to probe the tension between the critical erasure of the Baroness as a poet, artist and performer from modernist histories, and the indelible trace that her body has left on the footnotes of those histories. Delineating certain historical and cultural contexts informing the critical marginalization of the Baroness's *body-work* (i.e. both her body of work and her embodied art-labour), it is nevertheless possible to trace the ways in which the Baroness's (grotesque) *body* was anxiously appropriated and reconstructed by her contemporaries.

With her head shaved and lacquered in a high vermillion, her face sometimes daubed with yellow powder and cancelled postage stamps, her near-naked body rustling with an assortment of salvaged or stolen tin cans, toy soldiers and teaspoons, such accounts of the disturbing and sensational power of the Baroness's body are not hard to come by. Recording his first meeting with the Baroness, the memoirs of American artist George Biddle present a particularly striking example:

> I met her in my Philadelphia studio [...] in the spring of 1917, a few weeks before I enlisted in the officer's Training Camp. Having asked me, in her harsh, high-pitched German stridency, whether I required a model, I told her that I should like to see her in the nude. With a royal gesture she swept apart the folds of a scarlet raincoat. She stood before me quite naked – or nearly so. Over the nipples of her breasts were two tin tomato cans, fastened with a green string behind her back. Between the tomato cans hung a very small bird-cage and within it a crestfallen canary. One arm was covered from wrist to shoulder with celluloid curtain rings, which later she admitted to have pilfered from a furniture display in Wanamaker's. She removed her hat, which had been tastefully but

inconspicuously trimmed with gilded carrots, beets and other vegetables. Her hair was close cropped and dyed vermillion.[7]

Biddle's account here brings together recurrent themes in discussions of the Baroness by her contemporaries: a fascination with her 'boyish' body, a tension between her nudity and her visually sensational *couture d'ordures*, her foreignness and her dramatic, indomitable disregard for gendered and aesthetic convention. More pressingly for my purposes in this chapter, Biddle's account also records the need to record itself, to make sense of a sensorially dissembling encounter

The disorderly practices of the Baroness's body-work recorded here provoke confusion and the collapse of seemingly well-defined boundaries. While Elsa's appearance here as a female nude model in a male artist's studio should signal her conformity to a well-rehearsed gender script, Biddle's employment of masculine signifiers in his descriptions of her body which he describes elsewhere as that of a 'Greek ephebe, with small firm breasts, narrow hips, and long smooth shanks' speaks to the cognitive dissonance activated between Elsa's provocative displays and traditional constructions of femininity.[8] As later chapters will examine more comprehensively, the Baroness's body-work interferes with the gendered and voyeuristic gaze, dismantling the encoded practices of 'looking' which have reinforced notions of the model's passivity in relation to the artist's activity. Far from allowing the (male) artist unmediated access to the nude (female) body, any possible representation of the model here must first negotiate the active body of the model-artist as a work of art in its own right.

Importantly, as we shall see, the objects appropriated and re-contextualized in this provocative display – bird cages, discarded tin cans, stolen curtain rings – are also revealing as to the modes and functions of what I want to broadly term the Baroness's waste-based aesthetics. Recovering these devalued and discarded objects, and incorporating them into her performative self-display, the Baroness collapses anxiously negotiated distinctions between clean and unclean, inside and outside, dynamically reconfiguring her body *through* and *as* her art, and flatly refusing passive, specular models of detached contemplation of art from life. While this goes some way to delineating the methods through which the Baroness's *body-work* can be recuperated from the obsessive focus on her body which typically dominates representations of her in the memoirs and fictionalized accounts of her contemporaries, such a discussion must be grounded in an initial analysis of the *strategies of containment* activated in these textual reconstructions. As in Mumford's account of a rational modernism, the body and the designs built over it reinforce one another here. However, while Mumford's notions of modern design as functional and reduced to the essential elements of line and mass depended on a notably classical conception of the body as strictly delineated, contained and simplified, the dazzling body beneath the raincoat performs a perverse return of the ornamental excesses systematically discarded in accounts of the modern(ist) and the stripped down machinic modes of the Picabian mechanomorph or the Duchampian Readymade.

Far from recalibrating stabilizing ideals of the classical body (embodying aesthetic traditions of impenetrability, separateness and proportionality) for the modern, machine age, the body presented in this textual reconstruction is unambiguously grotesque – one that protrudes, extends itself and continually transgresses its own limits. Following Mikhail Bakhtin's reconfiguration of the category of the grotesque as 'a semiotics of the human body' we can clearly trace its contours in Biddle's account:[9]

> Contrary to modern canons, the grotesque body is not separated from the rest of the world. It is not a closed, completed unit; it is unfinished, outgrows itself, transgresses its own limits. [...] The body discloses its essence as a principle of growth which exceeds its own limits only in copulation, pregnancy, childbirth, the throes of death, eating, drinking, or defecation. This is the ever unfinished, ever creating body.[10]

Taken as a whole, Biddle's testimony certainly foregrounds the Baroness's infamously voracious sexuality and in the creative adaptation and application of used, rejected and stolen objects foregrounded here her body is rendered 'unfinished' and excessively (re)productive.[11] Giving special attention to that which protrudes from the Baroness's 'nearly' naked body as she dramatically sweeps aside the folds of her raincoat, Biddle's narrative situates the Baroness's body within the category of the grotesque as one that 'ignores the impenetrable surface that closes and limits the body as a separate and completed phenomenon'.[12] Transgressing and extending its boundaries, the body reconstructed here is instead one that connects itself to the world through the objects consumed and discarded by that world in an open system of perpetual renewal.

Reading across the memoirs of her contemporaries, the composite portrait of the Baroness that emerges is always already grotesque, built up as it is through multiple, fragmentary and intersecting readings. Furthermore, all employ the contradictory representational structures of the grotesque in making sense of the Baroness's corporeal performances. Rendering her through a language of ambivalent fascination and repulsion, such narratives employ the grotesque as a means of evoking 'the nonrational dimension of life as such, a dimension that, in principle, is both alluring and sinister, benign and devouring, and that defines itself against ideas of pattern and order'.[13] As this definition suggests, categories of the grotesque are intimately linked to structural systems of order and disorder. In rendering the Baroness's body through these already established categories, these narrative reconstructions attempt to buttress the binary logic of such structural systems, paradoxically re-inscribing her body as *neatly* disorderly to negatively reinforce more 'orderly' aesthetic and cultural modes, bodies and practices. In re-writing her performance of gender, sexuality and the everyday in sensationally visual terms, such accounts function as a strategy of 'calculated containment', a way of both rationalizing the unsettling encounter and shoring up the boundaries between artist subject and art object.

Looking across other contemporary chronicles, it is clear that these abject dynamics are formative in reproducing (and containing) the body of the Baroness. While Mary Butts and Ben Hecht rendered her body as a destructive, devouring and demonic force in their short stories, William Carlos Williams memorably evoked these abject dynamics in his attempt to work through the assault on his masculinity and identity as a modern American poet presented by her aggressive sexual advances and destabilizing corporeality.[14] Fictionalized as the avant-garde poet the 'Countess Sillivitch' connected to the hypermodern journal *The Shriek* (*The Little Review*) in Charles Brook's *Hints to Pilgrims* (1921), the stench of death, filth and decay clings to the literary reincarnation of this exotically European and visually sensational Dada poet.[15] From the bemused fascination expressed by painters, writers and editors for both her androgynous physique and her ornamental junk costumes, to the repulsive, smelly and sexually voracious figure that stalks the shadowy edges of modernist memory, this grotesque body never disappeared entirely from modernist mythology and memoir – albeit in the materially marginal form of unpublished manuscripts, letters, memoirs and footnotes.

This is an important point to emphasize. As Irene Gammel has eloquently suggested, the documentation of the Baroness's performances in the paintings, photography and narrative accounts of her contemporaries reads like a miscellany of 'exotic artifacts'.[16] However, if we consider the relegation of this fragmentary collection to the margins of modernism, it seems that this 'myriad of visual fragments' speaks less to the fragmentary nature of modernist narrative as Gammel suggests, than to the employment of the Baroness's grotesque body in the maintenance of narratives of modernist myth-making. To put it another way, while the fragmented body of the Baroness might, initially, seem to resonate with thematic and formal aspects of literary modernism, the processes by which her body is cast out, fragmented and re-contained within modernism's marginalia in the first instance are far more revealing. If modernism can be, as Tim Armstrong has proposed, 'characterized by the desire to intervene in the body; to render it a part of modernity by techniques which might be biological, mechanical, or behavioural',[17] how might we read attempts to regulate, contain and classify Elsa's body and bodily-practices? If, as Naomi Sawelson-Gore has convincingly suggested, 'the paradoxical irony of Dada is slippage. The movement of absolute rebellion was also one of repression', what does this case of the Baroness's confinement to modernism's marginalia reveal about the gendered and repressive rationalization of modernist production and subsequent constructions of modernist and avant-garde histories?[18] What role does the grotesque body or the structural dynamics of the abject have in informing or regulating this?

i. Marginality and modernity: Critical histories of exclusion and the case of Baroness Elsa von Freytag-Loringhoven

I am nauseatingly *tired* – tired of living in writing – or art – only – only only!

I hate myself – I spit on myself – I look in the mirror and see a neglected dispirited left over old woman!

And – the insane thing about it *is it is not true!*

But – it is true – in *America* –!

Elsa von Freytag-Loringhoven to Jane Heap

Through self-consciously modern experiments in modes of representation and living, and an oppositional critique of bourgeois thought and conventional artistic practices, the historical avant-garde has consistently adopted a peripheral or marginal relation to the centre in spatial terms, a deliberate positioning *against* prevailing social, cultural and aesthetic norms. As Susan Suleiman has detailed, the position of women within these historically predominately male-dominated movements thus emerges as a form of 'double marginality'. Women of the avant-garde, Suleiman suggests, have historically been faced with a choice: either accept and thereby reinforce patriarchal expectations, often subordinating their creative production to the codes of representation promoted by their male contemporaries in the process, or relegate themselves to the far-flung peripheries of these already marginal movements in developing critiques of these dominant avant-garde modes.[19] What I identify throughout this book as the regulation and containment of the Baroness within the marginalia of modernism – its letters, diaries, memoirs and unpublished manuscripts – certainly speaks to and informs this concept of 'double marginality', and in the following chapters I offer a reading of the mechanisms and motivations at work in this anxious regulation. Remaining sensitive to the gendered mythologies surrounding early twentieth-century avant-garde movements, it nevertheless becomes apparent that the treatment of the Baroness exceeds (even while it is obviously informed by) a straightforward misogyny, and speaks directly to anxieties regarding the definitions of modernism and modernity as 'dominant modes of rational practice'.[20]

As Amelia Jones and James Harding amongst others have recently noted in their queer(y)ing of established notions of the avant-garde itself, such movements are not only shaped by certain historical pressures and prejudices but continue to be organized and filtered through the rationalizing tendencies of art historical models. In a manner not dissimilar from the processes of remembering, forgetting and re-writing activated in autobiographical practices, the construction of critical histories testifies to a dependence upon narrative. Replicating the misogyny and heterosexism which Naomi Sawelson-Gorse has convincingly identified as a prevailing force in Dada configurations, critical histories have tended to privilege and promote the production of a selection of white, male, heterosexual and bourgeois artists in their (often Eurocentric and linear) narratives of early twentieth-century avant-garde formations.[21] In the context of New York Dada, the heroes are inevitably Marcel Duchamp, Man Ray and Francis Picabia, and the movement is typically defined by a small selection of visual objects which promulgate an imagined aesthetic coherence around the (Duchampian) Readymade, the mechanized fantasies of Picabia and de Zayas, and various playful attempts to bring art and the everyday into closer proximity.

Of course, the cultural landscape of this historical period was much more complex, and current critical reappraisals of the Baroness's work by no means stand alone in retrospectively challenging such monolithic constructions. Nevertheless, as the publication of the ground-breaking *Women in Dada* addressed some time ago, while studies of individual female avant-gardists have certainly appeared over the last few decades, art history more broadly has proved strangely reluctant to adjust or redefine its boundaries to accommodate new (notably feminist) methodologies and practices.[22] This is, ironically, especially pertinent for current discussions of the Baroness, and attempts to position her as the artist responsible for 'R. Mutt's' 1917 *Fountain*, which I shall address over the course of this chapter. While we can celebrate the rising popular profile of the Baroness and of her network of influences in the context of New York Dada and beyond, the terms of her movement from the peripheries to the centre of these discussions as a fetishized 'forgotten' figure are striking in their untroubled assimilation of Elsa into established art-historical categories. While no doubt well-intentioned, attempts to 'recover' the Baroness and establish her as a cult figure on these grounds in fact tend to demonstrate a tendency to neutralize the subversive threat of her performative, corporeal and waste-based practice in their rush to legitimize her as a significant artist. Rather than challenging the forms and functions of the Duchampian Readymade – which her work consistently does – she is made to stand for it, which not only attempts to legitimize her position through *Fountain's* iconic status, but suggests that feminist critique can be reduced to inserting women into masculinist histories, without challenging the terms upon which those histories have been made.

Building on feminist methodologies that have looked to the margins to recover 'forgotten female modernists' in recent years, I want to push this a little further in suggesting that attention to the forms and functions of the material accumulating on these boundary lines illuminates the process through which women and the work they were engaged in were systematically marginalized in early modernist and avant-garde critical histories in the first instance. Following Mary Douglas's model whereby 'if a person has no place in the social system and is therefore a marginal being, all precaution against danger must come from others', I read certain gendered strategies of containment activated across the historical avant-garde as a way of controlling and regulating these margins and the bodies and practices reproduced there.[23] Looking closely at the work that the Baroness produced from this position I want to suggest that waste proves generative, not only in its reuse in her costumes and sculptural objects, but in its provision of a methodological approach for a feminist project of 'recovery' that does not simply assimilate these figures into existing and overwhelmingly masculinist canons, but playfully engage with the disruptive potential of the margins in a radical challenge to the coherence and completeness of the notion of the canon itself.

An important aspect of this kind of canon-formation is not only the question of who is making art, but also of what kind of art they are making. As the pre-eminence of the Readymade suggests, in discussions of New York Dada's aesthetics, thematics and anti-establishment gestures, traditional theoretical models of avant-gardism have consistently foregrounded and fetishized the visual objects of Dada, despite Duchamp's own 'anti-retinal' stance.[24] As studies like RoseLee Goldberg's *Performance Art from Futurism to the Present* highlight: 'Despite the fact that most of what has been written today about the work of the Futurists, Constructivists, Dadaists and Surrealists continues to concentrate on the art objects produced by each period, it was more often than not the case that these movements found their roots and attempted to resolve problematic issues in performance.'[25]

James Harding's work in this respect has been incredibly illuminating, not only in highlighting the anti-performative bias at work in the traditional theoretical models of avant-gardism established by the likes of Peter Bürger, Renato Poggioli and Matei Calinescu in the 1970s, but in shifting the terms upon and through which we can discuss the historical avant-garde itself.[26] Of course, the interest (particularly tangible in Bürger's work) in retrospectively installing Dada, and particularly Duchamp, as the originary antecedents of a (then-contemporary) postmodern radical anti-institutionalism, speaks more to attempts to rationalize their own historical moment than to a discussion of the historical avant-garde more broadly. Nevertheless, this blind spot in relation to performance is telling, particularly given the fact that both Poggioli and Bürger foreground issues of antagonism, activism and anti-institutionalism in their definition of the avant-garde, certainly all highly performative gestures if nothing else. In his suggestion that contemporary models for approaching historical avant-gardes are filtered through a sedimentary layering of theories that 'fail to recognize, let alone conceptualize, the avant-garde gesture as first and foremost a performative act',[27] Harding identifies something important for developing here with regards to the Baroness. As a performative subject, Elsa is to Dada and modernism what performance is to the historical avant-garde more broadly: marginalized to the point of being actively repressed, and yet central to an understanding of the energies, gestures and impetus of avant-garde production in New York during these early decades of the twentieth century.

Insisting on 'performance as a pivotal category for defining the avant-garde itself', Harding identifies the marginalization of critical conceptions of performance while establishing its centrality in twentieth-century avant-garde praxis. Challenging these historiographical assumptions of the avant-garde and identifying an important dialogue between the 'centre' and the 'margins', Harding provides us with strategies for addressing the condition of 'double marginality' proposed by Suileman, and of Elsa's positioning in relation to this.

Taking into account the 'rather stunning absence of critical assessments that explore how the experimental work of women artists challenges dominant scholarly assumptions about the avant-garde', we can begin to see how the marginalization of both women and performance in rationalizing accounts of the avant-garde is mutually reinforcing.[28] Nevertheless, both Harding and Suileman's models open up possibilities for a gendered re-reading of the production, circulation and consumption of twentieth-century avant-gardes. Taken alongside an analysis of Elsa's own promotion of marginal forms (autobiography and performance) and aesthetic interest in jettisoned objects (the material waste she collected and used in her practice), such models can be usefully employed in engaging with the notion of the peripheries as potentially powerful sites of production examined by a selection of feminist historians.[29]

Between grinding poverty and frequent incarcerations on charges of petty theft or public indecency, the Baroness certainly existed on the fringes of society, and even a potted biography makes the very real material consequences of her marginalized condition clear. As Gammel's extensive biography describes in more detail, fleeing the conservative, repressive and violent conditions of her father's Swinemünde home in 1893 in typically dramatic style, Else Plötz, as she was then, made her way to Berlin where, after an irrevocable break with an aunt she had been staying with, she found precarious work as an erotic artist within the underground world of the city's vaudeville scene.[30] While this early experience provided good training for the artist's modelling through which she would be able to provide herself with some modest, if irregular income in the years to come, it also introduced her to a world of uninhibited 'sex-expression' that would occupy a central position in her life and art from this point on. Freeing herself from the relative security of bourgeois modesty and exploding into the territory being marked out by the sexually liberated New Woman, she embarked on a sex-quest through which 'now I began to know what "life" meant – every night another man […] I was intoxicated'.[31] Not without its consequences, this orientation to pleasure over propriety resulted in medical interventions and the inscription of her body as 'diseased' as she was treated first for gonorrhoea and then secondary syphilis in 1896. As well as marking her body physically through rash-like symptoms, the social stigma and anxiety surrounding syphilis would have marked as a fallen, and even dangerous woman, an illness she would later turn to metaphor in her attempts to channel pure artistic energy through her syphilitic, sexually desiring body to a horrified William Carlos Williams.[32] After pursuing several unconventional romantic entanglements across Germany and Italy, including her introduction of translator Felix Paul Greve into her own sexually dysfunctional marriage to architect August Endell, she followed Greve to America – after helping him fake his own suicide to avoid his debts – where she was eventually deserted.

Despite gaining an impressive title in her third marriage, she was no financially better off and was, again, abandoned when the German Baron rushed back to Europe to regain his honour with the outbreak of war in 1914.

Approaching middle age, alone and with a strident accent and inescapably German name, her circumstances in New York and Philadelphia (especially after America's entry into the First World War in 1917) were precarious, although even the poverty and outsider status endured during these years paled in comparison to the utter destitution of her years in post-war Berlin. With barely enough money to eat and heat her dilapidated apartments, which she shared with a collection of rats and mice that she apparently encouraged, the former Dada Queen was reduced to 'a shabby wretched female selling newspapers, stripped of all her rococo richness of her clothes, her speech, her personality', as Claude McKay records after a chance encounter with 'Frau Freytag' in the winter of 1923–4.[33]

Alongside painful letters where she pleads for financial and emotional support, several surviving poems from this period reflect the emotional, physical and psychological strain of her situation, vividly embodied in a piece such as 'Body Sweats' in which the tightly bound column of verse evokes the slim, tired and aching body of the Baroness herself:

Body
Sweats
Mind
Rags
Agony
Unceasing

Heartleach
Bloodseeps
Agony
Unceasing –[34]

Despite flashes of her dark humour and resolute sense of her own strength as an artist in the face of adversity who, like a 'Hellfly' will 'Buzz in spectral murderhouse', these poems are preoccupied with images of suicide and death as offering the 'one safe charm in life: distance'.[35] Violently rejecting Germany's 'decay reek […] Effect of brainsoftening backside', they nevertheless connect the Weimar Republic's dereliction to her own.[36] After two years of the extreme privation detailed in a series of desperate letters to Barnes in Paris, she spent most of 1925 between a home for destitute women and a psychiatric asylum. Continuing her correspondence with Barnes and producing the main body of her autobiography over this period, the Baroness tellingly conflates her own desperate situation with that of her mother's, whose escalating depression and undiagnosed uterine cancer led to an anguished few years marked by suicide attempts and dramatic disappearances before her eventual admittance to a Sanatorium in the months before her death in 1893. After an extensive reflection on her mother's condition and death in one particularly painful, long letter, the Baroness pleads with the younger Barnes:

> It takes <u>strong</u> people who love me – to rescue me – from pit I am in! <u>Pit</u> – <u>Pit I am in! I must be gotten out of Germany!</u> It <u>numbs</u> me – it drains all vitality – it makes me <u>useless</u> […] I am insane from Germany – as my mother was from 'home'.[37]

Although Barnes was able to call on enough friends to raise sufficient funds to secure the Baroness's passage to Paris in 1926, the Baroness's situation only vaguely improved. Her letters to Peggy Guggenheim and Mary Reynolds illustrate the extent of her financial precarity, and her admonishments to friends – including Barnes – for real or imagined slights became more frequent. Succeeding against the odds to open a modelling school in Paris, her immigrant status would once again prove decisive in pushing her to the margins, as her school was closed and her ability to work in Paris called into question.[38] In the particularly cold winter of 1927, she dies from gas asphyxiation in what was either a tragic accident, the vengeful act of a lover or suicide.[39]

During the last decade of her life, Elsa relied heavily on the financial support of friends and lovers, and her letters frequently admonish those who have forgotten her, or who have failed to acknowledge her unique contribution. Even in the slightly more prosperous New York Dada days, the Baroness was acutely aware of her marginalized position. Writing to Jane Heap in 1923 requesting money to pay her hotel bills (as she so often did), the Baroness launched into an embittered attack on the privileged 'insider' status of New York's avant-garde circles:

> I have to Pay! I am worried and unhappy[;] you are always invited and have a gay time – I am an outsider – only my art is good enough – then I get a bite – an alm – otherwise I am kicked – fi! I do feel like murder shit merde […] I am neglected – my welfare – my wishes – my feelings and [I] can starve to death […] because I can't even get gun for noble person's death.[40]

Invoking a 1921 letter from Man Ray in New York to Tristan Tzara in Paris in which Man Ray used a photographic still of the Baroness's contorted naked body to stand in for the 'A' of 'de l'Amerique', and thus metonymically for Dada in America, Elsa here further collapses associations with Man Ray's stammering 'merdelamerdelamerdelamerdelamerdelamer' and her own condition. Visually striking and immediately expressive of the Baroness's central but sublimated role in New York Dada configurations, as has been reiterated by scholars since Francis Naumann's identification of the model as Elsa in the 1970s, Man Ray clearly uses Elsa's body in order to transmit the *'mer de la merde'* between New York and Paris. However, given that the letter's intention is to announce the stillbirth of the movement in New York as 'all New York is Dada and will not tolerate a rival', Elsa's often-repeated status as the living embodiment of Dada here does not so much qualify or celebrate her as it's *'mère'* in Man Ray's eyes, but makes this maternity grotesque as she is reconfigured as a *'mère de la merde'* – an expulsive, contaminating and resolutely female producer of shit. Very tellingly, Man Ray measures the failure of New York Dada in economic terms, stating there is 'no one here to work for it, and no money to be taken for it, or donated to it'. In privileging economic stability as a mark of Dada's success, Man Ray not only reveals something about the avant-garde's relationship to the logic of capital and consumerism, but also activates the gendered mechanisms of 'double marginality' outlined by Suileman. Containing the commercial failure of New York Dada within an ageing woman's naked body, Man Ray is able to reject both as without value, as uncommodifiable, as waste, pushing both New York Dada and Elsa to the margins and protecting Paris – and himself – from contamination. Indeed, given that Man Ray's letter goes on to mention Picabia and Duchamp by name, it would seem that the reinscription of Elsa's body as a sign of failure does not just protect a broader Dada agenda, but specifically the reabsorption of her male contemporaries into a viable European avant-garde network.

Circulated between male Dadaists in order to uphold the binaries of New York to Paris, financial success to ruin, life to death, it is no surprise then that in trying to articulate the very real material consequences of her existences on the fringes of society to Heap, she would echo Man Ray's letter in identifying herself *as* the 'merdelamerde' that she symbolically represented here. Further than this, if we are to follow Gammel in her reading of the film project (itself a failure) from which this still was taken as a 'three-way film collaboration, Man Ray and Duchamp work[ing] two cameras, simultaneously filming the Baroness as she modelled in the nude',[41] her addition of the homophone 'murder' in her letter to Heap speaks to the success of this process of being made 'doubly marginal' as a kind of calculated expulsion. For Dada to survive in Paris, it must be murdered in New York, a performative gesture carefully contained within the borders of Man Ray's letter. While Man Ray and Duchamp had the means to leave New York, and the European networks to sustain and promote their work, the Baroness remained for several more desperate years, on the margins of modernist cultures

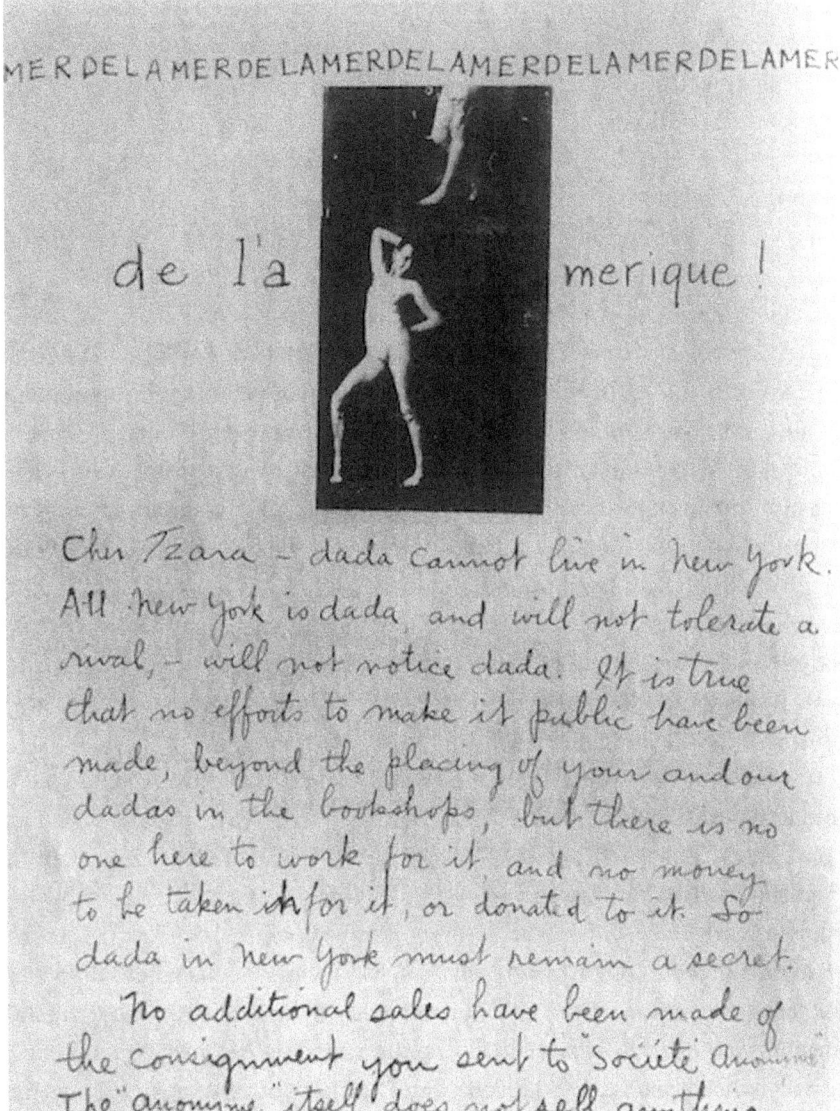

Figure 2 Man Ray, letter to Tristan Tzara with film still of Elsa von Freytag-Loringhoven posing. Postmarked 8 June 1921. Bibliotèque litéraire Jacques Doucet, Paris, Man Ray Trust/ADAGP, Paris and DACS, London, 2019.

of production, particularly after *The Little Review*'s more conservative turn in the wake of their own defeat over charges of obscenity for publishing *Ulysses*.

Having published some of her most provocative and innovative poetry and experimental criticism between 1918 and 1921, after the failure of the *Ulysses* trial in February 1921, *The Little Review* adjusted its stance on 'Making No Compromise with the Public Taste', which included its vocal promotion of the Baroness. Despite evoking the 'censor's gag-laden fist' in relation to the *Ulysses* battle, Harriet Monroe would make her own appeal to *The Little Review* editors directly to 'drop Else von Freytag-Loringhoven on the way' to Dada. In a clear move to purify Dada of its more subversive elements and to separate *The Little Review* from the controversy surrounding the editor's trial, Pound promoted Picabia as the magazine's Dada representative while the poetically and personally more difficult Baroness was increasingly sidelined. Although he would later chastise Anderson for not including the Baroness in an influential anthology of American poetry, his own ambivalent attraction to her Dada invective would play out in a tension between influence and censorship, as Gammel has described.[42] Legitimizing Picabia's mecanomorphic Dada, and his own avant-gardism in *The Little Review*'s pages, the Baroness's lived Dada, which 'laughs, jeers, grimaces, gibbers, denounces, explodes, introduces ridicule into a too churchly game' was brought under closer regulation.[43]

In the context of the Baroness's critical erasure, it is important to note that until 2011 no published collection of her poetry was available; until this point, accessing her writing was challenging, scattered as it was across archival fragments and the various Anglophone little magazines that published her work between 1918 and 1927. Her sculptural assemblages have been lost, destroyed or misattributed to other (male) artists, and for the most part only survive in photographic reproductions or in private collections, while her experimental memoir, written at the request of her friend and literary executor Djuna Barnes, although finally published in 1992, has since fallen out of print and into obscurity. Enlisting the help of Duchamp as early as 1957, Barnes had tried without success to have the Baroness's papers properly archived at Yale University, and it was not until the early 2000s that they were fully processed separately from the main bulk of Barnes's papers in the University of Maryland's Special Collections.[44] Because of the transitory nature of what critics have convincingly theorized as her proto-feminist performance art, and the perishable or otherwise temporary nature of her junk costumes, these provocative promenades and daring self-representational practices are virtually inaccessible, other than through photographs or the somewhat problematic records made by her contemporaries.⁴⁵ Despite being celebrated by many as the 'Original "Dada"' and maintaining a high profile across the pages of *The Little Review* between 1918 and 1922, Elsa has, until relatively recently, been consistently overlooked in subsequent critical histories of the period.⁴⁶ Mentioned only once in Robert Motherwell's seminal anthology of Dada practitioners and entirely absent from Arturo Schwarz's influential re-writing of New York Dada as the exclusive purview of Man Ray, Duchamp and Picabia, she still found herself relegated to the category of 'Others' in Francis Naumann's otherwise revisionist *New York Dada 1915–23*.⁴⁷

While it is obviously problematic to reclaim and celebrate the 'margins' as powerful sites of feminist resistance, an awareness of Elsa's negotiations with the material, social, economic and psychological implications of exclusion certainly adds another dimension to discussions of the disruptive potential of her *couture d'ordures* and highlights her antagonistic operation on the outskirts of fields of modernist production. Keenly aware of her outsider status, of her positioning at the edges of the 'safe' places occupied by the likes of Williams, Duchamp and Pound, the Baroness claims this space as a disarmingly alchemic site from which to produce art. As Williams describes in his rather lyrical account of her collecting practices, '[A] bride lost the heel of her left shoe at the tube station; lost, it becomes a jewel, a ruby in La Baronne's miscellany'.⁴⁸ It was in the very action of becoming lost or cast-out or useless that Williams suggests the Baroness found value, tapping into what Mary Douglas terms the 'energy' of the margins and transmuting matter into art by her recovery and eventual reconfiguration of it.⁴⁹ Occupying a boundary line in this way the Baroness, and the work that she produces from this position, are both open to the powerfully transformative energies of the margins; and to its contaminating power. As Mary Douglas memorably stated '[t]o have been in the margins is to have been in contact with danger, to have been at a source of power'.⁵⁰

As the many accounts of her outlandish costuming attest, gleaning the streets and recovering the broken, carelessly discarded and forgotten quotidian items that she found there was an essential component of her art practice, and yet the *practices* of collecting and composition that she developed are often treated as somewhat secondary to the visually striking nature of her sensational costuming. In drawing attention to these practices, later chapters will connect them to the structural patterns of recovery, reception and variation at work in her autobiographic projects, and propose ways of positioning them in an illuminating relation to Barnes's compositional practices and autobiographic poetics. As is memorably documented by those who visited her, the Baroness's apartment read like a strange archive of the life of the city as revealed through the objects it used and threw out. As George Biddle recalls:

> It was crowded and reeking with the strange relics which she had purloined over a period of years from the New York gutters. Old bits of ironware, automobile tires, gilded vegetables, a dozen starved dogs, celluloid paintings, ash cans, every conceivable horror, which to her tortured, yet highly sensitized perception, became objects of formal beauty.[51]

The 'horror' that Biddle records here seems less about the objects themselves than the confrontation with an unsettling archive of the used and compromised, an exhibition of 'matter out of place'. In recovering these objects and reusing them in her collages, sculptural assemblages, costumes and the decorative ornaments either gifted to her friends outside of a money economy or applied directly to her moving body, the Baroness presented a direct challenge to the systems that claimed to regulate the flows of consumer goods and capital in the modern metropolis. More than this, in applying these new constructions directly to her active body, the Baroness signals her refusal to keep her body in its proper place, proudly performing a recalcitrant femininity that defies conventional gender codes and expectations. This is pushed even further in Harding's reading of the Baroness's apartment as an 'antidomesticated space', its piled-up junk and the appalled reactions of Biddle and Williams revealing the limitations of an American avant-gardism whose loud claims for the dismantling of restrictive social codes and constricts such as marriage, religion and the family were built on a reaffirmation of gendered divisions of labour and the 'conventional domestic traditions of bourgeois society'.[52]

Deeply invested in a complex notion of artistic genius fused with a problematically racialized notion of 'Teutonic superiority' and worked out across her letters, poetry and criticism, the Baroness distinguished herself from the American artists around her whom she regarded as little more than 'plain working people, mixing up art with craft, in vulgar untrained brain'.[53] In doing so, she rejected democratic and pluralistic models of art and art production, favouring instead the isolated, individualistic notion of the artist-as-aristocrat. Setting herself outside of American society and its broad cultural definitions also liberated her from restrictive gendered and aesthetic codes and practices which would form the foundations of her shockingly provocative art:

> If I can write – talk – about dinner – pleasure of my palate – as artist or aristocrat – with my ease of manner – can afford also to mention my ecstasies in toilet room!
>
> If you can not – you are invited to silence – by all means![54]

Chastising others for staying safely within the bounds of bourgeois respectability and accepting the rewards for their conformity, the Baroness preferred to 'Say it with – – –/Bolts!'.[55] As well as her irreverent toilet humour, her pride in her anatomy and its functioning extended in her poetry to celebrations of oral sex, ejaculation, ageing and the 'rife – penetrating – rank – frank redolence' of her body.[56]

In what we could take as a manifesto statement for her aesthetic experiments with waste objects and the visceral qualities of her corporeal poetics, Elsa declared her intention 'to show hidden beauty of things – there are no limitations! Only artist can do that – that is his holy office. Stronger – braver he is – more he will explore its depths' [sic] (BS: 288). Djuna Barnes's recollection of the macabre beachcombing episode alluded to in my introduction confirms this tendency towards grotesque exploration explaining that 'she could – on the beach, on the beach of Croitoix [sic], stand over a drowned and decaying dog corpse –& poke a stick into its ribs – to see how it was "put together"'.[57]

Finding the hidden beauty in the cast-out, rejected and 'disgusting'; understanding composition through decomposition; plunging herself into decay in order to understand life – such were the conceits and contours of her aesthetic project. In her excremental ecstasies and liberated sexual expression, she certainly went further than other artists into the margins of socially or aesthetically acceptable notions of propriety and beauty. Given that performance itself can certainly be historized as a marginal art form, discussions of the Baroness's performative poetics must take this condition into account. Boldly flaunting gendered, aesthetic and spatial conventions in the development of her lived-Dada practice – often at great personal cost – the Baroness performed from the peripheries. However, it was from here that she could harness the transformative energy of the margins, sifting through the material and autobiographical 'wastes' rejected by others in her self-appointed quest to discover how things are put together, and what hidden beauty resides in them.

ii. Gods, mutts and Readymades: 'America's comfort – sanitation!'

> Toilets are made for swift cleanliness – not modesty!
> *Elsa von Freytag-Loringhoven, 'The Modest Woman' (1920)*

As outlined in my introduction, the identification of centre and periphery, and the relegation of certain objects, bodies, matter and practices to the margins of these schemas are essential functional aspects of the various rationalizing projects associated with techno/industrial modernity. As such, these distinctions not only structure the 'domain of the disgusting' which have informed a range of cultural, religious and historical practices, but were augmented and put to new uses in the period of rapid industrial and technological expansion which spanned the mid-nineteenth to early twentieth centuries. In emergent metropolitan centres, such as New York, urban rationalization was a matter of intense debate in the twilight decades of the nineteenth century. Flooding popular consciousness, volumes of literature, multiple reform movements, and new institutions targeting sanitation, health, waste management, class, prostitution, overpopulation and morality, all struggled to control and classify the changing topography of the city, and to manage the behaviours of those living within it.[58] Through such efforts, notions of 'progress' within the historical contexts of industrial modernity were deftly wedded to ideas that privileged the centre through a sublimation of the peripheries: waste disappeared underground in new sewer systems; deemed unsanitary, houses and communities were bulldozed and the urban poor that had populated them were relocated to new housing projects and factories outside the city limits. In clearing land for other, more lucrative ventures, such a move employed discourses identifying the urban poor as contaminants, thus justifying their economically driven relocation on the grounds of disease and moral degradation. Labour and labouring bodies were similarly subject to regulation, both inside and outside the Fordist factory. Where once ragpickers, street vendors and prostitutes had been an integral part of a labour economy, they were increasingly marginalized and forced underground through severe legal restrictions and regulations.[59]

The discourses surrounding urban and social rationalization across this period inevitably lead us back to the body, specifically the bourgeois body and its Other(s). The utopian texts of nineteenth- and twentieth-century urban reformers frequently invoke the fantasy of the coherent, contained body in their discussions of the ideal city: roads and boulevards like arteries facilitating the 'flow' of people, traffic and trade; large parks and green spaces metonymically refashioned as the 'lungs' of the city; the sewers and waste-management systems imagined as its bowels, hidden below and converting matter into waste; the signifiers of urban poverty on the surface of the city imagined as 'scum', which – if left unmonitored – would collect in small pockets of the city and multiply, threatening to suffocate the total structure of the city-as-body like a fatal, choleric disease. Such a corporeal re-imagining of the city's topography directly impacted on discourses of the coherent, clean and civilized bourgeois body, and the nineteenth and twentieth centuries witnessed an explosion of technologies and practices for regulating the body through diet, exercise, clothing and medical intervention.⁶⁰ Indeed, such technologies were not the exclusive purview of the bourgeois body, but were extended in disciplining recalcitrant bodies through extensive surveillance, classification and regulation. Just as the rationalized city relied upon corporeal metaphors for its expression, so too was the Bourgeois Imaginary tied to notions of the clean, the functional and the rational.

While the nineteenth century reinforced structural distinctions between the centre and the periphery, public and private, clean and unclean, the twentieth century perfected modes of maintaining and regulating such distinctions. As Amelia Jones has described in her study of 'irrational modernism', models of industrial production – specifically Taylorism and Fordism – emerged in order to both encourage and control 'the dangerous flows of labour and capital loosed by the new machine-age economies', ensuring efficient production through the regulation of labourer's bodies and the anxious containment of threatening surplus flows.⁶¹ In the realms of urban psychology, the theories of Gustave le Bon and Georg Simmel produced models for addressing the dangerous potential of the unregulated 'crowd' (Le Bon), and the disintegrating threat to the integrity of the individual experienced in the metropolis (Simmel).⁶²

From Simmel's concern for the 'intensification of emotional life due to the swift and continuous shift of external and internal stimuli' and his observation of the *'blasé* attitude' as an essential mechanism for the psychological survival of the individual in the metropolis, we are not so far from the theories developed by Sigmund Freud for addressing both the structure of the psyche and the relation of the ego to the outside world as one based on the sublimation of dangerous, unsociable desires. Famously, the structural model of the psyche developed in *Beyond the Pleasure Principle* (1920) and *The Ego and the Id* (1923) explored the tensions between instinctual desire and the drive towards instant pleasure (ascribed to the id), the regulating watchman of the Super-Ego and the Ego which, mediating between the two, seeks satisfaction through realistic and life-preserving ends.⁶³ Sublimation thus emerges as the necessary sociable outcome of the tensions between the Pleasure Principle and Reality Principle; desires are satisfied but only once transformed, via this defence mechanism, into 'healthy' drives and behaviours. Expanding on this model in his later text *Civilization and Its Discontents* (1929), Freud would posit sublimation as the preeminent symbol of civilization's 'progress' whereby excessive libidinal energy is carefully contained and regulated, allowed only a limited amount of expression once it has been re-routed to socially useful ends.⁶⁴

If modes of rational practice were central to projects of urban, techno-industrial modernity, as Tim Armstrong and Amelia Jones amongst others have convincingly argued, we can begin to usefully locate the role of waste (and its management) in developing and directing discourses around modernity and modernist practice. Indeed, the various social, spatial, industrial and psychological models briefly outlined here all rely to a certain degree of a process of identification, classification and removal; all are responding to the challenge presented by modern urban civilization to simultaneously produce surplus material and dispose of it, and to render that functioning as seamlessly and silently as possible. Essential to the smooth functioning of commodity cultures and capitalist economies, waste is of course the necessary by-product of production, both in terms of the surplus energy or matter generated through production, and in terms of the disposable commodities produced, consumed and replaced in the maintenance of such economies. Once an object has exhausted its use value within the context of the system which produced it, it is adopted by another system. Inscribed within a rational 'order of waste', it is ascribed a new value there. The important thing to emphasize here is that, so long as it passes seamlessly from one order to the other, it remains efficient. As David Trotter's excellent study of nineteenth-century encounters with 'mess' highlights, so long as it submits to its lowering of value within this taxonomic order, '[w]aste is the measure of the organism's ability to renew itself by excluding whatever it does not require for its own immediate purposes [...] It testifies, in its very dereliction to the power which cast it down and out'.[65]

Such spatial, industrial, social and psychological rationalizing tendencies and theories were profoundly inscribed on the bodies and texts produced within what we broadly identify as literary and visual modernism. Just as modernist architecture as exemplified in the theories of Le Corbusier and Alfred Loos sought to rationalize space and the bodies that moved through it through a focus on functionality and exclusion of ornamental excess, interesting connections made between the regulation of bodily practices and the production of modernist texts have established readings of literary modernism in light of its ambivalent responses to issues of efficiency, excess and waste.[66]

As Jones has explicated in her study of *Irrational Modernism*, twentieth-century avant-garde movements – as much as the later critical histories briefly outlined above – evidenced a subtle but strong rationalizing trend within themselves. As outlined in my introduction, while a rhetoric of purity and progress might be more immediately associated with the canonical modernisms of Ezra Pound and Le Corbusier, such motivations and practices cannot be straightforwardly divorced from a discussion of the avant-garde, and can certainly be traced within the Duchampian Readymade and Picabian mechanical fantasy. Keen to re-examine the revolutionary and critical stances taken by the avant-garde in the early decades of the twentieth century, recent scholarship has introduced nuanced readings of the Readymades as semi-autobiographical explorations of the compromised and equivocal masculinities experienced by noncombatant male artists during the First World War period, especially highlighting the recurrent themes of frustrated or dysfunctional heterosexual coupling that Duchamp's large glass construction *The Bride Stripped Bare by Her Bachelors, Even* (1915–23) makes so manifest. Nevertheless, while the Readymades certainly evidence an ambivalence with regards to machine-age optimism and the repetitive processes of industrial mass-production, I am struck by the ways in which the simplified clean lines and polished surfaces of the objects we most readily associated with New York Dada visually and materially align these Readymades with the structures and systems invested in the *maintenance* of modernity's flows, rather than any radical reversal of them.

It is unsurprising then that the most iconic Readymade is an inverted urinal, an object that is absolutely conceptually connected to waste in the age of industrial mass production. The shock value of *Fountain* rests on this – of course, and on its irrational presentation as an object out of place. Indeed, these were precisely the terms of the Board of the Society of Independent Artists justification for refusing the submission for their inaugural exhibition in April 1917 where they stated 'the *Fountain* may be a very useful object in its place, but its place is not in an art exhibition and it is, by no definition, a work of art'.[67] The conflation of the object's use and its status as art is very telling, and while the statement denies both, closer attention to the forms and functions of *Fountain*, especially in the context of its role in the later historicization of the avant-garde (and the Duchampian Readymade) reveals a deeper conformity to modes of rational industrial and aesthetic discourses than is at first assumed. Before we look more closely at the object itself in light of this, I want to briefly outline the narrative that has been built up around it, and the role this has played in legitimizing the historical avant-garde's production.

Between bicycle wheels, bottle racks and snow shovels, Duchamp had been experimenting with the possibilities of presenting 'a work of art without an artist to make it' since 1913.[68] It was only after his arrival in America that these 'distractions' took on the more formalized distinction of 'readymade', as he explained to his sister in a letter from 1916:

> Now, If you have been up to my place you should see a bicycle wheel and a bottle rack. I bought this as a readymade sculpture. And I have a plan concerning this so-called bottle rack. Listen to this: Here, in N.Y., I have bought various objects in the same taste and I treat them as "readymades". You know English well enough to understand the sense of "tout fait" that I give these objects. I sign them and give them an English inscription [...] This whole preamble in order to say to you: Take for yourself this bottle rack. I will make it into a "Readymade" from a distance. You will have to write at the base and *on the inside* of the bottom ring in small letters painted with an oil-painting brush, in silver-white colour, the inscription that I will give you after this, and you will sign it in the same hand as follows: [after] Marcel Duchamp.

Duchamp apparently exhibited Readymades in New York as early as 1916, although they went unremarked upon (or unnoticed) by critics.[69] The same fate would have perhaps befallen *Fountain*, were it not for the efforts of *The Blind Man*, a little magazine set up by Duchamp, Henri-Pierre Roché and Beatrice Wood in publicizing the affair. The Exhibition had been promoted in *The Blind Man* and elsewhere as liberating art from the conservative restraints of the French salon tradition, promising a progressive approach of 'no jury, no prizes'. The submission of a porcelain urinal by 'R. Mutt' proved too much of an affront however, and after a furious row between members of the Hanging Committee which resulted in the resignation of Duchamp and Walter Arensberg, it was decided not to include the work which was apparently hidden behind a partition when the show opened on 10 April 1917. As the story goes, a group including Duchamp and Wood retrieved the urinal and took it to Alfred Stieglitz to be photographed. Reproduced and circulated in the second and final issue of *the Blind Man*, this photograph is a key document in both recording the affair and legitimizing *Fountain* as an artwork.

Heavily critical of the Hanging committee's decision, the second issue stoked controversy surrounding what Wood's introductory comments dubbed 'The Richard Mutt Case' and set out to defend *Fountain*'s status as an art object.[70] This was done most convincingly through the careful staging of the Stieglitz photograph, published alongside Wood's first formal defence of the Readymade, and Louise Norton's editorial 'The Buddha in the Bathroom'.

While anecdotal evidence and testimony identified Duchamp as 'R. Mutt' from the outset, an assumption corroborated to some extent by Roché's photographic series of the Readymades arranged in Duchamp's West 67th St studio in 1917–18 intriguingly, despite continued interest in the affair, it was not until 1934 that *Fountain* was explicitly placed within the context of the

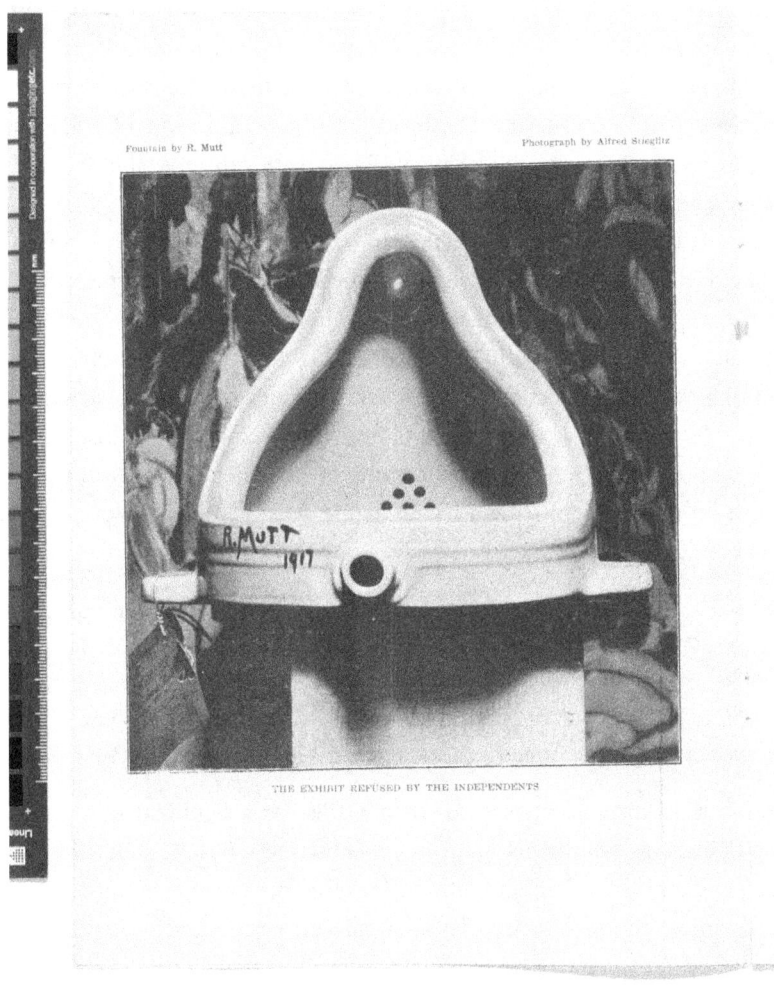

Figure 3 Alfred Stieglitz, *Fountain* by R. Mutt. The Blind Man (No. 2), May 1917. Philadelphia Museum of Art: The Louise and Walter Arensberg Collection, 1950. (1950-134-1053) © 2019. Photo The Philadelphia Museum of Art/Art Resource/Scala, Florence.

Duchampian Readymade.[71] While Breton's interest in the Readymade had much to do with his own attempts to contextualize the Surrealist object within a history of avant-garde experiment, it was during this period that Duchamp himself began to show an interest in documenting his production, collecting his notes related to the Large Glass construction in what became known as *The Green*

Box (1934), and working towards the miniature traveling museum *La Boîte en Valise (From or by Marcel Duchamp or Rrose Sélavy)* (1935–41) which included a miniature reproduction of *Fountain* alongside other prominent Readymades. With his profile as 'Dada Daddy' secure, it remained for the Readymades to be incorporated into official art historical channels, and from 1950 Duchamp began to issue replicas of the 'original' Readymades to meet the demands of museum and gallery collections.

In his research into the aesthetics and critical reception of the urinal in the late 1980s, William Camfield introduced some interesting ambiguities over the popularly accepted narrative surrounding *Fountain*. In an apparent contradiction of the account provided by Duchamp of *Fountain's* creation beginning with the selection of a standard Bedforshire model urinal from the J.L. Mott Iron Works on 5th Avenue with Aresnberg and Joseph Stella, Camfield produces a letter from Duchamp to his sister Suzanne, in which he presents an unidentified female friend as the artist responsible for Fountain's submission:

> Relay this detail to the family: the Independents have opened here with great success. One of my female friends under a male pseudonym, Richard Mutt, had sent in a porcelain urinal as a sculpture; as it wasn't at all indecent, there was no reason to reject it. The committee decided to refuse to show this thing. I have handed in my resignation and it will be a bit of gossip of some value in New York.[72]

Along with the discrepancies introduced in this letter, Camfield also highlights vague claims made in the popular press that the unknown artist 'R. Mutt' was a Philadelphian. While Camfield tests various theories – a female shipping agent, an early incarnation of Rrose Sélavy – none seem quite satisfactory, and these gaps in the *Fountain* narrative remained open.

Building on Camfiled's research some years later, Gammel's 2003 biography of the Baroness presents some compelling, although by her own admission circumstantial, evidence connecting Elsa to the infamous piece of plumbing ware. Spoken in a German tongue, the gender-ambiguous 'R. Mutt' of course invokes *mutter* (mother), or *Armut* (poverty), and her work also shows an interest in plumbing and sanitation. Certainly, the irreverent and scatological dimensions of the piece are consistent with the Baroness's own delight in toilet humour and anti-establishment gestures: she was vocal and creative in her insults, 'soulmonster' and 'shitmutt' getting particular mileage with those who had fallen short of her exacting standards, was comfortable loudly detailing her 'ecstasies in toilet room' and frequently bestowed scatological nicknames on her more illustrious contemporaries – Marcel Dushit and WC among her particular favourites.⁷³ Building her case, Gammel also draws attention to a comment made years later by Williams in which he refers to *Fountain* as a 'magnificent cast-iron urinal'.⁷⁴ Compellingly collapsing divisions between individual arts and between the products of the artist and the artist herself, Williams's comment not only conflates the porcelain *Fountain* with the Baroness's long poem 'Mineself – Minesoul – And – Mine – Cast-Iron Lover' (1919), or with the materiality of her sculptural assemblages *God* (1917) and *Enduring Ornament* (1913), but also resonates with Barnes's description of the Baroness herself as possessing 'a voice and a constitution of iron'.⁷⁵

In line with recent attempts to revise the overwhelmingly masculinist and misogynistic canons of the historical avant-garde, especially obvious in the contexts of Surrealism and Dada, Gammel's research has been indispensable in raising the Baroness's profile, and alongside the pioneering attentions of Francis Naumann, Amelia Jones and others, has rightly complicated and expanded our understanding of the practices and visual thematics involved with New York Dada. However, I am cautious about accepting claims built on Gammel's research that unproblematically position the Baroness as the rightful author of *Fountain*.⁷⁶ Indeed, while this would very neatly serve a basic aspect of feminist revisionist criticism – that of highlighting the systematic marginalization and misattribution of women's creative production in favour of her male contemporaries – the straightforward exchange of Elsa for Duchamp here does little else to address the real challenges that Elsa's proximity to Duchamp and the Readymade makes possible, and indeed perhaps overlooks key elements of her own art practice and critical thinking.

Whilst the recovery of those figures marginalized by an overwhelmingly white, heterosexual and masculinist canon has proved to be an essential step in challenging the prevailing hegemony, rather than assimilating the Baroness into the established aesthetic categories, codes and histories surrounding the (Duchampian) Readymade we must remain sensitive to the manner in which her distinctive waste-based practices and pointed gender critiques in fact destabilize the very aesthetic values upon which such canons have been constructed.

Certainly, the Baroness never claimed ownership over *Fountain*, and on more than one occasion her letters include vague references to it in their invocation to plumbing fixtures as a way of linking Duchamp to America, and to success.⁷⁷ As Gammel concedes, the final piece of textual evidence linking the Baroness to *Fountain* is ultimately missing. Given what Wood described as the 'small hurricane of controversy' surrounding the submission and rejection of *Fountain* it seems decidedly out of character for the famously outspoken Baroness not to have announced herself as its author, if that had indeed been the case.[78] She would later write a lengthy piece chastising American puritanical 'modesty' in relation to the suppression of *Ulysses* on similar grounds, and given the intense (if romantically one-sided) friendship between the two artists, it seems striking that Duchamp would not have included her in *The Blind Man's* defence, if she had been involved.

Although somewhat ambivalent over Felix Paul Greve's earlier appropriation of her life material for his novels, she nevertheless sharply acknowledged her collaborative role in the promotion of his literary reputation and success. Keenly sensitive to both her own outsider status and perceived slights by her peers, had she been deliberately excluded from the promotional activities of Norton, Roché, Wood and Duchamp after the event, we could expect her letters to bear some trace of resentment over the issue, especially given her bitter awareness of Duchamp and other's commercial success and notoriety in later years. In fact, even while she later claimed to dislike him on personal grounds, her letters to Barnes demonstrate a great respect for his authenticity and ingenuity, or as one letter puts it: 'I will be like he – without being counterfeit – that cannot be done – Marcel is priceless genuine – I will defy any person to "imitate" Marcel!'.[79]

Ultimately, the careful management of the Mutt case, in terms of both protecting the artist's identity and the management of the affair in the press after the event seems much in line with the cautious and savvy Duchamp than the impulsive Baroness, a distinction that in her own words marked the difference between Duchamp's 'prostitution' of himself and her own Amazonian self-possession whereby 'my swing will naturally go to desperation and "crime" instead [of] to: *prostitution*'.[80] Building on Camfield's research, Gammel's placing of the Baroness in Philadelphia over the period of the Independents is certainly compelling. However, while financial security was always somewhat elusive for the Baroness, George Biddle's recollections mark this period as a particularly desperate time for her. Given that Biddle records her sleeping on park benches with sailors and bathing in public fountains in lieu of a more stable arrangement, the suggestion that the Baroness could have purchased a urinal, arranged for it to be shipped to New York, and paid the six-dollar submission fee without enlisting the help of others starts to appear increasingly unlikely.

Nevertheless, all of this is to straightforwardly compare the case for Elsa as author with that of Duchamp, which somewhat misses the point. To return to the piece of textual evidence that most significantly troubles accounts of

Duchamp's authorship, what is compelling about his letter to Suzanne is the gaps and holes that it (re)opens around the notion of authorship and the avant-garde itself, ambiguities that were certainly at play with the original mystery cultivated around 'R. Mutt' but were later plugged, first by Breton's attempts to legitimize the Surrealist object, and later by Duchamp's creation of a neatly contained miniature archive and carefully controlled reproductions. In citing a truncated version of Camfield's extract, Gammel's influential reading of Duchamp's letter focuses squarely on the figure of the female friend, eliding Duchamp's broader involvement in the affair, and the instructions framing this comment as to how his sister should manage what starts to look more like a performance, with complicit actors and unsuspecting audience. Of course, this wouldn't be the first time that Duchamp had issued instructions to his sister with regards to the Readymades, the earlier collaborative gestures regarding the retroactive claiming of the Readymades he left in Paris made more explicit in the 'Unhappy Readymade' from 1919, and it is worth reconsidering R. Mutt (our mutt?) in this respect. While Wood, Stieglitz and Covert seem to have been peripherally instrumental in managing the affair, we can surmise that Charles Demuth, Walter Arensberg and Louise Norton were more directly involved. Writing to Henry McBride, Demuth reported that *Fountain* had been made by one of their set, and encouraged the critic to follow up this letter by contacting Duchamp or Richard Mutt directly. As Camfield details, had McBride followed up the invitation, he would have got through to Louise Norton, whose details have also been shown to have been written on *Fountain's* submission slip, visible in the Stieglitz photograph. Given the repeated references to the Baroness's advanced age compared to many of the younger Dada figures during this time (she was only forty-seven at the time of the Independents) compared to Norton's youthful twenty-five it seems more likely that she was the 'young woman' to which Stieglitz refers.[81]

Ultimately, the most extreme iteration of the challenge to the *Fountain* narrative – that Duchamp deliberately and illicitly claimed an object rightfully submitted by the Baroness – remains somewhat unconvincing. Nevertheless, bringing the Baroness and Duchamp into such proximity, these gaps and holes perform an important critical function, demanding that we rethink both the exchanges and interactions between these artists, and the processes through which the Duchampian Readymade is formalized as a privileged category of the historical avant-garde.

The Baroness was certainly directly involved in some of the photographic and film projects that Duchamp worked on in this period, not to mention the fascinating three-way collaboration with Man Ray that resulted in the single issue of *New York Dada* in 1921. Elsa was already selecting found objects on her urban perambulations and filling her studio space with her strange archive of 'bits of glass, wood, metal, paper and other decorative refuse collected from the street', and the opportunity for lively conversation and fruitful exchange was particularly rich during the period 1915–16 when they shared studio spaces in the Lincoln Arcade building as her biography details.[82] While their interest in the found or selected object appears contemporaneous (although there are important divergences, as we shall see), it is interesting to note that despite holding on to his Readymades when he left Paris, it wasn't until January 1916, some time into his tenure at the Lincoln Arcade Building and into his friendship with the Baroness, that Duchamp wrote to his sister and retrospectively elevated these objects to the status of Readymade.

Returning the Baroness and her abject aesthetics into the frame in this way doesn't simply complicate the story of *Fountain*'s authorship, but in doing so challenges the privileging of novelty and originality as essential categories of the Duchampian Readymade and broader theories of the avant-garde, exposing the intrinsic relations between these aesthetic categories and the dominant logic of capitalism and commodification within which *Fountain* is embedded.

The closer I look at *Fountain* the more divorced it seems from the forms and (dys)functions of Elsa's other sculptural objects, pieces which go considerably further in their identification with or even as polluting forms of waste and continue to be far more disruptive on this point than the urinal could ever be. As mentioned above, while *Fountain* initially might present as an irrational object – a urinal having no place in an art gallery – its forms and functions are deeply embedded within industrially and aesthetically rationalist discourses. The toilet and plumbing systems and sewers it was connected to were amongst the most important modern development in discourses surrounding and reproducing the 'clean' subject: toilets moved into private spaces, with working cisterns and powerful flushes that disposed of waste instantly and effectively, disappearing underground, relegated to another realm and symbolic order. Interestingly compromised objects, toilets sit on the boundary line between high and low, clean and unclean, the contained (Bourgeois) home and the contaminating sewer. As a functional object the toilet inscribes the downward verticality of the system of value – from the private home, to the public, mixed and compromising realm of the sewer – it removes waste from the body cleanly and efficiently, allowing waste to transition through it as it passes from one order into another.

Ultimately reassuring in its normal functioning then, the toilet identifies and polices that boundary, maintaining the civilized, clean and coherent body by removing waste and by regulating the vertical structure of the system that separates these two orders of matter. As an object, it is the outward sign of this ordering system at work. Performing these functions, it also acts as an oversaturated symbol of the fraught conceptual connections between cleanliness, godliness and purity continually shored up against discourses connecting material waste with more slippery notions of filth in the nineteenth century: slums, poverty, disease, moral degradation, dirt and decay. Of course, the urinal is a slightly more problematic object than the domestic toilet, given the tension between private bodily acts and public space that it combines. In its status as a public convenience, the urinal is coded as closer to the sewer, contaminated by its proximity to unknown bodies and bodily practices. Nevertheless, in spite of its association with intimate and private bodily functioning, *Fountain* itself is visibly clean and brightly polished – in fact it is brand new, uncontaminated, making its way straight off the assembly line, out of the hardware store and delivered into the hands of the Society of Independent Artists via 'R. Mutt'. Despite the rotation of the urinal interfering with the object's straightforward functionality, it hasn't been physically altered in any way, its prominent open pipes and holes have not been filled or blocked; while it presents itself as a somewhat irrational object, it in fact fails to confound its functional use as a piece of plumbing-ware.

The urinal is also very quickly assimilated into rational aesthetic discourse, obvious not only in *Fountain's* prominence in subsequent exhibitions and critical histories of the avant-garde, but in Norton's immediate defence of the object's 'chaste simplicity of line and form'. As alluded to above, the artful staging of Stieglitz's photograph is clearly instrumental in this respect. Arranged on a plinth and offset against the backdrop of a Marsden Hartley canvas, the dramatic lighting emphasizes the object's curvilinear form, its smooth polished surface and the sensuously undulating passages of light and shadow playing across its concave centre. While Norton would liken the object to a Buddha and the 'legs of the ladies by Cezanne', in describing the veil of shadow falling across the urinal Wood renames it the *Madonna of the Bathroom,* firmly positioning it within a Western art historical canon and legitimizing the urinal as an art object by drawing on the tradition of the female nude.

The title is interesting in this respect too. Playfully relating the object's physical rotation to a reversal of its normal functioning, the urinal is turned into a fountain. Read in this way, the literal inversion is meant to refer conceptually to a structural one. Reversing the downward verticality of the flow from high to low, that which should have been relegated is returned, playing on anxieties collecting around the urinal's compromised status as the regulating object between surface and sewer. In this context, readings that trace genital female forms within the curved and concave shapes, hollows and holes of *Fountain* add a troubling dimension to this reading of the rational Readymade. Contrary to Arensberg's notion that the reclaimed object revealed a 'lovely form [...] freed from its functional purpose', in drawing connections between the urinal's inversion, its potential threat to reverse the flows of its normal functioning and female genital forms, *Fountain* in fact re-inscribes conceptual connections between women, waste and contaminating flows, a point that gathers significance in light of one of the cryptic notes from Duchamp's 1914 box 'One has only, for *female* the urinal and one *lives* by it'.[83] While the object may no longer be 'functional' as a urinal for male use, it nevertheless continues to 'function' as a signifier of anxieties crystalizing around women, waste and modernity.

Speaking of the Readymades more broadly Duchamp claimed to have 'made them with no intention other than unloading ideas', and in this respect *Fountain* presents itself as a particularly obvious conduit for the 'flow' of Duchamp's creative thinking.[84] While the evidence allowing us to state categorically that Duchamp stole the urinal from the Baroness might be allusive, it is nevertheless possible to discern in *Fountain* an attempt by the younger male artist to 'unload' the Baroness and her transformative creative energy through the sanitized, insulated plumbing fixture. In stark contrast, The Baroness's sculptural objects – and I am reluctant to use Duchamp's term 'assisted' or 'rectified' Readymades because they are resolutely *handmade* – don't playfully evoke waste for shock value, but are deeply invested in the forms and functions of the used and compromised. Much like Duchamp, she issued her own instructions for collaborative 'Readymades', writing to Sarah McPhearson: 'Sarah, if you find a tin can on the street stand by it until a truck runs over it. Then bring it to me.'[85] She did not purchase manufactured objects, selected with 'visual indifference' but gleaned the streets looking for discarded and used material which she reinvested with value as she recombined in startling new forms.[86] Often made of rotting or otherwise perishable materials, most of these objects have not survived, and as such are conceptually and materially far removed from reproducibility of the Duchampian Readymade. Profoundly disrupting that downward verticality described earlier, the faintly repellent components of a piece such as *The Portrait of Marcel Duchamp* (1920–22), where wax, bones, feathers and cloth are brought together, are indicative of the Baroness's art practice more broadly. Impossible to replicate and yet fundamentally composed of bits of cast off, used and recovered material, these truly *mixed* media assemblages at once undermine the reproducibility of the Duchampian Readymade (made primarily for economic rather than aesthetic reasons), and highlight its anxious control of this process, the uncanny return of 'matter out of place' pointedly removed from Duchamp's carefully regulated repetitions.

Even a piece such as *God* which is most Duchampian in its readymade simplicity, stubbornly resists being brought back into the functionally and aesthetically rational categories that *Fountain* sits more comfortably within. Exactly contemporaneous to *Fountain*, *God* – a contorted plumbing trap mounted on a wooden mitre box – goes considerably further than the urinal in troubling the passages between high and low, clean and unclean, contained and contaminated. This is especially so given the plumbing trap's compromised

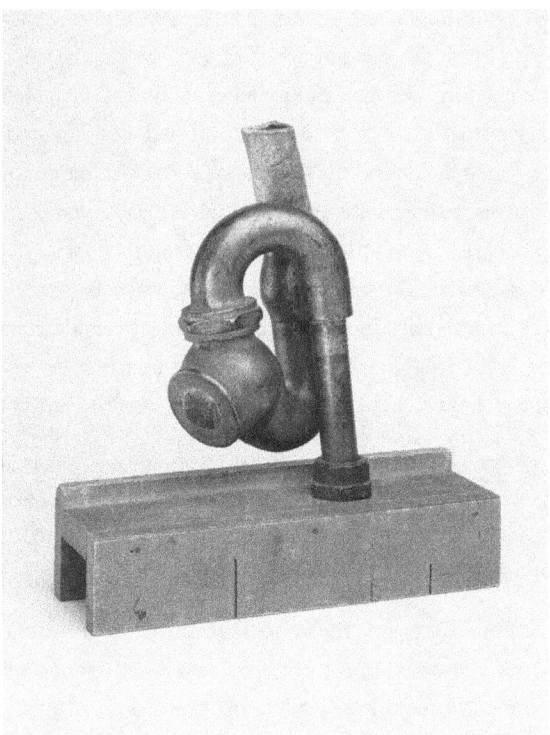

Figure 4 Elsa von Freytag-Loringhoven and Morton Schamberg, *God,* 1917. Philadelphia Museum of Art: The Louise and Walter Arensberg Collection, 1950. (1950-134-182).

status as a used and somewhat dysfunctional object itself; where the urinal was fresh off the assembly line, *God* was created when the Baroness ripped out a clogged pipe from Morton Schamberg's studio.[87]

The violence of this action is echoed in the composition itself, the visible saw marks on the mitre box recalling at once Duchamp's *Three Standard Stoppages* 1913–14 and Barnes's vivid depiction of the Baroness as some terrifying midtown Medusa, parading through the streets with a pack of dogs on gilded harnesses, live canaries in cages and once even a 'great plaster cast of a penis' which she 'showed to all the old maids she came into contact with'.[88] While the mitre box has been read as a *vagina dentata* by some, in placing it in direct dialogue with *Fountain* it seems to be making a more immediate point: if the crude humour of *Fountain* rests on the ideational conflation of women and waste and the visual play between urinal and vulva, *God* gets in on the joke by gifting the artist her own detachable penis.

Directly engaging with the misogyny of *Fountain*'s gendered thematics and sharing in the world of the Readymades, Elsa's decidedly more abject aesthetics direct us to their limits, returning the messy and corporeal matter that *Fountain* ultimately rejects. If we can read *Fountain* as re-encoding waste as feminine, Elsa here reverses the trope of woman-as-machine common to avant-garde vocabulary in order to expose the gendered connections between industrial rationalism, puritanical equivalences of material and spiritual cleanliness, and a contorted or congested masculinity, a reading well developed by Jones's study of Dada's equivocal masculinities.

Writing in response to the suppression of *Ulysses*, Elsa's polemic essay-poem 'The Modest Woman' bears some of these issues out. Proudly proclaiming the pleasure taken in her own body and its functioning, she lambasts America's puritanical attitudes towards corporeality and sexuality not only through mechanical imagery, but directly addressing the elevation of plumbing as machine-age deity and the renunciation of the messy and generative potentiality of the body.

> America's comfort: – sanitation – outside machinery – has made America forget own machinery – body! He thinks of himself less than of what should be his servant – steel machinery. He has mixed things! … Why should I – proud engineer – be ashamed of my machinery? (*BS*: 286)

Refusing distinctions between high and low, spiritual and material, heavenly and corporeal, the contorted plumbing trap reveals the precariousness of such ideological constructions, compounded by the wooden mitre block which, while theoretically supporting the assemblage, presents a constant threat of castration.[89] Conflating the 'high' concept of an abstract, de-corporealized God with 'low' bodily practices and material waste, the sculpture not only performs a destabilizing reversal of value, but violently collapses the conventional systems of order upon which such binary distinctions are founded. More closely aligned to the messy materiality of collage and the active dynamics of performance than to the coolly detached aesthetics of the mass-produced and contained Readymade, the Baroness's assemblage takes attempts to unite art and the everyday considerably further than her contemporaries, critiquing their approaches as she inverts the rationalizing and containing logic of their objects.

An intriguing footnote to the *Fountain* controversy is the claim that, in fact, *two* porcelain objects were submitted to the Independents – the urinal and a '"tastefully decorated" chamberpot by an unnamed artist'.[90] According to Charles Prendergast, William Glackens solved the dilemma by dropping and breaking one. While of course there is nothing more concrete to link the Baroness to this second pot to piss in, its description as 'decorated' puts it more in line with what we know of the Baroness's approach to making – echoed in Berenice Abbott's recollection of her invention of trousers 'with pictures and ornaments painted on them' – than the polished white surface of *Fountain*. Of course, a chamberpot is used by both men *and* women and, perhaps more importantly, in holding on to the wastes deposited into it, the pot occasions a more intimate relationship between waste product and its producer.

Perhaps we could even stretch this anecdote to bring in the 1923–4 gouache *Forgotten – Like This Parapluie Am I by You – Faithless Bernice*, executed to mark the end of Abbott and the Baroness's friendship. It is a remarkably cryptic image, for a scene so visually simple: if the heavily booted foot walking out of the fame is Abbott, what are we to make of the overt reference to Duchamp in the appearance of the overflowing sink/urinal, and the smoking pipe (Duchamp was rarely without one) left on its side? Are we to read this as Elsa chastising her New York friends for their careless treatment of her – leaving her behind and letting her work suffer from their wilful neglect? Given that *Forgotten – Like This Parapluie* was executed during the period of her artistic exile and destitution in Berlin, such feelings would not be surprising. And yet the umbrella leans affectionately into the piece of porcelain-ware. Could it be that Elsa is resurrecting old fantasies regarding the intellectual/sexual union of herself and Duchamp – and the exiting figure simply failed to understand the trailblazing work of these two avant-gardists? Compositionally balancing the pipe is a painted flower, one that, perhaps, recalls the decorative tendencies described by Abbott, and the smashed chamber pot by the unknown artist – perhaps recalls a set of exchanges that were more collaborative than Duchamp's mythologizing has admitted. Although in this later nod to *Fountain*, the contaminating flows from the blocked piece of plumbingware and the hand of Elsa are not so easily sanitised.

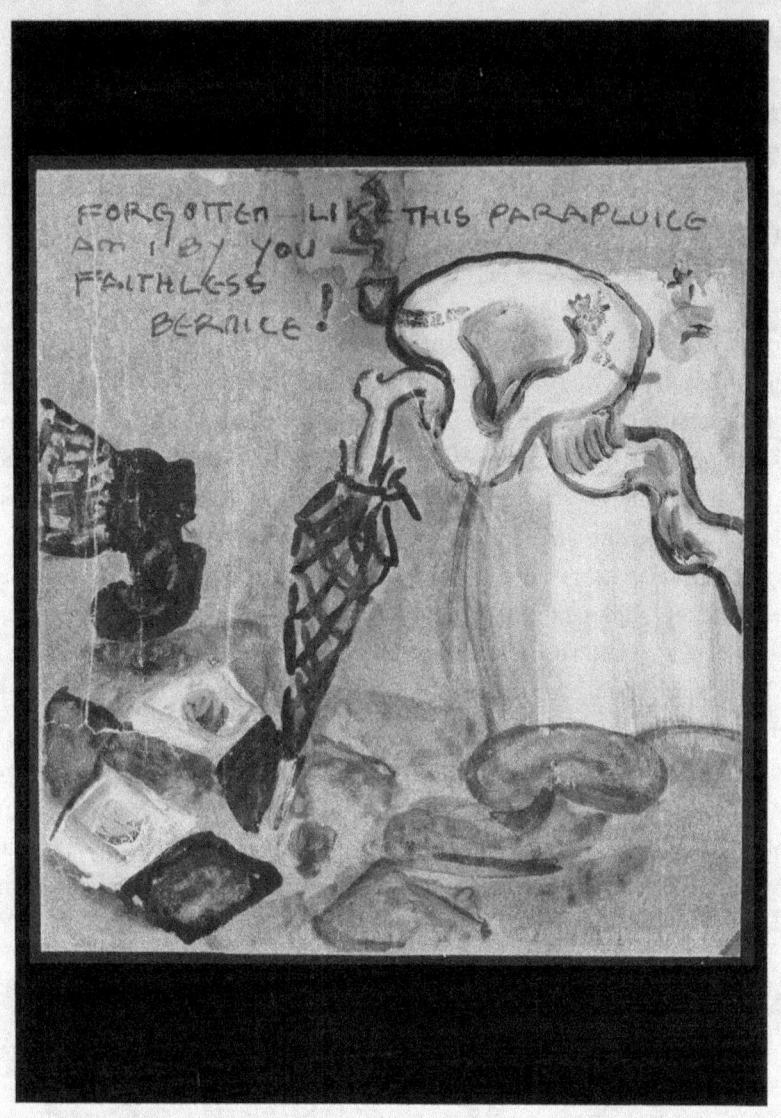

Figure 5 Elsa von Freytag-Loringhoven, *Forgotten – Like this Parapluie – I am by you, Faithless Bernice*, c. 1924. Gouache and ink. Elsa von Freytag-Loringhoven Papers. Special Collections, University of Maryland at College Park Libraries.

iii. Calculated containment: New Women and the New York Dada mecanamorphic portraits

Modernism can, in fact, be briefly defined: it is the emphasis of function and structure. Its canon is simplicity and directness.

Lewis Mumford, 1928

While the portraits traditionally associated with New York Dada seem to develop anti-corporeal modes of representation, rejecting mimesis and instead employing 'words, images, shapes, and sometimes even found objects so as to signify distinctive traits of each individual',[91] in their conflation of the human and the machine, and most pressingly in the persistent gendering of the machine in the work of Picabia and de Zayas, they are clearly still negotiating the messy terrain of bodies and subjectivity, and developing gendered strategies of containment in their modes of representation of brides, motherless daughters and ambiguously sexed machines. Indeed, reading these mechanical thematics alongside Huyseen's suggestion that '[w]arding something off, protecting against something out there seems to be a basic gesture of the modernist aesthetic', we can productively pose questions as to what, precisely, is being warded off in these images, and how such a project is attempted within certain examples of the mechanomorphic portraits traditionally associated with New York Dada.[92]

Negotiating between Enlightenment ideals of a coherent, closed, smoothly functioning and ultimately knowable machine-for-living-in, and the corporeal reality of bodies that leak, decay and transgress boundaries, several strategies emerged over the course of the nineteenth and twentieth centuries for the construction and representation of modern masculine subjectivities. As Klaus Theweleit suggests in his study of fascist masculinity, the maintenance of corporeal boundaries – that is, the re-inscription through language and metaphor of the male soldier body as an armoured, impenetrable, erect structure – emerged as an important strategy for re-affirming masculine subjectivity in the face of the shattering reality of war and the feminized 'flows' (the 'Red Flood' of revolution, femininity, cowardice, modernity, the masses) that threaten to engulf and dissolve him. Under Theweleit's treatment, anything that threatens the soldier male with the loss of his bodily boundaries – that threatens the 'tidy insularity of a person' – is intimately connected to the loss of mastery, a loss of identity.[93] Strategies of containment then, particularly in representations of the sexed and gendered body, emerge as of central importance not only in 'sustaining the illusion of masculine inviolability at the base of male social power', but in defining and regulating the modern masculine subject.[94]

What were these perceived threats to bodily integrity, and how might they be related to modernity and twentieth-century avant-garde practices? Innocuous in themselves, 'hybrid, fluid substances such as swamps or mires were regularly used to signify something other than themselves'.[95] Defined by their fluidity, ability to flow and hybrid status, such substances fit within structural theories of pollution and purity wherein the 'dangerous and contaminating are those which don't fit within the ordering structures'.[96] Of course, bodies themselves are the locus of such anxieties, being at once the site of this imagined inviolable wholeness, and the production of such 'contaminating' substances: the slime of sweat, the sticky pap of semen and other discharges, the mess of excrement and streams of urine. As Theweleit suggests then, 'whenever these things did turn up, they referred largely to the bodies of the men in question', emphasizing the threats presented by other bodies, notably women's, to their anxious conception of their own corporeal integrity and purity.[97]

Properly fixed in a domestic framework, women were conceived of as 'the living entities associated with hybrid substances [...] work[ing'] with and in things that were swampy, mushy' as they washed, cooked and took care of babies. Perhaps reflecting a blurring of the boundaries between female corporeality and these forms of domestic and embodied labour, their bodies similarly materialized anxieties regarding contamination and transgression, 'the swamp of the vagina, with their slime and mire [...] the slimy stream of menstruation', not to mention the fluids, fleshiness and (con)fusions involved in sexual intercourse and reproduction acting as powerful sites/sights at which the armoured male collapses.[98] In the face of this unstructured, oozing body, the soldier male not only encounters a contaminating threat from the outside against which he must insulate himself, but is also forced to confront his own feminized and fleshy interior. The armouring that Theweleit describes thus serves the dual purpose of insulating the subject and containing his own unsettling corporeality. Turning the 'periphery of his body into a cage for the beast within', the newly armoured masculine subject is thus able to identify with these disintegrative forces without being consumed by them; the more effective his armouring, the more successfully he repudiates and renounces these 'primitive' inner drives as utterly separate from his tidy insularity.[99]

This construction of female bodies as more threatening in their capacity to ooze, leak and transgress boundaries between clean and unlearn, ordered and formless, self and other readily lent itself to more abstract uses. In the context of the basic dualism informing the Cartesian subject and its projects, the masculine 'mind' (logic, reason, culture) is privileged over the feminine 'body' (passion, instinct, nature). Clearly at work in the maintenance of Primitivist and colonial discourses which collapsed gendered and ethnic 'Others' into the categories of 'instinctual', 'unformed' matter to be shaped by the rational, civilized white European male, we can also trace the reiteration of these gendered anxieties of dissolution and combative strategies of containment playing out across the projects associated with modernity and modernist cultures. As Huyssen amongst others has aptly demonstrated, not only would mass culture emerge as the 'hidden subtext of the modernist project' but, in the provision of a gendered discourse describing the anxieties provoked in the masculine, individual subject in his confrontation of the teeming masses and unmoored flows of urban modernity and industrial capitalism, mass culture was consistently gendered as feminine, ensuring that 'the fear of the masses in this age of declining liberalism is always also a fear of woman'.[100] Stepping out of the drawing room and onto the electrified streets of the metropolis, circulating through the city like the commodities they were encouraged to buy, the 'unnatural' New Woman provided a real body rapidly reconfigured through fashion and technology and circulated through novels, political pamphlets and the popular press within which to anchor these anxieties, and it is certainly possible to trace the various public debates over her economic, political and sexual autonomy within the artistic avant-gardism of the period.

Tellingly, gendered fears around the processes of modernity and mass culture were not neatly contained within the bodies of these New Women, but extended and made monstrous with her engagement with the machine, as Caroline Jones's persuasive reading of the problematizing of the sex of New York Dada's machines has suggested. While a Fordist remodelling of labour and labouring bodies had already troubled man's relationship to machine, the scale and horror the First World War shattered these bodies completely, and it was towards the *femme nouveau* that a significant amount of post-war rage was directed.[101] Riding bicycles and driving automobiles, taking on the factory work of absent men and learning new sets of skills related to stenography, a newly professionalized class of New Women emerged in an uneasy emancipatory relation to the machine. Certainly, the New Woman's alliance with the machine was not lost on New York Dadaists, as readings of Man Ray's object-portraits and Duchamp's bicycle wheels and empty typewriter skirts have aptly demonstrated.[102] In the discourses surrounding women's political and economic independence, sexuality and engagement with technology (of which the objects and images traditionally associated with New York Dada certainly participate) it is the New Woman's challenge to 'existing social relations and the distribution of power', her repudiation of that order, around which the most visceral responses to her are concentrated.[103]

Considering the persuasive arguments of Caroline Jones, Alex Goody and Amelia Jones amongst others, it would seem that the historical, geopolitical and techno-industrial contexts of New York during this period are of particular importance in formulating perceptions of masculinity, and its compromised relationship to modernity played out across the work of New York Dadaists during the war period. Developing Caroline Jones's reading of Picabia's neurasthenic gender trouble, Amelia Jones's convincingly revisionist argument for an 'equivocal masculinity' at the heart of New York Dada arising from the conflicted position of noncombatant *émigré* artists working in America during these years and Goody's notion of the uniquely American context of the challenges posed to both the masculine and feminine subject by technological modernity have all informed my thinking in this chapter's investigation into certain strategies of containment informing machine-age portraiture.

Read alongside Theweleit's theory of the processes whereby masculinity 'armoured' itself against the disintegrative and feminized floods of modernity, the negotiation of mechanical symbolism into the modes of (self)representation practised by a selection of New York Dadaists – and the gendering of these machine-human hybrids – locates an anxiously re-negotiated masculinity at the heart of these machine portraits. Furthermore, in identifying the strategies of containment through which these artists attempted to assert a masculine self against the conceptually connected threats of the machine-age and the New Woman, I want to present a model both for addressing the anxieties provoked by the Baroness's corporeal brand of lived-Dada, and for reading the attempts of her contemporaries to re-write and 'contain' these performances.

While Duchamp would later be heralded as 'Dada's Daddy',[104] his iconic *Large Glass* and carefully selected 'an-art' Readymades representative of New York Dada's love affair with the mechanical and mass-produced, it was Francis Picabia who altogether more publicly announced the arrival of New York Dada.[105] Alongside a series of newspaper articles in which he espoused a modern religion of machinery and celebrated America as its crucible, the French-Cuban artist published a series of object-portraits in the avant-garde journal *291* in 1915 which most explicitly engaged the anthropomorphic machine aesthetic through which Duchamp, Man Ray and Picabia would all explore their ambivalence to the New Woman and erotic desire in the machine age.[106]

Striking in their radical simplicity and absurd non-functionality, Picabia's mechanical portraits share the logic of the Duchampian Readymade in their apparent reproducibility and as their status as objects dislocated from their utilitarian uses and re-contextualized through a tension between object and title. Alongside Duchamp's frustrated bachelors and Man Ray's ambiguously sexed objects from this period, the mecanomorphic portraits also share in an anxious preoccupation with questions of erotic desire and compromised masculinity informing the visual thematics of New York Dada.

Charting the European artist's encounter with the new world of modernizing America in which 'the machine has become more than a mere adjunct of

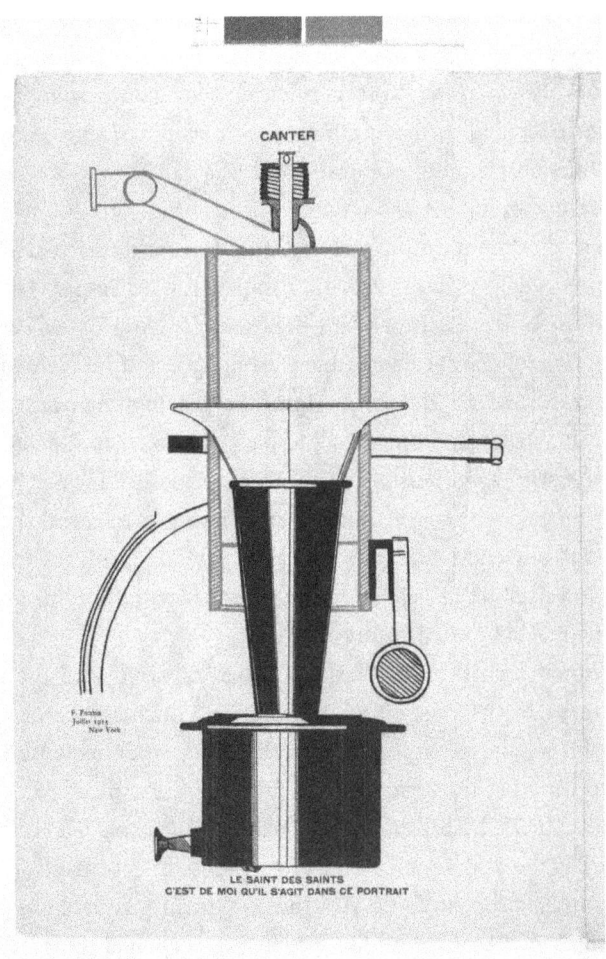

Figure 6 Francis Picabia, *Les Saint des saints*. From *291*, No. 5–6, July–August 1915. © RMN-Grand Palais/Francis Picabia.

human life. It is really a part of human life – perhaps the very soul',[107] Picabia's object-portraits employ the machine not only as playful symbolization, but as a means of connecting the transformative energies of technological modernity with the bodies it acts upon. In marrying 'Man to Machinery' and his lofty search for the artistic ideal, Stieglitz is celebrated by Picabia and de Zayas as having 'carried the Photography which we may call static to the highest degree of perfection'; as his portrait dramatizes, he at once transforms and is transformed by the camera he uses.[108]

This promiscuous play between machine and human is neatly captured in Picabia's own self-portrait *Le saint des saints*. While we initially read the suggestively erotic image as a straightforward celebration of early twentieth-century technology, the hydraulic/penetrative car horn loudly announcing itself as a modern saint in a machine-age pantheon, the colliding homophonic possibilities of *Les saint des saints* complicate a straightforward reading of this image, as does Picabia's insistence that '*c'est de moi qu'il s'agit dans ce portrait*'. While Picabia's proclaiming of himself and/as a car horn as some modern-age saint is certainly irreverent enough, the particular construction of '*le saint des saints*' here pushes the meaning of '*saint*' into '*holy*' and carries this iconoclastic Dada gesture even further. According to Hebrew scripture, God's presence appeared in the inner sanctum of the Tabernacle – the Holy of Holies – whose shape conforms to chamber component of the portrait here. While it is God's appearance recorded in Hebrew scripture, a blaring car horn appears here instead, Picabia's reconfigured machine (self)portrait announcing a '*saint des saints*'/'*saint dessin*'/'*santé dessin*' for the machine age. Is it Picabia himself who *is* the holy of holies – which in this image functions less to reveal the appearance of God, than to be penetrated by it – or are we to read Picabia's self-identification here with God itself, the car horn in the tabernacle and the (mechanical) hand that has brought this 'holy drawing' into being?

The pneumatic potential of both *Le saint des saints* and the strip-teasing corset activated in the portrait of de Zayas's as onanistic sewing machine is developed and further decorporealized in Picabia's simplified outline of a spark-plug that appeared at the centre of this July–August issue of *291*. Emblazoned with the motto 'FOR-EVER' and titled *Portriat d'une jeune fille Américaine dans l'état de nudité*, the sexual and sexist dimensions of this image are quite clear. Here she is, the European fantasy of the American girl made-not-quite-flesh, presented to us in a 'state of nudity' promising perpetual pleasure, energy and inspiration, the jolt that could kickstart this revolution of modern art in America. In Mumford's terms, this is a body stripped right down to its 'essential line and mass', both body and machine reconfigured in this new age. However, given Theweleit's discussion of the privileging of the sleek, hard and impenetrable surface in the construction of a masculine identity based on a deep-seated fear of contamination and disgust rooted in the female body and the disintegrating 'flows' telescoped into it, the visual thematics of the machine portraits and their relationship to established aesthetic categories of the female nude in their early twentieth-century contexts significantly complicate Mumford's straightforward celebration of aesthetic categories of reduction and simplicity.

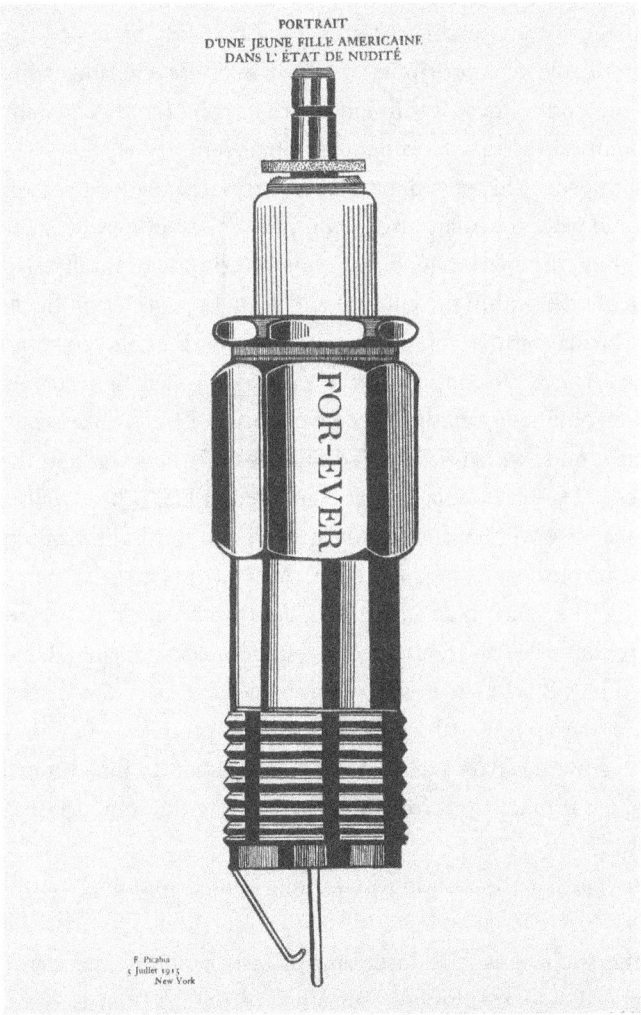

Figure 7 Francis Picabia, *Portriat d'une jeune fille Américaine dans l'état de nudité*. From *291*, No. 5–6, July–August 1915. © RMN-Grand Palais/Francis Picabia.

Barbara Zabel's work on the mechanamorphic New York Dada portraits is particularly interesting in this respect. Lending itself to masculinized metaphors of strength, durability, efficiency and structure, the machine aesthetic can certainly be read as a direct response to the experiences of modernity – not only in terms of replicating the imagery and experience of the newly engineered environment, but of articulating shifting conceptions and constructions of subjectivity and identity within this context. Significantly, Zabel suggests that in order to assert control over a burgeoning machine culture and their autonomy within it, the New York Dadaists attempted to link the machine with the human or natural worlds through an adoption of already established gendered and Primitivist ideologies. In this manner, they not only animated the machine through its ideological proximity to the female, sexual and primitive, they retained their control over it through the re-inscription of gendered ideologies relating to normative male power and dominance.

In this respect, while readings that trace the ambiguous sex of the Dada machines and place the infantilized *jeune fille* in the category of 'phallic woman' are compelling, the spark plug girl's pronounced state of nudity also demands that we situate her within the cultural and sexual categories of the female nude which, as Lynda Nead reminds us, is understood 'as the transformation of matter into form, as the containment of the wayward female sexual body within the framing outlines of aesthetic convention'.[109] Evoking classical traditions of the female nude which have relied on ideas of wholeness and the coherent arrangement of form, Picabia insulates and neutralizes conceptually connected threats of the New Woman and the machine, containing both within the smooth metal shell of the spark plug's contours. As Jones suggests, in her nudity and her ubiquity, the spark plug girl is rendered unthreatening, her combustible potentiality controlled and contained within her sleek, impenetrable metal shell. Neutralized in this way, she in fact seems somewhat inert, the spark plug being a *conduit* of energy rather than an independent producer of it, an association compounded by the spark plug's metonymic relation to the rationalized flows of Fordist labour practices through its proximity to the combustion engine and automobile.[110]

It seems particularly striking that while the surrounding portraits of the men of *291* – Haviland, Steiglitz, de Zayas and Picabia himself – all employ the machine as a means of re-inscribing or re-constituting the identity of their subject (indeed, it is only through Haviland's reconfiguration as a desklamp that the meaning of *'La Poésie est comme lui'* is made visually possible), the young

American girl at the centre of *291* is reduced by her machinic reconfiguration to an empty cipher and somewhat hollow joke. Surrounded by the named male contributors and financiers who collaborated on the *291* project, the *jeune fille* remains nameless – more than this, she is unnamed. Agnes E. Meyer was central to artistic activities and impetus of the avant-garde journal, and she is notably absent in this series of object-portraits; indeed she is the only significant contributor not to be included here.[111] Young, American and certainly possessing 'sparky' qualities in her disposition, artistic vision and financial support, it seems certainly plausible that Meyer was the exemplary *jeune fille Américaine* that so interested Picabia, especially if we are to consider the visual resonances between Picabia's later incarnation of the *jeune fille* as a lightbulb reflecting the words 'flirt' and 'divorce', and the typographic arrangement of Meyer and de Zayas's collaborative visual poem 'Mental Reactions'.[112]

In a clear demonstration of the gendered power relations structuring New York Dada canons and the historical avant-garde more broadly then, the only portrait of a woman in this issue is also the only figure to be presented to us as an anonymous nude. Given her positioning at the centre of the magazine and literally surrounded by the portraits of her (named) male counterparts, Picabia's machine-age nude dramatizes Carol Duncan's suggestion that 'art originates in and is sustained by male erotic energy […] When an artist had some new or major artistic statement to make, when he wanted to authenticate to himself or others his identity as an artist, or when he wanted to get back to "basics" he turned to the nude.'[113] The reformulation of representative modes for the machine age is performed on and through the female nude first. It is in their relation to her, and Picabia's demonstration of a mastery over both her form and the loosed libidinal energies she represents, that the identifiable (named) mecanomorphic portraits are thus organized.

As the most cursory glance at the role of the female nude in Western art histories highlights, such co-option of the female body in support of masculine artistic subjectivity and productivity is nothing new. Forming strong associations between (male) artistic identity and (hetero)sexuality, the mastery of the female nude metonymically standing in for Western art historical discourses thus also singled a mastery of those traditions in overtly gendered and sexualized terms. Tellingly, de Zayas's accompanying commentary on the mecanomorphs in this issue of *291* deploys a similar language of male virility and sexual conquest in its discussion of the condition of modern art in America where New York itself is figured as the coy ingénue who has 'taken all possible precautions against assimilating the spirit of modern art; rejecting a seed that would have found a most fertile soil'. While Stieglitz married man to machine and got issue in the static art of photography, de Zayas declares that Picabia comes to conquer America and brings forth a new plastic expression for the machine age in his mecanomorphs – the proper 'potentiality' of an 'inert' America finally brought out through the mastery of the conqueror/artist.

It is in the recurring fantasy of the daughter born without a mother that the female nude most fully emerges as a text (re)inscribed by gendered relations of power at working at once to contain the female sexual body and, in his mastery of her, make her his own machine-age daughter. Developing the mechanical imagery activated across Picabia's object portraits in the previous issue, Dadaist Paul Haviland contributed a statement to the September–October number of *291* in which he famously declared:

> We are living in the age of the machine. Man made the machine in his own image. She has limbs which act; lungs which breathe; a heart which beats; a nervous system through which runs electricity. The phonograph is the image of his voice; the camera is the image of his eye. The machine is his 'daughter born without a mother'. That is why he loves her. [...] After making the machine in his own image he has made his human ideal machinomorphic. But the machine is yet at a dependent stage. Man gave her every qualification except thought. She submits to his will but he must direct her activities. Without him she remains a wonderful being, but without aim or autonomy. Through their mating they complete one another. She brings forth according to his conceptions.[114]

The potentially destructive force of technology and mechanized modernity is thus neutralized in the reconfiguration of the machine, not as something which controls, regulates and produces male bodies (like the assembly line model of production), or that threatens to dissolve the boundaries of the armoured male individual (like the disintegrating experience of the metropolitan masses and mechanized warfare), but as a passive and dependent female love object – a fantasy of male reproductive capacity, control and autonomy in the modern age. His body is remade in the objects of the machine age, its cameras phonographs and electrical currents; the girl-machine makes his human ideal possible. Infantilized and feminized though, she remains dependent on him for her thought and action, her reproductive capabilities wedded absolutely to his patriarchal project, delivering his conceptions rather than producing her own.

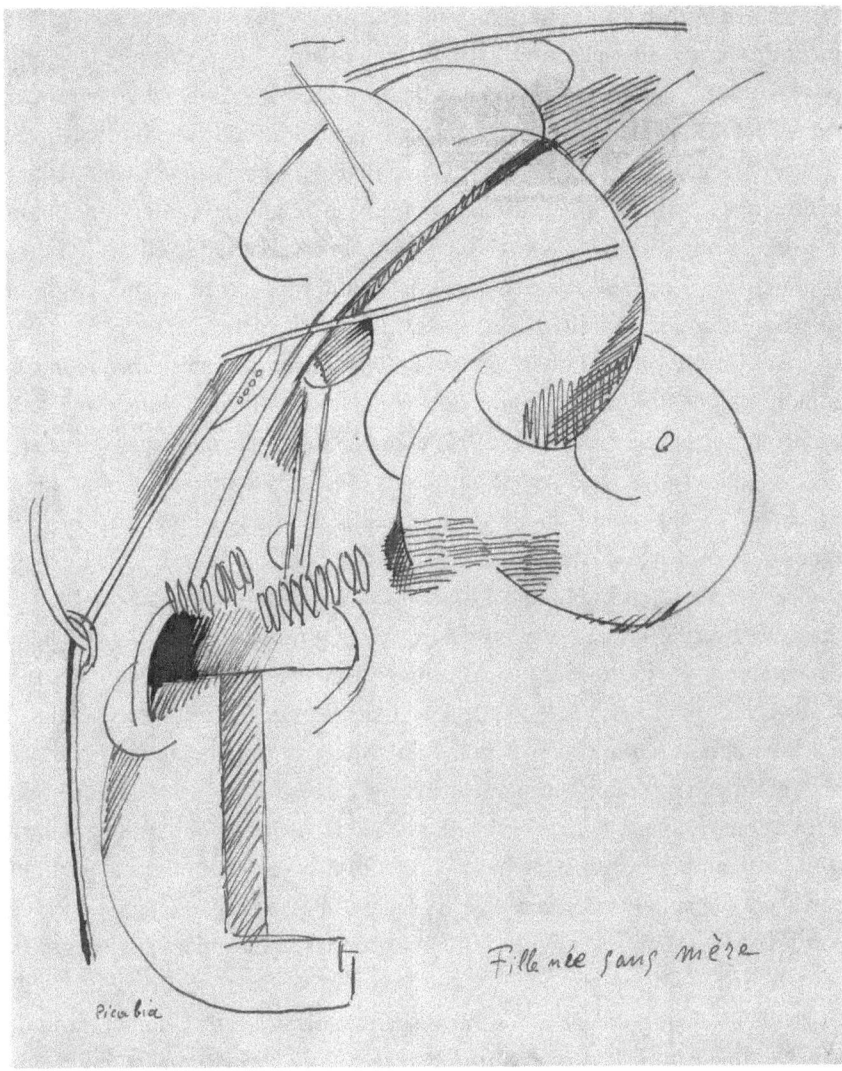

Figure 8 Francis Picabia, *La Fille Née sans Mère. c.* 1914–15 ink on paper, 10 ½ × 8 ½ in. Alfred Steiglitz Collection, 1949 (59.70.18). New York Metropolitan Museum of Art. © 2019. Image copyright The Metropolitan Museum of Art/Art Resource/Scala, Florence.

Referencing the biblical myth of origins when Eve was 'born' of Adam's rib, Picabia's own *Fille neé sans mère* to which Haviland is clearly gesturing appeared in the June issue of *291* and presents its own, modern myth of masculine parthenogenesis. As a reproductive fantasy, the messy corporeality of conception, gestation, birth and after-birth is done away with; this girl isn't born from the body of a woman, or even the rib of a man, but brought forward from his mind.

Stripped bare, her skeletal frame of interconnected gears, shafts, springs and mechanistic appendages seems to be making reference to forms of Duchamp's secret project, *The Bride Stripped Bare by Her Bachelors, Even* while the softer, somewhat insubstantial curves and hatched areas are suggestive of the frustrated erotics of Duchamp's construction.[115] Compared to the hard, impenetrable casing of the *jeune fille Américaine*, the girl here seems to be at a more embryonic phase, a 'working out' of Picabia's developing mecanomorphic style and his 'modern mythology of the sexes, in which cogs, wheels and rods served as a metaphor for sexual relations, albeit of a joyless, somewhat sadistic nature'.[116]

Given that Picabia's rather sudden shift from futuro-cubist abstraction to a more techno-mechanical mecanamorphic style (which Camfield suggests occurred during the summer of 1915) coincided with the outbreak of war and his own conscription and subsequent bouts of neurasthenia, Jones's reading of the drawing's exploration of a compromised masculinity at the heart of wartime culture is particularly convincing. However, while Jones reads the drawing as a castrated girl, pointing to her anatomical impossibility and gestural rather than engineering precise execution in order to pronounce her as 'a machine that cannot work', the *dependence* emphasized by Haviland's commentary nevertheless points us back to the way that the nude 'works' in relation to machine-age masculinity.[117] While the *fille* is clearly negotiating the equivocal masculinities reproduced through the period, possibly even functioning as a form of neurasthenic self-representation, Picabia's working out of the girl born without a mother before using her to bring forth his mecanomorphic portraits and Dada thematics underscores Nead's suggestion that 'the female nude within patriarchy [...] signifies that the woman/surface has come under the government of male style'.[118]

While Picabia's recourse to the established art historical tradition of the nude here certainly allows him to work through certain stylistic, formal and thematic challenges that the question of representation in the machine age presented him with, in the motherless machine-human forms that parade through traditional masculinist indexes of New York Dada, these artists were also directly engaging with the idea and reality of the New Woman.[119] Metaphorically bound as she was to notions of contaminating flows loosened by industrial capitalism, anxieties over a burgeoning consumer culture and the threat to (masculine) individualism posed by the potential feminization of culture in a technologically reconfigured age of mass production, the body of the New Woman was increasingly intersected in popular discourse with new technologies, new femininities and unbound libidinal energies.

While the New Woman was beginning to experience an extension of her own powers of self-determination, liberated from both restrictive corsets and strictly regulated gender codes defining the traditional concept of woman as the 'Angel in the House', her alignment in the machinic portraits to 'dangerous, unthinking machines that serve as metonymical representations of the mass-produced desires of a modern commodity economy' re-routes the unmoored, feminized and more threatening flows associated with commodity culture and the forces of modernity outlined above, projecting them back into her body where they can be recontained and regulated according to the voyeuristic structures of the male gaze.[120]

Published in the November 1915 issue of the journal *291*, Picabia and de Zayas's double-page spread is frequently invoked in discussions of the misogyny inherent in the machine images of New York Dada.[121] Composed entirely of verbal phrases, de Zayas's composition *ELLE* is a wholly negative assessment of emergent New Woman, ironically deploying the 'psychotope', 'an art which consists in making the typographical characters participate in the expression of the thoughts and in the painting of the states of the soul' to reduce this contemporary figure of femininity as, while sexually active, intellectually passive.[122] A '*HURLUBERLU*', she suffers from '*atrophie CéréBRaLE/CAUSée matériaLité paR purE*' and is consumed by her voracious and insatiable sexual desires. Mapped onto one another, de Zayas and Picabia's portraits present the liberty of the New Woman as a freedom from intellectual endeavour in favour of perpetual sexual gratification and possession of pleasure.

The liberated woman's pleasures which the artist of *ELLE* claims '*Je la vois dans sa pensée/et comme elle aime à son être*', are rendered explicitly sexual in the Picabia piece through the inclusion of the pistol and target. As Camfield has suggested, these function within the artist's visual lexicon as overtly sexualized symbols and, when reading the two images side by side the implication emerges that 'a target hit would cause the pistol to be re-cocked and discharged again in a repetitive, mechanical action'.[123] This reduction of female sexual pleasure to a nymphomatic hydraulic system is not only expressive of the (here explicitly misogynistic) thematics of New York Dada in which bodies are reduced to their machine counterparts, but is revealing as to the processes of effacement and reconstruction involved in such representations.

While several critics have pointed to the visually arresting typographical arrangements of De Zayas's *Elle* as 'espousing the shock tactics adopted by Dada and aggressively attacked the viewer', less attention has been given to the violent dismemberment of the female form enacted here before its reconstruction in the language of the (male) artist/viewer.[124] As De Zayas's signature above the piece's

Figure 9 Marius de Zayas, *ELLE*; From 291, No. 9, 1915. © RMN-Grand Palais/Marius de Zayas.

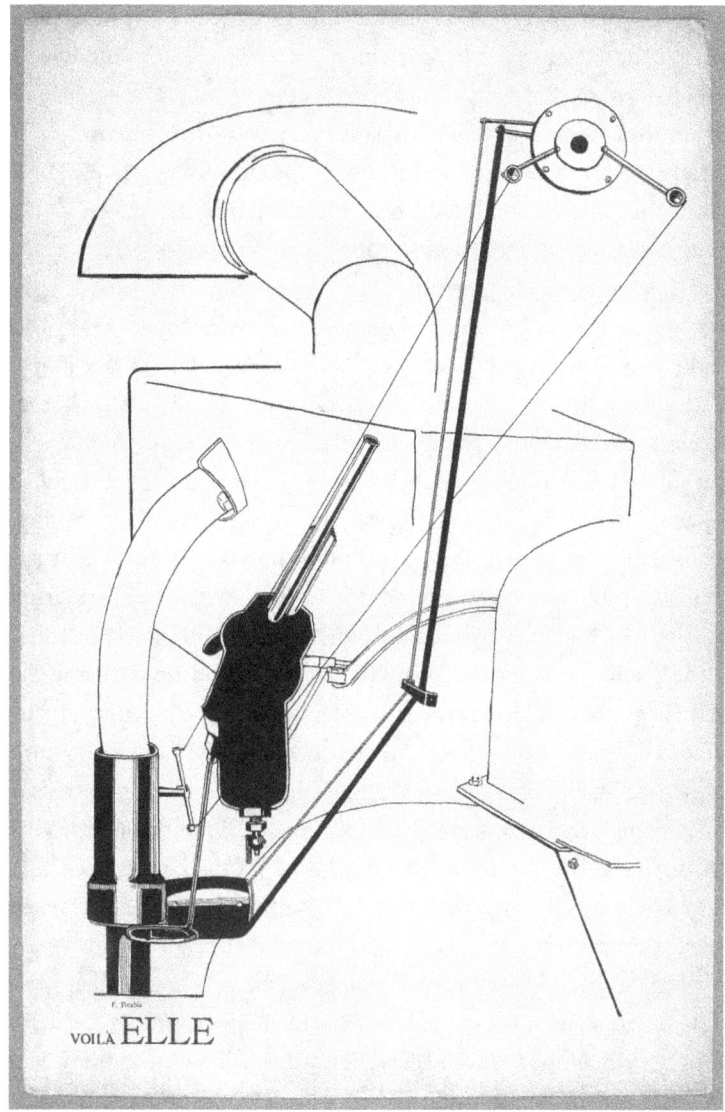

Figure 10 Francis Picabia *Voilà Elle*. From 291, No. 9, 1915. © RMN-Grand Palais/ Francis Picabia.

title attests to 'She' exists only as his verbal reconstruction, one that falls back onto the basic dualism of mind/body, masculine/feminine, intellect/instinct in violently repositioning her within the negative term of a binary logic designed to uphold an ideal of his own, inviolable masculinity. Taking the nude apart and putting her back together through the organizing structures of language, the nude and popular discourses surrounding the New Woman, de Zayas offers her up as a straightforwardly legible object. While De Zayas's portrait could be seen to dramatize the structures of the gaze in re-inscribing *ELLE* as an object of that gaze – that is, passively arranged to reflect its power back to it – Picabia's *Voilà ELLE* takes these representational dynamics a step further presenting her (the title literally translates as 'Here She Is') not as the sight/site of multiple, assigned projections, but having condensed the proliferation of discourses around this figure into a visually coherent and relatively uncomplicated image.[125]

Such a treatment would, perhaps, bear less significance if it were possible to read the two images as broader tongue-in-cheek representations of discourses surrounding the New Woman. However, this assessment fails to take into account the artist's own testimony, repeated by a contemporary critic that 'these works were portraits of the same woman made at different times and in different places "without collusion".[126] While it might be a stretch to propose that the unidentified model was the Baroness Elsa – a suggestion that would, it seems, be impossible to verify – there are nevertheless some compelling coincidences that I want to indulge in here. Elsa was certainly modelling in New York during this period: employed by Art Students League, the New York School of Art and the Ferrer School she posed for the American painters Louis Bouché, William Glackens, George Bellows, Robert Henri and Sarah McPherson. The latter, vividly recalling the Baroness as one of the models in her life drawing class in 1913, also introduced the Baroness to Duchamp in the same year.[127] Indeed, as Gammel points out, the two artists shared the address of the Lincoln Arcade Building on 1947 Broadway in 1915, so there is a strong possibility that she would have been known to Picabia and de Zayas through these networks, especially given Picabia's close and collaborative friendship with Duchamp during this time. Certainly, the insistent focus of both Picabia and De Zayas's drawings on the voracious sexual appetites of this unidentified woman fits within the sexually dynamic profile of the Baroness painted by her contemporaries and corroborated by her own testimony. Moreover, the identical compositional arrangement of verticals, prominent diagonals and curved protrusions in *ELLE* and *Voilà ELLE!* bears a striking visual resemblance to the poses struck by the Baroness in a series of photographs taken in 1915.

As Bohn suggests in his identification of the similar compositional strategies employed in the De Zayas and Picabia portrait both 'feature a vertical upright surmounted by a horizontal crossbar, both have a prominent diagonal extending from lower left to upper right, and both employ curved elements (on the left) to connect the vertical with the diagonal'.[128] In an interesting aside Bohn suggests, 'The reason her head is not visible, one eventually perceives, is because she is wearing a hat with a veil. The triangular outline indicates that the hat is secured

Stunning Subjects and Disruptive Body Practices   83

by a cloth band […] which is tied under her chin.'[129] While the riot of 'ROUGE/BLEU/JAUNE' crowning the De Zayas figure seems appropriately colourful headgear for the Baroness whose dyed red hair was frequently decorated with gilded vegetables and headdresses made from beads, feathers and stones, Picabia's pulley mechanism seems to visually echo the tight wrap of the cap construction and protruding feather worn by the Baroness in these photographs.

Figure 11 International News Photography, *Baroness von Freytag-Loringhoven working as a model*. 7 December 1915. Bettman/Corbis photo agency.

Obviously exaggerated by the bold stripes of the Baroness's costume, the striking diagonals of Elsa's elongated body, the curve of her buttocks and the upright line of her spine recorded in these photographs all seem to map rather neatly onto the drawings.

Regardless of the identity of the model, it suffices to say that there was one, one was circulated between these male artists and whose work has been effaced in the misogynistic and mechanical re-imaginations of form demonstrated by the drawings.[130] Ultimately passive and contained within the double-page spread, a straight line traced by a mechanical hand, this New Woman has *'Pas d'intellect-ualism'* and is *'Pas le mirroir de mone male'*. Without *'forme'*, she is defined only through a violent negation, a *'JOUissance à déchirer son être social'*. This effacement is put in high relief if we bring in a later iteration of Picabia's young girl theme, his *Jeune Fille* from 1920. A simple circle in the middle of a piece of paper, cut out and circled with the words 'Jeune Fille'. In a crude sexual pun the young girl is reduced to a hole, or, more graphically, a cut, one which when reproduced in Paul Eluard's magazine *Proverbe* in 1920, invites us to touch and penetrate the girl, to risk approaching the void and disappearing within it. We don't simply see through the young girl, she isn't even there.

iv. 'Not me. Not that': The Baroness Elsa von Freytag-Loringhoven and the grotesque protrusions of modernism's marginalia

> Immediately we saw the Empress in the middle of the shiny floor, her hunched body tied up in strips of gold lace, its rags torn in points, with the round bright lids that come off cigarette tins for tassels [...] Her head low she danced with such concentration it made me think of spells and witchcraft and the winding up of chains.
>
> Mary Butts, 'The Master's Last Dancing', 1932

In the cold, detached and single-minded pursuit of pleasure presented by Picabia and de Zayas's nymphomaniac New Woman we might trace elements of the grotesque; involved in a perpetual task of the renewal of pleasure, the visual focus on the erogenous zones of her breasts, buttocks and genitals conforms to a grotesque topography of the body which places special emphasis on those parts that seek to 'go out beyond the body's confines [...] and links it to other bodies or to the outside world'.[131] However, 'traced by a mechanical hand' and made legible these grotesque attributes are contained and mastered in the mecanamorphic portraits.

Reciprocally mapped onto one another anxieties surrounding the loosening of modernity's flows and the figure of the New Woman are organized and contained in the portraits; through the re-appropriation of conventional gendered modes of representation the male artist retains authority and control over both the Woman-as-Machine and the Machine-Woman as modernity. Neutralizing the disintegrative and transgressive potentiality of grotesque body-work, the reduction of the New Woman's body to simplified machine surrogates stages a recuperation of the grotesque in a sanitized and intelligible form, one that establishes a critical and aesthetic distance and mastery over her excessive sexuality and compromising ultra-modernity.

Turning to the reconstructions of the Baroness as an unambiguously grotesque body in the narratives of her contemporaries I want to consider how the grotesque functions as an aesthetic category of containment in the face of the Baroness's body-work. In the terms laid out by George Bataille's 'critical dictionary' published within the Surrealist journal *Documents* (1929–30), we could make a useful distinction here between the tendency to define words in terms of their *meaning*, rather than in relation to the *tasks* that they might perform. Bataille's brief discussion of *l'informe* is illuminating in this respect:

> A dictionary begins when it no longer gives the meaning of words, but their tasks. Thus formless is not only an adjective having a given meaning, but a term that serves to bring things down in the world, generally requiring that each thing have its form. What it designates has no rights in any sense and gets itself squashed everywhere, like a spider or an earthworm. […] affirming that the universe resembles nothing and is only formless amounts to saying that the universe is something like a spider or spit.[132]

Revealing as to the anxieties ascribed to form or, more pressingly, to formlessness, Bataille's comment dramatizes some of the differences I have been outlining in relation to the Baroness's body-work, the grotesque and specific strategies of containment at work in textual reconstructions of the Baroness's abject body. While neither the Baroness's body nor body-work is 'formless' in Bataille's sense, the grotesque protrusions of her corporeal art practices and the open connection with the world of used commodities established in her application of waste products directly to her body nevertheless reject 'form' in both its meaning and the task that it *per*forms, to simultaneously identify and generate a closed, completed and finished object.

As I have tentatively suggested, there is a slippage between the *meaning* of 'grotesque' (which links it to structural systems of order and disorder) and the '*tasks* that it performs' (which continually transgress, erode and dissolve such boundaries and binaries). Reconstructing this body and giving it shape as a grotesque *product*, such accounts strive to contain the unfixed, unfinished and destabilizing attributes afforded to the grotesque; they attempt to ascribe meaning to her body as a fixed object, overruling the disordering tasks performed by this body-work. Such an observation raises pertinent questions in relation to the methods and motivations of containment I am interested in exploring here: what 'meaning' is ascribed to the grotesque in these narratives? Why might it be preferable to define the meaning of the grotesque and locate it in a specific body rather than experiencing its tasks?

Given Bataille's assertion that *l'informe* performs the task of bringing down things in a world that generally requires that things have a coherent form, we can certainly trace the role of material and metaphorical notions of waste in structuring the contours of the Baroness's corporeal aesthetics in a position of critical resistance to the dominant forms of representation developed by her avant-garde contemporaries. Given the tendency of *l'informe* to not only bring things down in the world, but to threaten the dissolution of all structure in 'making the universe something like spit', the anxious containment of the Baroness's body and its grotesque protrusions within modernism's marginalia is, perhaps, quite obvious. At the most basic level, these accounts are all 'giving form', textually and visually, to her grotesquely open, protruding and transgressive body-work, work that without these accounts would, indeed, have been lost. However, in reconstructing this body as *neatly disorderly* in their narratives, such documents seek to replicate the structures of order and systems of value organizing the bourgeois imaginary, discursively re-locating and regulating this body in its 'proper place'. In rationalizing and re-writing her grotesque body, in claiming mastery over her own modes of self-representation and shoring themselves up against the disintegrative potential of this 'body-matter out of place', these narratives work to re-establish the coherence, integrity and impenetrability of 'the clean muslin souls of Yankeedom'.[133]

In her discussion of the abject, Julia Kristeva presents us with a useful theoretical model for addressing both the affect of anxiety and disgust experienced by the subject when confronting certain matter (the decaying, the disintegrating) and of theorizing this sensation in relation to psychoanalytical models of ego-formation. Identified by Kristeva as 'one of those violent, dark revolts of being' the experience of abjection threatens the integrity and coherence of the subject.[134] Opposed to the subject, the affect of abjection cannot, however, be easily reduced to a definable object and, as such, frustrates the oppositional structures of meaning (subject/object, self/other) central to the self-identification of the subject. Neither inside nor outside, the abject delineates and exposes the fragile and dangerously porous border between subject and object, self and other; it is the 'jettisoned object, [which] is radically excluded and draws me toward the place where meaning collapses'.[135] Driven out of the cultural world by the ever-watchful superego, it persists just outside the boundaries of the Symbolic Order, outside of language, challenging the structures that cast it down and out. In a moment of uncanny recognition, the subject encounters the repudiated part of itself as 'radically separate, loathsome. Not me. Not that. But not nothing either. A "something" I do not recognize as a thing'.[136] Primarily attached to the inaugural repudiation of the Mother, Kristeva posits this casting off – and the abjection which follows jettisoned objects – as essential to the emergence of the Subject, as the necessary violent prefiguring of the Subject's entrance into the (Lacanian) Symbolic Order and language.

The corpse and the skin formed on warm milk are presented as preeminent sites of abjection: the corpse in that it confronts us with the traumatic and cast-out knowledge of our own materiality and the conflicted identification and repulsion with the decaying body, and the skin on milk in its visualization of the fragility of the boundary between the skins of our own, seemingly 'contained' bodies and the world, and of the ease with which matter passes between realms. In Kristeva's terms, such encounters '*show me* what I permanently thrust aside in order to live'.[137] As these examples highlight, corporeal or material sites of exchange or (con)fusion are particularly privileged within the realm of the abject. The mouth, anus, vagina, nose, eyes and breasts all function as compromised borderlines; both ingesting and expelling objects (food, vomit, faeces, urine, tears, mucus, milk) such sites not only confuse the separateness of ingesting the 'good' and expelling the 'bad', but further compromise the subject in that it can no longer maintain the illusion of separating itself from the objects it ingests and expels. In identifying these boundaries and marking them as compromised, the abject 'threatens to dissolve the subject by dissolving the border'.[138] In spite of the subject's attempts to conceive of their body and identity as coherent and contained, abjection acts as a haunting reminder of the impossibility of such a task, exposing the fragile hold 'the subject has over its own identity and bodily boundaries, the ever-present possibility of sliding back into the corporeal abyss out of which it was formed'.[139] Imploring the subject to turn away from that which threatens meaning, the sensations of abjection – disgust, horror, vomiting, retching – might seem connected to a drive to protect the subject from poisonous, toxic or unpleasant substances. However, as Kristeva highlights: 'It is not thus lack of cleanliness or health that causes abjection but what disturbs identity, system, order. What does not respect borders, positions, rules.'[140]

Returning to George Biddle's narrative reconstruction of the Baroness's dramatic exposure of her 'nearly' naked body, we can identify the extension of her 'abject aesthetics' from her waste-based constructions to her corporeal art practices. The Baroness's recovery of material designated as waste interrupts the processes described by Kristeva through which the borders between subject and object are regulated, whereby matter passes from one order into another and persists there as a testament to the power that cast it down and out. As I signposted at the opening of this chapter, in the application of discarded tin cans and stolen curtain rings directly to her body the Baroness blurs the boundaries between herself and the organic, synthetic and mass-produced items she uses in her provocative self-display. Refusing the rules of expulsion, and erasing her own corporeal boundaries, her body is opened in a grotesque gesture of renewal. Radically disturbing system, order and identity, per Kristeva, the Baroness's performance here also interrupts and complicates the voyeuristic structure of the gaze and the gendered dynamics between (active) artist and (passive) model, as the following chapter will return to in more detail.

In recounting this event and reconstructing the Baroness's as a grotesque art-object however, Biddle's narrative is detached and impassive, establishing an aesthetic distance from the object before him as his recording 'eye'/'I' moves across her body and fragments it into its component parts in some cinematic close-up. With reference to Laura Mulvey's foundational theory of the gendered gaze as determining the representation and consumption of the female body in cinema, we can identify the ways in which Biddle's retrospective narrative works to reinstate certain gendered power relationships in this scene. As Mulvey states in her examination of the male socopophilic gaze: 'Woman is the image; man is the bearer of the look', power lies with him.[141] Specific contexts are important here. The encounter between female model and male artist occurs within his studio, and although the Baroness's performative display disrupts the gendered dynamics of that exchange in the moment, Biddle the biographer is able to record, recount and reconstruct this encounter through a critical distance afforded by time; the reconstruction of this body through the 'eye'/'I' that records this encounter also marks the restitution of his artist-identity. Dramatically (re)presenting Elsa as an erotically unsettling and grotesque art object, Biddle's narrative attempts to fix and stabilize Elsa's body as a 'signifier for the male other, bound by a symbolic order in which man can live out his fantasies and obsessions through linguistic command by imposing them on the silent image of woman still tied to her place as a bearer of meaning, not maker of meaning'.[142]

While the dramatic exposure of the Baroness's body-as-work does go some way to disrupting the terms of this encounter, the autobiographer's reconstruction of this body in his narrative firmly establishes Elsa as a visual art-object whose grotesque openness is ultimately harnessed within the contours of the artist/autobiographer's own representation of her. Reinstating this grotesque body within a fixed category, Biddle's narrative has shored up structures of meaning and symbolization against the threats to meaning and corporeal or psychological integrity presented by the abject. Reinstating this body as an ambivalently erotic and fetishized object provides Biddle with a clearly defined object of desire – if not straightforwardly sexual, then at least the desire to (re)posses himself through mastering his representation of her. Sublimated in this manner, the Baroness's disorderly and disordering body is kept under control and it is in this fetishized transformation of her as a newly defined 'bearer of meaning' that we identify the functioning of the grotesque in these accounts as a mode of calculated containment where 'abjection is reabsorbed in the grotesque: a way of living it from the outside'.[143]

However, outside of the more strictly regulated spaces of the artist's studio, the threat posed by the abject dynamics of the Baroness's body-work to the bodies of the avant-garde (non)soldier-males of New York is not so easily contained. Attention to the language of abjection deployed across these other narrative fragments and to the structural role played by these abject dynamics in reconstructing and representing this grotesque body also reveals just what is at stake in the containment of the Baroness's excessive body within modernism's marginalia.

The doubled narrative provided by modernist poet and Rutherford paediatrician William Carlos Williams in his reflective autobiography (1967) and retaliatory 'Sample Prose Piece: The Three Letters' (1921) is particularly interesting in this regard. Taken together, these two accounts roughly describe the narrative arc of their acquaintance. The first stage (only detailed in the later account) describes a primary encounter with her artwork in *The Little Review* offices, where he finds himself strangely drawn to a 'piece of sculpture that appeared to be chicken guts, possibly imitated in wax'. Discovering the Baroness to be the artist responsible, he decides to meet her upon her release from 'The Tombs' and takes her to breakfast. A second scene follows, briefly detailing her suggestion that he should 'contract syphilis from her and so free my mind for serious art', followed by the details of a later visit to the Baroness's

West Eighteenth street apartment, which mark a sharp cooling of relations on his part. The penultimate scene involves an explosive encounter outside his Rutherford home where he claims she had lured him out under false pretences and, following further rejection, 'she hauled off and hit me alongside the neck with all her strength'. In the later account denouement comes with a chance encounter on Park Avenue where the Baroness is arrested, but not before Williams, who had been anxiously preparing for their next encounter, 'flattened her with a stiff punch punch to the mouth'.[144] Clearly traceable even within this prosaic summary are the movements between attraction and repulsion, the threat to corporeal integrity presented by the abject and the ultimate restoration of order imposed by William's premeditated attack, the intervention of the law and the submission of this excessive personality to the structured confines of William's narrative.

Either focused on the useful biographical information and colour that this account provides, or indulging in the more lurid descriptions animating 'Sample Prose Piece', critical treatments of this narrative frequently collapse the two accounts together, glossing the fact that the two are separated by some forty years and the Baroness's death. While they essentially cover the same narrative ground, I want to highlight that, while the later account allows Williams to revise, rewrite and effectively contain the Baroness, reading it alongside the more hysterical 'Sample Prose Piece' reveals a more immediate need to contain her performances, and of the aesthetic strategies through which is attempted. In the revised version, Williams glosses much of the account, providing little detail of their relationship or of the infamous apartment scene, which he frames by explaining he was only there to offer her financial assistance. The authoritative first-person voice casts her as a somewhat pathetic figure throughout. A '*protegé*' of Duchamp's, Williams anxiously reiterates her middle age, and describes her as: 'a woman who had perhaps been beautiful. She spoke with a strong German accent and at that moment was earning a pittance in the city posing as an artist's model [...] she reminded me of my "gypsy" grandmother'.[145]

This alignment proves to be more narrative device than offhand comparison. In the middle of this telegraphic rendering of their relationship, Williams breaks off from the main thread of the narrative to flesh out other background scenes from 1918, including the death of his father. Despite seemingly being set to one side, Williams's reflections on death and loss in fact associatively connect the Baroness – via the figure of his grandmother – to death, decay and the submission of 'old' Europe to 'modern' America:

> The young woman [...] after an apparent delay of five years came to America in a sailing vessel loaded with car rails. [...] Grandma had wanted to be an actress; that was her objective in coming here.
>
> We brought Grandma's body from the shore [...] She lay in state in my front room where I did a pencil drawing of her really impressive features. The old cat slept under her coffin.
>
> But back to the Baroness.[146]

The associations made between his grandmother, death, old Europe and the Baroness here are telling, particularly if we consider the way in which art is figured here as a way of shoring up life against death, form against formlessness. In composing a portrait of his gipsy-actress grandmother, and in rewriting the Baroness's unsettling corporeality, the poet redraws their blurred boundaries and insulates himself from their contaminating excess; the portrait and the narrative reconstruction *stand in* for decomposing body. In this respect both the portrait and the textual narrative it is embedded within replace the fleshy reality of the abject body with the image of it, restating both Williams and the specifically home-grown American poetics that he represented as a source of creative vitality and life in the face of old Europe's death and decay.

With this embedded narrative Williams repeats and works through his relationship with the Baroness, demonstrating his mastery over her threatening corporeality in his ability to impose form in the face of dissolution. Blurring the boundaries between what is and is not us, the threat of liquefaction presented both in the corpse – the sign of death's intrusion into life – and in the smelly, repellent and excessive corporeality of the Baroness is, within the terms of ego-formation established by Lacan and Kristeva, central to the processes through which the subject attempts to identify himself. In terms established by Lacan's theory of the Mirror Stage, perceptions of bodily integrity and coherence are central to this process as the child (mis)identifies with its reflected image.[147] As this moment of self-realization is founded on a mis-recognition of the fantasy image as the material whole, Lacan's theory posits a profound alienation as inherent in self-identification. This alienation is not limited to the inaugural moment, but persists through this model of psychosexual development, determining the entrance of the subject into the Symbolic Order and beyond. The entrance into language and the need to construct reality in terms of language ensure, under Lacan's treatment, the perpetuation of some collective fantasy of 'reality' while the 'real' – that is, the materiality of existence that is beyond (or before) language and expression – is sublimated.

In locating the abject *before* the subject's entrance into the Symbolic Order and preceding narcissistic object-love and self-representation, Kristeva suggests that abjection 'preserves what existed in the archaism of the pre-oedipal relationship, in the immemorial violence with which a body becomes separated from another body in order to be'.[148] Focusing on the 'loss' of what is left out in Lacan's model of identity formation, Kristeva is able to identify that which resists incorporation into the body image as that which makes the (illusionistic) apprehension of a coherent, unified body image possible. In other words, in establishing the coherent subject capable of self-identification and representation, the subject must first abject a part of themselves. Acting as a boundary between self and other, self and world, the order of the abject is indispensable to the formation of the subject, one constituted through a series of losses that make identification as a projection possible.[149]

However, as theorists of the abject reiterate, this is a dangerous and porous boundary. The abject, and the bodies, material and spaces identified as such, demands constant vigilance and policing by the orders of language, law, taboo, culture and sociability broadly brought together within the notion of the Symbolic Order. Indeed, as Gail Weiss has underlined in her study of intercorporeality, it is the Symbolic side of the divide that must work to maintain, regulate and reinforce this boundary (between body image and what it is not), while that which is excluded to the 'unnameable, abject' 'other side' of the boundary constantly threatens to dissolve and overrun its limits. As Weiss states, 'the fragility of the border in turn undermines the stability and coherence of the body image'.[150] Excluded but not eliminated, from its position on the peripheries of the coherent subject (as both ego and body image in Weiss's terms), the abject continues to haunt the ego, threatening to disrupt the stability and integrity of its hard-won notion of corporeal coherence by staging a return of, or traumatic encounter with, pure materiality.

In this respect the sensation of abjection – disgust, retching, turning away – involves, as Elizabeth Grosz has explicated, 'the paradoxically necessary but impossible desire to transcend corporeality. It is a refusal of the defiling, impure, uncontrollable materiality of the subject's embodied existence'.[151] Just as categories of the grotesque were put to work in reconstructions of the Baroness's body to give form to the expressionless abjection experienced by those knocked down by her transgressive body-work and excessive sexuality, in describing their disgust, horror and turning away from the Baroness's abjected body, the various narratives that deploy it do so in order to transcend the messy corporeality and materiality that they encounter there. Transcending corporeality and materiality in this way they not only attempt to reclaim the Baroness as an object – one capable of bearing meaning – but to reaffirm their own (in Lacan's sense illusionistic) sense of bodily integrity and coherence given expression through language.

The extent to which the Baroness was viewed as a threat to corporeal integrity by her male contemporaries, and the compulsive need to contain these threats in their narratives in order to plug up their own bodies against her becomes strikingly clear in William's original account. Published in his own journal *Contact* in the summer of 1921, 'Sample Prose Piece' was written as a response to the Baroness's experimental poem-review of his *Kora in Hell*, Thee I Call 'Hamlet of the Wedding Ring' in which she criticized his bourgeois sexuality and his home-grown American values, which had both left their mark on his work as 'Inexperience shines forth in sentimentality – that masqueraded in brutality: male bluff'.[152] Written in the second person, Williams's piece dramatizes the struggles of the young 'Evan Dionysius Evans' against the voracious and devouring sexuality of the older European *baronne*: 'She was the fulfilment of a wish. Even the queen she held herself to be in her religious fervors of soul, so in actuality she was to him: America personified in the filth of its own imagination'.[153] An outrageous poet published by *The Little Review* and parading through New York in costumes constructed out of the trash of American consumer culture, the 'baronne' is a threatening male fantasy made flesh in this hysterical figuration. More than just an older European 'Other' to young America, this monstrosity was American-made, the fulfilment of a dark desire and deeply unsettling the ego ideal and body image of the young protagonist.

This is a body that refuses to remain contained, that not only exceeds its own limits in its opening to the world, but continually intrudes over the boundary line of the poet's own comparatively 'tidy insularity'. Even in the less physical early stages of their relationship, the ambivalent attraction to this kind of renewing openness, their conversation over breakfast passing as 'she talked and he listened till their heads melted together and went up in a vermillion balloon through the ceiling drawing Europe and America after them'.[154] Just as this original meeting is afforded more attention in establishing the grotesque qualities of the Baroness in this earlier account, the early stages of this relationship are tellingly fleshed out. Repulsed by her and 'that peculiar, pungent smell of dirt and sweat, strong of the armpit', he nevertheless draws closer, her 'broken teeth, her syphilis, everything' fascinating and engulfing him. This sensual fantasy of the couple dissolving from two into one is, however, shattered, rather than sealed, with a kiss.[155] Engulfed by the heavy sway of her body scudding into him like an old sailing boat 'Evan

Dionysius Evans was conscious, on his part, of two things: the very jagged edge of La Baronne's broken incisor pressing hard upon his lip and the stale smell rising from her body'. As his consciousness of the world around him falls away it is only the violated sense of his own bodily integrity that remains; while the jagged incisor points to the outline of his body, and of the permeable soft flesh of his lip, it is her emanating stench that is no longer simply a marker of her difference, but as a troubling transgression that pushes her body out into his.

The apartment scene is central in the representation of the Baroness as filthy, disordered and undeniably abject, and it is this emanating stench that emerges as a particularly privileged means of expressing 'Evan Dionysius Evans's' horror of her. Sublimated in the later version, the searing misogyny of William's account is at full tilt as he rails against the horror provoked by this 'dirty old bitch' and the flood of 'bloodygreen sensations' she spews over him in her declarations of love. Tellingly, the vertiginous horror of this scene is emphasized by the claustrophobic setting of the Baroness's disordered domestic space; sliding between material and metaphorical notions of 'filth' William's narrative struggles to identify and contain the destabilizing force of the Baroness. The two enter:

> the most unspeakably filthy tenement in the city. Romantically, mystically dirty, of grimy walls, dark gaslit halls and narrow stairs, it smelt of black waterclosets, one to a floor, with a low gasflame always burning and torn newspapers trodden in the wet. Waves of stench thickened on each landing as one moved up[156].

The associative references here to *Fountain* transformed from a polished porcelain urinal to a stinking 'black watercloset' are striking given my earlier discussion, especially with the Baroness appearing as a demonic sewage goddess at the close of the piece as the 'Filth stopped back in the pipes rose to her throat, bolted from her ears and her eyes like livid fountains from a broken sewer main'. With the references to blocked pipes and broken sewer mains we are closer to the thematics of the Baroness's *God* than the clean polished surfaces of *Fountain*, although here the imagined wastes are vividly rendered with the contaminating flows that are spewed from her own bodily orifices, rather than through a machine surrogate. Again, we see it is the vulnerable points mapped out in the topography of the grotesque body that preoccupy Williams here, although before this expulsive body can be properly drawn, Williams must recover himself from the boundary of himself – from the place where her stench has taken him.

Charles Brook's *Hints to Pilgrims* (1921) also takes us to this filthy tenement, repeating the key motif's in William's setting. However, while the poet in Brook's short story (an avatar of Hart Crane) ascribes the 'villainous smell on the stairs' to the proximity of an embalmer's school and thus to an identifiable and avoidable source,[157] the thickening 'waves of stench' here seem to assail 'Evan Dionysius Evans' from all sides, immersing him in an olfactory flood that slips between the grime of the walls, the black water-closets, the gas-flame and the wet newspapers. Comparing this lurid description to the later account we can see how the latter more successfully creates an aesthetic distance from this disintegrative experience and effectively 'contains' the destructive power of the Baroness:

> I called on the woman one day, gave her small amounts of money. Ashes were deep on her miserable hearth. In the slum room where she lived with her two small dogs, I saw them at it on her dirty bed.[158]

Emphasizing her wretched poverty, the picture he paints here is one motivated by pity, not desire, and establishes Williams as the benevolent benefactor. While the image of the dogs and the dirty bed remains, the overwhelming stench foregrounded in the original account is instead here replaced with the odourless *visual signs* of disorder: an unkept hearth, a slum room. In pulling back in this manner, the shifts between the two narratives dramatize the conceptual shift between the contaminating touch and the sanitizing gaze. While the first account foregrounds the fear of bodily disintegration provoked by the touch or smell of the Baroness, the second account can record the signs of disorder without being contaminated. The pattern here is reminiscent of Freud's discussion in *Civilization and Its Discontents* (1929) of the development of civilization as a privileging of sight and distance over smell and proximity as man began to walk upright.[159] With this in mind we could read the second account as a more confidently detached narrative. Visualization here ensures distance, marking a shift in Freud's terms from primitivistic olfactory sensorial modes to specular and civilized ones: distance thus protects the subject from that which threatens to dissolve its boundaries.[160]

Smell thus emerges as a particularly loaded carrier of the abject qualities ascribed to filth. Formless, invisible and permeating, it crosses corporeal boundaries indiscriminately, disintegrating the body as it refuses to remain contained or, indeed, traced back to a single, identifiable source. As Trotter points out, not only does smell evade visual identification, it also proves to be particularly slippery if we attempt to situate it within a semantic field. Lacking a vocabulary of its own, we are left to identify a smell by its cause (the smell of a flower, the smell of excrement), or by the effects that it generates (nauseating, appetizing). As Trotter states: 'It is the lack of an appropriate semantic field that renders the mere illusion to a bad smell in narrative so profoundly unsettling. [...] Meaning itself falters.'[161] In his insistence that 'close up, a reek stood out purple from her body, separating her forever from the clean muslin souls of Yankeedom' Williams attempts to use smell as an instrument of disgust in his narrative – a disgust that should serve to identify and maintain difference, and define the boundaries between the self and the other. 'Sample Prose Piece' struggles in its attempts to contain and separate the text and the speaker's body from the threat posed by the abject that it delineates. What it does reveal however is what is at stake in the collapse of meaning generated by such an encounter.

Williams's is by no means the only narrative that draws on smell to explore the disintegrating threat to the modern(ist) subject provoked by the Baroness.[162] In Ben Hecht's short story 'The Yellow Goat', published in *The Little Review* in 1918, the protagonist is drawn into a sexually charged encounter with a woman who he describes as a 'disease': 'Her flesh is insane. She is the secret of ecstasy and of Gods and of all things that are beautiful.'[163] The story is presented as an exercise in memory and meaning as the narrator attempts to reconstruct a sensorily destabilizing encounter and the sensations that provoked it – to attempt the impossible task of shaping and ordering the sensation of a total collapse of meaning in language. Painted against a frenetic background of bands and dancing bodies he tries to reconstruct the woman sitting opposite him:

> To this extent I am able to describe her. The face of a malignant pierrette or of a diabolic clown, stark and illuminated as under some strong lavender ray; the gleaming and putrescent eyes haloed in a gelatinous mist, full of reptilian sorcery. These are simple things to recount. But these were merely the mask for a bewildering thing which held me silent in a strange inertia. This thing hovered between us like a third person. It was an animation creating waves in the air that were neither of light nor sound. My thought grew dim and, during these moments that I sat returning her smile, an almost unbearable lust cried in my blood. (*YG*: 34–5)

Unlike the alterity ascribed to the *body* of the Baroness in the accounts of Biddle and Williams, Hecht goes further, highlighting that, while these artificial features bear significance to the sensations experienced upon encountering her, they merely act as the surface manifestation of the truly 'bewildering' thing. The 'third thing' in the air between them connects them, dissolves the boundaries between the two bodies and is understood as a form of *jouissance* as the world slips away. This is the point that descriptive language breaks down, unable to go any further in recounting and reconstructing the woman as a visual object. Moving to her apartment, the narrative instead turns to sensation and smell:

> We came breathless up a flight of stairs into a room lighted with a gas jet. The heavy sulfurous scent of tube roses stuffed the place but I could make out no flowers [...] She began to dance and throw her arms about and her mouth opened in a riveted laugh. The room became saturated with her. [...] She had ceased her dancing and thrown herself upon the grimy rumpled surface of a bed. A moan began to come from her and her fingers like claws scratched at the air. Her moving and the odors arising from her grew unendurable. I opened the door softly and ran. Pursuing me came the sound of laughter, rising in a howl. (*YG*: 35–36)

In his study of disgust William Miller asserts that 'the dangerous and contaminating are those things which don't fit within the ordering structures', namely the conceptual grid that structures the domain of the disgusting through binary distinctions of clean and unclean, organic and inorganic outlined above.[164] In recognizing and maintaining difference, disgust and desire function as important affective tools in defining boundaries between self and other, inside and outside.

Williams's attempts to classify the Baroness as 'filthy' exemplify the attempts made to rationalize her body-work through a re-writing of her body, to make her fit these 'ordering structures' as unambiguously 'disordered'. As the lingering final sentences of Hecht's short story suggest however, there are places that the ordering structures of language cannot reach:

> In the proper course of time I would fashion adjectives out of the thing the woman of the Yellow Goat had revealed to me and thus perhaps add to the progress of my race. But now there drifted before me a white-torsoed phantom and in my nose there remained the hot smell of a decay. (*YG*: 36)

The Baroness's reconstructed body in these narratives functions to manifest for the authors 'the border, the initial phantasmatic limit that establishes the clean and proper self of the speaking and/or social being'.[165] This is not to say that the Baroness was abject, or even identified her aesthetics as such, but rather to point to the ways in which her body-work is submerged in these accounts, expelled and cast out by the processes of abjection necessary for the self-identification of her modernist and avant-garde peers. As the 'Original Dada', the Baroness's critical erasure and the appropriation and confinement of her grotesque body to the margins of modernism speak to the processes of abjection as *self-purging* delineated by Kristeva: expelling the food I ingest 'I expel *myself*, I spit *myself* out, I abject *myself* within the same motion through which "I" claim to establish myself'.[166]

However, while abjection is necessary to establishing the boundaries and differences that individuate the self in these theoretical models, to respond to the demands to create or reaffirm these boundaries forces a recognition of 'the fragility of the self that is so constituted, and so not only the abject, but the very processes of abjection must also be buried, repressed, denied', as Weiss suggests.[167] While the processes of abjection seek to cast out the abject that 'demonstrates the impossibility of clear-cut borders, lines of demarcation, divisions between the clean and unclean, the proper and improper, order and disorder', this functioning must be, as Grosz suggests, rejected, covered over and contained.[168] Expelling the Baroness's body-work in order to define the contours of a modernist and avant-garde rhetoric concerned with progress, purity and the 'novelty of the new', modernism's marginalia attempts to cover and contain the modes and functions of this abjection. However, from this tapestry of lurid and sensational fragments, the power of the Baroness's *body-work* still resounds and, like the derelict and jettisoned objects returned to her body in her own waste aesthetics, it continues to challenge the power that cast it down and out.

2

Art dazzle: Modelling, performance and the Baroness's self-representational practices

> With me posing [is] art – aggressive – virile – extraordinary – invigorating – antestereotyped – no wonder blockheads by nature degeneration dislike it – feel peeved – it underscores unreceptiveness like jazz does.
>
> Elsa von Freytag-Loringhoven to Peggy Guggenheim, 1927

> The masculine can partly look at itself, speculate about itself, represent itself and describe itself for what it is whilst the feminine can try to speak to itself through a new language but cannot describe itself from outside or in formal terms, except by identifying itself with the masculine, thus by losing itself
>
> Luce Irigaray, *Women's Exile*

The Baroness has certainly been no exception to the recuperative trends of feminist criticism, and the small but steady stream of exhibitions, articles and full-length studies that emerged in the wake of the 1996 exhibition *Making Mischief: Dada Invades New York* – including Gammel's detailed biography, feminist revisions of New York Dada and historiographies of twenty-century performance art – have more recently been buttressed by the covetable *Body Sweats* collection, fictionalized treatments of her life and provocative Dada gestures and a deepening body of scholarly work that spans literary and art historical studies.[1] While such publications have certainly drawn on the continuing power of the Baroness to fascinate, they have also brought to light dimensions of a diverse and experimental art practice which combined a pioneering adoption of performance, early and important interventions into avant-garde practices of found object assemblage, collage and the Readymade, and an irreverent, idiosyncratic contribution to the early twentieth-century free verse movement.

In the wake of a surge of explicitly feminist performance art in the last decades of the twentieth century including Carolee Schneemann's messy transformation of the female body into painterly collage and dynamic critique of art history (*Meat Joy*, 1964; *Interior Scroll*, 1975) Hannah Wilke's modes of bodily display (S.O.S. Starification Object Series, 1974–82) and Rebecca Horn's auto-erotic costuming (*Cornucopia-Seance for Two Breasts*, 1971), a robust vocabulary developed around issues of gender performativity, the body, protest and the everyday.[2] It is no coincidence that concerted 'recoveries' of the Baroness date from the 1990s, a period of consolidation for Dada scholarship, of an overdue acknowledgement of the role played by mass-culture and modernity in the production of literary modernism, and in which critical vocabularies around feminist performance art and gender theory were assimilated into broader discursive frameworks. With these critical foundations in place, the written and visual documentation of the radical costuming practices and poses struck by the Baroness during what she described as the 'splendid years of my art dazzle in New York' has been enthusiastically engaged with and has certainly played an important role in organizing early revisionist gestures and grounding the sustained critical interest in her experimental poetry, art-objects and performative gestures.[3]

While the last chapter took the question of containment as its primary focus, detailing the attempts to erase, contain or reconstruct the Baroness's body in the letters and memoir accounts of her contemporaries, this chapter will bring the Baroness's own constructions to the foreground. It will examine the ways in which the Baroness's strategies of self-representation – her portraits, assertion of posing as art and the corporeal and autobiographic dimensions of her performative and artistic practices – do in fact, in Irigary's terms, develop a language for describing female embodied experience, of looking at, speculating upon and representing the female self. Disentangling herself from the web of visual and narrative discourses aimed at containing both the bodies of women and the range of material and metaphorical threats telescoped into them, attention to the modes of embodied self-representation developed by the Baroness simultaneously expands discussions of modernist and avant-garde practices through the processes of critical recovery while offering a compelling analogue to these processes of feminist projects of recuperation themselves. Correlating to these recuperative critical practices, the Baroness's own scavenging and recombination of used and devalued material push us to consider the radical potential of waste when it returns as 'matter out of place' – with implications for reading both the particular strategies activated in the Baroness's waste-based body-work and the work performed by contemporary feminist criticism.

Drawing out the various dimensions of this body-work goes some way to distinguishing the Baroness's own messy artistic practices from the disorderly but coherent representations of her body as a grotesque art object. However, this is a somewhat troublesome endeavour as, while the active and dynamic aspects of her self-representational practices certainly reconfigure the body as a site of artistic *process*, the reproduction of her own body as 'the greatest work of art that Elsa produced in her New York period' nevertheless necessitated an initial objectification of the body in spatial terms, as Richard Cavell has suggested in his study of Elsa's 'empathetic aesthetics'.[4] Rather than trying to elide these confusions and crossovers between the artist and the art work, I will be centralizing them in my comparative treatment of the Baroness's modelling, costuming, portraiture, literary criticism and autobiographic writing as a set of self-representational strategies that generate dynamic and transformative exchanges between model and artist, performer and audience. In representing and recreating herself as the preeminent *embodiment* of Dada, 'the only one, living anywhere who dresses dada, loves dada, lives dada', as Jane Heap famously put it, the Baroness exceeded avant-garde projects to bridge the divide between art and the everyday, and directly challenged the fetishization of the visual or purely intellectual within art historical traditions and claims for the radical newness of the avant-garde.[5]

While the centrality of the Baroness's body to her lived-Dada practice is immediately obvious in the reconfiguration of her outer limit as living, moving Dada canvas, her painted and assembled portraits, autobiographic and poetic practices all dynamically engage the body. Committed to notions of 'sex-freedom', in both life and literature, several of the Baroness's poems explore and expand representations of female desire as rooted in the body – through orgasm, oral sex and a physiologically registered yearning for a love-object. The broken rhythms and shifts between short exclamation and long exhalation in a poem like 'King Adam' (1919), for example, embodying the pulse and thrust of sexual climax:

Such mine love: electric fluid – current to thine wire – to make
Light –
Ah – h – h – such mine love! (*BS*: 55)

Revelling in sensual and explicitly sexual pleasure, the speaker here is firmly established as a woman in command of her own body and sexual expression, her clear instructions to 'Kiss me .... upon the gleaming hill .....' signalling a reclamation of female orgasm from the phallocentric act of penetrative sex.

Extending the linguistic acrobatics evidenced across her entire *oeuvre* – where she would frequently combine German, English and imagined words into new, expressive compounds – the interaction of visual and sonic elements in the Baroness's (Dada) optophonetic poetry most clearly exemplifies her corporeal poetics. As the editors of the *Body Sweats* collection elegantly put it: 'Emerging from her own inner ear, the sound poems effect an extralexical sensory stammering that questions traditional representation and signification, locating the body itself as the site of meaning' (*BS*: 176). Like some intratextual echo-chamber, these 'Crimsoncruising yell[s]' emanate from, and always return us to her body, and her body-work: the 'Swish – sh – sh – sh – sh/Sish' of 'To Home' (1923) acoustically connecting us to the 'Castle cloud's/Leafy limbswish' of another poem, 'Ostentatious' (1926–7), which in turn is related to the sculptural assemblage *Limbswish* which, it has been suggested, the Baroness wore on her belt as a decorative kinetic accessory she paraded through the streets of New York. Highlighting the centrality of practices of recovery and re-use to her collage aesthetics, the juxtapositions between the organic, the synthetic and the mass-produced directly engage the viewer/reader in their production of meaning, transgressing boundaries between the body, the city it moved through and the objects and sensory perceptions she found there.[6]

Decorating her body with vegetables, tin cans, foreign postage stamps and bicycle lamps as she moved through the city, she both mirrored and challenged contemporary consumer culture. Animating Dada aesthetics in this manner, she not only rejected the organizing principles of containment informing the misogynistic and arrested mecanomorphic drawings, but sharply identified the modes of aesthetic and industrial rationalism underpinning the Duchampian Readymade. While these costumes sensationally reworked her body as a living canvas, she would also work directly on the surface of her skin, a striking self-fashioning practice vividly recalled in accounts of her lacquered scalp, black lipstick, early adoption of nail varnish and flashes of her face painted in shades of emerald green or lurid yellows. This practice was also repeated in several portraits of her friends and avant-garde peers.

As Barnes's notes and Williams's telling insistence of poet Wallace Stevens's refusal to come below 14th street testify to, Elsa terrorized the streets – sometimes wrapped in only a Mexican blanket or brandishing a plaster-cast penis, sometimes in the marginally more decorous costumes constructed out of tea spoons, coal scuttles and curtain rings.[7] Combining sexually explicit poetry, phallic props and provocative costumes constructed out of discarded and re-appropriated junk, the Baroness's public Dada performances were profoundly anti-social, and quite distinct from the safe, sanctioned spaces of high art and theatre, though they certainly mocked the dry solemnity of such institutions. In this respect, the intersections of the carnivalesque as a literary mode and the performative dimensions of Swabian Fasching practices explored over the course of this chapter illuminate a set of relationships between costume and critique that the Baroness exploited in the pursuit of her Dada critique of bourgeois respectability.

Refusing to adhere to gendered spatial codes and practices, these performative gestures, like her art-objects, costumes and poems, were certainly viewed as an invasion in the institutional and public spaces – the subways, art galleries, editorial offices and streets – of New York itself, and were monitored, regulated and censored accordingly. Perhaps unsurprisingly, the Baroness was arrested several times during her stay in New York. With charges ranging from petty theft to violent encounters and frequently disciplined for public indecency, she was also accused of being a spy after the passing of the Wartime Act. Recollecting her time in Philadelphia, Biddle suggests she was arrested on more than one occasion for 'trying to bathe in the public pools' while Margaret Anderson records that when having 'Tired of conventional living, she became an artist's model. Tired of conventional dressing, she began creating costumes which resulted in her arrest whenever she appeared on the streets. Tired of official restraint, she leaped from patrol wagons with such agility that policemen let her go in admiration'.[8]

Whether such accounts are accurate documentations of the Baroness's brushes with the law, they make clear that a certain level of regulation and censorship was felt to have been enacted upon her body and strikingly public corporeal performances. Interestingly, the first mention of Elsa in New York is in fact the report of her arrest published in the *New York Times* on 16 September 1910. Under the appalled heading 'SHE WORE MEN'S CLOTHES', the article goes on to detail how 'Mrs. Else Greve [...] was arrested in crowded Fifth Avenue this forenoon while walking by the side of her husband, F.P. Greve of New York, dressed in men's clothes and puffing a cigarette'.[9] Her arrival in New York is thus marked by a public act of gender defiance, appropriating the symbols of masculine power and privilege in order to unseat their 'naturalness' in ways that pre-figure both feminist performance art and theories of gender performativity.[10] Importantly, this challenge to codes of feminine propriety and proper public conduct (which the article attempts to remedy through its anxious insistence on her social status as a married woman) is organized through her costuming and posing practices which are radically extended in her appropriation and reanimation of the quotidian and domestic in her collage couture.

It was not only the restrictive expectations of gender norms that the Baroness critiqued through her costuming and performance. She frequently used her poems, portraits and experimental approach to literary criticism as vehicles to expose the limitations of avant-garde projects and anti-establishment pronouncements, and in rerouting these Dada energies through a dynamically open set of self-representational practices she similarly opened avant-garde experimentation to renewal through a series of collaborative and transformative gestures.

Invited by Biddle to review an exhibition of his at Wildenstein's on Fifth Avenue, the Baroness presented herself as the embodied energy of disruptive techno-industrial modernity. As Biddle recalls:

> She made a clean sweep of Schwartz's Toy Store that morning; and she had sewed to her dress some sixty or eighty lead, tin or cast-iron toys: dolls, soldiers, automobiles, locomotives and music boxes. She wore a scrapbasket in lieu of a hat, with a simple but effective garnishing of parsley; and she led, tied on one string and fastened at different intervals, seven small, starved, and terrified curs. The gallery was crowded. The Baroness had her say, remorselessly, in front of every painting.[11]

A dazzling example of what Alex Goody has described as the Baroness's provocative mode of Dada self-display as 'a lived transgression of the boundaries of human – animal – machine', in incorporating these quotidian objects in her elaborate handmade costume she evokes and mocks the limitations of Biddle's brand of social realism to fulfil its agenda to capture life, remorselessly delivering her critique through a mode of embodied, visual, kinetic and acoustic Dada performance.[12] The particular items of her costuming here, the toy soldiers, automobiles and locomotives not only playfully represent the modern world, but evoke the kind of play that encourages boys to grow up to be soldier-men, which given the blasting apart of those male bodies on the battlefields of Europe reads from a twenty-first-century perspective as a wry warning about the uncritical repetition of performative masculinity. Beyond the cross-dressing performance detailed by *The New York Times* then, Halberstam's notion of female masculinity as at once subordinated and essential to the analysis of the construction of masculinity offers a useful keynote for thinking about Elsa's self-performance more broadly, particularly in the context of her penetration of the construction and performance of modernist masculinity and the critique of the gendered politics and poetics of gazing and 'posing' activated across her *body-work*.

i. Self-Representational practices, collage and the Baroness's Dada portraits

> Women have always collected things and saved and recycled them because leftovers yielded nourishment in new forms. The decorative functional objects women made often spoke in a secret language, bore a covert imagery.
>
> –*Miriam Schapiro and Melissa Meyer, 1977*

Much like the Armory Show of 1913 which loudly announced itself as the event which established New York as the site for the production and consumption of modern art, *Making Mischief*, curated by Francis Naumann and Beth Venn and held at the Whitney Museum at the close of the twentieth century, makes a revisionist claim for the importance of New York – and New York Dada, as it was subsequently termed – in the history of twentieth-century avant-garde production. While more recent work has been keen to expose and correct the exclusion and marginalization of minority modernists within these movements, it is worth emphasizing that until relatively recently New York Dada was itself considered a marginal movement in twentieth-century art histories.

Alongside the persistent Eurocentric focus of early influential art histories of the historic avant-garde, the highly politicized and explicitly anti-war focus of the Dada activities unfolding in Zurich and Berlin ensured their more immediate relevance to the building the anti-establishment brand of Dada which had initially largely overlooked the New York groupings in this context. Seemingly a-political and geographically removed from the events unfolding on the European stage, the retrospectively identified New York Dada moment was, in comparison to its European counter-parts, a transitory one emerging from the collaborations and conversations of European émigrés and American artists, writers, visual artists, patrons and editors between 1915 and 1923. Since the resurgence of Dada scholarship during the 1990s, this picture has become more complicated as considerations for performance and poetry as well as visual experimentation have introduced new lines of inquiry focused on the political and cultural contexts of New York Dada, opening up discussions about gender, non-combatant masculinity, patronage and technology in the promotion and production of Dada and important theoretical treatments of the intersections of Dada politics, poetics and performance.[13]

Growing out of Francis Naumann's extensive and invaluable work on New York Dada, the 1996 exhibition *Making Mischief* proved hugely influential in galvanizing this revisionist trend. Limiting its focus to the circle of artists, writers and visitors who frequented the lively Arensberg salon on 33 West 67th Street (as opposed to the Mabel Dodge or Alfred Stieglitz groups) the exhibition presented work by over twenty European and American artists, placing significant works such as Duchamp's *Tu'm*, early Readymades, Man Ray's 'rayographs' and the mechanical portraits of Picabia and de Zayas alongside photographs, letters and magazines. While the show gave predictable prominence to the 'Dada Daddies' French artist Marcel Duchamp, French Cuban expatriate Francis Picabia and American photographer and artist Man Ray, its thematic and literal focus on the Arensberg salon as an epicentre of avant-garde production gave equal space to other more marginal members of the group including Juliette Roche, Morton Schamberg and John Covert. Forcing a reconsideration of Man Ray as more than a photographer and producer of second-rate Readymades, the exhibition showcased several of his paintings and drawings alongside reproductions of Duchamp's more infamous works, and brought to light a vast range of portraits, drawings, paintings and assemblages by more marginalized players, including Beatrice Wood, Clara Tice, Charles Demuth and the Baroness Elsa von Freytag-Loringhoven.

Given the discussion of the gendered dynamics of portraiture presented in the previous chapter, it is worth noting the prominence of portraits in the *Making Mischief* exhibition and the revisionist impact that this focus has on historical narratives of New York Dada. Underpinning the central narrative of the exhibition – establishing a sense of intimacy of the Arensberg salon – the opening room of the exhibition was hung with the portraits produced by New York Dadaists of themselves and each other. Amongst Picabia's more familiar mechanomorphic portraits of De Zayas, Stieglitz and '*La Jeune Fille Américaine*', the work of Beatrice Wood, Florine Stettheimer and the beadwork portraits of the Baroness also enjoyed prominence. Such focus not only places women artists (as opposed to female muses) at the centre of a revised narrative of New York Dada, but introduces a range of art practices seemingly at odds with the dominant machine aesthetic common in treatments of Dada's formal thematics.

While the dematerializing bodies of Florine Stettheimer's fragile watercolours and Clara Tice's playfully animated calligraphic figures present a direct challenge to the 'hypermasculine and confrontational rhetoric espoused by most male Dadaists',[14] and are certainly incongruous within the dominant 'machine-centred, anti-humanistic, and masculine stance' of Dadaist aesthetics, the aggressive and confrontational objects and practices developed by the Baroness 'in anything-but-traditional-media' problematize any straightforward categorization of a coherent 'feminine' – that is, as straightforwardly anti-mecanomorphic – Dada aesthetic.[15] Indeed, whilst they certainly share an aesthetic interest in found objects and modern commodities, and deploy the irreverent humour that Naumann identifies as 'the most salient, consistent, and powerfully operating factor behind the creation of all great Dada artefacts',[16] her assemblages, objects and portraits remain in striking ways distinct from the Readymades and techno-mechanical re-imaginings of form explored by the more familiar New York Dadaists.

In the messy materiality of her plastic and performative art practices, and the autobiographic poetics activated in her portraits, poems and performances, the Baroness's challenges to both gendered and generic conventions went considerably further than her spectacular subjectivity as re-written in the fragmented portraits of her contemporaries. Through sexual confession, sexually explicit and collaged poetry and corporeal performance, the Baroness developed forms and vocabularies for embodied female self-representational practices; she not only gazes at herself, but looks – and talks – back. These self-representational and decidedly autobiographic practices are underpinned by her idiosyncratic waste-based aesthetic, and are particularly apparent in the multi-media (self)portraits she produced. Retrieving and re-applying waste material the Baroness both took ownership over her 'double marginality' and challenged the naturalized binaries of self/other, masculine/feminine, inside/outside, clean/unclean ultimately upheld by her avant-garde contemporaries.

Close attention to the forms and functions at work in the Baroness's lively *Portrait of Berenice Abbott* (c. 1922–26) usefully illustrates some of these ideas. Bold and brightly coloured, the portrait brings together a wealth of diverse materials including coloured tinfoil, glass beads, cut and pasted paper, tinted lacquer, celluloid, feathers, brooches, stones and hand-stitched scraps of fabric. Recovered and re-used, discarded items become ornamental and decorative in a visually riotous play between foreground and background, while the juxtaposition of man-made and organic materials complements the techno-primitivism at play in the rendering of Abbott as both Primitivist fetish and mechanomorphic fantasy. Rather than straightforwardly subordinating her subject to 'symbolic machine surrogates',[17] the Baroness re-creates a striking physical resemblance through the gestural language of juxtaposed and newly symbolic materials. The sweep of a feathered brooch invokes the smooth and androgynous curve of Abbott's 'modern' cropped hair, while the complementary curvilinear lines of the pouting lips and moustache allude at once to her attractive femininity, her 'masculine' attractions towards women and her New Woman androgyny.

The elegant line of Abbott's elongated neck is offset by the chunky beaded choker, itself highly reminiscent of the elaborate wearable ornaments that the Baroness was known to gift to her friends. Highly decorative, the shimmering cantered squares of pasted tinfoil arranged across her shoulders at once evoke the luxurious golds and richly textured patterns of Gustave Klimt's canvases, and the Baroness's own waste-based costuming practices.

Further than a playful observation of the physical characteristics of her subject, Elsa also includes important and celebratory references to Abbott's status as an artist of the vanguard; her large earrings like miniature reproductions of Duchamp's *In Advance of a Broken Arm* identifying her as a significant contributor to New York Dada, while the foregrounded black orb, crowned with

Figure 12 Elsa von Freytag-Loringhoven, *Portrait of Berenice Abbot c.* 1923. Mixed media collage of synthetic materials, cellophane, metal foils, paper, stones, metal objects, cloth, paint, etc., 8 ⅝ × 9 ¼ in. New York, Museum of Modern Art (MoMA). From the collection of Mary Louise Reynolds. 336.19 © 2019. Digital image, The Museum of Modern Art, New York/Scala, Florence.

flashing spikes and skeletal camera-stand in the bottom right corner of the piece reference Abbott's recent transition from sculpture to photography. Against the luminous gold of the lacquered passages, and the busy, highly decorative sections of looped markings, pasted elements and textured fabrics, Abbott's eyes literally stand out, the bright, ruby-like glass beads recreating the sharp, focused eye of the photographer as she meets our gaze.

With its fractured forms, range of distinct, stitched together materials and complex spatiality, the Baroness's collaged portrait rejects notions of the picture surface as smooth, contained and finished. Rupturing the surface of the picture in this way, the juxtaposition of fabrics, fragments and urban flotsam also self-reflexively highlights the hand-worked and constructed nature of the portrait, raising questions about the construction of identity and the work of representation. Connecting Abbott's body with the technological tools used in the production of her art, and material from the world she reproduces in her photographs, the Baroness is not 'describing' Abbott from the outside, but generates a kind of collaborative, dynamic dialogue between her recombined materials and her subject; in terms set down by Rozsika Parker she 'transform[s] materials to make sense'.[18] In this respect, the work of representation is not engineered through a coolly detached arrangement of forms performed from an insulated somewhere-out-there, but produced through the 'new possibilities of signification' arising from the juxtaposition of flat zones of colour, pasted elements and hand-stitched fabrics, and fostering an open exchange between the various compositional elements of the portrait, the material word it is connected to and the dynamic interchange between artist and subject that occurs in its making.[19]

In its incorporation of Readymade material elements from the world outside of itself, the *Portrait of Berenice Abbott*, of course, recalls Picasso's *Still Life with Chair Caning* (1912), which, as Christine Poggi has reiterated 'has acquired legendary status in the history of art as the first deliberately executed collage'.[20] However, rather than conforming to Cubistic notions of collage (particularly to Formalist treatments of collage as involved primarily in the identification of the picture surface as flat), and the later critical histories that have privileged 1912 as the invention of the medium, in its dense accumulations the Baroness's portrait recovers more than just scraps of fabric and lost jewelled beads, but connects itself to a marginalized and more explicitly *feminine* history of making practices and *feminist* strategies of composition that unpicks art historical categories separating high from low, private from public and the gendered distinctions between art and craft.

With an emphasis on the 'cut' and the implied violence of that gesture, conventional readings of Cubist collage, or more precisely, *papier collé* theorize the medium as a strikingly subtractive process in the first instance, formalizing a 'procedure of destruction and negation' whereby the imagined whole (newspaper, printed wood-grain paper) is cut apart before being reassembled in a set of new spatial and formal relationships.[21] Rosalind Krauss's influential framing of Cubistic collage within the field of structural linguistics corroborates such formulations on intellectual terms, the subdivision of the Sausurrean sign into signifier and signified usefully describing the relationship of collaged material to referent. As Krauss acknowledges, Picasso was less interested in the illustrative possibilities of collage, than its referential qualities: a torn piece of newspaper might refer to the whole, or cut into certain shapes and printed with certain letters, might refer instead to a bottle, a violin or a glass; illusionistic oil cloth or *broderie anglaise* patterns at once referring to their real word equivalents (chair caning, lace table cloths) and a tongue-in-cheek acknowledgement of their own uncertain status as *trompe l'oeil* referents in the material world.

In this respect, important theorizations of early twentieth-century avant-garde experimentation have grounded theories of collage on the structural conditions of *absence*, the system of collage inaugurating 'a play of differences which is about and sustained by an absent origin'. Under this treatment, negation is echoed through the various compositional stages of Cubist collage: the absent referent from which the bottle, violin or glass takes its meaning, the 'forced absence of the original plane by the superimposition of another plane', and the primary gesture of cutting into material to produce the collaged fragments.[22] As Krauss writes:

> If one of the formal strategies that develops from collage, first into synthetic and then into late cubism, is the insistence of figure/ground reversal and the continual transposition between negative and positive form, this formal resource derives from collage's command of the structure of signification: no positive sign without the eclipse or negation of its material referent.[23]

Just as the Saussurean sign operates through a process of negation or *difference* whereby meaning is determined by the terms that it is not, under this treatment the cut-out can only refer to the cut-away, to what George Baker has described as the *disjecta membra* of form. Within this system waste can only be conceptualized as the negative term in the binary, as loss and absence referencing the 'inescapable fact that something has been removed, that matter has been cut away, and that we are gazing at a field of parts and pieces, an accumulation of broken fragments'.[24]

In the context of this book's interest in fantasies relating to an ideal contained and insulated modernist body and text, such formulations are striking both in their initial privileging of a whole or sealed object that has been violently cut into and broken open, and of their renegotiation with the 'proper functioning' of waste as material which falls away and is removed.[25] While such structuralist readings are still useful in approaching the play of negative space and referentiality at work in Cubist collage or Matisse's later paper cut-outs, they do not fully engage with the materiality of certain elements of Dada collage (photomontage or the Merz constructions of Kurt Schwitters and the Baroness's own waste-based practices), and certainly fail to account for traditions of collage practices that operate outside the narrowly defined terms of Cubist experimentation.

Involving a rich history of anonymous folk art and the undocumented domestic labour of women, collage aesthetics were, in fact, widely practiced and developed outside of the masculinist Western art histories, as Miriam Schapiro and Melissa Meyer's 1970s theorization of 'Femmage' has established. Complicating the notion of collage as modernist invention, an account of the traditions of femmage also troubles theorizations of collage's relationship to waste. In its emphasis on processes of *combination* rather than *cutting*, femmage allows for a focus on the generative recovery and *re-use* of waste material, rather than a fixation on the processes of its production alone. Obviously related to the domestic work of darning, mending and making, such practices rely on the salvaging and collecting of scraps of fabric, threads and leftovers, and reveal a rich but marginalized mode of making historically performed by (or at least assigned to) women who 'have always collected things and saved and recycled them because leftovers yielded nourishment in new forms'.[26]

With its generative reuse of material scraps and fragments, handmade quality and intimate nature of its production and circulation, the *Portrait of Berenice Abbott* can clearly be situated within the context of femmage and as such signals a radical challenge to the emphasis on impersonality and objectivity advocated by the Duchampian Readymade and the Picabian mechanomorph.[27] As Meyer and Schapiro explain, the personal is elevated in femmage not simply in its privileging of the diarist's point of view and the 'woman-life context' of the work, but imbedded in the act of recovering and recombining the materials themselves. As they write:

> Collected, saved and combined materials represented for such women acts of pride, desperation and necessity. Spiritual survival depended on the harbouring of memories. Each cherished scrap of percale, muslin or chintz, each bead, each

letter, each photograph, was a reminder of its place in a woman's life, similar to an entry in a journal or a diary.[28]

As opposed to the production of waste material through the cut-out and cut-away, it is the processes of recovery and collecting that take precedence here, ones that take on a distinctly feminist and autobiographic function. In a striking departure from the claims to objectivity and impersonality made by the Duchampian Readymade, or Krauss's theorizations of Cubism's privileging of the 'impersonal operations of language' itself, the act of selection here is highly personal, driven by the artist's desire to recover or save something saturated with personal significance.[29] Tellingly, Krauss's essay is framed by a rejection of autobiographical readings, what she terms an 'art history of the proper name'. The tension between autobiographic reading and certain autobiographic strategies is subtle and complex, as we shall see in relation to Barnes's work, but this persistent critical resistance to the personal (and implicitly feminine) in conceptualizations of literary modernism and the historic avant-garde has certainly eclipsed the compelling connections to be made between waste, collage aesthetics and the structural patterns of auto/biography that this book is invested in.

Later chapters will deal more explicitly with the deep connections between autobiographic practices and the cutting and stitching of material as worked out across the collaborative 'Baroness Elsa' biography, but I just want to touch on the connection made by Meyer and Schapiro between the combinations of femmage and the self-representational strategies employed by the diarist as she recalls and rewrites the personally significant and otherwise ephemeral moments in her life.

The deeply personal nature of the salvaged and archived material described by Meyer and Schapiro certainly chimes with descriptions of the (con)fusion between the Baroness's domestic and working spaces as her 14th street studio, the anchoring of her costuming practices in her personal autobiography, and of the distinctive self-representational practices activated in her portraiture, as Anderson recalls:

> During these later years she lived in a tenement of two rooms with three dogs. She wrote or painted all day and all night, produced art objects out of tin foil, bits of rubbage [sic] found in the streets, beads stolen from the ten-cent store. She considered that she was at the summit of her art period.[30]

Using the 'cherished' material from her strange miscellany in her representation of Abbott, the Baroness brings the two artists together within her portrait, just as her incorporation of collecting and making practices conventionally associated with gendered modes of amateur craft work into her

Dada aesthetics brings these marginalized practices into proximity with high modernist aesthetics. Given the predilection for puns and innuendo that greased the wheels of so much of the Baroness's bilingual Dada wordplay, the alternative meaning of collage in contemporary slang to refer to a non-marital 'shacking up together' would no doubt have amused her. Indeed, while the Baroness was by her own admission resolutely heterosexual, the portrait does seem to play with this 'pasting together' of the two women, especially pertinent given the Baroness's attack on 'Faithless Bernice's' rescinding on her promise that 'as soon as you had an apartment large enough – "you would give me a little room all to myself to work in"'.[31]

As the Baroness's furious letter predicts, the two women would never be roommates, and yet as far as a generative intersubjectivity imagined between two artists goes, the portrait certainly creates a space of co-habitation. While Gammel has read the small, sculptural figure crouched on the table in the left-hand side of the composition as 'a sketch of Abbott holding an umbrella crowned with beads',[32] I would suggest that, given the intimate domestic setting of the composition, the presence of the Baroness's own dog Pinky, and the familiar crouching pose of the figure, we could in fact read this small, vaguely mechanized idol as a self-portrait of the Baroness herself. Certainly, the figure bears a striking resemblance to a photograph of the Baroness taken in 1915, who, draped in chiffon exposing the flesh of her arms, bends her body into a similarly exaggerated contrapposto pose, arms foreshortened and folded tightly into the body with her weight offset as one foot is raised on tiptoe. In this photograph, just visible in the alcove behind the door stands a black umbrella, connecting the cluttered interiors of the Baroness's live/work spaces with the busy composition of the Abbott portrait, and to the slightly later gouache *Forgotten Like This Parapluie*, dated between 1923 and 1924, but obviously completed after the two had fallen out. Sadly, despite the Baroness's expectation that Abbott would photograph her striking poses 'for business reasons', no such images exist, and yet the portrait still opens up interesting readings of the intersubjectivity of the artist, model and subject activated in the alternative modes of female self-representation developed in the Baroness's Dada portraits.

As Ina Lowenberg has suggested: 'Women have been frequently used as subjects (for which we can read "objects") in the arts, including photography, that self-portraiture is a way to keep control of their own representation.'[33] Indeed, while the inscription of the Baroness's initials above the relic's head could simply be read as the artist signing the work as a whole, its prominent positioning here above this 'self-portrait' dramatizes Elsa's continued employment of her

Figure 13 International News Photography, *Baroness von Freytag-Loringhoven working as a model.* 7 December 1915. Bettman/Corbis photo agency.

body-as-art in an assertion of her independence of other's representations of her, and as a means of maintaining her ownership over her own self-presentation. By representing herself as an inscrutable art-object here, Elsa subtly refuses the claims to objectivity made by the camera/photographer in their ability to 'capture' and 'contain' their subject; while it can record her postures and performative gestures, she remains somewhat elusive.

In fact, neither figure can be reduced to a single, fixed identity in this composition. While the combination of masculine, feminine and androgynous features ensures that the representation of Abbott resists identification through the signs of sexual difference, the relic-as-self-portrait captures the multiple identities of Elsa as artist, art-work and model. Given Abbott's own training as a sculptor, it would be tempting to read the figure as a straightforward primitivist reworking of the model into art-object, one which is particularly striking in its rejection of the contained contours of the classical nude in favour of an open spiral or zig-zag curve. However, given the strong visual resonance of this form with the helix of Elsa's kinetic sculptural assemblage *Limbswish,* we can begin to identify the ways in which her aggressive approach to modelling-as-art, and the interconnectedness of her performative, autobiographical and waste-based practice radically disrupts the voyeuristic structures of looking that have dominated Western art histories.

In her textured representation of artist and art-object within the same physical and temporal space, Elsa's (self)portrait dismantles traditional binary hierarchies of subject and object, artist and model, drawing closer to the dynamics of performance in collapsing the objective, contemplative distance afforded by more traditional pictorial treatments of the female nude. Rather than reinforcing the unequal power relations traditionally enforced between artist and model, painting subject and painted object, Elsa seems to be celebrating the shared vision of the two female artists in this portrait as the strong diagonals of the composition reinforce the 'arrow' created by the umbrella connecting the body of the sculpture with the eyes of Abbott. Delineating a field of vision, the beaded umbrella shape here could be read in either – or both – direction: while Abbott the photographer gazes upon her model with a sculptor's eye, the model/relic gazes back. Mutually representing, their red-ruby eyes gaze upon each other, reformulating one another in that – female – exchange. Indeed, while the terms of the model's reconfiguration according to the eye of the photographer/sculptor are more immediately obvious, if we look again at decorative ornaments displayed by Abbott and the swirling contours of colour that make up the surface of her skin here, it seems that the model has similarly remade the artist.

With her sharp, exaggerated gilded eyelashes and painted face, the portrait of Abbott vividly connects the subject to the artist's own well-documented modes of self-display, directly recalling the Baroness's elaborate costuming on visiting the French consulate:

> I went to the consulate with a large-wide sugarcoated birthday cake upon my head with fifty flaming candles lit – I felt just so spunky and affluent! In my ear

I wore sugar plums or matchboxes – I forget which. Also I had put on several stamps as beauty spots on my emerald-painted cheeks and my eyelashes were made of gilded porcupine quills – rustling coquettishly – at the consul – with several ropes of dried figs dangling around my neck to give him a suck once and again – to entrance him. I should have liked to wear gaudy coloured rubber boots up to my hips with a ballet skirt of genuine gold paper white lace paper covering it (to match the cake) – but I couldn't afford that!

As a relatively rare account of the Baroness's costuming practices by the artist herself, this narrative reconstruction of her birthday performance is fascinating as a document of her modes of self-display. Turning her body into a living collaged canvas she freely applies paint and postage stamps directly to her skin, extending the limits of her body through the application of vegetable and animal products as she transforms herself into a sugar-coated birthday cake burlesque in honour of her fiftieth birthday. Mixing her mediums, and transferring material from her collage portraits to her body and back again, the Baroness connects her more explicit modes of self-display with her work in more established forms and genres – including portraiture.

As we shall see, in using the space of the portrait as a vehicle for claiming her identity as an artist, she also directly engaged the decorporealized machine modes which would eventually be canonized under the term 'New York Dada', her blend of organic, synthetic and industrially produced (and often used) materials challenging the cold detachment of chrome, glass and steel selected with 'visual indifference' and traced by a mechanical hand. In an intriguing pastel and collage portrait of Marcel Duchamp from the early 1920s the Baroness goes against the established New York Dada grain by representing Duchamp in rich, warm, earthy tones, his roughly hewn face taking on the contours of a carved wooden mask. The detached head appears like a reliquary bust, arranged with other items including a stoppered bottle and spoked wheel referencing his early Readymade experiment. However, writing against the script of New York Dada, beneath the now iconic symbol of machine age art production Elsa includes a web of delicate lace, which along with the roughly hand-stitched edge introduces the hand-made, the feminine and the autobiographic into the frame.

ii. Making mischief, or looking through a glass dynamically

Tri-ri-ri-ri-ri-ri-ri-ri-ri – art oozes – gushes out of cautionlifted tap – champagne!

–Elsa von Freytag-Loringhoven, 'Thee I Call "Hamlet of Wedding Ring"'

As we have seen, *Making Mischief*'s focus on the portraits associated with New York Dada was central to its revisionist intentions, which are particularly upheld in a piece such as the *Portrait of Berenice Abbott*. Such a revised focus on the modes of self-representation practised by female artists challenges entrenched assumptions about New York Dada practices – not simply over questions about who is making art or indeed what kind of art they are making, but in re-framing a 'dominant mode of avant-gardism [which] is predicated on the erasure of the subjectivity of the artist – the messy and potentially compromising aspects of her or his sexuality and other biographical vicissitudes – from the artistic encounter'.[34] Of course, while this exploration of subjectivity, self-representation and autobiography is more immediately obvious in examples of self-portraiture, it is important to highlight the compromised status of portraiture in this respect: exploring the problematic boundary between self and other, portraiture always threatens to 'collapse into self-portrayal'.[35] In exploring ideas about personal identity and forms of self-representation these portraits and self-portraits are, by these terms, messy and compromised in their auto/biographical focus.

Significantly in this respect Naumann, whose pioneering work in 'recovering' the Baroness should not be understated, chose to use Charles Sheeler's photographic image of the Baroness's assemblage *The Portrait of Marcel Duchamp* (c. 1920) on the front cover of the exhibition's catalogue. Clearly central to the revisionist focus of the show as a previously overlooked poet, performer, model and visual artist, Elsa's objects and images also expanded definitions of New York Dada thematics and practices themselves. As a portrait, the Baroness's piece is visually and materially at odds with the familiar visual thematics of Dada – Picabia's mecanomorphic fantasies, Man Ray's gender fluid egg beaters and priapic paperweights, Duchamp's coolly ironic Readymades. As Zabel suggests, 'the handmade and the organic predominate' in this sculptural assemblage consisting of chicken bones, fishing wire, springs, gears, fabric and sprays of ornamental feathers all arranged in a vertical composition seeming to sprout from a wine glass like a strange forest fungus.[36] If Dada is 'invading' New York here, the unavoidable prominence of the Baroness and her own contributions to machine-age portraiture not only places her on the front line in such an invasion, but asks us to identify the challenges of this 'highly personal and sensual art, which incorporated human and animal forms, organic materials, and her own body', not only to 'New York' but to New York Dada itself.[37]

While the choice of an unfamiliar object by a hitherto relatively unknown female artist (as opposed to a Duchampian Readymade, for example) speaks quite plainly to the revisionist impetus of the exhibition, in choosing a portrait

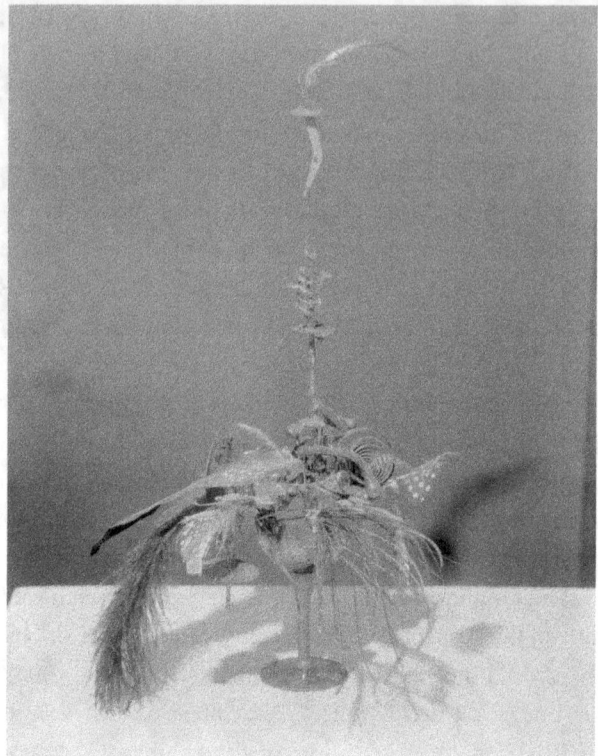

Figure 14 Elsa von Freytag-Loringhoven, *Portrait of Marcel Duchamp*, c. 1920. Photograph by Charles Sheeler. Bluff Collection, photograph courtesy Francis M. Naumann Fine Art, New York.

for the cover of the exhibition catalogue, Naumann also appears to foreground the centrality and importance of modes of self-representation in developing revisionist narratives of New York Dada. In stark distinction to a criterion based on impersonality and objectivity, with their focus on the autobiographic, the organic and the used, the Baroness's sculptural assemblages foreground not only the aesthetic choice of the artist, but evoke the moving, desiring body of the artist herself. While this is perhaps more immediately obvious in the decorative, kinetic constructions such as *Limbswish* (c. 1920) and *Earring-Object* (c. 1917–19) which evoke both the techno-industrial cityscape and the moving body of the artist within it, we can also trace the resolute presence of the Baroness in her portraits from this period, the interplay of organic and synthetic materials in a piece such as the *Portrait of Marcel Duchamp* not only modelling the 'interaction between the artist and his machine environment', but dramatically performing the transformative exchange between artist and subject.[38]

A strange and striking piece, the Baroness's *Portrait of Marcel Duchamp* has offered itself up to a range of interpretations. While some have read it as a 'toast' to the artist and object of her sexual and romantic desire, others have pointed to the champagne glass as encoding a biographical reference to Duchamp's infamous *Large Glass* construction that preoccupied him during this period, or as an allusion to Man Ray's photographs of Duchamp's female persona Rrose Sélavy, one which certainly seems suggested here through the arrangement of feathers around the rim of the glass that visually echoes the feathered hat cutting across Duchamp/Sélavy's eyes in the photograph taken by Man Ray and reproduced as the collaboration *Belle Haleine, Eau de Violette* (1921).³⁹

Figure 15 Man Ray and Marcel Duchamp, *Rrose Sélavy*, 1921. © Man Ray 2015 Trust/ADAGP, Paris and DACS, London 2019.

Figure 16 Man Ray, *Marcel Duchamp*, 1916. © Succession Marcel Duchamp/ADAGP, Paris and DACS, London 2019/© Man Ray Trust/ADAGP.

It is also possible to trace Duchamp's tall, willowy frame and delicate, elongated features in the fragile verticality of the composition. Supported by the slender stem of the champagne glass, the delicate bird-like construction seems at once perched upon and emerging from this transparent body. Following the diagonal curve generated by the drooping feathers and material spilling out of the glass we find the delicately crossed legs of a figure seated in three-quarter profile. As the long, thin and knotted wire construction evoked the straightened, upright spine, the opposing curves of bone and feathers crowning it trace the aquiline nose and sloped forehead. Several of Man Ray's striking photographic portraits of Duchamp survive, one in particular – dated from 1916 and featuring Duchamp seated in profile on a cane chair, his folded hands holding a book and resting on his crossed legs – makes for an interesting comparison to Elsa's 1918 sculptural assemblage.

Highlighting the impermanence and ephemerality of so much of the Baroness's production, and revealing as to the role of collaboration in the circulation of her work, it should be emphasized that this sculptural portrait only survives in reproductions of Sheeler's silver print photograph, originally published in *The Little Review* in 1922. This paradoxically renders the otherwise animated portrait rather static, the gently kinetic and sensuously tactile aspect of the feathers arrested in the still image. Interestingly though, in arranging the piece to be photographed, the positioning of the light source in relation to the assemblage has added another dimension to the photograph, casting an amorphous shadow away from it, almost like a bird caught in flight. While we could leave this collaborative photographic by-product as an accidental addition to the Baroness's composition, nevertheless, in the flirtatious relationship between object and shadow reproduced on the flat surface of a single photograph, it does present a further Duchampian reference that is worth exploring in relation to Elsa's own auto/biographical poetics here.

Throughout this period Duchamp's notebooks, writings and compositions express an interest in the aesthetic possibilities of shadow play, particularly his experiments with 'the execution of the picture by means of luminous sources. And by drawing the shadows on these planes simply following the *real* outlines projected [...] all of this to be completed [...] to relate with the subject?'[40] The 1918 canvas *Tu'm* explicitly explores this slippage between objects and shadows. In addition to the 'proper' relationship of object and shadow established with the prominent extrusion of a bottle brush and the 'real' shadow that it casts as it protrudes through the torn canvas, the ghostly painted outlines of shadows removed from their objects are also traced across the picture surface. Tracing the shadows cast by Readymades hung from the ceiling of his studio and projected onto the canvas, Duchamp not only reverses the relationship between that which lies within and that which sits outside and in front of the picture frame, but uses this shadow-without-an-object to explore the idea of representation itself.[41]

Amongst the notes and diagrams collected in *The Green Box* documenting the completion of both *Tu'm* and the *Large Glass*, Duchamp includes a note on the shadow play at work in *Tu'm* wherein: 'shadows cast by 2, 3, 4, Readymades. "*brought together*"'.[42] Collectively, the traced shadows 'bring together' a selection of Duchamp's Readymade objects and the canvas itself can therefore be read as a representational *résumé* of Duchamp's work to date, as the artist himself suggested.[43] Following Rosalind Krauss in her inclusion of shadows in the category of the index, we can also see how the representational capabilities of the traced shadows bring the Readymades together in other ways. In 'establishing their meaning along the axis of a physical relationship to their referents', the indexical trace of the shadows alone signifies the objects, bringing them back into a direct relationship with the painting.[44] As the notes suggest, Duchamp's primary interest in executing a picture 'by the means of luminous sources' was the representational quality of the shadows themselves, their ability to signify the Readymades while disrupting the fetishization of the material objects themselves:

> 'to *inscribe* a readymade' – The readymade can later be looked for. – (with all kinds of delays)
> *The important thing then is just* this matter of timing, this snapshot effect[45]

The metaphorical proximity between the shadow, the Readymade and photographic technologies in Duchamp's comment is particularly interesting in light of Sheeler's photographic reproduction of Elsa's lost *Portrait of Marcel Duchamp* where several things are indeed 'brought together' in the shadow and re-inscribed in this (literal) snapshot. As the only evidence of a lost object, the photograph – like a Readymade – records the 'physical transposition of an object from the continuum of reality into the fixed condition of the art-image by a moment of isolation, or selection' and in doing so has, in Krauss's terms, brought icon and index together in a single image.[46] While the photograph does, of course, record a literal absence – that of the assemblage itself – the dialogue that the photograph captures between shadow and object both documents the material, three-dimensional existence of this lost object by a marginalized artist, and visually references the dynamic, symbiotic relationship between the two artists that Elsa always insisted upon.[47] We might even go a step further in suggesting that the blurring that occurs in the shadowed zone visually manifests the dissolution of boundaries between self and other, subject and object that Zabel insists is inherent in all portraiture.

Importantly, it is the feathers that stand at the boundary edge of object and shadow, spilling out of the champagne glass and down to the table it is presented on. In referencing Duchamp's performance of Rrose Sélavy, the blend of feather and shadow in the photograph certainly brings Duchamp and his female alter ego together in one portrait. However, the feathers encode a further intertextual reference if we consider their proximity to the Baroness's own costuming practices. As James Harding has highlighted, the feathered hat worn by Rrose Sélavy and reproduced on the front cover of the single issue journal *New York Dada* in April 1921 sits in a direct visual dialogue with two smaller portraits of the Baroness on the end page of the journal, one of which features her wearing a feathered headdress of her own creation beside the inverted poem titled 'Yours with Devotion/Trumpets and Drums'.[48]

In this respect, the portrait repeats the work of the journal in bringing herself and Duchamp together as collaborators at the cutting edge of defining New York Dada in its moment, especially significant given that this single issue of *New York Dada* is still predominately treated as a collaboration between Man Ray and Duchamp, overlooking the Baroness's treatment of modelling as a dynamic art form in its own right. In this respect, just as the distinct and disparate elements of bone, feathers, fabric, glass and wire are brought together in the composition of her portrait, the cast-shadow, in being 'rigorously contemporary with the object it doubles, [...] simultaneous, non-detachable, without exchange value', brings the modelling artist and her cross-dressing subject together in the erotically charged interplay of feathers and shadow, a union sealed with a small gold ring just discernible amongst the material collected in the glass.[49]

Elsa's desire to be sexually and intellectually united with Duchamp has been well documented.[50] Following a pattern of pursuit echoed by Williams's experience and her own autobiographic account, Elsa made her sexual desire for the young French artist clear. Indeed, the *Portrait of Marcel Duchamp* under discussion here was only one of several known visual and verbal representations of Duchamp, including a later pastel and mixed-media collage portrait, and George Biddle's record of at least one other piece painted on celluloid. As Biddle ventriloquizes:

> It was painted on a bit of celluloid and was at once a portrait of, and apostrophe to, Marcel Duchamp. His face was indicated by an electric lightbulb shedding icicles, with large pendulous ears and other symbols.

> 'You see, he is so tremendously in love with me,' she said.
> I asked: 'And the ears?'
> She shuddered: 'Genitals – the emblem of his frightful and creative potency.'
> 'And the electric bulb?'
> She curled her lip at me in scorn. 'Because he is so frightfully cold'.[51]

The interplay of the sexual with the autobiographic at work here is ground that the Baroness would retrace later in her detailed letters to Barnes, and is typical of her portraits, poetry and literary criticism. While the transparent nature of celluloid intertextually connects this portrait to Duchamp's *Large Glass*, it's development during this period for early animation and film intriguingly invests this piece with a kinetic or performative potential, while also gesturing towards the collaborative film and photographic projects that Duchamp, Man Ray and the Baroness worked on together. As Biddle suggests, this work is two things at once – a portrait and an apostrophe to Duchamp. In taking on her would-be-lover as the subject of her portrait, the Baroness not only works through the more frustrating elements of their relationship, his infamously cold impenetrability repeated through the transparency of the celluloid, the glass lightbulb and the icicles surrounding the face, but turns this sexual rejection into 'a critical strategy to read his artwork' as Gammel has suggested in a nuanced reading of the Baroness's 1918 poem 'Love – Chemical Relationship'.[52]

Displaying a characteristic blurring of form and genre, the poem moves between dramatic text, free verse poetry and ekphrastic verbal portrait and can certainly be read – as Gammel has demonstrated – as an ironic dramatization of the perpetual suspension of sexual consummation and erotic satisfaction presented in Duchamp's *Large Glass*. Slipping between French, German, English and the Baroness's own idiosyncratic neologism, the poem's opening lines invoke theatrical convention in order to introduce:

UN ENFANT FRANÇAIS: MARCEL (A FUTURIST)
EIN DEUTSCHES KIND: ELSA (A FUTURE FUTURIST)
POPLARS – SUN – ACLAYHIGHWAY (*BS*: 253)

Establishing linguistic, national and gendered differences in the character's identification of themselves, and setting the scene for what the narrator 'Elsa' hopes will be the synthesis of these oppositions, the poem goes on to explore the frustration of unconsummated desire. Proceeding through a pattern of repetition and variation, the opening lines are languorous, drawing out the discursive elaboration of the narrator's pleasure in the embodied, sensual experience of her partner. Dream-like in its imagery, the opening of the poem figures this pleasure through the couple's shared communion, underscored by their easy assimilation and incorporation into a rich organic world which, in turn, mirrors them:

> The poplars whispered THINE DREAMS Marcel!
> They laughed – they turned themselves – they turned themselves
> To turn themselves – they giggled – they blabbered like thineself – they smiled!
> [...] with the same French lighthearted sensual playful MORBID smile like thineself
>
> <div align="right">–Marcel! (<i>BS</i>: 253)</div>

These opening lines are vibrant and vibrating with energy, the repeating turns of the poplars invoking a playful sense of dynamism and malleability in this *vignette*. The deep sensuality of the poem builds to its climax, which is sharply interrupted by Marcel's sudden emotional detachment and the glacial glassiness through which he insulates himself against her.

> Poplars thou lovedst and straighthighways with the smell of
>   poplars which is like leather as fine – like morocco leather in
>   thine nostrils – and thine nostrils are of glass!
> Thou seest the smell uprise to the brain!
>
> Sensual thine eyes became – slanting – closed themselves!
>
> Thine smile turned pain – died –
> Then thou diedst!
>
> Thereafter thou becamest like glass.
> The poplars and the sunturned glass – they did not torture thee
>   any more! (*BS*: 253)

As Gammel suggests, the opening of the poem presents a 'syntactically disjointed modernist portrait of the artist', a poetic exploration of his physicality, personality and his art that progresses through the fragmentation and reconstruction of selected body parts, notably the mouth, nose and eyes.[53] As explored in the previous chapter, Bakhtin's examination of grotesque imagery placed a special emphasis on conceptions of the body as a whole, and of the limits of that whole. Unlike the classical body, the grotesque body is not closed, finished or completed, but continually outgrows itself and transgresses its own limits. Thus, in the topography of the grotesque a particular emphasis is placed upon 'those parts of the body that are open to the outside world, that is, the parts through which the body goes out to meet the world [...] the open mouth, the genital organs, the breasts, the potbelly, the nose'.[54] The opening of the poem celebrates the construction of the lover's body as open and interpenetrating with her own and the world around them through its 'connective orifices and protrusions, as a vessel through which life flows as it pursues its eternal process of self-renewal'.[55]

At the erotic (anti)climax of the poem the ripe sensuality of the outside world – vividly figured through the rich smells of the poplars – transgresses his corporeal boundaries, the notes of the heady scent piling up, shifting and becoming confused as it is taken into his body. Turning to something *like* 'morocco leather' as he breathes it in, this rich sensual experience nearly overwhelms him as the smell is both transformed and transformative. Turning his nostrils to glass as it moves through him, the smell is similarly transfigured into a visual rather than purely olfactory sensation, moving through his body and rising to his head he seems ready to submit himself to its waves of sensual pleasure. This moment of pure synaesthetic harmony, however, remains unconsummated. Instead of affirming life and renewal at the moment of the body's relaxing into the warm, undulating pulse of the poplars, 'Marcel' insulates himself against the sensual world in a kind of glassy death. Refusing to submit to the grotesque possibilities of that which 'swallows the world and is itself swallowed by that world', this movement into the body is suddenly reversed as the body stiffens as it metamorphoses into glass.[56] While the narrator opens her body to these experiences, renewing herself through the world and remodelling herself until she can proudly proclaim 'I AM FAT YELLOW CLAY', 'Marcel' is overwhelmed by the sensorially dissembling encounter with the 'straight yellow highways – the/whirring poplars – the fat colour of clay'. Threatened with the dissipation of his corporeal boundaries – of becoming like the smell that creeps into his body – he detaches himself, shoring up these compromised boundaries as he casts himself in cold, dead glass:

> Thou now livest motionless in a mirror!
> Everything is a mirage in thee – thine world is glass – glassy!
> Glassy are thine ears – thine hands – thine feet and thine face.
> Of glass are the poplars and the sun (*BS*: 255)

Like the bachelors in Duchamp's *Large Glass*, 'Marcel' here is forever separated from his 'bride'. However, in refusing to cast herself in glass alongside her love-object, this separation is presented as one ultimately determined by 'Elsa' the narrator and, by extension, by Elsa the poet. Rejecting both the position of bride and bachelors in her forceful refusal of this dead glass world, and without a bride to shoot at, the swirling gas trapped inside Marcel's glassy shell seems fatally trapped. Going even further than Duchamp then in her articulation of thwarted desire, and taking aim at a kind of frigid masculinity, it is in 'Elsa's' triumphant difference after 'Marcel's' metamorphosis that can enjoy her love as an aestheticized eroticism:

> BUT I LOVE THEE LIKE BEFORE. BECAUSE I AM FAT YELLOW CLAY!
> THEREFORE I LOVE THAT VERY THIN GLASS WITH ITS COLOR-
> CHANGE; BLUE – YELLOW – PURPLE PINK.
> So long must I love it until I myself will become glassy and every-
>   thing around me glassy.
> Then art thou I! I do not need thee anymore-! (*BS*: 255)

Indeed, while becoming 'glassy' might present a final consummation of her desire, the moment of becoming like him and thus overcoming her desire for him, the poem quickly turns to a celebration of this difference. Realizing that 'Thou standest beside me – and art NOTHING beside me!', the poem closes with an affirmation of her messy corporeality: 'I must bleed – weep – laugh – ere I turn to glass and the world/around me glassy' (*BS*: 255). Refusing to seal herself against the world, a gesture that also refuses the cycles of life-affirming renewal that such an interpenetration promises, the narrator instead celebrates the leaking, flowing fluids that connect her to the world, the tears and blood that cross the boundary line of her body and undermine the fantasies of corporeal integrity and solidity that the glass anxiously attempts to reinforce.

Visually, the *Portrait of Marcel Duchamp* complements and reproduces the drama of 'Love – Chemical Relationship' and the two pieces certainly seem to gesture out beyond their own limits to one another.[57] As suggested above, approaching the sculpture as a straightforward portrait it is certainly possible to identify the delicate features and elongated profile as static representation of a seated Duchamp, while the glass, cogs and springs reinforce this identification in their referencing of New York Dada's machine aesthetic. In its resolutely handmade status, and its blending of the organic, synthetic and autobiographic, the portrait challenges the detached erotics of New York Dada; animated by her poetry, the sculptural portrait becomes sensual, performative and dynamic.

While Rudolf Kuenzli has read 'Love – Chemical relationship' as an attempt by the Baroness to 'transcend her passion and her joy in life, and to join Duchamp in the cerebral, deathlike world of his *Large Glass*',[58] placing the poem alongside the *Portrait of Marcel Duchamp*, I would propose other ways of reading the linkages and slippages between representation and desire, self and other activated dialogically across these portraits. Kuenzli, recognizing the expression of the Baroness's erotic desire to blend and become indistinct with Duchamp-as-love-object, presents the space of Duchamp's *Large Glass* as the site of this (con)fusion: 'In becoming Duchamp, and Duchamp becoming she [in the glass], there would be no need for "I" and "Thou", since they would be one'.[59] However, this reading, especially in its privileging of Duchamp's glass as the space of this dissolution, seems to run contrary to the poem's avid insistence throughout on the differential signifiers 'I' and 'thee', the celebration of the narrator's messy corporeality at the close of the poem-portrait and the visual dynamics of the sculpture.

Interestingly, contrary to Kuenzli's reading of the poem, 'Elsa' does not become indistinct in the glass but, rather, *confirms* her narrative 'I'/'eye' after her confrontation with the glass 'Marcel'. Structurally, the poem can be roughly divided into three sections: the opening address to 'Thee', the closing insistence on the desires and corporeality of the narrative 'I', and the pivotal central section which marks the transformation of the love-object into glass. Such linguistic patterning is suggestive of the slippage between self and other, painting subject and painted object implicit in Western histories of portraiture.[60] Capturing the dynamic moment of change realized in the poem – where sensual, sensorial experience touches and spreads through the glass nostrils before the total petrification of 'Marcel' – the sculptural portrait holds the conflicting materials and emergent subjectivities in tension. In this sense, the erotic climax of the poem, while still not totally realized, is nevertheless held in anticipation here. Metonymically inscribing Duchamp as a 'purely aesthetic subject', the champagne glass, insisting at once on its material kinship to the epochal *Large Glass* and its presentation of an alternative to the impersonal aesthetics of the Duchampian Readymade, supports rather than swallows the composition. The dramatic moment captured in the sculpture visually represents not only the erotic (anti) climax of the drama, but the moment of Elsa's own aesthetic self-identification through, or against, Duchamp and his aesthetic project.

While the glass, cogs and springs could very well be read as visual signifiers of the individual works and visual thematics associated with Duchamp and New York Dada more broadly, the organic materials – bone, feathers, wax – belong entirely to Elsa's own, 'messy' aesthetics of waste. The dominance of the organic materials here, often read as engulfing the cogs and springs and excessively spilling out of the wine glass, can be interpreted – contra Kuenzli – as the erotic fusion of Elsa and Duchamp according to her own aesthetic and erotic principles. While the glass attempts to 'contain' the organic materials, they overflow its boundaries, the feathers and the shadow they cast exceeding and compromising the 'tidy insularity' of the subject just as their intertextual referencing of the Baroness's own costuming practices collapses the boundaries between artists and subject, reconfiguring the sculptural assemblage as a kind of double exposure, or (self)portrait. Offering a mode of reading the portrait and the poem together, the shadow always leads us back to Elsa as producer. As the triumphant close of the poem attests to, Elsa resists becoming 'glassy' through an aggressive reassertion of the corporeal, sensual and organic, dissolving boundaries between the body and the world, self and other, male and female, in defining herself and her subject through her own androgynous mode. Resisting her own transformation into glass, 'Elsa' here effectively refuses the work of the gaze in containing and defining its objects; refusing to live flat and 'motionless in a mirror' she resists becoming a surface to reflect or 'mirror' that gazes back to itself.

From the early writings of Otto Rank and Sigmund Freud, to Jacques Lacan's later theorizing of the 'Mirror Stage' and the expansions of Object Relations Theory made by Melanie Klein and Donald Winnicott, the concept of narcissism has played a central role in psychoanalytic theory and might prove useful here in illuminating what we might playfully term Elsa's 'looking through a glass dynamically'. The myth of Narcissus, the beautiful Greek youth who fell fatally in love with his own reflection provided psychoanalytic theory with a thematic basis for developing theories of subjectivity and sexual identity in relation to a dynamic of seeing and not seeing. Freud's 1914 essay 'On Narcissism' is particularly important in this respect, allowing Freud to develop his earlier ideas on narcissism and psycho-sexual development, and pointing towards the later tripartite model of id, ego and super-ego (foreshadowed here with the postulation of an 'ego-ideal'). Developing Paul Näcke's notion of 'narcissism' as useful for describing one 'who treated his body as one normally treats a sexual object', Freud reframed the concept as 'the libidinal complement to the egoism of the instinct of self-preservation'.[61] In establishing differences between the neurotic and the schizophrenic – whereby the neurotic maintains erotic relationships to objects outside of herself while the schizophrenic withdraws from the outside world completely, redirecting this focus back onto the self – Freud refined his thinking on the psycho-sexual implications of the shifts between 'object-libido' and 'ego-libido'.

In this essay the ego is shown to develop in relation to a departure from a primary narcissism, a necessary redirecting of libidinal energy outwards which, nevertheless, the ego attempts to recover through 'narcissistic object choice, identification, and by trying to fulfil the ego-ideal', all of which revolve around seeing, identification and self-observation.⁶² Importantly, the moment of 'seeing' is also central to Freud's developing thought on the centrality of the castration complex in psycho-sexual development, generating anxiety about the penis in male children and envy for the penis in female children. As subsequent feminist revisions of psychoanalytic models have been keen to point out, this dynamic of seeing/not seeing as centred upon the phallus, later developed by Lacan, excludes and alienates women from the primary processes of identity formation inscribing them instead as the symbolic 'lack' upon which the castration complex and male psychosexual identity are founded.⁶³ As Whitney Chadwick has put it in the context of the implications for modes of representation, the female self is doubly alienated by this process, as the consistent privileging of male sexuality proposed by these models has 'left woman in the position of signifier for the male other, her subjectivity (or "femininity") determined by the discourses of patriarchy'.⁶⁴

While Freud's early and important proposal of the role of narcissism in the individual ego as a 'necessary intermediate stage between auto-eroticism and object-love' is of some interest here, Lacan's concept of the Mirror Stage developed in the 1930s and largely indebted to Henri Wallon's earlier research seems to lend itself more readily to the poem-portrait's dramatization of the emergence of the self against/through the glassy Other. As touched upon in the previous chapter, building on Freud's theories of 'specular subjectivity', Lacan's model describes the role of identification in ego formation – the moment of the child's self-identification through her reflected image. Within Lacan's formulation however, this self-identification is one of imagined wholeness at odds with the fragmented experience of the real self; self-identification here is thus figured as inaugurated through a primary misunderstanding and alienation. As Jacqueline Rose has succinctly put it:

> Lacan's account of subjectivity was always developed with reference to the idea of a fiction. [...] The mirror image is central to Lacan's account of subjectivity, because its smoothness and totality is a myth. The image in which we first recognise ourselves is a *mis-recognition*.⁶⁵

There is certainly room for a reading of the poem-portrait in Lacan's terms – indeed, the narrative 'I' only emerges after the narrator's confrontation with the glass, and she continues to love both the glassy material and the phantasmagoria she finds there. However, rather than reading this emergence of the poem's narrative 'I' as founded on a primary misidentification – and one that posits Woman here as 'lack' – I want to suggest that in looking at the glass/mirror/aesthetic subject 'Marcel', Elsa recognizes her *difference from* this motionless site of mirage and, more pertinently, her ability to animate the glass which is empty without her: 'Thou standest beside me – and art NOTHING beside me'. She refuses to recognize herself in the mirror as its kaleidoscopic colour changes, while mesmerizing, lack the substance of her embodied materiality. In this sense, Elsa refutes the coherence and uniformity suggested as a salutary cover for the ego in Lacan's model, renouncing the 'myth of subjective cohesion which the concept of the unconscious properly subverts'.[66]

This inscription of self-presentation more evident in the poem, but also possible to trace in the *Portrait of Marcel Duchamp*, acts as a powerful testimony to Elsa's desire to realize the embodied female self by deflecting the gaze which attempts to reiterate the work of Lacan's mirror stage – to contain its objects in a coherent and unified image. Encountering the mirror and recognizing what she is not, Elsa refuses a model of subjectivity and self-representation built on a glassy 'mirage'. Thus, the emergent narrative 'I'/'eye' does not describe itself in visual terms, but through the powerfully embodied sensations of crying, laughing and bleeding. In dramatizing this action the poem-portrait performs this realization of the self through an act of embodied self-representation, one that reclaims 'the female body from its imprisonment in art as a beautiful, voiceless object to be judged by male spectators'.[67]

Through the construction of the poem-portrait of the aesthetic subject 'Marcel' who is transformed into his own glass construction, Elsa the poet not only defines herself against the artist, but against his aesthetic vision. While the glass of the 'Futurist' is rigid, motionless and unworkable, the materiality of the 'fat yellow clay' by comparison is defined by its capacity for dynamic change and renewed form. Our 'Future Futurist' then is materially defined as an active and embodied subject that refuses any fixed and final subject position, but that can shape and form herself at will.

iii. Chimera in the croquis class: Spectacle, performance and the Baroness's body-work

I am not merely the model who poses, I seek as best I may to give artistic expression, to show forth something of the thoughts within me.
Elsa von Freytag-Loringhoven, 1915

In the gaps between the absence of fleshy bodies and female artists in foundational histories of the first American avant-garde groupings, and the persistent interest in the spectacular qualities of the Baroness's abject body – her painted face, startling costumes, advancing age and aggressive sexuality – sits her own embodied and dynamically performative body-work, that is, the modelling and costuming practices performed on and through her body. The oppositional dynamics between movement and stasis, dynamic plasticity and passive 'glassiness' explored in both the *Portrait of Marcel Duchamp* and 'Love – Chemical Relationship' thus emerge as central, not simply to a more comprehensive understanding of the disruptive potential of the Baroness's waste-based aesthetic, but in reclaiming the embodied, performative and autobiographic dimensions of this body-work from the anxious sublimation of this reconstructed body within modernism's marginalia. In line with more recent feminist revisions of modernist histories which have tackled the gendered historicizing and mythologizing trajectories of Dada which, in Sawelson-Gorse's words, 'embodied the male as a term and a movement', the remainder of this chapter will focus on questions of specularity and performativity in order to delineate the extent to which the Baroness's body-based art practice with its focus on the kinetic, the erotic and the autobiographic engages and transforms certain gendered scripts relating to early twentieth-century avant-garde practice. Through this body-centred, erotically charged performance, the Baroness not only threatened to shatter the boundaries of bourgeois respectability, but aggressively pointed out that despite all their avant-gardism and boundary-breaking poetic and visual experiments, her contemporaries remained more or less complicit in the maintenance and reinforcement of the patriarchal socio-cultural judgements of the late nineteenth century.

As previous chapters have established, despite the rallying cries of Tristan Tzara's 1918 Dada manifesto to overcome an insipid bourgeois culture of morality and sentimentality, the mechanized fantasies and mechanical portraits associated with New York Dada seem to bear more of a renegotiation of normative gender codes within the context of a new, technologically and commercially re-worked landscape than any radical reappraisal of gendered, classed or primitivist codes of representation. In this respect, such work ultimately reinforces these organizing structures and reproduces the 'specular focus and voyeuristic gaze of Western representation'.[68] In this sense, the model of 'rebel masculinity' adopted by many of the heterosexual, white, male and middle-class avant-gardists of the early decades of the twentieth-century allowed, to reverse Halberstam's paraphrasing of Gertrude Stein, already grown men to play at being rebel-boys.[69] Problematically, while modernist myths of male creativity frequently 'collaborated in fusing the sexual and the artistic by equating artistic creation with male sexual energy, presenting women as powerless and sexually subjugated', subsequent critical art histories, in privileging works which wrested 'their formal and stylistic innovations from an erotically based assault on female form' in the formulations of modernist canons, not only propagated such myths, but participated in the marginalization of alternative modes of representation and production.[70] However, rather than throwing out claims for Dada's radicalism as 'an infantile parody of the *logos*, a babbling *Urwort* aimed at echoing and cancelling the name of the Father and the authority of his Law',[71] attention to the marginalized modes of Dada – notably its performative energies as processed through the pioneering body-work of the Baroness – reinvigorates discussions of the movement's challenges to language and representation.

Importantly, the Baroness would figure her difference from – and critique of – these bourgeois male avant-gardists in terms of movement and stasis. In the experimental prose poem review of Williams's *Kora in Hell*, 'Thee I call "Hamlet of the Wedding-Ring"', controversially published in two parts in *The Little Review* (March 1921), Elsa attacked Williams directly as one 'shackled to cowardice of immobility' (*BS*: 299) who, despite his anti-bourgeois stance in fact preferred 'sex – with kitchenmaid' to a dynamic, sexually experienced female artist – an equal who understood poetry in fundamentally embodied and active terms (*BS*: 305). Including biographical references to the profession, family heritage and private life of this 'wobbly-legged business satchel-carrying little louse' (*BS*: 312), the review moved beyond the boundaries of art criticism, blurring into poetic collage and autobiography as she explored and attacked his refusal of her sexual advances and his limited contribution to avant-garde poetics.

While some critics have read the satirical invocation of Shakespeare's Hamlet here as a deflation of high culture typical of the avant-garde, in casting Williams as a diminutive Hamlet, obsessed to the point of paralysis over questions of his own bourgeois existence, she pokes fun at his inflated opinion of his own contributions to culture, his continued adherence to such notions despite his avant-garde pretensions and, more pointedly, his fundamental misunderstanding and distortion of the question of 'eckshishtensh' itself – his bourgeois life as a married doctor living in the suburbs having protected him from any dynamic experience:

> true to formula – male brute intoxicated bemoans world – (into
> that he never stepped) – his existence – all existence! (*BS*: 293)

Invoking Hamlet in her critical treatment of Williams's containment within the boundaries of social convention, Elsa insists upon a correlation between the valuation of the products of high culture and the reinforcement of repressive social conventions regulating the expression of sexuality and gender – and the debilitating paralysis generated by both. Williams's adoption and maintenance of these models reduce his work to the 'stray words of unourished –unevolved – decaying imagination' (*BS*: 295), the manifestation of a fundamental weakness perpetuated through a separation of body and mind, words and action:

> Strength of you: brutality – makebelieve – phantasmagoria –
> cheating before limelight – hysteria! such it is.
> Grace – rhythm of juggler is strength
> Grace – rhythm is strength: body – mind (*BS*: 295)

Developing through the Baroness's idiosyncratic grammatical and syntactical arrangements, abrupt breaks and playful neologism, the poem-review implicates all American modernists, presenting America itself as a 'helpless giant on infants feet – knuckles for brains [...] destroyer of values – creator never' (*BS*: 298-99), fundamentally opposed to her own notions of poetry as an intoxicating embodied sexual and spiritual energy, a '[f]eeling of something exquisite – extraordinary – great – joyful' (*BS*: 312).

Tellingly, in establishing differences between Europe and America, herself and Williams, active and passive, Elsa's diagnosis of Williams's and America's fatal 'stagnation' lies in its inauthenticity, and emphasis on appearance. As a 'Boil proclaims disease', the Baroness claims that America attempts to cover its cultural or historical deficiencies through an elaborate cover-up: 'Look pretty – quick! paint! – powder –! perchance culture will be deceived' (*BS*: 294). Despite its aping of (European) high culture and its puritanical, prohibitionist 'clean' culture, Elsa's stinging critique of American-grown avant-gardism, especially with respect to sexual and artistic matters, insists that 'One does not help soul in merely depriving it of dung'. While appearances can be arranged even with 'feet encased by faulty foundation decay – debris' (*BS*: 300), the 'disease beneath artificial complexion' – inauthenticity and stagnation (*BS*: 298) – is quickly exposed when it comes to the dynamic action of performance. Drawing out an extended comparison between the work of the artist and the circus performer, Williams is outed as one 'cheating before limelight', who 'trying to step into tights/Juggle words – as balls – about feelings – impressions'. Playing the part of the juggler, he nevertheless lacks the 'rhythm – curves – science – conviction – background – tradition!' to flesh out this performance convincingly, his 'stray words of unourished – unevolved – decaying imagination [...] juggled before public' only deceiving himself (*BS*: 295).

Strongly echoing her various statements regarding modelling as physically demanding and emphatically embodied art practice, the Baroness draws a clear distinction between Williams 'vain vanity' and her muscular poetics, and of the real risk involved in the production of her art:

> Nothing in circus funny – easy – for performer – unless in breathing-space during rest.
> Performance – action – work: breathless – highest tension.
> Force ripples – vibrates life – muscle in action one visible form.
> You: brittle – breaking – decaying iron – eaten by rustworm (*BS*: 296)

Like the glassy 'Marcel', Williams is reducer here to a brittle, corroded and broken machine, a mute force against Elsa's acrobatic, muscular and strikingly performative gestures.

Whereas the juggler-imposter 'W.C. Attacks art –/*when has time*' (*BS*: 307), the Baroness lived her art – clear enough by this point in the repeated refrains of her as the living embodiment of Dada's iconoclastic energy – but also literally true to the extent that she transformed the source of her livelihood into a mode of art. The acrobat who discovers that 'rhythm *is* strength: body – mind' (*BS*: 295) as she performs in the brightly lit circular arena of the circus is also the model posing in the life drawing class. This connection is made more explicit in the unpublished dramatic fragment 'Chimera' from 1927, after the Baroness had returned to Paris and started modelling again. The opening directions strongly evoke the circus arena described by the Baroness in her criticism of Williams's *Kora in Hell*

> Large – brightly lighted croquis classroom
> In grand chaumiere
> Face aged – body ageless in excentric [*sic*] attire
> Upon podium stands nude

The various versions of this poetry-play all open with the juxtaposition of a statuesque nude, who sometimes stands in 'dynamic attitude upon podium' with a young, knickerbockered American man passing through. Their dialogic exchange structures the drama and moves from quick fire colloquialism to longer, philosophical mediations on the culture and commerce, the obsolesce of marriage and gender and class relations explored through the figures of the materially poor but spiritually wealthy 'artist-aristocratic' and the 'grubby' but wealthy American capitalist. At once drawn to and repulsed by the vision of her 'glitterself expanding', the man repeats the pattern of many of the Baroness's own failed American romances, exclaiming: 'you've such scary way of expressing yourself – pulpity! Turns my bile up – can't stand it! […] – though – there's something about you – that pose – that incisive eye glint'. Acknowledging that 'posing aint digging diamonds' the man hands her a bill and the 'shadownaked' somnambulist – who in one version had previously thrown herself 'down into eloquent pose of wrathful vanquishment' – becomes animated, jumping 'erect in victory pose'. While the chimera of money seduces the 'dream-walker' model with the promise of a life beyond the podium where she might 'exhibit my pictures – finish my frames – write', she nevertheless asserts her posing as an embodied mode of art production, as 'one of my expressions'. Indeed, it is from this strikingly embodied position that her art proceeds.

While the Chimera of the title refers to illusion and the wished-for fantasy of the nude's artistic and financial independence, its mythological roots as a female-headed monster combining the parts of other animals present a striking model for ways of reading the self-representational practices and collaborative autobiographic projects developed by the Baroness. As we have seen, her portraits certainly take on Chimeric dimensions, folding representations of the gazing subject and gazed upon object into mutually determining relationships, and in her proud articulation of posing as art she collapses traditional hierarchies between nude and painter, insisting upon the labour of the model as a vital aspect of the artistic process. Tellingly, in uniting the model's desires for artistic expression and financial autonomy, a deleted addition to one of the handwritten drafts of 'Chimera' includes her plan to start her own life-modelling class. Calling on a range of friends and associates including Barnes, Biddle and Peggy Gugenheim, the Baroness followed the same path, as a letter to her friend Sarah Freedman details. A chimeric document in its own right, the letter creates a fascinating interchange between word and image, the letters written content – detailing her plans to start her own modelling school – on the recto interacting with a series of fragmented self-portraits of the model in action on the verso. In its visualization of the dynamic poses of the life model by the artist/model herself it clearly positions the model as an artist in command of her own image and in dramatizing the dynamic relationship between her modelling and more conventional modes of representing the self the letter clearly articulated the ways in which the Baroness was experimenting with 'way[s] to present a story about herself for public consumption' in her own script.[72]

After detailing a debilitating loss of confidence in her ageing body the Baroness triumphantly declares her rebirth as a model, and although she claims that the venture is one driven by economic necessity, she nevertheless positions

Figure 17 Elsa von Freytag-Loringhoven, letter to Sarah Freedman, undated. Black ink on paper. Previously unpublished. Elsa von Freytag-Loringhoven Papers. Special Collections, University of Maryland at College Park Libraries.

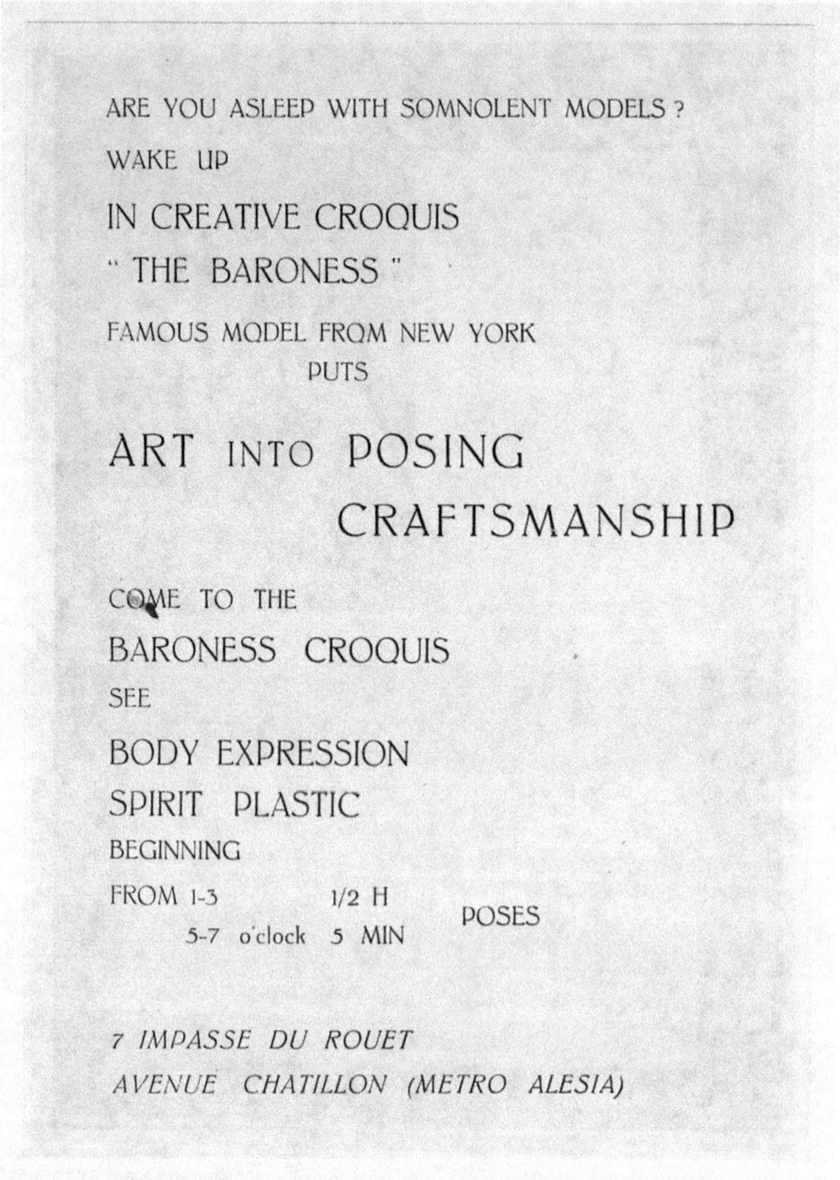

ARE YOU ASLEEP WITH SOMNOLENT MODELS?

WAKE UP

IN CREATIVE CROQUIS

" THE BARONESS "

FAMOUS MODEL FROM NEW YORK

PUTS

ART INTO POSING
CRAFTSMANSHIP

COME TO THE

BARONESS CROQUIS

SEE

BODY EXPRESSION

SPIRIT PLASTIC

BEGINNING

FROM 1-3   1/2 H
   5-7 o'clock   5 MIN   POSES

7 IMPASSE DU ROUET

AVENUE CHATILLON (METRO ALESIA)

Figure 18 Elsa von Freytag-Loringhoven, Advertisement for 'Baroness Croquis' Modelling School, 1927. Elsa von Freytag-Loringhoven Papers. Special Collections, University of Maryland at College Park Libraries.

modelling as central to her entire art practice, a recovery of 'the one thing I know how to do – that I had known – discovered again'.[73] As her 'last dream' and final chance for economic and artistic self-determination, the Baroness returned to modelling, and a surviving advertisement for the short-lived creative croquis evening class emphasizes the tensions between movement and stasis, active and passive through which she would define her practice.

Repeating the trope of the somnolent model that connects 'Chimera', the collaborative Barnes/Baroness autobiographic project and *Nightwood's* Robin Vote, whose passive presentation of herself 'to the spectator as a "picture" forever arranged' is a consequence of her somnolence, this model promises to dynamically reshape the work of those who encounter her 'spirit plastic'. Far from passive, the labour-intensive modelling that the Baroness describes to Freedman provides a valuable insight into the muscular 'body expression' that she developed:

> For *2 hours* posing croquis – (quick sketch) I get *8 fr* from the grand[e] chaumière – *10 fr* from the others – every 5 minutes a different pose. Maybe – you can imagine what dull school mechanical poses the other models give – and – how excellent I am! *I am!* More so – than ever before!'[74]

Counterpointing active with passive, embodied and self-directed with mechanical and arranged, the Baroness circles back to the privileged space of the circus presented in her criticism of Williams's *Kora in Hell* – as a space where the model's dynamic body and expressive art are brought together in her poses. Of course, the circus doesn't just involve the athletic acrobatic bodies of the performers, but directly engages the bodies of its spectators in the gasps, cries and applause that it elicits. In staging this dynamic interaction between performer and audience, the circular arena of the circus big top is a privileged site of transformative exchange whereby the dazzling contortions and aerial feats of the acrobat are registered in the bodies of the spectator.

It is also the stage upon which Nora Flood and Robin Vote first meet, a scene which is closely focused on these ideas of transformation and exchange. Critical approaches to Barnes's privileging of the circus and modes of spectacle have been wide-ranging, and do not need rehearsing here, although the well-established tradition of reading Barnes's texts in relation to the Rabelaisian carnivalesque should be emphasized.[75] The prominent featuring of the circus and modes of spectacular performance in both Barnes and the Baroness's work clearly connect the two at the surface level of their own texts, and within broader critical frameworks organized around the carnivalesque, grotesque and modes of spectacular performance. It also provides its own 'arena' within which to think about the broader transformative exchanges activated between Barnes and the Baroness that later chapter will explore in more detail. Putting Barnes to one side for now, in my discussion here I am keen to draw out the Baroness's own thinking on modelling as a radically transformative activity – one that involves

Figure 19 Theresa Bernstein, *Woman with a Parrot c.* 1917. Oil on canvas, 40 × 25 inches. Formally of the Martin and Edith Stein Collection.

not only the effort and labour of the model in twisting her limbs and turning her body into sculptural poses – but also an active collaborative force in the art*work*, that is to say, in the work undertaken in the completion of the painting, drawing or textual portrait.

The Baroness was a well-known and popular model in her years in New York, as the testimonies of Sarah McPherson, Louis Bouché and George Biddle all support, and Gammel's biography fleshes out in more detail.[76] Theresa Bernstein seems to have been particularly taken with the Baroness's poses, as several of her striking portraits attest to. Better known for her *plain-air* paintings and impressionistically rendered scenes of everyday life, these portraits stand out. In one such portrait, *Woman with a Parrot* from 1917, the hitherto unidentified Baroness stands, her back to us and partly exposed by the low back of a dress tightly bound through the waist with a vivid green and decorated wrap.

One arm drops down at a slight angle inclined into the curve of her buttocks. The other arm is extended out in front of her and balances a red parrot on her hand. Her jewellery and headpiece crowning her cropped red hair are familiar from the various photographs and accounts that document her costuming and modelling practices, and the parrot was, in all likelihood, part of her own menagerie.[77] Turned from us, her open contrapposto stance is exaggerated with the positioning of her arms, and the physical effort of this pose is registered in the luminous, thick strokes of paint building up the areas of her exposed skin. While the ground is left bare in places, and only roughly treated with fast, wide strokes in others, the Baroness's body is carefully built up in wider gestural sweeps and finer detailed areas and it is the bright rounded contours of her muscular back that move forward towards the viewer and draw the eye in. It is a striking portrait, one that is expressive of the embodied labours of both painter and model, as a preparatory life drawing sketch of Bernstein's from 1917 also makes clear.

A better-known portrait of the Baroness by Bernstein stages this dynamic interaction between model and artist in more overt terms. Vividly rendering the thick musk described by Williams and reappearing in several anecdotal accounts of the Baroness's excessive corporeality, in 1917 Bernstein painted at least two portraits where the proudly displayed and thickly rendered body of the nude model is set against a rich ochre background, her stretched and open body heavily outlined in a chunky band of dark paint, like an emanation pushing out from her body.

Recalling the Baroness's celebration of her own body as the malleable 'FAT YELLOW CLAY' in 'Love – Chemical Relationship', these pulsing auras seem to speak to the transformative dynamics I am describing as central to

Figure 20 Theresa Bernstein, *Elsa von Freytag-Loringhoven* (*c.* 1917). Oil. 12 × 9 inches. Photograph courtesy Francis M. Naumann Fine Art, New York.

her modelling practice; the model stands in front of the painter, in 'dynamic attitude upon podium' as 'Chimera' puts it, engaging the artist in a gaze the terms of which she seems to be setting. This gaze does not present the smooth, polished surfaces of the classical nude, whose impenetrable surfaces uphold work ideationally to share up the female body itself, but in its openness and emanation into the air around itself this nude functions in the terms described by Mary Russo's 'female grotesque'.[78] Subverting both the male gaze and the gendered power dynamics of representation typically structuring the artist/nude relationship, Bernstein's painting, in its celebration of the ageing, stinking Baroness and its own painterly excess, embraces certain taboos surrounding female representation and ideals of feminine beauty, and the model and painter together.

Visiting the men's life drawing class at the New York School of Fine and Applied Arts in December 1915, a *New York Times* reporter tracks down a new model who has apparently been 'much discussed in art circles in this city'. Under the promising title 'Refugee Baroness Poses as a Model: Woman Who Puzzled New York Art Students Reveals Her Identity' the reporter broadly connects ideas surrounding the New Woman (her economic independence, sexual liberation and transgressive behaviours including her fashion and lifestyle choices) with the Baroness. Unsurprisingly, given the need to makes sense of the figure of the New Woman discussed in Chapter 1, and the network of gendered conventions and codes governing representation of the female nude, in identifying the mysterious Baroness the article places considerable attention on the traditional markers of her femininity, diligently recording that 'she is lithe in future and graceful as a leopard. Her hair is red and her eyes a turquoise blue'. While emphasizing the conventionally feminine features of her eyes and hair, the muscular body of the man-eating leopard unsettles this portrait, at once pointing to an aggressive, devouring femininity and attempting to neutralize it through an attractive exoticism.

Just as the reporter struggles to contain the Baroness and her 'bizarre attire' within more conventional representations of woman-as-art-object, the 'posing' of the title reveals more than it intends to, referring in this case to not only the various poses struck by the model for the artist to work from, but the identity of model itself one of many 'poses' struck by the Baroness. Disrupting the traditionally silent, passive and feminized role of the artist's model, the Baroness loudly asserts that her independence and her personal creativity are assured and sustained through this employment:

> I do not mind telling you who I am. I am the Baroness von Freytag-Loringhoven. […] Why do I pose? The answer is very simple. I was penniless. […] But here is trouble. I long always for self-expression. I paint pictures, but they do not sell as yet. They perhaps never will. As I stand in my place on the model throne I feel within me the rhythm of life. I would dance, but one must have lessons.

As I have outlined, the Baroness tuned her work into body-work, that is to say, she claims the modelling body as a medium through which to express her 'body expression/spirit plastic', and in doing so attaining a level of financial and artistic independence. Complicating the gendered subject position that the article attempts to articulate for this exotic 'Oriental' refugee as a model and a wife, Elsa's appropriation of the traditionally passive, sexualized and feminine role of artist's model as a route to 'self-expression' underscores her refusal to be contained in the discursive constructions of femininity, 'New' or otherwise.

In trying to pin down this New Woman two years later and just weeks before America's official entrance into the First World War, a frequently referenced *New York Evening Sun* article presents the free-verse writing Mina Loy as the representative '"modern woman" that everyone is talking about'. Unlike the (German) Baroness, it would appear that (English) Loy's elegance and beauty make her more readily acceptable as the feminine face of modernity, as the inclusion of a large photographic portrait of the striking poet suggests. The article itself is less an investigation into the shifting social and political agency of the New Woman, or of specific women's role in shaping the first American avant-garde as artists, patrons and editors than a profile of the 'English Poetess Who Writes About Blue Dolls and Such Gay Things'. Reduced to a somewhat twee list of 'Dos and Don'ts' the article frames the New Woman as one who, while styling herself provocatively against the sentiments of 'Grandma', can still be identified and situated within the familiar discursive category of 'Woman'. While Loy clearly presents herself as 'a woman determined to create her own image' as Carolyn Burke has suggested, the article's commodification of her particular brand of feminine modernity limits her expressive or transgressive agency.[79]

Set within the society pages of the newspaper, the unchallenging familiarity of the article's tone takes on a sharply gendered aspect when we consider it in light of its paratextual apparatus, the various charity benefits, engagement announcements and Valentine's Day dinner advertisements which it is surrounded by. The caption running beneath the large portrait of Loy articulates this concession between avant-garde iconoclasm and conventional gender scripts; the painter, poet and playwright, it asserts, 'Doesn't Try to Express Her Personality by Wearing Odd Looking Draperies – Her Clothes Suggest the Smartest Shops, but Her Poems Would Puzzle Grandma'. Even while her poetry may puzzle, her chic dress and beauty allow for an assimilation of Loy into a sanctioned mode of New Woman artistic expression by virtue of her commodifiable femininity. In this respect the article functions within what

Judith Butler has described as the 'regulatory practice that produces the body it governs, that is whose regulatory force is made clear as a kind of productive power, the power to produce – demarcate, circulate, differentiate – the bodies it controls'.[80]

Like the Baroness, Loy makes her own costumes, however, while Loy's are suggestive of the 'smartest shops', Elsa's are radically unsettling, subtly alluded to here in the reporter's rejection of 'odd looking draperies' and refusal to visit Greenwich Village, which the costumed Baroness of course terrorized. While Loy's costumes can be imagined *as* commodities, unique designs sold in smart boutiques, the Baroness's *are* commodities, or at least the collaged remains of them. Rejecting a form of commodity fetishism which places the value in the limited life of the commodity, the Baroness's costumes and constructions invest instead in the commodity's after-life. Acknowledging that 'some might call her bizarre in attire', the 1915 'Refugee Baroness' piece makes a subtle but direct connection between her costumes, which 'are all her own, for she designs them and makes them' and her modelling practices. She states: 'I am not merely the model who poses. I seek as best I may to give artistic expression, to show forth something of the thoughts within me', and while these thoughts are clearly expressed in her appropriation of the female nude as an embodied, autobiographic mode of performance and her insistence on taking 'the hardest poses nobody would have dared to ask and keep them [...] for ambition and curiosity – to test my strength', they are also activated in her *couture d'ordures,* signalling at once her refusal to be alienated from her labour, and her commitment to direct her artistic production.

iv. Übermarionettes and living statues

I wish – and how wonderful, – that she could dress herself in Mr. Wriggley's Broadway sign or the Brooklyn Bridge, using in either experiment all the flags of all the old countries of Europe and Asia [...] as a headdress. A most difficult medium; the creating of a legend

Charles Henry, 1920

Drawing on the subtle and incisive distinctions between theatrical spectacle and performance drawn by David Graver in his comparative treatment of the directorial practices of E. Gordon Craig (1872–1966) and Antonin Artaud (1896–1948) whereby 'the spectacle is the image created on the stage; the performance is the activity involved in the creation of that image', we can begin to separate out the modes and functions of the Baroness's performative art practice from the reconstruction of her grotesquely spectacular image.[81] Recovered from the letters, diaries and memoirs of her contemporaries, critics have reconstructed a startling photomontage of the Baroness in her New York 'art dazzle' days in recent years. While the shock of her strange spectacularity – her shaved head, tin can bras and elaborate headdresses – has proven to be enduringly fascinating, more attention is now also being given to the activity involved in the making of those images, the collecting, collaging and stitching into the early hours of the morning that the 'Refugee Baroness' article refers to. These practices are deeply interwoven with fabric of the Baroness's life; her childhood in Swinemünde and the 'strange handiwork' produced by her mother as later chapters will explore in more detail, her training as an erotic artist in Berlin, her time amongst the avant-garde circles of turn- of the century Munich and her sex-quest around Italy.

As is frequently reiterated, her early and formative experiences as an artist model and *tableaux vivant* in the Berlin Wintergarten underscore and inform these later practices, and the aggressive approach to modelling as a dynamic and collaborative mode of performance and collaboration opens up a way of reading her later performances and of aligning her with, rather than setting her against various avant-garde practices of the 1910s. In returning to these earlier encounters of the self-representational possibilities of embodied performance, I am not only interested in tracing the genesis of the Baroness's art practice, or presenting a case for the importance of performance in developing revisionist feminist historiographies of the avant-garde, but attempting to make a distinction between the Baroness's own construction of herself as a performative subject, and later reconstructions of her as a grotesquely stunning art-object.

Long before she made her first provocative excursions through New York, or began developing the jarring, a-tonal rhythms replete with neologism and vibrating with kinetic energy that would mark her idiosyncratic contribution to the free verse movement and Dada poetics, the Baroness was experimenting with modes of spectacle and performance. As her later recollections detail, after running away to Berlin in 1893, Elsa Plötz (as she was then) supported herself as an actress and chorus girl. Too overcome with 'bashful shame' to ask for a job as a shop-girl, she nevertheless 'died with curiosity' when she chanced upon Henry de Vry's advertisement 'clamouring for "girls with good figures"' to perform at the Wintergarten vaudeville theatre as part of their *tableaux vivant* which would mark a decisive turning point in the young girl's life:

All dreams materialized miraculously. Marvellous things happened to me. I was told to strip [...] Then I was clad in tights and 'Henry de Vris' [*sic*], boss of 'living pictures', looked me over, though I did not then quite know what for. Being safe inside my meshell – I liked that scrutiny.

Importantly, as Gammel points out, in his rewriting of the Baroness's life material in his 1905 novel *Fanny Essler*, Felix Paul Greve's Elsa-avatar fails not only to graduate from the amateur stage, but also to place this pivotal first encounter with the *tableaux vivants* after her official dramatic training it is used as an effective narrative device to demonstrate 'a (naturalistic) social fall and entrapment rather than an artistic development'.[82] As it was, Elsa in fact entered the Wintergarten prior to any formal training and went on to perform at the Zentral Theatre in 1895 which was, in her words: 'The most fashionable stage then for chorus girls looking for adventure and money – and I was engaged, with not a sound in my throat nor a note in my ear – but I was handsome – with a straight figure and nimble legs.'[83]

While clearly both early experiences laid the groundwork for her later New York promenades and Dada costumes, they also highlight several important features which, taken together, contribute to an understanding of her development of dynamic and embodied forms of self-representation. Both extracts place a heavy emphasis on her figure. In doing so they highlight her understanding of – and pleasure in – the visibility of her body, and the ways in which such a specularity connects her through her body to forms of art, as outlined above. However, the presentation of the Baroness's body and its seemingly uncomplicated reproduction of the dynamics which have historically organized the female body 'as a site of male viewing pleasure, a commodified image of exchange, and a fetishized defence against the fear of castration' are in fact not so straightforward.[84]

As one of the first theorists to promote the notion of the director as the supreme authority in the creation of the theatrical art work, E. Gordon Craig prioritized control and manipulation (over actors, scenery, soundscapes) in the creation and control of the theatrical art work. Craig's ideal then was one of authority and uniformity, bringing all the elements involved in the theatrical event under the control of the director whose expressive intentions (and his alone) are realized through a carefully arranged and repeated spectacle. In his definition, then:

> Acting is not an art [...] Art arrives only by design. Therefore, in order to make any work of art we may only work in those materials with which we can calculate.[85]

The charismatic de Vry (like the master of the life drawing class) seems to fit this model as overseer of the vision, composition and execution of these static living pictures; the carefully constructed illusion of 'clothed nudity' corresponding to the director's manipulation of limbs and poses of the performer's bodies involved in the recreations of mythological scenes.[86] De Vry's living pictures bear an interesting resemblance to what Graver has described as Craig's dream of a 'primordial "Ubermarionette" whose moves were not constrained by the limits of human bodies and could be repeated without variation when so desired'.[87]

Without a will of her own, controlled and regulated by the director and carefully manipulated to execute his artistic vision, we could certainly trace a salient connection here between Craig's übermarionette and the reconstructions of the Baroness's body in the memoirs and fiction of her contemporaries. Such a relationship is set in high relief when we consider that Craig's ideal form of theatre, enabled through the predetermined and rigorously controlled actions of the übermarionette, would provide a 'centre and a focus for a perfectly planned and ordered spectacle'.[88] Such fantasies of directorial control in creating a spectacle to be unproblematically consumed by audiences might bear a special relationship to the living pictures which walked a particularly fine line between artistic expression and illicit entertainment. Foregrounding working-class women's bodies, the living pictures effectively contained a potentially disordering or contaminating excessive sexuality by literally re-casting these potentially grotesque bodies in the smooth, impenetrable surface of the classical body through the application of padding, tights and *malliot*.[89]

However, what initially seems like a static spectacle, a well-lit, highly artificial staging of silent and still costumed figures artfully arranged in a live reproduction of historical paintings becomes more complex under closer inspection. A borderline art form as Peter Webb suggests in his study of *tableux vivants* and *pose plastique* these living pictures are at once static and active, artistic duplications and corporeal appropriations, achieving the illusion of nudity by painting, covering and building upon the body, as Elsa's autobiography goes on to detail:

> I was taken right away for the 'marble figures' – which – as I later learned – takes the best figure – even though I was to be upholstered considerably with cardboard breasts and cotton hips – but it was great fun – and I felt the pride of a primadonna.[90]

Elsa's appropriation of this mode of costuming as construction with its focus on the body and its augmentation through the application of other materials into her own, performative art practice disrupts the director-mediated, ordered spectacle and, importantly, the relationship of the spectator to it. While the living statues developed through the eighteenth and nineteenth centuries as a pre-cinematic form of bourgeois entertainment and erotic titillation – an artful and coolly detached form of voyeurism – the Baroness's later recollection emphasizes the erotic charge of spectacular performativity, which is supercharged when it is taken out of the spaces designated for erotic entertainment and played out on the streets. Foregrounding her erotic experience over the audiences, the pleasure that she articulates in being scrutinized and in retaining control over her built-upon body distorts and disrupts more traditional notions of the female nude in a Western art-historical tradition as shaped and controlled by male desire and power.[91] Prefiguring her later employment of stolen and jettisoned items of consumption as a radical performance of her disruption of ordering structures which sought to control, contain and fix both women and waste within systems of value and codes of representation, these early embodied performances thus collude with such notions of female specularity in order to radically destabilize them.

Drawing attention to the eroticized female body these performances evoke the familiar dynamics of woman-as-spectacle only to expose it as a sight/site of overlaid constructions – literal in the cardboard breasts and hips built over Elsa's body as a *tableux vivant* and more figurative in the panorama of characters assigned to the actress. Despite de Vry's request for 'girls with good figures', their bodies are consistently reworked and recreated through their cardboard constructions: the nude marble figures registered and recreated by the spectating gaze as recognizable art works or scenes in fact the result of the costumes and constructions built over the nude body. Similarly, as stage acting involves the necessary adoption of a series of different roles, access to the actress herself must always be mediated through a series of assigned and fabricated identities and costumes. Taking this fluid play of identities a step further, Fanny (which we can read here alongside Elsa's own testimony), anxious about forgetting her lines, began to cross-dress on stage in a strategy to paradoxically distract attention from her acting by showcasing her ability to manipulate these fabricated identities.[92] In revealing that these performances rely on the construction and application of material to the body in their compositions they not only interfere with the dynamics of the gaze (insisting on constructing themselves rather than being constructed via the gaze exclusively), but expose the female body as an overdetermined zone of projected desire. In doing so this 'posing' not only exposes femininity as cultural construction, but highlights the appropriation of female bodies 'as a passive medium on which cultural meanings are inscribed or as the instrument through which an appropriative and interpretative will determines a cultural meaning for itself'.[93] In examining the Baroness's compelling early experiences with modelling and performance, there has been a tendency within this growing body of scholarship to connect these directly with a discussion of her later urban promenades. While I certainly agree that her work as a model and *tableau vivant* is foundational to her later development of a consistent performance aesthetic, before going forward we might also think back through the European folk traditions surrounding Karnevale, and its connections to a grotesque corporeality.

Widely practised across Europe, pre-lentern karnevale traditions blend the Christian calendar and its dedicated period of fasting with the seasonal shift from winter into spring as a time of rebirth observable in nature and replicated in the image of the resurrecting Christ. Sharing in the carnival traditions of parades, masked balls and satirical performances designed to signal a subversion of the orders and rules of everyday life, the particular traditions surrounding *Fasching* or *Fastnacht* specific to Southern Germany, including Munich, where the Baroness spent a formative period between 1900 and 1903, are striking in their incorporation of elaborately carved masks, a celebration of the profane, bawdy and licentious and loud, or otherwise disruptive performative elements. Visually arresting, the costumes themselves are designed to be moved in, decorated with a range of acoustic and kinetic elements including feathers, beads, wool tassels, clacking wood pieces or small bells and cymbals in a manner that is certainly sympathetic to the Baroness's ornamental embellishments. Attended by cow bells and wild dancing and including screaming witches, large ferocious bears and masked characters, the performative elements of fasching break down boundaries between spectator and participant as elaborately costumed figures stalk through the villages with the main body of the parade, but also break away, running into crowds and performing a range of disruptive behaviours. Illuminated with reference to Bakhtin's study of Medieval Carnival, we can see that fasching similarly 'does not know footlights, in the sense that it does not acknowledge any distinction between actors and spectators'.[94]

The costumes and carved masks are of particular importance in this respect. Generating a spectacular anonymity echoed by the Baroness in her recollection of being 'safe inside my meshell' as a *tableau vivant*, the masks obscure the identities of the participants, the costumes facilitating the collapse of social hierarchies and the mixing of all people that Bakhtin identifies as an essential aspect of the carnivalesque. Indeed, it is through the mask, this 'most complex theme of folk culture', that Bakhtin connects two central concepts relevant to a discussion of the Baroness's costuming and performance – the carnivalesque and the grotesque body. Connected with 'the joy of change and reincarnation [...] and with the negation of uniformity and similarity' the mask dissolves the distinctions between individual bodies and reimagines the carnival crowd as a universal body – one opened to the world and constantly reformed and renewed by it. It is this relationship to 'transition, metamorphoses, the violation of natural boundaries' that is perhaps most illuminating with regards to the Baroness's later costuming practices, particularly in her transformation of waste materials into performative extensions of her body.[95] Not only do the usually stratified groups of young and old, rich and poor, male and female blend and become visually unidentifiable in the carnival body, but the specific costuming traditions associated with fasching also place gender performance and the fluidity of boundaries between the human and animal as a central element in the carnivalesque reversal of order as young boys dress as old crones, women behave like men and men dress as animals.

Divorced from its medieval contexts and subject to the same gender codes and conventions that structure modern life, carnival has similarly been subjected to certain regulations, and masking specifically has been more of a man's game in carnival practices since the medieval period.[96] However, while the heavy, carved masks and handmade costumes appear to be inherited through families according to the patrilineal line in more recent generations, Làszló Kürt has identified certain subversive elements within the performative contexts of Swabian fasching which are 'eroticized differently from the heterosexual male's perspective'.[97] In the specific contexts of fasching, these include a 'woman's ball' run by and for women exclusively where they 'dance with each other, sing bawdy sons, and drink heavily; they may dress as males, perform male dances, and parody manly sexual prowess'. While this obviously represents the anxious regulation of carnival's most subversive elements, it is nevertheless interesting to consider Elsa's appropriation of gendered masking privileges and her own performance of conventionally 'male' behaviours in her aggressive sexuality, bawdy and irreverent humour and anti-domesticity in light of these practices. Certainly, the carnivalesque is a useful framework within which to think about Elsa's performances and writing. While her costumes clearly connect her body to the world in an open exchange that unsettles in its grotesque openness and presentation of junk material as radically 'out of place', in its humour and subversion of certain dominant stylistic trends, her poetry and literary criticism can also be read as developing a mode of carnivalesque critique.

As Russo has succinctly summarized, there are three main forms of carnival folk culture in Bakhtin's formulation:

> Ritual spectacles (which include feasts, pageants and marketplace festivals of all kinds); comic verbal; compositions, including parodies both oral and written; and various genres of billingsgate (curses, oaths, profanations, market place speech).[98]

Elsa's profane declarations, delight in expletives and attacks on puritanical 'modesty' certainly chime with this description, and throughout her poetry and literary criticism we can trace the carnivalesque as a literary mode which subverts and liberates dominant modernist styles through humour and chaos. Her focus on corporeality, on her body's rhythms and anatomical functioning and her costume-constructions similarly situate her within Bakhtin's topography of the grotesque.

As is clear in her insistence of posing-as-art detailed above, the Baroness – to paraphrase Simone de Beauvoir – is not born, but rather becomes a model and performer. The model is clearly not reducible to any one of the various 'poses' executed and repeated over time, even if it is reconstructed in an image produced by someone else. Elsa's costuming and modelling then, and her insistence upon these activities as embodied modes of self-representation in their own right, implicitly challenge the seemingly stable identities ascribed through and to gender. Exposing the ways in which female bodies and female identity are constituted through the repeated performance of various acts expected of them, Elsa's 'poses' and costumes resonate with later gender theories in exposing 'Gender [as] what is put on, invariably, under constraint, daily and incessantly, with anxiety and pleasure'.[99] Attention to Elsa's modelling practice highlights what, in Butler's terms, constitutes the performance of gender:

> Gender is in no way a stable identity or locus of agency from which various acts proceed; rather it is an identity tenuously constituted in time – an identity, instituted through a stylized repetition of acts.[100]

However, in her gender performances the Baroness is not consistent in the acts she performs; an artist's model, arrested for wearing men's clothes, her junk costumes and challenges to gendered codes of propriety transgress and frustrate the binary logic that would otherwise attempt to fix her in any one, stable 'feminine' category.

Connections between spectacle, performance, femininity and representation are of central importance in addressing the tensions between the anxious reconstruction of the Baroness's abject body in the memoirs and fiction of her contemporaries and her own modes of self-representation. The extent to which these recollections of her early performances place an emphasis in her own ability to gaze upon herself and the pleasure taken in that action should be emphasized. Juxtaposing Elsa and Irigaray's comments on female self-representation in the epigrams opening this chapter, I have gone on to explore the various ways in which Elsa's embodied self-representation attempts to create a language for female experience that, while still relying on a dynamic of 'seeing', resists modes that determine her subjectivity as a fetishized art-object. Resonating with Irigaray's notion of the double-bind that ties female embodied expression to an internalized specular subjectivity, John Burger has famously stated:

> A woman must continually watch herself. She is almost continually accompanied by her own image of herself [...] From earliest childhood she has been taught and persuaded to survey herself continuously. And so she comes to consider the surveyed and the surveyor within her as the two consistent, yet always distance elements of her identity as a woman [...] Her own sense of being herself is supplanted by a sense of being appreciated as herself by another.[101]

Elsa certainly expressed a keen understanding for these multiple subject positions, as she put it herself: 'I am keenly conscious of (my) own self, as if I were both theatre and spectator in one, not only the author'.[102] The important thing to highlight here is that beyond the doubled role proposed by Burger – that in internalizing the gaze, 'woman's' subjectivity and identity are only determined in relation to her status as object, one that she is complicit in reproducing – Elsa casually accepts the doubled-identity of being both the gazer and the gazed upon, transcending its binaries to some extent by introducing a third term. Conceiving of herself as author above all else, Elsa re-frames the terms of the discussion in order to prioritize her performance, and her authorship over this production.

Importantly, in discussing the pleasure taken in viewing herself as a performative art-object of her own construction she is not founding a specular identity based, in Berger's terms, on the desire to 'be appreciated as herself by another', but to reclaim looking on her own terms as mode of strategic resistance for embodied female subjectivity to reassert itself against a gaze which has attempted to cast 'woman as image, man as bearer of the look'.[103] In reclaiming the right to gaze upon herself, to describe and speculate upon her own performances as dynamic and embodied art-works, and in engaging her spectators in her own transformative exchange, she reverses the notion of the 'privileged links between seeing, knowing and possessing as functions of the masculine',[104] positing the female artist, model and autobiographer, as at once the product, audience and author of these performances.

Returning to George Biddle's recollection of his first encounter with the Baroness detailed in the previous chapter, we can more fully appreciate the role of performance, spectacle and the carnivalesque in developing her self-representation practices. A snapshot of the Baroness in the full swing of her Dada Queen days, Biddle's reconstruction brings both the early *tableux vivants* and the more infamous New York performances together, and presents a compelling case for the imbricated nature of her modelling and costuming practices. Exchanging the cardboard breasts and cotton hips for tomato tin cans and quotidian objects, the treatment of the body as a site of perpetual renewal that is present in the living statues – but regulated by the actions and vision of the director – is pushed into more grotesque territory in the Baroness's fully realized body-work.

The stolen curtain rings, gilded vegetables and used tin cans decorating her body of course represent a prominent example of her waste-based and collage aesthetics during the period, but they also signify an aggressive appropriation and reinterpretation of the role and history of the female nude itself. As Lynda Nead has suggested, 'More than any other subject, the female nude connotes "Art" [...] it is an icon of western culture, a symbol of civilisation and accomplishment.'[105] Despite presenting herself to Biddle as an artist's model, his comment traces the difficulties in containing her in this position, and the challenges that her self-display present to the artist attempting to represent the female nude. Far from the sooth, closed, impenetrable surface of the classical nude, she is 'nearly' naked, his access to her body interrupted by her own art constructions. What Biddle sees as she parts the raincoat (which in itself frames this narrative with a troubling 'opening' of its own) is not the smooth surface of her skin, the boundary line of her body, but its grotesque openness, the tomato tins and celluloid curtain rings shockingly displaying the body's interpenetration with the city that she moves though. Recovering the old, the used and useless, and connecting them with her own body, her self-display also enacts the processes of perpetual renewal that not only characterize the grotesque, but disrupt the flows of commodities and capital activated within consumer capitalism.

As such, it is unsurprising that the Baroness's employment of junk material and her appropriation of the female nude as living, autobiographical performance art refuse, as the studies of Amelia Jones and Irene Gammel have both emphasized, to work within the spaces of the art institution or the artist's studio. Indeed, these were not the only officially sanctioned spaces of high culture that she infiltrated. While examples of breaking into museums, art galleries and editorial offices abound, one particularly striking example of her deployment as embodied performance as affecting spectacle is worth repeating here. Margaret

Anderson recalls a particular highlight of the 1921 social calendar, a benefit concert arranged by Anderson in the Provincetown Theatre at which the opera singer Marguerite D'Alverez performed. Arriving late – which she claimed was the unfortunate result of painstakingly preparing her costume, the Baroness shocked the room into a hushed silence. As Anderson recalls in her autobiography:

> She wore a trailing blue-green dress and a peacock fan. One side of her face was decorated with a cancelled postage stamp (two-cent American, pink). Her lips were painted black, her face powder was yellow. She wore the top of a coal scuttle for a hat, strapped on under her chin like a helmet. Two mustard spoons at the side gave the effect of feathers.[106]

Exposing the construction of the diva personality by performing as the ultimate prima donna and upstaging the opera singer, the Baroness's performance evokes the trappings of sensational spectacle, but refuses the aesthetic distance necessary for voyeuristic contemplation and digestion.[107] The unfixed nature of these performances, clear here in her appropriation of the spaces of high culture and perversion of its normal practices, and evident in the active dynamism of her public promenades, disrupts the theatrical event itself. As Graver suggests: 'without a fixed meaning to be conveyed, a theatrical performance cannot be consumed. It can only be entered and experienced'.[108]

Elsa's performative authority generated a kind of spectacle akin to Artaud's notions of cruelty – that is, not a theatre of sadistic violence, but a spectacle that refuses to offer itself for contemplation and pleasure, but is instead pressed upon an audience to 'overwhelm and disorientate it'.[109] Artaud's notion of a spectacle that would be more felt than seen is useful in thinking through the nature and impact of the Baroness's spectacular performances:

> We abolish the stage and the auditorium and replace them by a single site, without partition or barrier of any kind, which will become the theatre of the action. A direct communication will be re-established between the spectator and the spectacle, between the actor and the spectator, from the fact that the spectator, placed in the middle of the action, is engulfed and physically affected by it.[110]

Elsa's appropriation of New York and her own body as the stage and site of her autobiographical performances chimes with Artaud's comment. In combining spectacle and performance, the Baroness's methods of self-representation engulf the spectator, radically de-centring the 'implicit authority of their all-encompassing gaze'.[111] This is not a spectacle that is registered, digested and reconstructed in the eye of the beholder, but a performance that emanates out of her body in her 'body expression/spirit plastic' and in her *couture d'ordures* and is registered in the bodies of those who encounter it. Abolishing the stage and the auditorium, Elsa preferred the 'arena', a space of dynamic interaction and transformative exchange between performer and spectator that she used to great effect in her modelling and costuming practices and recreated in her (self) portraits, literary criticism and in the collaborative 'Baroness Elsa' project, as we shall see.

Rather than suggesting that this erotically charged, corporeal and challenging performance placed Elsa on the limits of the avant-garde, the pioneering work of early scholarship on the performative dimensions of the Baroness's Dada practice has established rich ground for tracing the lines of her influence from within Dada and beyond. As Amelia Jones has highlighted, Duchamp's later performance of his ultra-feminine alter-ego Rrose Selavy not only echoes Elsa's androgynous gender-play, but also places eros-as-life at the centre of Dada experimentation.[112] While James Harding has rightly placed the Baroness in a revised historiography of feminist performance art, Gammel's extensive research has established valuable connections between the Baroness's personal history and her aesthetic practices that are indispensable to this study.

Alongside readings that place the Baroness in proximity to the feminist performance art of the 1970s and beyond, or, in read her work in the context of the international avant-garde, compelling connections could be drawn along lines of gender, materiality and performance histories between the Baroness's New York costuming and her earlier experience as a 'living picture' to the scenic art of Lavinia Schulz and Walter Holdt, the Dada Balls, Bauhaus costume parties and Cabaret Voltaire events. Including Marcel Duchamp and Brogna Permutter-Clair's live recreation of Lucas Cranach the Elder's *Adam and Eve* (1528) performed as part of Picabia and Satie's ballet *Relâche* in a history of the *tableaux vivants* form, Webb's history of the erotic arts places New York Dada within art-historical lineage that blends the erotic and the spectacular, that transgresses the boundaries between high and low; in doing so he also places posing at the centre of New York Dada activity.

3

'Not dead': Djuna Barnes's mature autobiographic poetics

>Man cannot purge his body of its theme
>As can the silkworm on a running thread
>Spin a shroud to re-consider in.
>
> Djuna Barnes, 'Rite of Spring', 1982

Writing to his sister Djuna Barnes in 1958, Thurn Budington expressed his frustration with her recently published verse play *The Antiphon*. Located less in the Baroque excesses of her pseudo-Elizabethan verse or the ornately overwrought patterns of family, history and memory structuring both the sinister tragedy's polyphonic surface textures and the counterpointed movement of weaving and unravelling that propels the dramatic action, Thurn's complaint focused on questions of revenge and personal biography:

> I am reading your play for the second time to try and understand what seems to me to be a fixation or sort of revenge for something long dead and to be forgotten. The writing itself is tremendous but after that I can only wish the subject could have been different. One which could live as a monument to the genius of your mind.[1]

While seemingly untroubled by the textual difficulties normally identified by critics as problematic to *The Antiphon*'s reception, Thurn nevertheless establishes his own strategies for making sense of this 'tremendous' writing. Identifying personal biography as the motivating energy behind this powerful drama, Thurn chastises Barnes for her choice of subject matter and in doing so falls back upon critical assumptions of autobiographic writing as performing a full disclosure of uncomplicated 'truths' relating to both the author and her work. Foregrounding notions of truth and facticity in his approach to reading this text, Thurn's demonstrated 'confidence in the referentiality of language and a corollary confidence in the authenticity of the self' clearly rely on notions of linguistic transparency and coherent subjectivity as the source and product of autobiographic writing.[2] In challenging Barnes with this reading of *The Antiphon* as a mode of biographic revenge, Thurn drastically undercuts the polyphonic textual strategies activated in the play, wherein the plausibility or authority of any 'official' narrative is consistently disrupted through the multiple and competing voices of the Hobbs family as they repeat, revise and contradict the different versions of their shared traumatic history.

While *The Antiphon* can certainly be examined as representative of Barnes's mature autobiographic poetics, the application of a straightforwardly biographical mode in critical approaches to Barnes's texts is deeply problematic on ethical, critical and aesthetic grounds. In addressing the persistence of this 'biographic impulse' in critical treatments of Barnes's work, this chapter proposes a more nuanced treatment of the intersection of the biographic and fictive in Barnes writing, suggesting in fact that such biographic framing aims at a reduction and simplification of the stylistic complexities of her autobiographic poetics and of the textual messiness of her writing practice. Moreover, in attempting to impose a confessional dimension onto her texts, such readings are complicit in the re-entrenchment of the 'unequal, nonreciprocal relation[s] of power' that have traditionally structured the reception of female-authored modes of autobiographic writing through a co-option of the confessional's effective 'normalization of the speaking subject and thus the elimination of any transgressive potential which might exist'.[3]

While biographic readings demonstrate an overt concern with the status of the text as a final, coherent and complete *product*, close attention to the productive potential of the messy textuality and disruptive patterns of recurrence activated through Barnes's autobiographic practices in fact allows for a reconsideration of the *processes* at work in the construction of her texts and in the development of her mature autobiographic poetics. As well as exposing critical tensions between modes of autobiographic writing and biographic models of reading, attention to the persistence of this 'biographic impulse' within Barnes criticism is highly suggestive of a set of anxieties surrounding the un-contained and incoherent 'messiness' of the autobiographic text and subject and of the strategies through which this messiness was managed.

Barnes herself was no stranger to the tensions between the cleanly represented and easily digestible biographic ideal and the messy realities of the autobiographic text and subject. In addition to the complex autobiographic patterns at work in her more famous texts, Barnes worked on a series of more conventional memoirs recording her life in 1920s and 1930s Paris and her early childhood. Alongside the multiple drafts and revisions of these manuscripts, Barnes also worked in collaboration with Elsa von Freytag-Loringhoven on a book project including an account of the German artist's pre-Dada biography intermittently from 1924 until the end of her life, as earlier chapters have touched upon. Imagined as an accompaniment to a collection of the Baroness's Dada poetry which also failed to appear and reconstructed through the Baroness's long and detailed letters from Germany transcribed by Barnes, the younger woman struggled with the restrictions and demands of the genre, as her correspondence suggests.[4]

Agonizing over this project long after the death of the Baroness in 1927, Barnes's failure to complete the biography reverberates across her correspondence as a painful refrain, interrupting and interfering with her discussions of other projects years later. Indeed, the urgency with which Barnes returned to the aborted manuscripts in the 1930s, the 1950s and again during her organization of the Patchin Place poetry in the late 1970s underscores its intertextual relevance in considering some of Barnes's most productive periods and of the disruptive powers of recurrence itself. Raising important questions about the ethics and aesthetics of recovery, the mass of fragments, aborted manuscripts and near-identical drafts that make up this 'failed' auto/biography thus presents an illuminating intertext for any discussion of the engaged practice of return and revision that structures both the patterns of Barnes's mature autobiographic poetics and the messy textuality of her writing practice.[5]

As highlighted in my introductory comments, tensions between communication and obfuscation, strategies of containment and concerns over excessive textual mess have remained prominent features of Barnes criticism and have been instrumental in framing responses to her work. Early readers including Emily Coleman frequently connected issues of communication and constructional coherence as intimately connected and problematic issues within Barnes's texts.[6] While for Coleman, issues of art, life and communication are straightforwardly and necessarily connected, Barnes's texts not only resist communication in these terms by insisting on 'speaking to themselves', but also refuse the tidy constructional unity traditionally offered by the structuring frameworks of character and plot. As Barnes lamented in her reply to Coleman's letter:

> I can't, I have never been able to plot or plan a book or give it, apparently any structure, I don't really think I know what a structure is, in the accepted sense, or isnt [*sic*] it I don't believe in it, for me? Perhaps it is all right for others, but for me it seems so queer to write a synopsis of chapters and plot and all that sort of thing, and then hang your feelings on it. I am trying desperately with the Baroness to think of something which you would call structure, and I can't, it has always been my failure, people from the beginning have cried for plot, I can't think one up.[7]

While Barnes's writing frustrates conventional forms of structural coherence imagined as linear sequence or the tropes traditionally associated with narratological development ornate and complex structures are nevertheless erected across the corpus. To what extent then might the Baroness's waste-based practices illuminate Barnes's rejection of the clean, contained and straightforwardly referential text? Are there mutually illuminating connections to be drawn between the Baroness's modes of recovery and re-use and the messy (inter)textuality of the Barnes corpus and its patterns of return, repetition and variation that unpick 'assumptions on which historical progression and developmental models are based'?[8]

Drawing generative comparisons between textual patterns of repudiation, return and variation and the structural functioning of waste already outlined I want to propose compelling new perspectives for addressing the material messiness of Barnes's textual practice and compulsive intertextuality, the generative and disruptive nature of her mature autobiographic poetics and of the fraught relationships established between the Barnes corpus, literary history and modernist practices more broadly. Like the externalized drawing out of the silkworms life-labour that Barnes found so compelling, her own texts develop complex architectural patterns to accommodate the processes of recovery, repetition and revision that structure and support her autobiographic poetics.

Nothing is closed or final in the Barnes corpus as can be illustrated by her treatment of the 'failed' 'Baroness Elsa' biography, the cycles of poetic fragments that make up her late production, and her illuminatingly enthusiastic response to the French biologist and prominent eugenicist Alexis Carrel's theory of 'inner time' in the 1930s.[9] With a close consideration of Barnes's late verse tragedy *The Antiphon*, the Patchin Place poetry cycles, the 'Baroness Elsa' manuscript and its complex relationship to *Nightwood*, this chapter will present an analysis of the patterns of Barnes's autobiographic poetics and their relationship to, or even *as*, modes of modernist wastes.

i. 'This generations vulgarity': Djuna Barnes and the 'biographic impulse'

> Yes, certainly a great deal of my writing is intuition, remembrance of time and pain, but good heavens do you think that the book was written without a great deal of thought?
>
> Djuna Barnes to Emily Coleman, 1935

Appropriately, the unwelcome return of a repressed and decidedly messy family history is the central narrative concern of *The Antiphon*. Set within its own richly intertextual and intergenerational framework, published in 1958 but set 'during the war of 1939',[10] the play opens as the far-flung members of the Burley-Hobbs family return to a decaying ancestral home at the request of the Puckish and mysterious 'Jack Blow' (later revealed as the absent brother Jeremy). The densely overwrought pattern of three generations of conflicted family history is gradually unravelled through the counterpointed narratives and voices produced as mother, daughter, uncle and brothers repeat, revise and re-remember this contested shared history. While these voices are clearly presented in an antagonistically antiphonal relationship to one another, the play also reverberates with the absent but not forgotten voices of the paternal grandmother Victoria, the 'Free-soiler, free-thinker, nonconformist' (II, 64), and her son Titus Hobbs whose shared philosophy that 'all love was truth and honor' (II, 68) was finally realized in his serial adulteries and 'monstrous practice of polygamy' (II, 70).

As the play's dialogue proceeds through a language preoccupied by haunting as much as it is itself haunted by its referents, we learn of the infidelities and sexual philosophies of the deceased father Titus – 'That old Ram! Cock-pit Bully Boy!' (II, 103), the 'merchant' brother's murderous intentions towards mother and sister, the true identities and relationships between the more mysterious characters, and the bitter memories of a family history punctured by pain and cruelty. Orchestrated by the disguised 'Jack', the drama at the centre of this sinister family reunion revolves around the exposure of such abuses, most climactically, the elaborate re-staging of the rape of the daughter Miranda as a young girl 'not yet seventeen' who was then 'thrown to a travelling Cockney thrice her age' (II, 151), a traumatic and horrendous act arranged by her father and silently accepted by her mother, Augusta. With the aid of a crude dollhouse structure complete with marionettes named by Jack/Jeremy as 'Hobbs Ark, beast-box, dolls house' (II, 144), Augusta is finally forced to bear witness to her daughter's trauma and her own complicity in this violent history. Retreating wildly from her own guilt and culpability, Augusta insists on her own victimization; refusing to accept her part in the various atrocities woven through the family history the older woman unravels and the stage is set for the final act in which the mother and daughter are drawn closer together and both destroyed as Augusta bludgeons her daughter to death before collapsing dead herself.

As Thurn's reaction implies, certain aspects of the play are in fact familiar to Barnes's own biography, to the accounts of her unconventional childhood documented across various letters and manuscripts, and to her earlier experimental family chronicle *Ryder*. Less focused on questions of revenge or recrimination than in detailing and deflating the pompous exploits of the patriarch Wendell Ryder and the immediate consequences of his polygamous utopian philosophies on the women and children around him, the Rabelaisian *Ryder* nevertheless establishes the narrative ground upon which its later, bleaker incarnation takes root. Both dissect the free-love philosophies propagated by a domineering paternal grandmother and father, detail the disturbing and damaging effects of a fervently practised polygamy and, more pressingly for Thurn, both invoke characters, locations and situations familiar to the Barnes-Chappell family biographies.[11] Given Barnes's own insistence in conversation with critic James Scott that 'Ryder and Titus, they are my father. Where did the basic story come from? From my life',[12] the part played by personal autobiography in the composition of these texts might, initially, seem to be unambiguously straightforward. However, looking across Barnes's published texts and the reams of unpublished and repeatedly revised manuscripts and textual fragments now collected in the Djuna Barnes Papers at the Special Collections, University of Maryland, the relationship between the Barnes corpus and modes of autobiographic writing as straightforward disclosure becomes increasingly fraught and complex.

From the distillation of personal experience and observation evident in her early New York journalism, to the playful satire of Natalie Barney's left bank lesbian coterie in *Ladies Almanack* (1928), the composite characters, settings, and examination of desire, memory and pain that inform *Nightwood* (1936), and the familial dynamics shaping both *Ryder* (1928) and *The Antiphon* (1958), it is apparent that the autobiographic is deeply woven into the textual fabric of Barnes's literary production. Such a notion is closely explored over the lengthy correspondence between Barnes and Coleman chronicling the gestation of *Nightwood* as questions of narrative structure and textual production are interrupted and subtly restated through reflections on her relationship with Wood, anecdotes about her family and anxieties about the development of her 'next book', the collaborative 'Baroness Elsa' auto/biography. Across these letters Barnes frequently identifies an active autobiographic ingredient in her fiction: as one particular reflection has it, 'I suppose its possible that I only have two books in me, my life as a child, "Ryder", and my life with Thelma "Anatomy of Night" – I can not imagine spending years writing fiction, things made up entirely out of thin air and without a foundation in some emotion.'[13]

Nevertheless, Barnes was famously suspicious of 'being biographied' and being made the focus of some '"tell all" to the idiot public'.[14] Frequently refusing to comply with requests for interviews, Barnes consistently ignored or angrily despatched fans and scholars interested in her work in later life, and famously responded to the *Little Review*'s 1929 questionnaire sent out to 'the artists of the world' with the glib response: 'I am sorry but the list of questions does not interest me to answer. Nor have I that respect for the public.'[15]

In 1978 a horrified Barnes wrote to her friend and patron Peggy Guggenheim to berate her for offering a letter of introduction to the young and hopeful biographer Daniel Halpern who, despite having already been informed about Barnes's 'opinion of people trying to write my biography', nevertheless accosted her in the street to request an interview.[16] While the same letter derisively debunks connections between biography, authenticity and immortality that the genre has traditionally reinforced, another earlier letter from Barnes to Guggenheim goes considerably further in illuminating Barnes's opinions regarding the application of biography in readings of her work.

> A biography, against my protests, both to author and proposed publisher, will in all horrible probability appear in 1972. The awful point in all of this sort of ridicuouls [sic] "publicizing" of a person, is for the publisc [corrected to public] [sic]pleasure, I can't stop it so I shall suffer one more of those cheap 'interpretations' as they are called. This generations vulgarity. God help my work, which is all they should be interested in.[17]

Deeply opposed to the idea of a biography Barnes's basic suggestion here is that the reproduced image of the writer – the facts and intimate details of a life inauthentically arranged into a composite and coherent picture – distracts and detracts from the work itself, obscuring what she describes elsewhere as the essential 'disturbance' of her writing which, she felt, should be experienced rather than analysed.[18]

In this respect, Barnes's resistance to biographic modes of reading resonates with the excision of the personal familiar to canonical modernist poetics and expressly advocated by T.S. Eliot's influential 1919 essay 'Tradition and the

Individual Talent' – at least to the extent that 'honest criticism and sensitive appreciation [be] directed not upon the poet but upon the poetry'.[19] While Barnes's work sits somewhat uncomfortably within the stabilizing framework of legitimacy, conformity and literary history provided by Eliot's 'impersonal theory of poetry' and its demands that the pursuit of art equates 'a continual self-sacrifice, a continual extinction of personality', motifs and ideas raised in this essay regarding the 'historical sense' indispensable for poetic composition certainly challenged and informed aspects of Barnes's own poetic projects, as we shall see.[20]

However, enforcing connections between order, history and contemporary poetics, Eliot's suggestion that entrance into the temporally disruptive 'present moment of the past' is stabilized through a fundamentally 'impersonal' approach to art (which, in turn, forms the basis of the contemporary poet's promotion into the pantheon of the 'traditional') stands in a distinctively antagonistic relationship to Barnes's attitudes and aesthetics.[21] While the 'historical sense' exhibited across Barnes's texts could certainly be interpreted as exhibiting the 'timeless and temporal together', she nevertheless refuses to conform to Eliot's model. Rather than guaranteeing stability, coherence and impersonality – (and thus reinstating 'tradition') – Barnes's recuperation of literary history through discontinuous scraps and fragments, alongside her 'extreme stylistic mannerism', 'runaway figurative language' and 'promiscuous blurring of categories' deconstruct and challenge the grounds upon which Eliotian 'tradition' sits.[22]

While the question of Barnes's adherence to a poetic 'extinction of personality' is certainly contestable, she is nevertheless clear in emphasizing the negative consequences of biography's excessive and distorting publicizing of personality in relation to her work. Reinforcing a clear distinction between the original and disturbing 'work' and the reproducible string of 'cheap interpretations' of both text and author generated by such biographic scrutiny, Barnes highlights the unstable ground between text and author, truth and fiction, representation and selfhood upon which such biographical analysis attempts to establish itself. While being deeply immersed in autobiographic practices and patterns, Barnes's texts nevertheless continually challenge and deconstruct the critical foundations of facticity, stability and intelligibility upon which the genre of autobiography has traditionally been founded.

A famously slippery and unruly genre, autobiography has been disciplined to some extent by a body of criticism that retrospectively examined eighteenth- and nineteenth-century forms of life-writing from twentieth-century perspectives. Contextually related to literary modernism's rejection of 'eminent Victorians' and the promotion of poetic impersonality popularized by Eliot and Pound, early twentieth-century commentators either overlooked or pointedly derided auto/biographical modes of writing and the apparently connected implication that it was preferable or even possible to trace a text back to its source in order to reveal a stable and easily identifiable authorial intention beneath.[23] However these notions of facticity and intentionality were revived to a certain extent by mid-century critics in establishing the foundations for critical approaches to autobiography as the narrative reconstruction of a life achieved through a 'coherent shaping of the past' and insisting upon a 'certain consistency of relationship between the self and the outside world'.[24]

According to this scholarship, while written records celebrating exemplary lives either in their public achievements or commendable moral standards can be traced back to Plutarch and beyond, the form and function of modern auto/biographical writing can best be understood in the context of a post-Enlightenment period of positivism that the more clearly defined genres of autobiography, biography and the novel emerge from. Richard Altick's observation that biography was 'the literary emblem par excellence of Victorianism' illuminates both early twentieth-century rejections of the genre and the appeal of the close connections established between the nineteenth-century popularization of literary realism and the auto/biographic project.[25] While the novel moved away from realism and into more experimental territory in the early decades of the twentieth century, biography and a burgeoning field of biographic theory remained dedicated to it.

As Liz Stanley has elaborated in her discussion of the 'realist fallacy' upon which such notions of biography are based, the emphasis on reconstruction and expertise promoted by this model of thinking underscores an imagined correspondence between the accumulation of a series of verifiable and apparently irrefutable 'facts' arranged in a chronologically logical narrative and the unproblematic *realization* (rather than representation) of the essential character and intentions of the biographic subject. While this might not pose immediate problems for the biographic text itself, the extension of such a biographic mode of reading which 'proposes that there is a coherent, essentially unchanging and unitary self which can be referentially captured by its methods',[26] into the critical analysis of other texts has proven especially prevalent in the treatment and criticism of the stylistically challenging work of marginalized twentieth-century figures, notably at play in the projects of recovering 'forgotten female modernists' including Barnes, Mina Loy and H.D, amongst others.

Rather than simply providing historical or biographical context, statements and speculation surrounding Barnes's sexuality, her tumultuous relationship with Thelma Wood, her unconventional childhood, and possible abusive or incestuous early sexual encounters have been directly employed in order to ground and guide a significant amount of Barnes scholarship. Promising the disclosure of some originary biographic truth, such readings have frequently been privileged as a necessary preliminary stage in textual interpretation. Responding to the ornate and anti-realist aspects of Barnes's prose, her problematizing of language as straightforwardly referential, and her 'persistently non-communicative and transgressive' aesthetics,[27] such biographical approaches have positioned an initial illumination of the life as essential in untangling and organizing the ambiguities of the work. Suggesting that the two are bound together but have been overworked to the point of unintelligibility, the biographer/critic equips himself with the tools to identify and stabilize the 'woman' and the 'work' as two separate but internally coherent and mutually illuminating objects of study. As Barnes's posthumous biographer Philip Herring put it, 'Before I could understand the novel [Nightwood], I believed I had to understand Djuna Barnes.'[28]

Herring's 'understanding' of Barnes revolves around two conflicting impulses that, under his analysis, lie at the root of her character and work: 'the desire to scream to the world of the outrages that had been committed against her, and the more ladylike impulse to endure her bitterness in silence'. Herring locates this 'ladylike' second impulse in her much-documented need for privacy in later life, even noting that had she been alive 'she would have opposed by every possible legal means the writing of this biography'.[29] This, coupled with the insistence that this first impulse was satisfied through her writing, presents the biographer/critic with an irresistible puzzle: uncover and reveal the sources of these 'outrages' and you have the key to decoding and demystifying an otherwise obscure and evasive text.

Under the terms of Herring's analysis, Barnes's resistance to biographic scrutiny tautologically serves to reinforce the principles of such a critical approach. Extending Philippe Lejeune's notion of the 'autobiographical pact' in which the convergence of authorial and readerly consciousness is focused within 'a contract of identity that is sealed by the proper name',[30] Barnes's fictional characters are taken as avatars which, once identified as their historical counterparts, reinforce the tripartite stability of author, narrator and protagonist originally proposed by Lejeune. Through this biographical approach Herring adapts the terms of Lejeune's pact to extend to the work of the biographer/critic: what emerges in this instance between the subject, the biographer and the reader is an implicit contractual obligation to 'truth', withheld by Barnes but discernible through the work of the biographer/critic and expected by the reader. Going considerably further than attempting to extract an explanation or confession from Barnes's work, such biographic modes of reading work to contain, organize and 'clean up' the messy materiality of Barnes's writing practice and the disruptive patterns of her autobiographic poetics while providing a stable platform from which to tackle the stylistic 'difficulties' presented by these texts.

In the challenges that it presents to reading, performance and interpretation, *The Antiphon* is widely regarded as Barnes's most cryptic and 'difficult' text. Perhaps unsurprisingly, in its self-conscious anachronism, delight in language and intertextuality and interest in the complexities of memory and autobiography, the play has also been considered 'the most "Barnesian" of the author's texts'.[31] The proximity of textual difficulty and Barnesean poetics highlighted here, coupled with Barnes's troubled relationship to autobiographic practices, proved influential in shaping early critical readings of Barnes's work through enabling and encouraging the activation of this 'biographic impulse' in approaches to the corpus. Given that both *Ryder* and *The Antiphon* deal obliquely with questions of rape and incest, in returning to Thurn's letter we can assume that his concern with the play's 'subject' refers to her treatment of these issues and their proximity to such tantalizingly recognizable avatars.[32] The extent to which he located some form of sexual violation as a key biographic event returned to and recurring across her work is clear and Thurn has certainly not been alone in using biographic information to anchor and understand the play.

While Barnes's first biographer Andrew Field went so far as to suggest that 'the Barnes oeuvre may be said to be one of the best instances of deep auto-analysis outside of the Freudian canon in modern English literature',[33] important early contributions to Barnes scholarship foregrounded biographic details but overlooked the complexities of her autobiographic poetics in developing textual readings.[34] With regard to Barnes's late play, Field built on Lynda Curry's extensive 1978 study of the cuts and excisions across the five major draft variants charting *The Antiphon*'s gestation in order to expose 'the story behind the story in Barnes's writing, either removed or disguised, or only obliquely told'.[35] While Curry used the textual evidence of Eliot's extensive cuts in order to draw comparisons between an original sexual violation of the corporeal body and a later violation of the textual body,[36] she also highlighted the significance of the excision of the now infamous hayhook scene in Act II, the obfuscation of the details surrounding Miranda's rape and the roles played by her parents in the various violences committed against the daughter.[37]

Forging connections between textual opacity or ambiguity and forms of biographical violation (sexual and textual), Curry's analysis – while still invaluable to Barnes studies – nevertheless provided the ground for future simplifications of the stylistic, linguistic and aesthetic difficulties presented by Barnes's play as encoded biographic confession of sexual crimes so traumatic they can only be discerned through a fragmented and encoded language of evasion and allusion.[38] With recourse to significant studies in incest discourse, Louise DeSalvo's influential contribution to the *Silence and Power* volume insisted that in order to understand Miranda, readers must 'learn her language, the language of the incest-victim, which simultaneously masks and reveals'.[39] In presenting the play as a preeminent 'example of modernist literature of revenge',[40] DeSalvo's analysis has done much to cement readings of *The Antiphon* as a biographic testimony to modes of patriarchal violence and oppression, despite not employing biographical models itself.

The question of whether or not Barnes was abused by her father or raped on his invitation is not the issue here, rather it is a question of the strategies through which Thurn and subsequent critics have fallen back on biography as a way of anchoring these texts, of reinstating an official and coherent narrative to stabilize the messy autobiographic poetics developed throughout the play. Particularly striking about Thurn's letter are the ways in which his re-framing of Barnes's text as a revenge-driven form of literary confession provides him with a model for rationalizing and making sense of both the text and of restating control over his sister's narrative. Silencing the play's intersubjective and antiphonic reverberations, Thurn also silences his sister, pathologizing her as a woman with an 'unhealthy' relationship to a past 'long dead and to be forgotten'. In a mode strikingly similar to the Baroness's 'containment' in the memoirs of her contemporaries explored previously, Thurn's letter attempts to correct and re-contain both the messy eruption of repressed traumatic memory that *The Antiphon* dramatizes through the counterpointed narratives of the reunited Hobbs family and to finally close or seal off the repetitious and disturbing narrative.

However, Barnes refuses to be silenced and in a move that I would position as characteristic of the forms and functions of both the Baroness's and Barnes's autobiographic poetics and the messy textuality of their writing practices, Barnes ruptures the 'official' narrative re-presented by Thurn's letter. Disrupting both the 'clean' page of his letter and the neatly organized account of *The Antiphon* as 'a fixation or sort of revenge for something long dead and to be forgotten' that it insists upon, Barnes interrupts his analysis by annotating his letter. Challenging

Thurn's notion of 'revenge' she replaces the word with 'justice'; responding to his dismissal of 'something long dead' she scribbles the rejoinder 'not dead'.⁴¹ If to be dead is to be finished and silenced, Barnes's rejection of such a state in relation to both her life and art is expressed here not only in her choice of words, but in the violence with which this reply is textually performed. Cutting into the page 'not dead' challenges the finality of Thurn's analysis and contravenes his ruling. Rupturing his clean and contained narrative in this way Barnes privileges the active process of 'remembering' over the more passive 'memory' and, in doing so, demonstrates the disruptive and messy potential of her autobiographic poetics.⁴²

Writing to Coleman in November 1937 Barnes further illuminates the significance of these annotations in explicitly addressing the tensions between untroubled narrative clarity and messy ambiguity – between exposure and secrecy – as they are balanced in her writing. She writes:

> I am very happy that you have come into a knowledge of what a home, family, blood ties mean. [...] I've said nothing to anyone: what a victory that you know now why I am so 'secret' [...] You see now why one must be secret? One must not betray that place, or it will heal up, and you'll know nothing more of it clearly, only to so few, a John [Homes], you, and ones [sic] secret book that one day becomes public, but still secret if written as it should be. Why did I just say 'will heal up'? That's exactly it, it just came out. The wound in the side of Christ.⁴³

In imposing this biographic framework and thinking himself capable of speaking for Barnes in 'betraying' the place from which her texts are woven, Thurn's letter attempts to clean up and cauterize the open 'wound' which Caselli and Taylor have more recently addressed as essential to an understanding of the 'complex relationships between personal disclosure and modernist art' traced by Barnes's autobiographic poetics.⁴⁴ Echoing the biblical episode of the incredulity of Thomas related in the Gospel of John in which the open wound testifies to both the identity and trials of Christ, and thus of his resurrection, Barnes's bleeding text is here directly connected to a conception of her autobiographic poetics. The open wound is a validation and a testimony to the disruptive power of return and recurrence; in exposing this 'secret place' the wound is healed, the connection between the past and the present severed, and intuitive understanding is lost. As Caselli has succinctly described:

> The revelation of the secret does not imply consolation, but a betrayal that obfuscates clarity. The secret, rather than producing obscurity, preserves clarity of vision, which would be lost once the secret goes public. The wound in the side of Christ needs to stay open as testimony: a healed wound is lost knowledge.⁴⁵

Just as Barnes expressed frustration at the repression of artistic intuition in favour of prescriptive analysis that she identified as central to the psychoanalytic method of revealing the secrets of the unconscious,[46] Barnes here equates the healed wound with a form of exposure and erasure – a reductive cleaning up or simplification of material which must be read alongside her 'innate dislike of parading, or "telling on" the innermost secret'. The 'secret' cannot be straightforwardly told or exposed except through art, and only then is it 'lifted into its own place, given back to itself'.

As many feminist critics have subsequently demonstrated, the models of subjectivity promoted by the methods of (auto)biographical analysis outlined over the course of this chapter have been almost exclusively masculine, white and middle class.[47] Such an overwhelming trend can be linked in the first instance to the historical tendency to record the public lives and achievements of 'great men' and the popular tendency to turn to these more accessible and established records in developing the field of autobiographical studies.[48] However, this historical gendering of autobiographic theory and practice also highlights ideological foundations for the genre's retrospectively and anxiously defined proximity to notions of facticity, truth and stability.

As outlined in my earlier discussion of the gendering of waste and certain anxieties related to the representation and experience of masculinity in the modern machine age, a rhetoric of containment, inviolability and wholeness became increasingly prevalent in attempts to stabilize masculinity in the face of the feminized flows of urban, industrial modernity. Circumventing these messy, fragmented and anxiously policed models of subjectivity, the return to essentialist notions of selfhood as at once unique and universal, transcendent and internally consistent, offered mid-century critics of autobiography a stable model of the self to draw on. When defined as requiring 'a man to take distance with regard to himself in order to constitute himself in the focus of his special unity and identity across time,'[49] autobiography could be celebrated as providing a 'vital impulse to order' in the construction and conception of an otherwise fragmented self.[50]

As such, the history of auto/biographic theory itself illuminates the tensions between the fantasies of a coherent, fully realized subject 'fixed' by the auto/biographic method and the representations of messy (inter)subjectivity that is put into high relief by Barnes's clearly stated aversion to biographic models and the disruptive patterns of her autobiographic poetics. In her resistance to the biographic project and her conception of writing as an open 'wound' outlined here, Barnes refuses the promise of textual disclosure that the genre purports to provide just as her texts consistently frustrate the biographic readings that they appear to invite. Instead, they present 'repetitions of a narrative that temptingly offers itself up as biographical and yet fails to work as a key to "disclose" the text'.[51] Returning to Barnes's evocative treatment of writing as a wound that Taylor identifies as central to Barnes's treatment of trauma and allows Caselli to develop her analysis of *Ryder* and *The Antiphon* as 'intertextual anatomies of revenge' which 'dissect the dead body of literature, study the politics of the family, and figure their own illegitimacy',[52] we can identify the importance of these repetitious patterns in structuring Barnes's mature autobiographic poetics according to a model wherein a 'realist version of "truth" as something single and unseamed is jettisoned'.[53]

Mediated through the wound which works as the sign and condition of these disruptive repetitions and antiphonal reverberations, Barnes's texts produce a 'narrative destabilisation' which insists that 'things are not over, that the story isn't finished, can never be finished, for some new item of information may alter the account that has been given'.[54] Moreover, whereas traditional accounts of autobiographic discourse promote developmental narratives within which individual growth occurs and is charted through time and both are presented as consistent, coherent and linear, the intertextual reverberations of Barnes's repetitious narratives and the pages of revised and rewritten manuscripts produced through her writing practice seriously disrupt Eliotian assumptions of the 'order' of history, narrative, linearity and genealogy and, with it, notions of legitimacy, originality, progeny and inheritance.

Considering the visceral qualities of the image of the open wound, the ways in which it ruptures the present by testifying to the past and providing the conditions for its resurrection, and Barnes's performance of this 'wounding' in her puncturing of the clean surface of the page containing Thurn's sealed account, the processes of repudiation and return involved in the structural model of waste examined throughout this thesis become increasingly relevant in addressing the 'disturbances' identified by Barnes as so essential to her work. Attention to the workings of waste in this way not only highlights the ideological imperatives shaping the various interpretative devices retrospectively used to contain these excessive narratives but allows us to frame a discussion of the production of textual mess and retrieval of repudiated and compromised material as active ingredients in Barnes's 'improper modernism', one which interrupts linearity and obscures narrative clarity in its complex, messy relationship to the patterns of memory and history.

As Stanley has emphasized in her authoritative account of auto/biographic discourse as announcing the 'interplay of one life with others', by its very definition autobiography is a messy and hybrid genre, which slides between literary and personal histories and generic classifications (confession, sexual confession, memoir, biography, fiction) collecting and collaging disparate and discarded material.[55] Just as nothing appears as new or original in the Barnes corpus, but is compromised by its retrieval of repudiated or used material, autobiography itself is highly revealing of the messy materiality and complex intertextuality structuring the Barnes oeuvre. However, as Barnes's 'wounding' of Thurn's letter exemplifies, the patterns of rupture and reverberation detailed here are not simply the result of the recurrent resonances of memory, history or narrative explored by autobiographic practices but can be identified within the unruly material messiness of the Barnes corpus itself.

ii. Textual waste and the structural patterns of Djuna Barnes's re-made modernism

> Barnes used red, blue, and green pens, often combining the colours on a single page. Some of the severely edited pages took on a visual life of their own, apart from any literary content.
>
> *Hank O'Neal, Life Is Painful, Nasty and Short*

As outlined in my introduction, from the editorial advice offered by Eliot and Coleman, to the introduction of O'Neal into Barnes's Patchin Place apartment in 1978, or the more recent publication of the *Collected Poems* (2006), a pervasive compulsion to 'clean up', order and make sense of Barnes's corpus and writing practice has been central to the shaping of Barnes criticism over the last decades and has proven particularly prevalent in relation to Barnes's later (post-1940) production, a period relatively slim in publications but voluminous in production. Careful attention to the ways in which Barnes's writing practice is documented across this late period as a form of compulsive revision is particularly revealing as to the importance of textual mess in the production of Barnes's 'improper modernism'. Elaborating on the accumulative and messy nature of Barnes's writing practices observed during his time assisting Barnes in the years 1978–1981, O'Neal describes her creative process in these later years as follows:

> She does have a tendency to save everything that is on a piece of paper, and to compound the problem she is forever making notations on anything in sight, and it then must be saved for future reference. Poems on grocery lists. All these papers are just piled up on her desk in no apparent order. She said there are many good poems buried under the heaps and scraps, but a mine-detector will be needed to find anything.[56]

Rather than repudiating mess and identifying waste, she actively produces and accumulates it, confounding distinctions between finished poem and obsolete draft.

The densely material and retentive nature of this process can be illuminated with reference to the messy intertextuality of the Barnes corpus itself. Generating temporal and generic instabilities Barnes's texts together act as palimpsests of literary history, disrupting notions of linearity and coherence as they re-inscribe antiquated echoes and estrange more attributable images or phrases. This macro disruption of the grand narratives of literary history is also replicated on the micro level of Barnes's own textual production, where extensive revisions and repetitions structure her corpus according to internal patterns of return, refrain and variation. Intimately linked to the forms and functions of Barnes's mature autobiographic poetics, these persistent processes of revision and the disorientating textual refrains and echoes that such practices engender enable the mobilization of individual phrases, powerful images, poetic fragments and the estranged echoes of other texts across nearly seventy years of work and through a range of journalism, poetry, drama, prose and personal correspondence, confounding notions of a definitive original or final text as a stable referent to uncover.[57]

At once cannibalizing itself and borrowing at will from other literary, biblical, mythological and historical sources the Barnes corpus demonstrates what Daniela Caselli has memorably described as a 'poetics of impropriety', an 'inopportune modernism [that] has never been fully absorbed within the literary history of the twentieth century because of its inherent scepticism towards genealogy and timeliness and of its staged illegitimate and belated self-conception'.[58] Anachronistic, stylistically challenging and linguistically perverse, Barnes's texts revel in their untimeliness – in their estrangement. From the loosely Jacobean verse structures reanimated by *The Antiphon*, to the imitation of woodcut illustrations or dripping Beardsleyesque ink drawings that Barnes chose as visual accompaniment to so much of her prose and poetry, or the fatally estranged Felix and Robin Volkbein – the one fixated by lineage, blood and his own ancestral illegitimacy, the other figured as 'the infected carrier of the past [...] who is eaten death returning' (*N*: 36) – the Barnes corpus resists opportunities to 'make it new' but returns again to the worn-out and debased, to the wastes of literary tradition and history.

As Caselli makes clear, notions of tradition, lineage and genealogy are invoked in Barnes's works only to be exposed as inauthentic, illegitimate and impure, a tendency which I apply as an essential component of her interest in experimentally autobiographic modes. Advocating a 'formal multiplicity' and 'excessive productivity' as more recent feminist theorists have been keen to point out, autobiographic modes effectively disrupt notions of a historically transcendent and coherent self, favouring instead a model of identity as contingent, conflicted and various.[59] Adopting Terry Threadgold's definition of poetics as the working on or with texts, we might productively discuss Barnes's 'belated' and 'illegitimate' modernism as directly informed by an active *poiesis*, a generative making and rewriting which is intimately linked to autobiographic modes in its disruption of 'official' narratives and complication of temporal cycles of birth and decay.[60]

As Julie Taylor has subsequently elaborated in her study of Barnes's 'affective modernism', the concept of belatedness is central to psychoanalytic studies of trauma which build on Freud's early observation that '*hysterics suffer mainly from reminiscences*'.[61] The return of repressed material so integral to the psychoanalytic process is of course also central to autobiographic forms in which a belated 'witnessing' is evoked at the point of writing, reading or performing the text. Similarly, both place considerable emphasis on the power of repetition and revision to disrupt the seemingly coherent categories of identity, memory and temporality evoked by the psychoanalytic or autobiographic subject.[62] Given that – as both Caselli and Taylor agree – Barnes's modernism spurns notions of 'originality' and 'authenticity' in its involvement with a kind of scavenging through literary histories and the perversion of those traditions through the jarring return of earlier literary forms, concepts and languages, structural relationships between textual mess, a poetics of waste and gendered modes of autobiographic discourse become increasingly apparent.

Operating at once as a strategy of containment and a radical means of disrupting identity, system and order, the structural functioning of waste – detailed in its historical and theoretical contexts previously – certainly provides a compelling model for addressing the extent to which the patterns of Barnes's mature autobiographic poetics and the messy materiality of her writing practice work together to 'keep the wound open'. In positioning the disruptive patterns of recurrence activated in the late poetry alongside Barnes's anxious revisions of the 'Baroness Elsa' biography we can see how the forms (messy revisions and incessant intertextuality) and functions ('keeping the wound open') of Barnes's writing might be effectively reconsidered according to a destabilizing logic of return familiar to both the structural functioning of waste and the regenerative processes of autobiographic modes of writing. Challenging the persistent interpretative emphasis on critical narratives of order, coherence and clarity, such a focus enables an effective repositioning of rupture, discontinuity and return as central to the production of Barnes's mature autobiographic poetics and writing practices – to her 'improper modernism'.

With recourse to the self-representational practices and the prominence of waste in the embodied aesthetics developed by the Baroness, I have already established a framework within which to consider the connections between the perceived 'messiness' of the Barnes corpus – its baroque excesses and opacities, the complex inter- and intra-textuality structuring her oeuvre, and the multiple fragments, drafts and revisions peppering the archives – and the 'biographical impulse' outlined above. Rather than approaching the complexities or difficulties of Barnes's texts as obfuscatory challenges to interpretation which might be overcome through biographic detetctive work, considering the Barnes corpus as preoccupied with forms and functions of waste not only illuminates the potentially disruptive dimensions of her 'poetics of impropriety' but exposes the methods and motivations behind attempts to 'clean up' the messy ambiguities of her texts.

Given the organizing focus imposed by the biographic impulse delineated above, it is perhaps unsurprising that discussions of what is commonly regarded as the most confusing, repetitive and seemingly chaotic period of Barnes's creative production are strongly inflected with popular representations of the writer as an elderly and uncommunicative recluse from this period. Popularized by Hank O'Neal's conflated account of his time with the *writer* and his organization of her *work* between 1978 and 1981, this version of Barnes – the Trappist living in alcoholic and misanthropic isolation and suffering from an inability to work – establishes conceptual connections between the body of an ailing, elderly woman and an unruly, secretive and evasive body of work.

As a way of grounding the textual instability and unreliability produced across the enormous bulk of material comprising the late period of Barnes's creative production including the Patchin Place poetry, *The Antiphon*, the posthumously published *Creatures in an Alphabet* and assorted prose fragments, discussions of this work frequently invoke the image of an ailing and aggressive Barnes, unable to keep her apartment, her writing or her own body in order. Detailing Barnes's physical condition alongside vivid descriptions of the messy Patchin Place apartment, Hank O'Neal's 'Barnes Diaries' archived in the Frances McCallough Papers at the University of Maryland are particularly illuminating in this respect. On first meeting her in September 1978, O'Neal carefully documents her physical condition alongside a detailed account of her living and working conditions. In his analysis, the elderly woman had a 'difficult time getting about', a frustrating immobility that is clearly echoed in his account of the stagnation of her writing process. As he catalogues she

> suffers from arthritis, emphysema, hardening of the arteries and has cataracts on both eyes [...] the desks are piled with papers, mostly poetry that is being worked and reworked. It is all typed and looks as though it is undergoing rather severe editing. Under the desks are more piles of paper, apparently being filed in some order.[63]

Certainly, such a slippage between textual and corporeal issues was not unfamiliar to Barnes's own correspondence which frequently moved between discussions of her latest projects and complaints about her health and distrust of doctors.[64] However, the direct conflation between the 'failed' attempts to organize her poetry and her 'failing' body tends to suggest that this work suffers from a form of textual unwieldiness and messiness which demands some form of critical interference. Working directly with Barnes in organizing her papers and preparing a list of 'approved' poems, O'Neal rectifies a disorderliness that he connects with her physical condition. Unable to make progress with her poetry, despite her efforts, O'Neal records that 'she added that there are pieces of poems scattered about; one part of a poem is here another part is over there and she can't see well enough to put all the pieces together'.[65] Like the tooth that needs filling and the bills that need paying, the critic – after Hank O'Neal – appears charged with the responsibility of imposing the order that an elderly and decidedly disorderly Barnes could not. In this respect, it is the critic himself who is metonymically reimagined as O'Neal's mine-detector, blasting apart the 'heaps and scraps' to salvage the valuable poetic fragments buried underneath.[66] Justifying the imposition of such organizing frameworks, the material bulk of this production is re-imagined as waste which must be identified and repudiated before order, sequence and clarity can be reinstated and the final or definitive version extracted cleanly and entirely.

Just as the employment of biographic models as interpretative tools for decoding Barnes's more obscure texts could be traced as attempts to seal up the 'open wound' essential to her autobiographic poetics, this critical concern with organizing and streamlining the textual mess produced by Barnes's accumulative and retentive writing practice insists on re-imposing the organizing frameworks of linearity and chronology disrupted by the open and repetitious cycles produced by these discontinuous fragments and revisions in the first place. Such textual unruliness is reiterated as a matter of critical concern by the editors of the *Collected Poems*. Describing their project an attempt to 'bring order to chaos', the editors invoke O'Neal's account in presenting this body of work as disruptive, repetitive and at times incoherent.[67]

Recapitulating what Nancy Levine articulated as the 'rescue work' of Hank O'Neal, such critical approaches to the Patchin Place manuscripts demonstrate a tendency to validate a sometimes ruthless process of selection and exclusion with extensive reference to the 'struggles of the mature poet with poems that are more in draft stage than complete' (*CP*: 4).[68] The editorial aim in organizing this work and preparing it for publication is thus explicitly stated as an attempt to 'bring order to late drafts so that the reader can appreciate Barnes's poetic skill and see her literary efforts as a continuing process' (*CP*: 4).

Densely accumulative and refusing straightforward distinctions between polished draft and obsolete waste, Barnes's messy writing practice is thus rationalized through a critical emphasis on continuity and coherence, as is elaborated in this illuminating reference to her laborious process of revising and working over manuscripts:

> Rather than continuing yesterday's draft, she would usually begin anew each morning. She would first set down by hand the makings of a poem, type the text, and then correct it time and again, thus producing multiple versions of the same poem in a sequential order which is normally unclear. Typically, she typed an original with two carbon copies, and in almost every case the handwritten corrections on the three versions are different. Then she would incorporate some of the previous day's corrections, type a new version, and make new corrections by hand. (*CP*: 8)

In a highly suggestive reiteration of O'Neal's documentary account, Herring here emphasizes the existence of a temporal sequence of improvement and evolution, postulating an inherent but obscured structure at work across the multiple versions and possible variants of any one poem. This desire to uncover the sequential order of the drafts clearly locates textual value in linearity, transparency and coherence while the model of textual evolution and refinement proposed by the editors privileges a final and most fully realized version or poetic *product* at the expense of close attention to the *processes* at work in Barnes's poetic production.

The extent to which Barnes's own writing demonstrates a consistent interest in such processes is evident from her early days as a journalist in New York. Visiting the Hippodrome and interviewing its artistic director Arthur Voetglin in 1915, Barnes's journalistic attention is focused less on the large-scale performances incorporating dancers, animals and impressive pyrotechnics than on the organizational structures of the spectacle itself. In a rich *tableaux vivant* which is worth considering here in an illumination of the processes at work behind Barnes's own creative production, the young journalist complicates the smooth functioning of the spectacle by drawing attention to the labour involved in its production:

> Under lights that glowed like oppressed glowworms trellised in, and under the strain of the hums of many machines, some twenty tailors and dressmakers sat, backs towards us, like people in a dream. [...] They turned and sewed and turned again, and always silently, but for the sound of the wheel – the machine went on – a half-circle of half-finished garments for the season 1915.[69]

As Laura Winkiel has elegantly demonstrated, this piece is particularly representative of the deep interest demonstrated across Barnes's early journalism in the changing forms of public culture and her interest in documenting the 'shift from live, interactive forms of entertainment to mass culture spectacles'.[70] In highlighting the extent to which the show is reduced to the technologies of its production, Winkiel's examination of the 'smooth, polished surfaces of commodified spectacle' clearly resonates with Siegfried Kracauer's elaboration of the workings of the 'Mass Ornament', as Goody has elaborated upon.[71] Certainly, the mechanized and carefully regulated bodies of the workers here directly echo the alienated action performed by the fragmented bodies of the Tiller Girls and recall the discussion of 'übermarionettes' in the previous chapter. Like the 'indissoluble girl clusters whose movements are demonstrations of mathematics',[72] or the fetishized mecanomorphic portraits familiar to New York Dada, human and mechanic qualities are blurred as the mechanized workers move 'like people in a dream' in unbroken unison to the metronomic whirr of the wheel maintained by their 'booted feet', their activity overseen by the tyrannical 'Silver King' in the production of his spectacular Hippodrome fantasies.

However, while the arresting image of faceless workers toiling away in silent and dimly lit monotony might, initially, seem to support a case for the alienation of the modern artist and spectator under the conditions of the 'transformation of public culture from local, heterogeneous sites of entertainment to the capitalized, homogenized culture industry', such a reading overlooks a subtle but suggestive metaphor for the activity involved in the production of Barnes's somewhat excessive textuality and of her mature autobiographic poetics.[73] If we are to dissociate the writing process from the notion of a final, ideal product to which it is working towards, the working bodies of the seamstresses, stitching together bits of old material in the construction of 'half-finished garments', present a powerful image of the writer recycling fragments and scraps in a generative making and unmaking. Proceeding through a process of revision, repetition and variation, material is 'turned and sewed and turned again' by the writer and seamstress alike whose hands both work 'over a thing not complete, ever catching up to a perfection that would never be quite understood'.

While the critical 'rescue work' detailed here might task itself with the uncovering of the author's ideal intention – the perfect, final and pared down 'version' of a text – Barnes's messy writing practices and conception of her autobiographic poetics as an open wound complicate the possibility of finality or 'closure' in these terms. Indeed, following the example set by Barnes's Silver King, we might suggest that the author's idealized intentions must remain similarly unrealized in material reality as completion and 'closure' in this sense is itself a fantasy, thus binding the seamstresses and the author alike to this mode of perpetual production. As Levine details, Barnes perfected a form of 'endlessly protracted composition' throughout this later period.[74] Acutely aware of the accumulative nature of a set of writing practices which produced 'literally tens of pages to one stanza', Barnes also confessed her compulsion to revise, to 'change it, over and over, until the room is ten feet high with one canto'.[75] This practice involved not only the rewriting of typescripts, but cutting into existing manuscripts in the same way that her annotations reopened the sealed account provided by Thurn's detailed above, until her manuscripts were refigured as 'palimpsests encrusted with addendum in red, green, and black ink written in her painfully crabbed hand'.[76]

iii. 'Circulation in the theme': Repetition, refrain and variation across the Patchin Place cycles

> Beware old women, like dried wasps (or small spiders) that can come out of the crystal stage, and bite again.
>
> *Djuna Barnes, 'As Cried' Manuscript*

As even a cursory reading of the *Collected Poems* highlights, the linear and sequential approach to the Patchin Place poetry proposed by the editor's treatment of it as a document of progressive improvement or an interrupted attempt at the extraction of slim volume from the mess of material is immediately frustrated by the densely woven webs of intertextual exchanges animating not only the work from this late period, but reverberating across the entire corpus in un-contained and unwound echoes and refrains. As Herring points out (and Scott Herring has more recently engaged with) attempts to put these pieces in their proper place by organizing them into cleanly divided cycles according to motif or theme is continually frustrated on the grounds that 'it is difficult to recognise disparate themes for the various cycles, with names like "As Cried", "Gardens for old men", "Dereliction", "Nativity", "Obsequies", "Rakehell", "Sardonics", "Tom Fool", "Jackdaw", and "The Laughing Lamentations of Dan Corbeau", because she often transferred lines from one cycle to another' (*CP*: 6).[77]

Reading across these pieces is not simply a matter of charting the repetition or replacement of words, images and poetic fragments in order to trace the successive stages of a poem's gestation but points to the development of a complex system of retention, return and reclamation at play across Barnes's 'bewildering' corpus. Engaged in an ongoing process of revision, poetic fragments and images slide unfixed across this body of work, and language itself loses its referential function as words are dislocated from their meanings and re-contextualized within new images and archaisms. In a strikingly organic manner, it is possible to trace the ways in which poems 'start out singly, develop offshoots, become longer affairs, split like amoebae'.[78] However, rather than supporting a biologically grounded notion of evolution in which processes of selection and recurrent traits might be traced as a pattern of improvement in the cycle's genealogical structure, such biological metaphors are undercut and temporal sequence is confused by the doubling and dividing of lines, words and phrases. Echoing Levine, it is this process of substitution, recurrence and reverberation that informs Caselli's notion of an illegitimate and even incestuous production, a 'poetics in which genealogy and descent are challenged but not replaced by an alternative lineage [...] but constantly evoked and undermined'.[79]

In her refusal to repudiate textual or literary 'wastes' and in the overproduction of her texts, Barnes does not develop a poetics of *refinement* but of *recovery* and *regeneration*.[80] As Levine details and the archives attest to, multiple variations of individual poems were produced and retained without seeming to privilege a 'final' version. While over ninety versions of the poem

'As Cried' were filed by Barnes, the material relating to the 'Man cannot purge his body of its theme' pieces exceeded some five hundred drafts and continued in other cycles. Tellingly, rather than approaching the voluminous drafts and multiple variations comprising this material as related to a larger project involving the elaborate construction of interrelated poetic cycles divided across various 'cantos', Phillip Herring emphasizes contraction and refinement in his treatment of this material: 'Her technique, as always, was to write numerous versions of the same poem [...] out of this multiplicity of drafts Barnes finally managed to distil a poem of only three lines called "Rite of Spring"' (*CP*: 16). Published in *Grand Street* in 1982 and obviously related to the mass of other (often much longer, messier) manuscripts, this crystalline tercet might initially seem to conform to the principles of refinement and distillation proposed by Herring:

> Man cannot purge his body of its theme
> As can the silkworm on a running thread
> Spin a shroud to re-consider in. (*CP*: 145)

However, while it might be tempting to position this published version as a definitively final and self-contained poem and to thus rationalize the messiness of Barnes's writing practice during this period as reflective of an unfinished editorial process, such an approach ignores the (re)generative capacity activated within a poetic economy where words, images and whole lines do not move in one refining direction through one cycle, but across a series of intersections and involutions, mapping complex patterns of recurrence and refrain more familiar to musical composition.[81]

In his commentary on this published poem, Phillip Herring highlights Barnes's typed annotation on the otherwise clean typescript: 'twenty years trying to finish this poem' (*CP*: 145). While this note might appear to uphold chronological readings of the drafts as leading to this endpoint, the formulation of 'trying' in the continuous present is significant. Used as a transitive verb here it is clear that the effort is expended in attempts to complete the poem. However, the slippery nature of 'trying' when isolated as intransitive verb or adjective also conflates the act of expending effort with its effects: neither the attempt at finishing the poem nor the 'trying' nature of these efforts is complete.

Indeed, any attempt to read this poem as final and finished is further undermined by Barnes's extended comments on another typescript of the same, three-line poem. On this undated version Barnes details her frustration at *The New Yorker*'s initial rejection of the piece after Barnes (characteristically) refused to change a word in her submission. She describes the piece as 'a totally new idea, as a poem "in progress" as Joyce's "Work in Progress" was to become "Finnegans Wake" [...] the booby [Howard] Moss was too stupid to see, and lost the first new move, in poetry, a poem waiting, to be continued' (*CP*: 145). Any notion of the 'finished poem' becomes impossible under Barnes's conceptual and grammatical formation here; the poem that Barnes has allegedly spent twenty years 'trying' to finish cannot be completed while the expenditure of this effort and its effects on her are still being felt, and so the poem must instead be re-imagined as the basis for the production of further pieces.[82] Interestingly, in citing a letter from Barnes to Frances McCallough, Levine identifies this 'new idea' as a poetic *cycle* rather than an individual poem. Positioned at the opening of the 'Late Unpublished Poems' section of Herring and Stutman's *Collected Poems*, 'Dereliction' (Man cannot purge ...)' is, as the editors suggest, related to both the published 'Rite of Spring' and No. 19 in the approved 'List'.

> Man cannot purge his body of its theme,
> As goes the silkworm ferrying her thread,
> To baste a shroud to metamorphose in
> From a silk-proud mouth
> But no sanctuary in the fossil's eye,
> Pander, pass by. (*CP*: 149)

One of three versions completed over three days and archived in the same folder, this poem is dated 1 June 1971 and is clearly related to 'The Rite of Spring'. While the opening of the poem points one way, the fifth line of the poem intertextually connects both 'Dereliction (Man cannot purge ...)' and 'Rite of Spring' to a series of poems including the line 'There is no gender in the fossil's eye' with variations on 'gender' including 'bargain', 'sanctuary', 'heaven', 'seasons' and 'sessions'. These poems are distributed across several folders including *There is no gender in the fossil's eye*, *Dereliction* and *Descant* and connect seemingly distinct pieces including 'Dereliction (Man cannot purge ...)', 'Descant (There is no gender ...)', 'The Honeydew', 'Dereliction (There is no sanctuary)' and 'Satires (Man cannot purge ...)'.

Identifying 'Dereliction (Man cannot purge ...)' as a draft 're-working' of 'Rite of Spring', the editors divide the heterometric poem into an opening, blank verse quatrain and closing couplet 'unconnected to the previous four' (*CP*: 149). Bisecting the poem in this manner, they not only arrest many of the intertextual reverberations briefly alluded to here but also gloss the densely imbricated nature

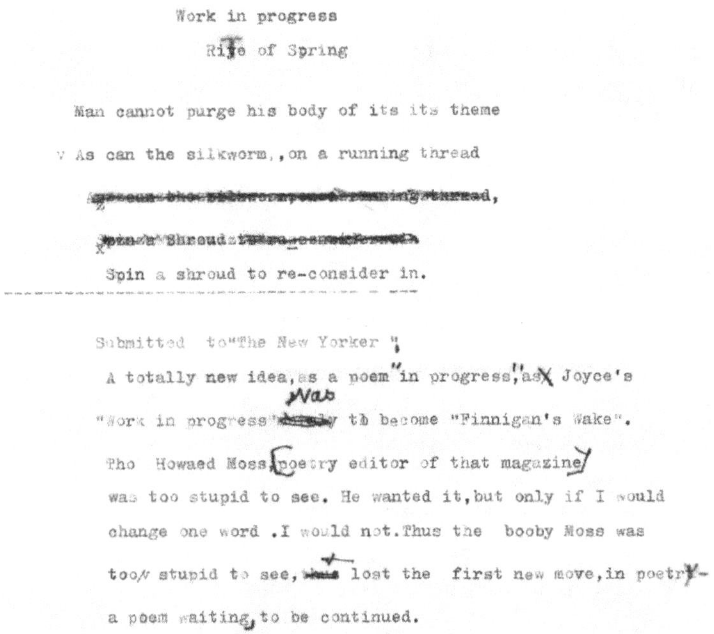

```
          Work in progress
             Rife of Spring

  Man cannot purge his body of its its theme
v As can the silkworm,,on a running thread
  ~~green the silkworm spinning thread~~,
  ~~spin a Shroud to re-consider in~~
x
  Spin a shroud to re-consider in.
------------------------------------------

  Submitted to "The New Yorker ",
                      "
  A totally new idea,as a poem in progress,"as Joyce's
                          was
  "Work in progress" ~~simply~~ to become "Finnigan's Wake".
                         ^
  Tho Howaed Moss[poetry editor of that magazine]
  was too stupid to see. He wanted it,but only if I would
  change one word .I would not.Thus the  booby Moss was
                           ↑
  too/ stupid to see, ~~has~~ lost the  first new move,in poetry -
  a poem waiting,to be continued.
```

Figure 21 Djuna Barnes, 'Work in Progress: Rite of Spring'. Typescript, undated. Special Collections, The University of Maryland at College Park Libraries.

of these cycles and the connections forged between these two poems. As the editors highlight, the closing couplet of 'Dereliction (Man cannot purge ...)' – 'But no sanctuary in the fossil's eye / Pander, pass by' – reappears and is recycled across several of the other poems: a variation on the couplet closing 'Dereliction (Man cannot purge ...)' opens 'Dereliction (There are no sessions ...)', which in turn lends material to 'Discant (Pregnant women …)' and appears in 'Descant (There is no gender …)' and so on. Opening with a variation of the closing couplet from 'Dereliction (Man cannot purge …)', 'There is no sanctuary in a fossil's eye / *Voyeur*, pass by', 'Dereliction (There is no sanctuary …)' develops Barnes's mediations on the themes of time, ageing, death and resurrection that preoccupy many of these poems.

Echoing the opening lines of Nos 30 and 31 from the approved 'List' which call for 'gardens for old men' to 'twitter' and 'whimper', respectively, in collapsing the cycle of birth and death with the affecting image of the 'breastmilk in his lamentations still', this poem also intertextually reconnects the two parts of 'Dereliction (Man cannot purge …)' deemed unrelated by the editors. A variation of this line reappears in 'Satires (Man cannot purge …)', part of a thirteen-page 'canto' dated March 1968 which opens with a revision of the silkworm couplet familiar to 'Rite of Spring' and 'Dereliction (Man cannot purge …)':

> Man cannot purge his body of its theme,
> As does the silk-worm ferry forth her thread,
> High Commander, tell me what is man
> And what surmise?
> Is breast milk in the lamentation yet?
> O predacious victim of the wheel,
> St. Catherine of roses, turn your gaze
> Where woe is;
> Purge the body of its dread,
> As does the bombace from her furnace heave
> To weave a shroud to metamorphose in?
> To re-consider in
> What bolt of havoc holds your dread?
> On what cast of terror are you fed?[83] (*CP*: 150)

Identified by the editors as unrelated, the two sections of 'Dereliction (Man cannot purge …)' presenting the image of the silkworm and fossil's eye, respectively, must then be reconsidered in closer proximity once this multi-directional circularity has been established. While the opening two lines are nearly identical to those of 'Dereliction (Man cannot purge …)', this sonnet in blank verse expands the meditation by posing a series of questions which visually separates the activity of the silkworm from the effects of these labours; that is, her spinning thread and the luxury of detached self-reflexivity that such activity affords.

The first of these questions reintroduces the 'what is man theme' which opens both 'Laughing Lamentations' and 'As Cried' and appears in the second stanza of the tellingly titled 'The Rounds' from 1965. In its strict patterns of rhyme and metre 'The Rounds' is strikingly formal: three stanzas composed of seven, chain rhymed lines in iambic and trochaic pentameter. These tight formal patterns enable both the interplay of narrative and bleak commentary across the stanzas and a circulation of theme and poetic material through and beyond the limits of the poem. While the poem is not a roundel, the metrical regularity, internal rhyme schemes and repetition of words certainly reference the form popularized by Swimburne in the patterns of return and refrain that it establishes. Indeed, Barnes's handwritten comment 'Not in proper sequence' on an otherwise clean typescript of this page not only elucidates the process of substitution and exchange at work across these poems in which the opening lines of a second stanza in one poem spawn a series of seemingly distinct pieces, but encourages a broader reading of the poems together as a looser form of roundel in which patterns of refrain and return are (re)generated across metrically familiar items. If we are to consider the recurring lines 'Man cannot purge', 'what is man' and 'there are no sessions' along with their variations as *refrains*, their positioning at the opening of so many of these pieces is striking considering the roundel's specification of the repetition of the beginning of first lines in its formal construction.

The second question posed by 'Satires (Man cannot purge ...)', 'Is breastmilk in the lamentation yet?' tightly binds the intertextual relationships between this poem, 'Dereliction (Man cannot purge ...)' and 'Dereliction (There is no sanctuary ...)' and weaves further reverberating patterns through other poetic fragments and 'cantos', as has been suggested above. Intimately related to each other and echoing out beyond themselves to other recurring images and motifs at work across the Barnes corpus, this 'messy' late period of Barnes's poetic production generates a fluid, multi-directional network figured through a regenerative series of exchanges, substitutions and variations. Facilitated by the messy materiality of Barnes's writing practices and intimately related to the forms of her mature autobiographic poetics, the open networks activated in the Patchin Place poetry in which nothing is cast off but is allowed to circulate, attach to other fragments and generate new poetic sequences problematize conceptions of the poetry as autonomous, single and self-contained structures.

The mobility and mutability of Barnes's poetic process outlined here are not restricted to the work of the mature poet but, as Melissa Jane Hardie has suggested, can be identified as early as the 1915 chapbook of 'rhythms and drawings', *The Book of Repulsive Women*, in which a process of echoing and substitution moves through the slim volume as 'poems are referred to each other both through subject matter and placement in the volume'.[84] Close structural and metrical similarities compound this process of replication, refrain and variation across this volume as 'Corpse A' is mirrored by 'Corpse B' and 'In General' is counterpointed by 'In Particular', generating an uncanny poetics which destabilizes and complicates the belief in an authentic original from which to deviate in the first place. As Hardie demonstrates, 'Repulsion' itself figures this reflexive 'turning' as a structural trope throughout the volume, referring not just to the decadent and 'repulsive' women who refuse to function as points of attraction, but the structural patterns of rhyme and replication which maintain tensions between the forces of attraction and repulsion throughout the volume.

Looking closely at the figuration of the turned/turning women in *The Book of Repulsive Women*, Hardie makes compelling connections between Barnes's treatment of rhyme and her extensive textual revisions. Considering the way in which rhyme operates according to a logic of substitution through aural familiarity and connecting the figure of the turning woman with this aural logic, Hardie positions rhyme as effectively problematizing conceptions of a poem as a fixed and closed system of reference given the production of a range of possible phonic substitutions produced beyond each word; indeed, 'rhyme instantiates revision' here.[85] Structurally operating according to an 'internal system of derivation', Hardie's analysis of the working of rhyme thus establishes the critical ground from which to consider Barnes's messy writing practices as a deliberate strategy of deferral and retention, one that works with the corpus's retrieval and estrangement of the outdated and antiquated from literary history in order to mark the 'dialectical relationship between modernity and history as its returned repressed'.[86]

Considering the activation of these arrangements across the early and late poetry and their re-emergence in the structures organizing Barnes's late tragedy in blank verse, *The Antiphon*, it might be valuable to highlight that the English usage of 'verse' is somewhat fluid and can be used interchangeably as a definition of a single unit, a stanza, and 'poetry' itself. Moreover, emerging from the Latin *vertere*, 'to turn', the term 'verse' is also etymologically infused with the mobility described here, particularly interesting if we consider this alongside the etymological root of 'poetry', 'to make'. Barnes's versification is quite pointedly a *making* from *turning*, a notion that is set in particularly high relief given the recurrent and metamorphosing image of the worm across these cycles.[87]

While obviously linked to the evocative and pervasive image of the silkworm to which we shall return presently, Barnes's specific use of the 'inch-worm' in the opening line of 'The Rounds', repeated in the opening of 'Dereliction (Does the inch-worm …)' not only compounds the relationship between the spinning silkworm and the 'what is man theme' explored throughout the collaged 'cantos' and cycles collected here, but is particularly well-suited as a metaphor of processes of return and refrain. Specifically referring to the larvae of Geometer moths, so named for their particular looping movement through which they appear to be measuring the earth they pass over, the expansion and contraction of the inch-worm's body as it moves are not unlike the pattern of stressed and unstressed feet propelling the sequence(s) forwards through longer quatrains and shorter tercets bridged with a central, matched rhyme, drawing material apart and together across this poem and the repeating cycles.

If the inch-worm offers a compelling natural analogy for the metrical structures of these poems and the drawing together and separating of material that occurs across the cycles, the evocative and recurring image of the labouring silkworm so effectively deployed across these poetic variants and beyond provides an illuminating insight into Barnes's conception of her messily regenerative writing practices and 'wounded' poetics. In keeping with the formal traditions of the sonnet, the juxtaposition of the silkworm's embodied activity and the 'what is man theme' maintained in dialectical antagonism in 'Satires (Man cannot purge …)' is 'resolved' to a certain extent with the subtle introduction of a third party – the writer. While man is unable to make the material of his life at once a part of himself and a separate shroud from within which to self-reflexively review this life, the silkworm's embodied and perpetual (so long as it does not complete its task) activity presents a natural metaphor for the labours of the writer, especially the writer who self-consciously reworks narrative material from life into their literary projects.

In his commentary for the published 'Rite of Spring', Herring includes an aside attempting to explain the silkworm's recurrence across these pieces with reference to a marginal note on an apparently unrelated poem 'Laughing Lamentations of Corbeau' dated 19 June 1966. As Herring suggests, the quote – 'The silkworm after having spun her task, lays her eggs and dies' – is taken from Joseph Addison's Essay No. 111 in *The Spectator* (1711), which, upon first inspection, seems like a strangely inadequate 'clue' to Barnes's use of the silkworm. Indeed, such brevity and finality seem to sit uncomfortably with the emphasis on resurrection, regeneration and mobility outlined here.[88] However, considered in the context of the essay as an extended meditation on the 'Immortality of the soul', a more nuanced picture emerges. As Addison surmises, to be able to imagine the human soul as capable of achieving perfection places it in a state of decline; assuming it can no longer improve, the soul is rendered 'incapable of further enlargements, I could imagine it might fall away insensibly, and drop at once into a State of Annihilation'. Instead, the argument for the immortality of the soul must be driven by notions of 'the perpetual progress of the Soul to its Perfection, without a possibility of ever arriving at it'. By contrast, 'Man, considered in his present state seems only sent into the World to propagate his kind. He provides himself with a Successor, and immediately quits his Post to make room for him.'[89]

Ideas of succession and irresponsible procreation feature prominently in Barnes's work, most notably forming the narrative focus of *Ryder* and *The Antiphon*'s examination of familial dynamics. Rather than upholding bourgeois notions of inheritance and lineage, the burden of succession in both texts does not fall to an individual but to Wendell's/Titus's philosophy unfolded in the lives of his children, an intrusion of the past into the present. The tragic action of *The Antiphon*, the malevolence of some of its characters and the final act of filicide all dramatize the working out of the deceased patriarch's 'inheritance' and it is significant that the silkworm reappears in the third act during Augusta and Miranda's final exchanges. Throughout this act, it is Augusta who continually protests her innocence, alternating between fierce attacks on the daughter who refused to 'make me something' (III, 186) and plaintive requests to undo time and be reborn through Miranda. Giving voice to years of unspoken abuse and betrayal, Miranda demands:

> How is it that women who love children
> So often damn the children that they have?
> Would you propose a beggared silk-worm draw
> From out her haggard poke so brave a silk
> Could card a paragon? (III, 187)

In this passage the expatriate writer Miranda recasts herself as the 'beggared silk-worm' whose 'haggard poke' is not equal to the task of casting a shroud for her mother to metamorphose in.[90] With no children of her own this 'well-used spinster' (II, 137) not only refuses Addison's notion of Man's interest in succession but refuses to provide the narrative through which Augusta might be reborn to a new account. On the contrary, Augusta is left to fear, 'May God protect us! I wonder what you'll write / When I'm dead and gone' (III, 182). Retaining the gendered pronoun favoured by Addison and familiar to manifestations of the silkworm across Jacobean literature, Barnes's silkworm is not merely an animal 'formed for our use' and limited to the action of procreation, but involved in a dynamic and creative activity that, in *The Antiphon*, is explicitly connected to the labours of the writer. While 'Man' remains limited to his condition, the gendered activity of Barnes's silkworm appropriates the perpetual process of deferral described by Addison as the soul's progress towards an impossible to realize perfection.

This tonal shift might be further illuminated with reference to a further set of intertextual echoes incipient in the image of the silkworm. As Caselli has highlighted, further than the Addison reference, Barnes's invocation of the silkworm carries other intertextual resonances including John Donne's *Sermons* and Thomas Middleton's *The Revenger's Tragedy*, both owned and annotated by Barnes. While the gendered pronoun remains in Middleton's tragedy, the expenditure of the silkworm's labour figured as finite and brief is markedly reworked in the famous lines delivered by Vendice to the skull in Act III, scene v:

> Does the silkworm expend her yellow labours
> For thee? For thee does she undo herself?
> Are Lordships sold to maintain ladyships
> For the poor benefit of a bewitching minute?[91]

Directly challenging the limited scope of Addison's silkworm, who spins, procreates and dies, the 'yellow labours' expended by Middleton's silkworm are re-framed as a dynamic and perpetual creativity.[92]

While the more oblique published 'Rite of Spring' directly contrasts man's inability to separate his 'theme' from his body with the easily 'running thread' of the silkworm, 'Dereliction (Man cannot purge ...)' develops this meditation by further compounding associations between the image of the spinning silkworm and the messy materiality of Barnes's own wounded poetics. Establishing a metonymic relation between the activity of the silkworm and a compulsive form of remaking familiar to the laborious revisions undertaken by the writer, Barnes here develops the image of the running thread with the introduction of the line 'To baste a shroud to metamorphose in'. Taken from the Middle English *basten* and old French *bastir* (to build), the process of basting alluded to by Barnes here refers specifically to the process preferred by seamstresses whereby pieces of material were sewed loosely together with large, running stitches to temporarily hold them together while the garment was being made. A substitution of the more reflective 're-consider' for the active image of resurrection and renewal evoked by 'metamorphose' is thus grounded upon the reintroduction of stitching and sewing imagery powerfully evoked by the Hippodrome's toiling seamstresses.

While this 'basting' is absent from several variants, its traces remain and it serves to bolster the dense figuration of the silkworm as a condensed metaphor uniting the messy revisions and repetitions involved in the *activity* of Barnes's writing, with the unfinished *subject* of her poetic cycles and wounded poetics. In terms of form and content then, Barnes's silkworm poems artfully deploy a strategy of revision, repetition and variation in order to radically destabilize linearity and singularity. Conceptually connected to the repetitive action of the seamstresses stitching, the basting silkworm brings together the multiple variants and heterogeneous pieces of these poetic cycles and exposes them as engaged in an ongoing process of revision and metamorphosis. Furthermore, intimately connected to the autobiographic text and subject in the mode of embodied and perpetual labour that it represents, the condensed image of the silkworm 'discloses the autobiographical subject as unfixed; as fragmented, discontinuous, heterogeneous; as engaged in continuous revision and transformation'.[93]

In this respect, the closing couplet dismissed by Herring as 'unrelated' takes on a new significance. In counterpoint to the generative making and unmaking presented by the spinning and stitching silkworm, the 'fossil's eye' initially appears as an image of arrested movement, of stasis and belonging, definitively, to the past. At once belonging to a past geological age, fixed and time-frozen, the fossil as it reappears in the present moment has performed an incredible leap through time, staging the return of something that should have disappeared and tuned to dust centuries ago. However, as something *pre*historic, the value of the fossil is that it exists outside of time, a place before recorded history, before the division of time into years, 'seasons', 'sessions' or 'quarters'. Just as Jack and Miranda's return to the decaying ancestral home in *The Antiphon* introduces the themes of return and remembering as a form of rupture, the surfacing of the fossil stages its own 'rip in nature' (I, 8), fracturing the supposedly stable frameworks of 'nature', time and history. As a concentrated palimpsest of time and existence, the fossil record acts as a mode of spatialized natural history; produced through a process of sedimentation, the fossil returns through a temporal vortex, enacting a vertical disruption of the supposedly linear sequences of time and history.

Following the example of the silkworm whose self-made shroud simultaneously evokes the cloth within which the dead are wound in mourning rituals and the means of remaining hidden from view or concealed, Barnes similarly collapses this notion of time experienced as linear sequence – a coherent line from birth to death – across these pieces. This process is figured in 'Satires (Man cannot purge ...)' through the confusion and infusion of 'breastmilk' with the tears from 'the lamentation' and clearly activated across the multiple drafts and revisions relating to this cycle. Like the axial movement of the silkworm's spinning which effects a simultaneous unwinding and spinning, temporal sequence is externalized, not as a straight line to walk down, but as a circularity to be cast within, reinforced by the sliding substitutions from St Catherine's spiked wheel to the ornamental Rose windows familiar to Gothic architectural embellishment invoked by the poem.

With the thumping repetition of 'dread' in the second half of the poem, clear connections are established between the ability to 'Purge this body of its dread' and the activity involved in the weaving of 'a shroud to metamorphose in? / To re-consider in'. Sliding across a range of substituted signifiers, the recurring references to St Catherine implored to aid in this purging ritual reinforce the circularity and mobility involved in such activity. Unlike the spinning silkworm, the poem can only rhetorically reflect on the torture of man's arrested stasis: 'what bolt of havoc holds your dread'. The positioning of circularity rather than sequence as a guiding principle of the spatio-temporal organization of the internal structures of these pieces is of course replicated through the accumulative seriality instantiated by Barnes's extensive revisions and annotations. An individual poem does not proceed in time through various sequential drafts but lines are unpicked and re-stitched at different points in time, their threads looped across drafts in recurring patterns and motifs until the text starts to resemble the densely interwoven structures more common to textiles than texts, connecting the poem intertextually to other pieces in an impossibly 'unfinished' process.

The axial movement described by the silkworm's activity here in relation to the unspooling of time and accretion of memory is strongly reminiscent of French philosopher Henri Bergson's theories relating to time and consciousness, most notably that of his foundational theory of 'duration' first proposed in his doctoral thesis *Time and Free Will: An Essay on the Immediate Data of Consciousness* (1889) and developed throughout in the later essays *An Introduction to Metaphysics* (1903) and *Creative Evolution* (1907). Approaching the question of reality through an inward contemplation of the self, Bergson details the 'layers' of perception accreted to the surface of our 'inner life' including perceptions which come to the self from the material world, memories near the surface of the mind which remain somewhat detached from the stuff of the self, and repeated, habitual action bound to these perceptions and memories.[94] Radiating from the inside out, these layers 'form, collectively, the surface of a sphere which tends to grow larger and lose itself in the exterior world'. Tracing these layers 'beneath the sharply cut crystals and this frozen surface', Bergson suggests, we find this 'inner life', 'a continuous flux […] a succession of states, each of which announces that which follows and contains that which precedes it'.[95] In a famous description of duration, Bergson presents the doubled image of unwinding and rolling up familiar to the labour of the silkworm favoured by Barnes:

> This inner life may be compared to the unrolling of a coil, for there is no living being who does not feel himself gradually to the end of his role; and to live is to grow old. But it may just as well be compared to a continual rolling up, like that of a thread on a ball, for our past follows us, it swells incessantly with the present that it picks up on its way; and consciousness means memory.[96]

Refining this idea of duration, Bergson proceeds to present the image of the 'myriad-tinted spectrum' and, finally, that of 'an infinitely small elastic body, contracted, if it were possible to a mathematical point'. Focusing less on the line that is generated than the *action* by which it is traced, Bergson privileges movement, 'the act of tension or extension; in short, pure mobility' in describing the image of the self in duration.[97] While Bergson ultimately rejects such metaphors as capable of fully expressing the dual action of duration, this notion of 'pure mobility' allows him to shift his discussion from 'a thing already made' to an emphasis on duration as *process*, something 'continually in the making', as it does for Barnes.

'Pure mobility' and 'multiplicity' certainly present themselves as attractive terms through which to explain the regenerative series of exchanges, substitutions and variations that characterize this 'messy' late period of Barnes's poetic production. Facilitated by the messy materiality of Barnes's writing practices and intimately related to the forms of her mature autobiographic poetics, the fluid, multi-directional networks activated in the Patchin Place poetry in which nothing is cast off but is allowed to circulate, attach to other fragments and generate new poetic sequences problematize conceptions of the poetry as autonomous, single and self-contained structures. Intimately related to each other and reverberating out beyond themselves, the intertextual echoes of these poems not only reach beyond the formal boundaries of their internal metrical, syntactical and thematic patterns, but ensure that nothing in the corpus remains fixed or final, but is continually remade, not simply by the interlaced patterns of substitution and recurrence connecting these poetic cycles, but in the ongoing processes of revision and repetition and that characterizes the dense materiality of Barnes's writing practice.

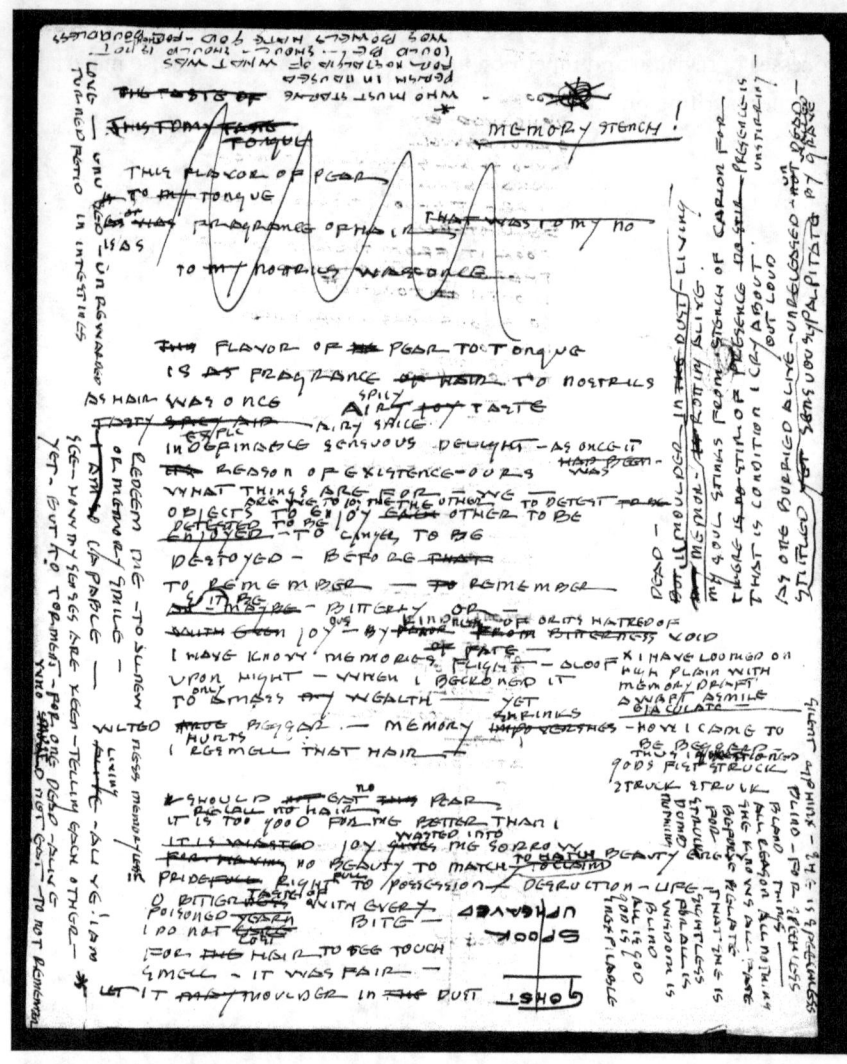

Figure 22 Elsa von Freytag-Loringhoven, 'Memory Stench', handwritten draft. Ink on paper. Previously unpublished. Elsa von Freytag-Loroinghoven Papers. Special Collections, University of Maryland at College Park Libraries.

4

Troubling structures: Inner time and the 'Baroness Elsa' manuscript

> Myself is timeless/That is my occupation/Hense [sic] D – my movement violated – in this time – I am out of time – I have no occupation – I am stalled.
>
> *Elsa von Freytag-Loringhoven to Djuna Barnes, 1924*[1]

This sensation of violated movement, of being stuck 'out of time' that Elsa articulates in one of her desperate letters to Barnes is vividly explored across her correspondence, her poetry and her autobiographic writing, and is powerfully spatialized in the handwritten drafts grouped under the evocative title 'Memory Stench'. Addressing the question of 'how I came to be beggard thus' does not simply involve a charting of chronological time in a manner familiar to the *Bildungsroman* tradition, but generates complex spatial and temporal patterns of repetition, refrain and variation as the narrative threads of a life are unspooled. Such concerns with being 'out of time' resonate with recent discussions of Barnes's stylized anachronism, her '*late* late modernism', and of the troubling temporal structures activated both within her individual texts, of those texts to each other, and in their relationship to critical histories of literary modernism.[2] Importantly, this sensation also informs Barnes's stuttering progress with the collaborative 'Baroness Elsa' manuscript, the failed project that would return to plague Barnes throughout her life, and as such casts significant light on the 'troubling structures' of Barnes's own autobiographic poetics. In turning my attention to the collaborative project that the two women embarked on in the mid-1920s in the context of these closing chapter's broader discussion of the messy textuality of Barnes's writing practices and mature autobiographic poetics, this chapter presents itself as an interruption that 'troubles' the structure of this book – one that I hope enacts the very patterns of return, repetition and variation that I am describing.

In assisting Barnes with the organization of the accumulated correspondence, drafts and heavily annotated revisions related to this project, O'Neal draws connections between Barnes's working practice in the 1930s with that of the late 1970s:

> She had started the project in 1932 and then started again and again, always beginning from page one. Even then it seemed she had difficulty in beginning a story, poem, or in this case a loosely autobiographical novel, and continuing through to a conclusion. She would begin, type a number of pages, and stop. Then she would repeat the process with minor alterations. The project was never completed.[3]

Although O'Neal is quite correct in his observation of the messy compositional practices employed by Barnes, his assessment of it as a failure not only has significant implications for a reading of her later Patchin Place production, but marginalizes Barnes's own concept of the open, or wounded text as a fundamental and formative element of her writing. Moreover, in dating the composition of this 'thin folder' from the early 1930s, O'Neal also effectively silences the Baroness's part in the collaboration, while also shutting down a discussion of the Baroness as a formal and formative influence on the younger woman's work. As we shall see, his assessment that Barnes's had been silent about the Baroness in the fifty years since the publication of her *transition* obituary is also not entirely correct, and her recurring figure can, in fact, be traced throughout Barnes's writing.

i. The Baroness's interruptive poetics

> Thought about holy skirts – to tune of "*Wheels are growing on rosebushes*"
> Beneath immovable – carved skirt of forbidding sexlessness – over pavement shoving – gliding – nuns have wheels.
>
> Elsa von Freytag-Lorinhoven, 'Holy Skirts'

We can easily read the Baroness as an 'interruptive' force. Her loud, barking voice, her arresting public promenades and the various critical interventions she imposed on the literary and artistic projects of her would-be lovers all foreground the shock effect of interruption. Similarly, in their abrasive and arresting patterns, her a-tonal sound poetry and verbal collages stage themselves as strikingly interruptive, interrupting themselves as much as they interfere with the free verse experiments of her contemporaries, snatches of dialogue, remembered scenes, urban noise and detritus colliding 'Two-in-one – all in nix mix up mess'

What here for – ?
To good? ah-!? hurry – speed up – run amuck – jump – beat it!
    farewell! Fare-thee-well – good-bye! bye!
ah – by-ye-ye!
['Holy Skirts']

Her waste-based constructions, costuming and collecting practices also interrupt the downward verticality of systems of order based upon the proper positioning and behaviour of matter, and the collaging practices worked out in her poetry, portraits and assemblages produce similarly jarring structural contrasts and juxtapositions.

Of course, interruption is deployed to great effect across a range of key modernist texts, even to the extent that it can be claimed as an 'instrumental element of an emerging cultural paradigm', as Asradur Eysteinsson has described.[4] While the Baroness develops similarly disruptive or interruptive modes to those of Eliot or Joyce as described by Eysteinsson, in her marginalized status as a poor German woman working from the boundary of the historical avant-garde, and in her critically marginalized status in relation to those avant-garde groupings the stakes of her interruption are that much higher. Moreover, in her waste-based and embodied art practices her interruptions also resound in a somewhat different register to the structures of high modernist aesthetics, even while we could productively trace certain intersections here. In the context of this chapter however, I want to use interruption as a means of addressing the interpolative techniques at work in the 'Baroness Elsa' project, and of positioning these as informative to a discussion of Djuna Barnes's messy writing practice and mature autobiographic poetics. In recovering and reusing the life material that she had permitted Greve to use in his naturalist novels *Fanny Essler* (1905) and *Maurermeister Ihles Haus* (1906) the Baroness not only interrupts his narrative, but also disrupts the broader projects of the naturalist novel. Of course, given the complex temporalities of this project, the extent to which Barnes and the Baroness also frequently interrupt themselves, their other texts and each other is also of interest.

Alongside the desperate and detailed letters sent from the Baroness to Barnes in 1924, the earliest surviving manuscripts relevant to the 'Baroness Elsa' project include a short preface signed by 'D.B' and dated 7 December 1924 in which she highlights the extent of the Baroness's destitution in Germany, describing her memorably as 'a citizen of terror: a contemporary without a country'.[5] Although this succinct preface only obliquely references the much larger and decidedly messier autobiographic project that Barnes would struggle to contain 'herein', the impetus of the project at this early stage is clear. As Barnes writes: 'In gathering together her letters, in offering some of her works, my hope has been that a country will inherit her life, offering in return peace, and decency, and time.'[6] In extending the Baroness's own painful understanding of herself as an exile in her homeland to a sense of her as estranged from her own historic moment, Barnes not only sketches out the wandering unhomed and untimely *détraqués* familiar to us from *Nightwood* and the exiled Miranda's homecoming staged in *The Antiphon*, but signposts the project as one of critical recovery.[7]

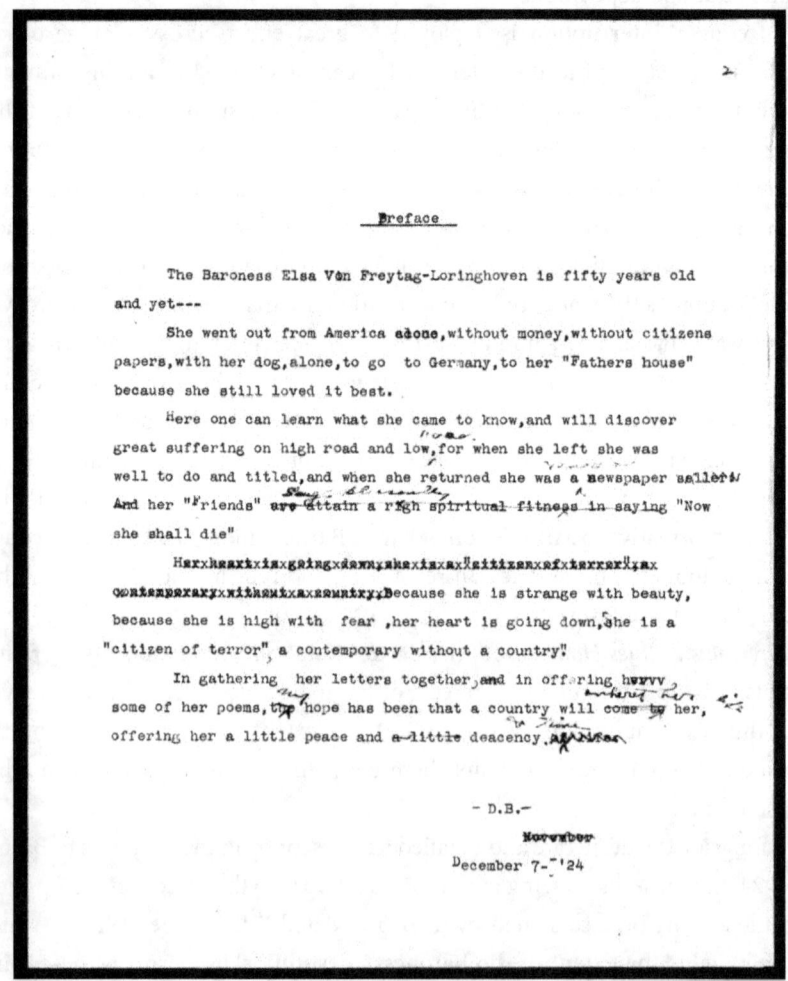

Figure 23 Djuna Barnes, 'Baroness Elsa' Preface. Typed and annotated page dated 7 December 1924. Elsa von Freytag-Loroinghoven Papers. Special Collections, University of Maryland at College Park Libraries.

Originally imagined as a collection of the Baroness's poetry, the thought of which sustained the exiled Baroness through a particularly dark period, the project gradually evolved to incorporate these biographic elements, and by the early months of 1925 she was absorbed in preparing the pages of her autobiography.[8] Unsurprisingly, the project began to take on more significance for the Baroness and mentions of it become increasingly urgent in her letters, even writing to Barnes in the months before her death that 'There is only one ambition now in me – to finish my biography'.[9]

As Lynn DeVore has insisted, the surviving manuscript is 'a fascinating and sensational memoir', documenting the Baroness's idiosyncratic and radically disruptive approach to the English language and punctuated by 'digressions and interior interludes'.[10] While in 1924 Barnes had imagined the project as a slim book of verse with a framing biographic statement, the material kept coming, the long sections of the neatly handwritten memoir complicated by equally long, decidedly messier letters, which interrupt and retrace key scenes and themes from the more linear narrative provided by the biography. Although the autobiographic account was presumably intended as a device for framing the Baroness's experimental poetry in the context of New York's machine age avant-garde cultures, the detailed and highly textured document instead returned to the years before she arrived in America, focusing predominantly on her childhood in Swinemünde, her violent, domineering father and suicidally depressed mother, her formative experiences as a chorus girl and performer, and the series of often quite disappointing liaisons that map out her personal sexual odyssey before her arrival in America.

From its very conception, the writing of her memoirs in a series of dense instalments to Barnes was already staging a recovery, not only in the recuperative action involved in the recollection of her childhood and formative sexual experiences, but as a pointed reclamation of her life material from her second husband Felix Paul Greve's two novels *Fanny Essler* (1905) and *Maurermeister Ihles Haus* (1906).[11] The intertextual relationship between the Greve's earlier novels and the Baroness's 1920s memoir has been drawn out by Hjartarson and Gammel, the latter convincingly positioning the autobiography within the generic conventions of the female sexual confession and identifying its functioning as a sophisticated gender critique, not only of the *fin de siècle* circles within which Elsa moved, but of the naturalist style adopted by Greve which 'ultimately controls and limits the exuberance of the female protagonist'.[12]

Given my earlier tracing of the various attempts to control and contain Elsa's threatening New Woman energies within the narrative reconstructions of her contemporaries, it is worth briefly detailing the distinctions between Greve's and Elsa's treatment of her life material, especially given the discrepancies between their representations and treatments of female sexuality. While Greve positioned himself as the chivalrous 'epitome of rational and sexual control' in the figure of Freidrich Karl Reelen, Elsa's later account not only represents a 'parodic reversal', as Gammel suggests, but restates the by now familiar pattern of abject recoil and sexual withdrawal that her provocative sensuality provoked in her Greenwich Village days.[13]

Causing controversy at the time of its publication, the novel – published under Greve's name – followed the sexual awakening of the young Fanny as the aspiring actress moved between the stages and seedier sides of Berlin's avant-garde in the 1880s. Detailed through a series of letters from Elsa to Greve during his imprisonment for fraud, the novel recreates the various aspects of Elsa's experiences in Berlin familiar to us from the Barnes collaboration: her unchaperoned perambulations of the city and the conservative aunt that she lodged with over her first two years there (1893–5), her sexual experimentation, immersion in avant-garde circles centred around Stefan George (1868–1933) and marriage to architect August Endell (1871–1925). Importantly, these texts also detailed her experiences in dramatic training and stage performance, as both an erotic artist and cross-dressing actress. Despite its sensational content and ambiguous stance on the politics of the New Woman, the novel's style and narrative structure were resolutely naturalist. Carefully detailing the salacious details of Fanny/Elsa's sexual history through a dialogic question and answer format familiar to confessional narratives, the male narrator and various other lovers she engages with gain access to her history and her body, one which is then reconstructed within the frameworks of the male-authored naturalist novel, and directed per its voyeuristic gaze.[14]

Clearly this novel, and two of Greve's later texts *Maurermeister Ihles Haus* (1906) and *Settlers of the Marsh* (1925) which detail the familial drama of Elsa's childhood, and the breakdown of the couple's marriage in Kentucky, bears much relevance to the politics and poetics of containment discussed earlier. As Gammel has suggested, *Fanny Essler* 'exemplifies the problematic appropriation of the female sexual confession into *fin-de-siècle* naturalist fiction [...] the male author, narrator, and characters all listening to, and exploiting, Elsa's sexual confessions'.[15] Further than a problematic appropriation of Elsa's narrative, Greve effectively contained and controlled Elsa's sexuality and artistic expression through his carefully framed narrative reconstruction. Rewriting Elsa's own life experience into popular novels, Greve denied the trajectory of Elsa's success; this is to say that while Elsa would use these early experiences as foundational to her later New York performances, both *Fanny Essler* and *Maurermeister Ihles Haus* contain this character within the narrative arc familiar to the naturalistic trope of the 'fallen woman'.

First institutionalized by her husband Eduard after being convinced that their unsatisfying physical relationship is a sign of her 'sickness', and then dying before the discovery of her first husband's suicide, Fanny's sexual identity remains circumscribed within the contexts of male sexual gratification and seduction, just as the narrative imposes severe punishments and limitation on projects of female self-realization. Fanny is killed off at the novel's close in adhering to formal convention and in homage to Greve's literary hero Flaubert, and similarly, the radical challenge to patriarchal rule that bristles underneath the surface of Greve's second novel and explodes with the daughter's final challenge to the father is effectively silenced with the death of the mother, Bertha, and the novel's swift resolution to marry off the disobedient Susie (Elsa) to Consul Blume.

Alongside the strict adherence to gendered codes of literary convention despite their controversial or subversive content, Greve's novels lack any of the experimental approaches to grammatical structure and syntactical arrangements associated with the Baroness's later writing in English. While they were collaborations to the extent that Elsa provided the imprisoned Greve with the narrative material from her young life in a series of detailed letters, they were published under Greve's name, and bear little trace of her stylistically or aesthetically. Adopting the antagonistic role of artist-critic publicly taken by the Baroness in her denouncement of the limitations of her male avant-garde contemporaries in later years, her own manuscript details her thoughts on this appropriation:

> He had written two novels, they were dedicated to me in so far as material was concerned, it was my life and persons out of my life. He did the executive part of the business, giving the thing the conventional shape and dress. […] I remember I disliked the 'style' already then, […] I did not cherish his abrupt style … that seemed to me dry and artificial … having no carrying power nor convincing quality of its own.[16]

In place of Greve's 'dry and artificial' style, Elsa puts her messy and expressive body centre stage, finding a language through which to articulate the 'sex atmosphere unconsciously eminating [sic] from me' (105), and through which to explore female-centred heterosexual desire and climax divorced from misogynistic constructions of feminine sexuality that impose the ideals of virginity or maternity. Literally silencing her much sought-after orgasm in one episode related by the Baroness, Greve also figuratively silences the young Elsa in his novelistic treatment of her life material. Interrupting Greve and recovering this material Elsa signal her refusal to be complicit in patriarchal projects organized around silencing women and denying their sexual agency. As a result, the revisionist impulses of Elsa's project, along with the various textual strategies mobilized through this powerfully embodied writing, frustrate the stabilizing frameworks traditionally associated with modes of auto/biographic discourse, stylistically and structurally demonstrating her refusal to be 'contained within the male system of order'.[17]

As has been established, the Baroness developed a strikingly corporeal mode of writing in her poetry and prose not only obvious in their sexually explicit and erotically charged content, but in their treatment of the processes of ageing, of death and decomposition, and of a living body moving through the city. These embodied qualities can also be traced in the formal relations that her writing establishes between the self-representational practices of her waste-based body-work, and the visual, acoustic and grammatical challenges of her poetry and prose, particularly apparent in her assault on the compositional structures of English grammar. In her study of the interplay of the erotic and the textual informing what she termed 'Sapphic Modernism', Shari Benstock proposes the development of a Sapphic practice antagonistically related to the high modernism. In these practices, language itself is radically reformed through the distinct challenges to what she reads as the patriarchal structures of grammar and syntax.[18] Through close attention to Jane Marcus's earlier examination of the gendered textual strategies activated in Virginia Woolf's *A Room of One's Own* (1929) which, Marcus suggested, enlisted 'punctuation in the service of feminism with the use of ellipses for encoding female desire, the use of initials and dashes to make absent figures more present and transforming interruption [...] into a deliberate strategy as a sign of women's writing', Benstock presents a promising line of inquiry for considering certain formal aspects of this revisionist project.[19]

As the editors of the recent *Body Sweats* collection have rightly insisted, alongside her deployment of neologism, portmanteau construction and anachronism, the dash serves a particularly muscular function across her poetry, evoking the moving body as it activates a dynamic and kinetic rhythm across looser lines of connected fragments and chains of associated or juxtaposed words and images.[20] In this respect the dash of course also connects the Baroness's poetry to her distinctive collage aesthetics, the dash marking at once the 'cut' and the 'stitch' as her collected fragments are brought into new expressive, aesthetic or interpretive relationships through juxtaposition. That the Baroness's distinctive punctuation was a deliberate textual strategy is supported by a fascinating passage in a long letter to Barnes in which she discusses the autobiography and repeats certain detail relating to her early life at length. With regards to her punctuation she writes:

> Tell others of my inventive brain! Maybe – oh – maybe? I will even be able – feel necessity (for then am I able –) to invent happiness – joy mark! Not only exclamation mark. Djuna – as I just see now – our interpunction [sic] system is puny! One should be able to express almost as much in interpunction – as words – yes – at last even – after gradual evolution – in this new strange thing – to express absolute in it! As I did in sounds – like music! Yes! Wordnotes!!! You Djuna – you must have felt yourself already often some disgust with poverty of interpunctional material![21]

Identifying the interpretative possibilities of musical sounds, patterns and structures released from the rigid (and in Benstock's terms patriarchal) structures of grammar and syntax, the Baroness directly connects the ringing 'wordnotes' of her experimental Dada sound poetry with the expressive and subversive potential of this dynamic 'interpunction'. She also tellingly draws Barnes into collusion in this secret expressive mode, identifying her not only as an artist sympathetic to her need for more malleable expressive modes, but as the writer she could trust to execute her vision.

Written in her strangely runic hand, the Baroness's extant handwritten manuscript clearly displays the stylistic elements, the dash used prominently as a tool to connect seemingly distinct or disparate images, ideas and time frames together. Indeed, the dash seems to function to some degree as the 'interpunctional' symbol of the recovery work being done through the autobiographic process, visually rendering the Baroness's sense that 'nothing is past and buried – ever! All are links in a chain [...] I am slow – I need much time – but I am thorough – I forget nothing'.[22]

Alongside her tendency to cross through lines of her manuscript, looping lines guiding the reader back to her revisions and afterthoughts squashed around the deleted phrase, or included in the margins at right angles to the main body of the text, we can read the dash – through Benstock and Marcus a deliberately strategy of recovery and revision. In stitching together two or more distinct ideas, time frames or reference points, the dash not only functions to show, rather than attempt to elide, certain temporal and self-representational instabilities associated with the composition of an autobiographic project of this nature, but also 'wounds' the closed and contained bodies of Greve's texts, opening them up in a grotesque gesture of perpetual renewal. Identifying the connections between her own biography and Greve's novels, and emphasizing the stylistic and gendered limitations of latter, the Baroness develops a model of collaborative auto/biographic writing which self-consciously demonstrates its own repetitive and irreverent intertextuality and transgresses generic boundaries through a consistently 'interruptive' poetics.

In this respect, while Gammel's treatment of the memoir as a confessional document situated within the contemporaneously emergent genre of the female sexual confession is compelling, I want to suggest that its 'effectiveness as a gender discourse' is also figured through the disruptive patterns of recurrence, repetition and revision that structure the document itself, and position it as a somewhat troubling intertext between the divergent stylistic traditions and autobiographic practices represented by Greve and Barnes.

Importantly, Elsa does not only interrupt Greve's narrative, but her own, which quickly becomes particularly apparent when we take in the full range of material related to this project that is collected in the Elsa von Freytag-Loringhoven papers held at the University of Maryland. Including the Baroness's

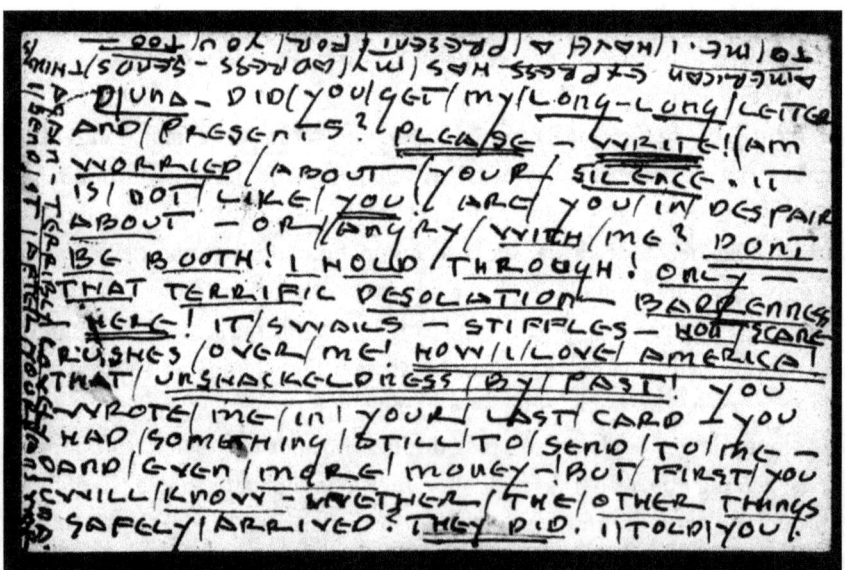

Figure 24 Elsa von Freytag-Loringhoven handwritten letter to Djuna Barnes, c. 1924. Elsa von Freytag-Loroinghoven Papers. Special Collections, University of Maryland at College Park Libraries.

original handwritten manuscript, the papers also include Barnes's full typescript, the various drafts and fictionalized rewritings that Barnes returned to over the years and the long, detailed letters filled with rapid cuts between the present day, her time in America, her relationship with Greve and her childhood.[23] Slipping between the past and the present, particular scenes and images from the main body of the text are picked up by the letters, compulsively unpicked and embroidered in more detail there. In handling these materials, in cutting material from the letters and the biographical account and weaving them together through her own compositional and writing practices, Barnes's 'Baroness Elsa' document testifies to a tactile and collaborative practice, one that draws text and textile together in illuminating ways.

ii. Cutting, stitching, weaving: Ida-Marie's 'strange handiwork'

> It is written like half mad in syntax – later it becomes a little better. There are reasons for it: 1: I am half mad – as is only sensible … 2: I Cannot tell events but be carried by emotion into a fancy world of spatial reality – as you know. 3: I begin to be clumsy with English expressions not coming readily any more – doing damage to my sentences – so I must leave all work to you – picking out and presenting – if you think it worth while.
>
> Elsa von Freytag-Loringhoven to Djuna Barnes

In the context of Barnes studies, this autobiographic project has been given surprisingly little attention, and it is striking that when it has been discussed in relation to the Baroness, attention has been directed primarily at the material relating to her New York art persona: the early interest in forms of spectacle and performativity, and her sensational sex confessions. In shifting my attention to the figure of her mother, Ida-Marie Plötz and this earlier phase of her biography I want to draw out particular compositional structures relevant to a discussion of this project, and of Barnes's autobiographic practices more broadly, and offer ways of thinking about this textual waste as an effective gender discourse.

While Barnes was clearly as struck by the ekphrastic possibilities of the Living Statues as later critics have been, selecting it as one of the working titles for the autobiographic project and having the 'borderline art form' reappear in *Nightwood*'s Frau Mann, I want to suggest that it is in the cutting and stitching and figure of Ida-Marie that bind Barnes and Elsa together, illuminating the patterns of their collaborative labour, compositional practices and auto/biographic structures.

Importantly, in focusing my attention on this area of Elsa's biography, I am signalling a mode of reading that engages with the messy materiality of Barnes and the Baroness's writing practices, that resists reading the typescript as a 'finished' or complete document and that instead works on 'keeping the wound open' through the commentary that Elsa and Barnes supplied in the margins, in their letters and in the various drafts and revisions made by Barnes over the years. Indeed, in the body of the 'official' biography, this early stage of the Elsa Plötz's life is afforded relatively little space, although it reports in somewhat telegraphic detail her mother's 'mental brooding' and 'dreadful death by cancer of the womb, occasioned by my father's thoughtless mental as well as physical conduct'.[24] In turning to the letters though we find the Baroness compulsively returning and reiterating certain details of her mother's life, notably her 'strange' behaviour in the months leading up to her death, which Greve's second novel *Mauremeister Ihles Haus* also traces, and the more gruesome details related to her death, which the novel does not.

Detailing the education and violently turbulent home life of the two young Ihle girls, Greve's novel closely follows the shape of the account provided by Elsa's letters, particularly with regards to the father's physically abusive outbursts and the anti-social and erratic behaviour of the mother. Alternating between overt displays of affection and cold detachment towards her children, Berthe is also described as mortifyingly rude to her friends and neighbours, takes to reading excessively and to private bouts of religious mania, and to spending alarming amounts of money on blue eiderdowns and richly embroidered linens.[25] Following Elsa's recollections of this period almost exactly, the narrative observes Berthe's increasingly alarming behaviour, the denouement coming with her disappearance and suicide attempt after which we are curtly informed she was taken directly off to the Frauendorf Asylum near Stettin.[26]

However, just as Greve contained the exuberant sexual excesses of a younger Elsa in the figure of Fanny, so too are the various threats to patriarchal order and gender conventions presented by Ida-Marie carefully regulated in this second novel. While Greve details her furious outbursts, her refusal to conform to normative standards of conservative, late nineteenth-century Prussian femininity through her careless dress and closely shorn hair, in having Bertha die silently beyond the scope of the narrative gaze, he effectively side-steps both the gruesome details of her death and, importantly, Elsa's interpretation of it as an act of patriarchal violence inscribed on the mother's body.

As the biography obliquely states and the letters more explicitly detail, her mother's death from uterine cancer was expedited by her 'secrecy about troubles of that sort prompted by female shame – to be examined in those parts';[27] a secrecy no doubt informed by the belief that the cancer was related to the syphilis that Elsa claimed she contracted from her husband after their marriage. In Elsa's account the transmission of the disease, the invasive 'cure' and the 'female shame' that Ida-Marie was made to feel are all unambiguously treated as acts of patriarchal violence perpetrated on her mother's body. In contrast to Greve's silence, Elsa's narrative directly challenges the father for his part in her death. Refusing to call his hastily wed second wife 'Mamma', she retorts by 'telling my father my mamma lay dead in the graveyard by his fault', an act of filial disobedience that was swiftly met by an extremely violent response, which the Baroness later claims could have made him a murderer twice over.[28] Preoccupied by the figure of her mother in her letters, Elsa returns again and again to these scenes, and to the more macabre details of the latter stages of her illness and death, the graphic shock of these images powerfully expressive in their violence.

Shattering the detached and artificial peace of the dead body lying in repose Elsa returns us to the corporeal realities of death. Leaning in to kiss her mother we are made to feel the 'overpowering smell abyss of space – sudden smack into the face and the appalling hardness of flesh – that was not marble nor ice'.[29] The corpse, like the open wound is a privileged site within Kristeva's topography of the abject 'blurred between the inanimate and the inorganic, a transitional swarming, inseparable lining of a human nature whose life is undistinguishable from the symbolic'.[30] While Greve's account rejects the sight of the corpse and the 'breaking down of a world that has erased its borders', the eighteen-year-old Elsa not only stands before it, but dredges it up from within her it over thirty years later. Where language and representation fail in *Mauremeister Ihles Haus* Elsa falters, her language stutters, but she persists:

> My mother my mother dead
> My dead mother – I had a dead mother
> Dead dead dead – do you know that – ?
> I did not

It is not only in the grotesque reanimation of the mother's corpse that Elsa's narrative refuses to conform to the silence imposed upon Ida-Marie in life, in death and in Greve's novel. In abruptly removing Berthe from the novel's action at the point at which she enters the asylum, Greve also silences Berthe/Ida-Marie's 'open war declaration – against family', and the effective strategies of gender disobedience that she exercises during this period. In a rather radical move, Elsa insists that Ida-Marie's presentation of 'madness' was a deliberate strategy to subvert the oppressive patriarchal codes that strictly delimited her behaviour per the roles of wife, mother and petite-bourgeois woman.[31] Remodelling herself as 'homeless in midst of great house – comfort – secure position' she effectively abdicated responsibility from the oppressive gender roles imposed on her.[32] Refusing to see her husband, Elsa describes Ida-Marie's newly found freedom in the sanatorium, where she 'shyly, giggling, smirking gay insisted she wasn't mad'.[33]

Having been forced to sacrifice her own artistic inclinations as an accomplished musician after her marriage, it is in this newly liberated state that she turns to needlework as Elsa describes in passage that is worth quoting at length:

> She began to make strange 'handiwork' (when she had been such 'skilled worker' in fine embroidery – needlework!!) now she did things – nobody would think of putting together – spoiling elegant material with cheap trash – she was 'tired of doing "fine handiwork" everybody could do that – and: 'Was this not nice? Something new – what? Now – next time I will put together some of Papa's remanats [sic] from that square patterned rust-brown heavy wollen [sic] suit – with the little reddish squares – don't you know –? That look like little fat squares – bacon squares – fried goldenbrown – don't you think so – don't you like them –? I love them – just the little squares! Oh! You know nothing! You are all such dull unobservant fools' [...] she was speculating about – maybe – putting with 'such and such stitch some velvet of special tint or silver braid – or lace – on it – to make "handkerchief holder"', the usefulness had ceased to interest her, the putting together was what mattered! And – now listen–! Who had ever heard about 'remnants of a mansuit – that showed themselves distinctly as what they were – to be used as "hankerchief holder" with velvet and silver lace?'[34]

As Rozsika Parker explored in her landmark study *The Subversive Stich*, the history and practice of embroidery itself present a complex, double-sided model for thinking through Ida-Marie's production here, embroidery having historically 'provided both a weapon of resistance for women and functioned as source of constraint'.[35] In its domestic contexts, embroidery was, by the nineteenth century largely divorced from its economic status as paid production, instead occupying a central place in the education of young girls in properly feminine conduct. Deeply imbricated in the construction of ideological histories of domestic femininity as Parker's history shows, the long hours spent in silence, in private, bent over their needlework encode a passive, subservient and obedient feminine ideal ensuring women 'remain at home and home and refrain from book learning'.³⁶ With the popularization of sampler work, this emergent ideal of domestic femininity is at once repeated and confirmed in the biblical, moralistic and domestic lessons that are used to teach girls their craft. Successfully intertwining notions of natural femininity with embroidery as a sign of the inherently feminine, by the nineteenth century needlework proficiency was 'intended as evidence of a woman's self-denying, loving, giving, effortless yet never idle femininity', and most pressingly, employed in the service of her husband's comfort.

In rejecting her 'fine handiwork' Ida-Marie also rejects her ascribed role as a petit-bourgeois woman in an industrial capitalist society; that is, engaging in a mode of unpaid labour whose value is derived from both her demonstration of industriousness and her selflessness in labouring for the comfort of her husband and children. However, rather than rejecting embroidery in its deep imbrication with feminine ideals outright, she instead reclaims the craft as a powerfully expressive strategy of gender resistance. Using the tools that have been most closely allied to her femininity, she radically strikes out against the master to bring down his house.

Indeed, it is not only in her rejection of the conventional forms and gendered practices of embroidery that we can read Ida-Marie's 'strange handiwork' as laying down a decidedly subversive stitch, but in the tactile pleasure taken in her materials, and her treatment of them. The basting together of the thick woollen cuts of Adolf's suits with the overtly feminine delicate lacework seems to evoke a crude rendering of their relationship, its sexual overtones telling considering Elsa's later accusations. If the suit stands in a metonymic relationship to the man, Ida-Marie's cutting up of the 'mansuit' similarly deconstructs the tyrannical patriarch and turns him into a pile of useless (and harmless) 'remnants' repurposed through her own transformative labour.

Given the international popularity of Berlin woolwork during this period, we can roughly assume that Ida-Marie's accomplished needlework would have included this form of embroidery, alongside more delicate sampler work. Heavier than fine needlepoint, Berlin woolwork used dyed yarn to create colourful, durable designs for furniture, screens and bags. While obviously possessing a clear use value, this work was also popularized through the mass production of printed patterns for the needleworker to follow carefully. The description that Elsa provides of her mother's work realigns the tactile and embodied processes of needlework to more liberated, materially explorative and associative processes. In Ida's juxtaposition of different materials, emphasis on the processes of construction, and rejection of 'usefulness' as a marker of value, her work clearly mirrors the daughter's later experimentation with hand-made constructions and elaborate costumes.

Considering the historical gendering of this mode of production, its centrality in the forging of mother-daughter relationships is perhaps obvious, the mother often described as passing her skills – and their coded lessons on sanctioned femininity – down to her child. As Parker describes, the mother-daughter relationship was a highly idealized and popular subject for embroidered pieces, whereby:

> sewing a sampler declaring the child's intention of continued goodness and obedience was a means of maintaining a sense of one-ness with the mother whom embroidery and sampler-making signified. At the same time, perhaps the protestations of love and appreciation denied the guilt/ambivalence that characterises the mother/daughter relationship, thus stilling the guilt death inevitably brings in its wake.[37]

Ambivalence is certainly a salient feature of Elsa's treatment of her mother across these documents, veering between adoration, self-identification, resentment and indifference. Engaged in her own, sympathetic cutting, stitching and weaving as she recalls and records her mother's 'strange handiwork', this 'oneness' with the mother is activated through the interruptive, associative and autobiographic practice itself. Drawing direct comparisons between her mother's 'insanity' and her own desperate situation, this dense passage overlays the image of the two women to the point where mother's uterine cancer recurs as a 'spiritual' tumour swelling in the womb of the daughter.

> I am insane from Germany as my mother was from 'home'. She tried to escape – and did – in some way! Then returned – for her death? Should this be – my return? But – my body is unharmed – it could only be suicide […] I harbour it – I carry it around – Djuna – like embryo in womb – and as such it grows! It grows by law of natural necessity – through air I am in – if I am not operated! It will swallow me – my cancer? Djuna – have I spiritual cancer of womb – […] you see – this very terrible logical – speculation – occurred to me just now – by writing –

As she acknowledges, it is only in the process of writing that the daughter comes to recognize her mother in herself, and tellingly, it is through this detailed recollection of the mother's stitching that brings the daughter to a sudden reflection of her own autobiographic practices. Interrupting herself to apologize to Barnes for the disorganized form of her narrative in a way that recalls Barnes's own letters to Coleman regarding *Nightwood*'s messy composition she writes:

> Excuse my clumsy rambling telling! But – it is very hard to tell and – I am not used to tell 'stories' – And I can not pay attention to anything like 'style' at all! I don't know – what make me tell you this –anyway – unless – yes – I wish to show you myself – my origin –

Like Ida-Marie's unconventional stitching, the biography, lacks the formal qualities of the naturalist novel, its narrative is not sequential but proceeds according to a notion of personal time, to which Barnes was highly receptive, as we shall see. Looped with the lines of her underscored words and connected by the running stitch of her dashes, the written page itself starts to resemble a densely worked piece of fabric. In fact, just at the point where Elsa questions her reasons for committing all of this to paper, there appears a strange crescent marking, with small lines running across its curve like a stitched cut.

The needle and the pen both wound the surface of the text/textile, but in their treatment of these materials as surfaces to be cut into, turned and reworked, they also emphasize their openness to the processes of renewal, reparation and revision. As the visual artist Louise Bourgeois has written, the needle – and we could add, the dash – 'is used to repair damage'.[38] As Parker points out, 'reparation' in the psychoanalytical theories presented by Melanie Klein is not only understood to drive creativity, but is rooted in the guilt and ambivalence characterizing the mother-infant relationship.[39] In light of this, we could approach these dashes and/as stitches as the older Baroness externalizing internal childhood trauma and 'facing loss and damage and making efforts to repair and restore one's objects'.[40] Certainly, Elsa's relationship to her mother could be described as ambivalent, and the insistence with which she returns to

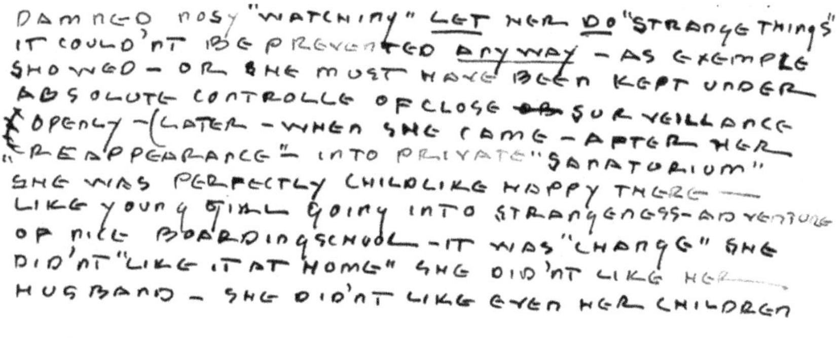
DAMNED NOSY "WATCHING" LET HER DO "STRANGE THINGS"
IT COULD'NT BE PREVENTED ANYWAY – AS EXEMPLE
SHOWED – OR SHE MUST HAVE BEEN KEPT UNDER
ABSOLUTE CONTROLLE OF CLOSE ~~OR~~ SURVEILLANCE
OPENLY – (LATER – WHEN SHE CAME – AFTER HER
"REAPPEARANCE" – INTO PRIVATE "SANATORIUM"
SHE WAS PERFECTLY CHILDLIKE HAPPY THERE —
LIKE YOUNG GIRL GOING INTO STRANGENESS – ADVENTURE
OF NICE BOARDINGSCHOOL – IT WAS "CHANGE" SHE
DID'NT "LIKE IT AT HOME" SHE DID'NT LIKE HER
HUSBAND – SHE DID'NT LIKE EVEN HER CHILDREN

Figure 25 Elsa von Freytag-Loringhoven handwritten letter to Djuna Barnes, 12 July 1924. Elsa von Freytag-Loroinghoven Papers. Special Collections, University of Maryland at College Park Libraries.

these scenes speaks to a desire to recover or repair the lost object (the mother in Klein's terms). Outside of the field of Object Relations Theory, what is clear is that while Greve's narrative focused on the power struggles between the father and daughter, in recovering this material and reworking it across her letters, it is the mother and daughter relationship that becomes more prominent.

Following Liz Stanley's treatment of the salient epistemological, theoretical and technical issues existing between the seemingly distinct genres of 'biography' and 'autobiography', we can identify the ways in which this densely intertextual manuscript functions as a mode of auto/biographic writing that is 'concerned with the intertextuality of biography and autobiography, and also of fact and fiction, the spoken and the written, and the past and the present'.[41] Promoting hybridity and intertextuality, Stanely's discussion is particularly useful for framing a feminist analysis of the Baroness's recovery and reuse of the material used by Greve, and of the compositional practices involved in the collaboration with Barnes. It also raises pertinent questions with regards to the ethics and aesthetics involved in Barnes's treatment of this material after the Baroness's death.

Interestingly, in transcribing the pages of Elsa's handwritten manuscript, Barnes made a subtle but suggestive editorial decision. Retaining most of the elements common to the Baroness's linguistic and syntactical idiosyncrasies, Barnes introduced another grammatical element in her organization of the manuscript, the ellipse. As emphasized by Marcus and Benstock's accounts, the ellipse is a particularly loaded sign. Marking an omission and absence within the text the ellipse, in both its grammatical and rhetoric functions, 'figures as absence, a fault, a defect: it marks the impossibility of figurabiltiy and the failure of representation'.[42] Pointing to itself as a textual gap, the ellipse stands for the unspoken and unrepresented and can thus withhold the 'sense' of the sentence. At this stage, Barnes does not cut or radically re-write anything from Elsa's manuscript so the ellipse does not address a material absence, but figures the necessary 'wounding' and openness centralized by Barnes's thinking through modes of autobiographic writing. Just as Barnes had used the asterisk to powerful effect in *Ryder*, scarring the page and marking the textual absences generated by the censor's demands, the ellipse here functions similarly to point to an absence. Yet in testifying to Elsa's handwritten narrative, the ellipse also functions as the sign of its presence, paradoxically opening the typescript by stitching it to Elsa's text. As we can trace in the patterns of recurrence, revision and substitution activated across the Patchin Place cycles, Benstock's suggestion that the ellipse works to interlock texts together, turning tropes inside out 'so that deviation constitutes a new form of structure' opens up possibilities for reading the structural role of this intertextual manuscript in shaping both Barnes's 'failed' biography and the patterns of her own autobiographic poetics.[43]

The question of how to extract a new form of structure from a model of deviation is precisely what preoccupied Barnes in her struggles with the 'Baroness Elsa' project. From the initial preface written at close of 1924 the project evolved through 1930s from a straightforward typescript through a series of abandoned drafts and manuscripts titled 'Elsa', 'Baroness Elsa', 'The Beggars Comedy' 'The Fury' and 'Living Statues'. Alongside Barnes's correspondence from the period, these material documents demonstrate the range of Barnes's attempts to re-work the Baroness's first person narrative into an experimentally biographic account, one that would neither uphold the 'realist fallacy' promoted by traditional biographic writing by re-containing Elsa's sensational body in its pages as a guarantee of the text's authority and legitimacy nor 'take liberties' with its subject. In this initial stage of re-writing, Barnes was already experimenting with the generative textual, temporal and generic instabilities presented by the Baroness's manuscript which moves between her address to Barnes in the present and her hopes for the future of this project, her own memories of the past, their changing impact on her at intervening points over the years and her dialogue with Greve's text.

iii. Alexis Carrel and *Nightwood*'s troubling structures

> The wish to be disembodied in order to travel into the past that has brought these things to our notice and at the same time to carry on with them into our own future, but Elsa, unlike the average child, had little ability to hatch her eggs in private. Man only commits beauty in the remembrance of things past. It's his broken recollection that makes the appeal of the wax work, for memory is not only what a person has himself seen or come into contact with, it is also what he has imagined.
>
> Djuna Barnes, 'Baroness Elsa' fragment

Given the frequent reference to Marcel Proust and his lengthy novel cycle *À la recherche du temps perdu* in Barnes's letters from the 1930s, we might surmise that she was similarly interested in the philosophies of time and inner experience presented by Henri Bergson (1859–1941), considering the close critical and personal relationship popularly established between the two.[44] We might well imagine the core Bergsonian concepts of *l'étendu* ('clock-time') and *durée réelle*, ('inner time') would have resonated with Barnes, as they have been shown to have influenced other members of her circle and the high modernist aesthetics they developed.[45] Certainly, Coleman was keen to discuss these theories with Barnes, and, although the latter claimed to have attempted Bergson, a letter dated 13 November 1939 puts into question the extent to which his philosophies influenced her thinking: stating that as she couldn't get on with his ideas, she suggests she gave it up. However, there was another, now considerably less familiar, theorist of time and consciousness whose work was enthusiastically received by Barnes and whose thinking illuminates compelling connections between early articulations of Barnes's use of 'spatial form' and of her own approach to writing and personal time as necessarily, and somewhat grotesquely, open.[46] Connecting the spatial and the temporal in compelling ways, turning to the 'Baroness Elsa' project we can see how Barnes developed the structures and motifs that appear to dazzling effect in *Nightwood*, and recur across the later Patchin Place production.

A French surgeon and biologist, Alexis Carrel (1873–1944) came to prominence with his pioneering techniques in surgical treatment and invention, for which he was awarded the Nobel Prize for Physiology in 1912. An enthusiastic advocate of eugenics in the years leading up to the Second World War, Carrel was directly involved in the implementation of eugenics policies under the Vichy regime and openly supported the policies aggressively pursued by the Third Reich, which perhaps explains his absence from discussions of Barnes's aesthetics during this period. In 1935 Carrel published *L'Homme, cet inconnu* (*Man, the Unknown*) which presented these views and prescriptions for society alongside a more nuanced treatment of the relativity of what he termed 'inner time'.

Carrel's concept proposed that the experience of time differs from organism to organism as it is measured by what occurs within the individual, rather than from mathematical time which we 'conveniently compare [...] to a straight time, each successive state being measured by a point'. In opposition to the measurements of the clock which correspond to 'certain rhythmic events, such as the earth's rotation on its axis around the sun', this tracing of duration along a continuum does not account for the 'value of physical time [which] seems to differ according to whether we look back to the past or forward to the future'.[47] Invoking Bergson and other contemporary theorists working in the fields of physiology, physics and biology, he makes a case for the inadequacy of mathematical time to account for man's extension through time and space, to account for his existence in four dimensions. Observing that a 'rock, a tree, an animal cannot be instantaneous', Carrel approaches the question of inherent time as it occurs in space and within bodily tissues, rejecting linear measurements of time for a more dynamic and mutable model. As he asserts:

> Duration consists of the superposition of the different aspects of an identity. It is a kind of intrinsic movement of things [...] Each inanimate or living being comprises an inner motion, a succession of states, a rhythm, which is his very own. Such motion is inherent time.[48]

As the 'expression of the changes of the body and its activities during the course of a life', inner time is thus explained as distinct and separate from externally measured 'mathematical' time, and can itself be separated into its component parts of 'physiological time' – the beating of the heart and slow degradation of tissue – and 'psychological time'. Compared to the complex movement of physiological time which is at once a fixed dimension and a succession of sates, psychological time – consciousness – 'records its own motion'. Quoting directly from Bergson's *Creative Evolution* he writes, 'Duration is the continuous progress of the past which gnaws into the future and which swells as it advances [...] The piling up of the past upon the past goes on without relaxation.'[49]

This accumulative, somewhat digestive sense of the past's encroachment into the future features prominently in Barnes's writing; her texts are littered with fragmented accounts from historical record, myth, nursery rhymes and a range of literary modes; the interiors of *Nightwood* and *The Antiphon* in particular are cluttered with old paintings, artefacts and crowded rooms 'teeming with second-hand dealings with life' (*N*: 59); and her characters are, as Julie Abraham established, 'obsessively concerned with their relations to history', and to their legitimacy in relation to these official records.[50] Indeed, given the messy materiality of her compositional practices and the dense accumulations of material relation to the Patchin Place production we could go so far as to say that her archive similarly maps duration as a process of dense accumulation, as opposed to a model of improvement as refinement, as Herring's treatment of a 'geriatric avant-garde' suggests.[51] However, while Herring's discussion is necessarily focussed on the compositional practices of the older Barnes, I want to consider the particular patterns of recovery and re-use structuring the Patchin Place production in relation to her complex response to Carell's 'inner time' in the 1930s, its formative role in the 'Baroness Elsa' project and of the 'troubling structures' emanating across *Nightwood* and beyond.

Within T.S. Eliot's dictum of the historical sense indispensable to the production of poetry as involving 'a perception not only of the pastness of the past, but of its presence [...] a sense of the timeless and the temporal together' we might trace similar Bergsonian resonances. However, while Bergson and Carrel's formulations rely on metaphors of fluidity and blending, Eliot's language of 'existing monuments' forming an 'ideal order among themselves' has decidedly clearer edges.[52] Of course, as is well established, Eliot's relationship to tradition, and particularly his repudiation of modernism's closest living relative, Romanticism in favour of Classical or mythic models is more vexed than his essays from this period might suggest.[53] Nevertheless, Eliot's pointed insistence on the poet's ability to absorb literary history and organize its discontinuous elements until they cohere into a 'simultaneous existence and composes order' is somewhat at odds with Carrel's description of simultaneity and the individual patterns of 'inner motion' whereby 'man is constituted, in his fourth dimension, by a series of forms following, and blending into, each other. He is egg, embryo, infant, adolescent, adult, mature and old man'.[54]

Importantly, while Eliot's model draws on the *external* referents of literary history and an inherited European identity, Carrel proposes that duration, and the 'inner motion' of which it is composed, is located *internally* as a 'succession of states'. Experienced subjectively and registered within the body's organs and tissues, its patterns are entirely distinct from organism to organism. Reinforcing the logic and coherence of our sense of the past through the 'explanatory logic of narrative', Eliot's notion of this structure of recurrence is ultimately reassuring and affirmative, organized through the external referents of European cultural history and stabilized through poetic 'impersonality'.

It is striking that in the depth and breadth of more recent critical interest in Barnes's relationship to Eliotian impersonality, the fact that she was directly engaged in a collaborative autobiographic project with the Baroness during a formative period of *Nightwood*'s composition is rarely acknowledged.[55] In making a case for Barnes's outsider status in relation to Eliot's model of poetic tradition that 'stressed the continuity and wholeness of that order', and her scepticism of the processes involved in poetic depersonalization, Tyrus Miller succinctly identifies the 'extreme stylistic mannerism and runaway figural language [...] radical loss of boundaries, the promiscuous blurring of categories' that is characteristic of Barnesean aesthetics. Nevertheless, in identifying elements of 'Joyce's flamboyant displays of style, Eliot's borrowings from literary history and Pound's thematic montage of fragments' in Barnes's literary output, Miller overlooks the Baroness as an influence that sat much closer to home.[56] Given her significant contribution to the thematics of montage and Dada poetics in the late 1910s and early 1920s, the prominent publication of her work alongside the likes of Joyce and Pound in *The Little Review* and elsewhere, and Barnes's own involvement with her on both a personal and literary level, she seems as likely a source of stylistic inspiration as the farther-reaching Pound.

In its activation of strategies of recovery, revision and repetition, the Barnes corpus by contrast stages a much messier and more discontinuous mode of return which calls into question the stability of the referents of 'nation', 'identity' and 'history' re-stated in Eliot's account. Like Eliot, Barnes turns to mythic, historical and literary models and yet, in looking well beyond the boundaries proscribed by Eliotian tradition, and incorporating the low, the devalued and the decidedly feminine, she unpicks the border line of Eliot's pattern, and opens her texts to renewal from outside of such narrow proscriptions.[57] Pushing this further, it is possible to identify a reverse movement in Barnes's deployment of tradition – whereas Eliot's ideal 'really new' poet finds his place through his organizational labour, establishing himself in relation to tradition, Barnes's temporalities work from the inside out, subordinating the structures of history, myth and literary heritage to the patterns of this inner time.[58]

Far from coherent or stabilizing, history functions in Barnes's texts as it does on Sophia Ryder's walls, a stylistic artifice of artfully arranged and juxtaposed fragments that covers over instead of removing, where meaning is not given whole, but presented as an interpretive act occurring between discontinuities, and subject to 'the obliterating and relentless wave' of change. History, as displayed on Sophia's walls and in Barnes's texts, refuses the universal, instead presenting itself as something personally constructed, the 'telltale rings of the oak' coming forward in the pattern (R: 13).

If, as Melissa Jane Hardie suggests, Eliot's notion of this mode of historical consciousness can be traced in broader accounts of the 'temporal dynamics of the modern' as the interpenetration of 'nostalgic traditionalism' and 'the transformative promise embedded in the idea of modernity as constant change', Barnes's proximity to Eliotioan tradition not only troubles the claims for its inherent stability, but also complicates definitions of the modern(ist) that it was so influential in shaping.[59] Operating across (rather than simply outside of) the limits of Eliotian aesthetics and recovering the outmoded and antiquated from beyond its boundaries through the processes of retrieval and estrangement described by Caselli, it is possible to see the ways in which the Barnes corpus effectively uses the disruptive and generative potential of waste and mess that this book has been tracing to mark the 'dialectical relationship between modernity and history as its returned repressed'.[60] This is not to reiterate readings that suggest Barnes makes a 'modernism of marginality', but to trace the ways in which the structural principles of recurrence and return identified as an organizing principle of the Baroness's practice function similarly within Barnes's writing, and to identify the biographic project and Barnes's enthusiastic reading of contemporary theories of time and consciousness as informing these patterns in noteworthy ways.

Certainly, the rhythmic patterns of Carrel's inner time, and the aesthetic problems related to its representation preoccupied Barnes throughout her writing. The later Patchin Place production pointedly returns to this issue on both a formal and thematic level, with the silkworm emerging as a powerful condensed metaphor of the writer's labours as at once durational and externalized. In shifting my focus back to this earlier and fruitful period of Barnes's production, I want to highlight the ways in which her reading of Carrel and her engagement with his thinking are worked out across the 'Baroness Elsa' manuscript, which is itself structurally interwoven into the fabric of *Nightwood*, and which reaches full expression towards the end of her own life in the reiterative modes of the Patchin Place production.

In one particularly illuminating letter to Coleman towards the end of *Nightwood*'s production, Barnes explicitly relates Carrel's theories to her own thinking:

> I have just read Dr Alexis Carrel's "Man, the Unknown" get it immediately. It is superb, about eighty percent of it is what I have been screaming about for years and no one would listen to me. His theory of inner time pleases me, and of the outer boundary that we know nothing of, or how far it goes. […] and how Carrel loves past time, of which we are compiled.[61]

Moving from this explicit discussion of Carrel, Barnes's letter proceeds like an experimental enactment and examination of the compositional qualities and rhythmic patterns of this 'inner time' as Barnes explores the embeddedness of memory and its involuntary interruption into the present. Significantly, Barnes's creative expansion on the simultaneity and 'inner motion' involved in this theory is figured through reference to the Baroness, and Barnes's ongoing struggles with the biographic project. Meditating on the nature of her writing practices and the source of her narrative material, Barnes laments the slow progress of the 'Baroness Elsa' project:

> Darling, I have written still almost nothing on the Baroness; I am apprehensive that perhaps I've written my best, my life and love. What shall I write now that will be as good? Nothing I should think, because I write from the heart, being a female, or can I now write like a female Proust, not so much from the heart as

from the head in the heart (that good doctor Carrel knows that we think with our whole body, live and have our being in the whole).

Barnes's conception of the interconnected autobiographic, corporeal and gendered dimensions of her own writing is striking here, and it is significant that she invokes both Proust and Carrel in her articulation of a 'thinking heart' as the source of her writing. In reflecting on her own modes of production here, Barnes engages suggestively with provocative questions about the poetics and politics of (self)representation, notably on the fraught positioning of auto/biography as a 'privileged form of expressing embodiment'.[62] After a seemingly digressive account of a recent lunch with the Bouchés to which I shall return, Barnes's letter circles back to the issues of embodiment and formal composition in establishing the particular problems presented by this biographic project.

> What shall I do with Elsa, make her part of myself and the rest biographical? There is no other book idea that I have any thought of, she would be excellent for me if I would bring my conscience to take liberties with her, and why not? Shakespeare or anyone else would, only in her case she was so peculiarly passionate about her individuality and identity, that it seems a sort of breach of faith.

Having testified to the embodied qualities of a set of distinctly autobiographic writing practices conceptualized as an 'open wound' or 'thinking heart', Barnes finds herself presented with certain ethical and aesthetic dilemmas. Keenly aware of Elsa's own 'passionate individuality' and the centrality of self-representational modes in the development of her own Dada practice, Barnes acknowledges the 'breach of faith' involved in assimilating her subject in her own writing; however, I would also suggest that the letter's focus on questions of structure – of *Nightwood*, the 'Baroness Elsa' project and of Barnes's examination of the functioning of memory in the letter – articulates her attempts to work out these compositional issues according to the patterns of inner time that she intuitively felt and confirmed through her reading of Carrel.

In this respect, the letter identifies two core problems that Barnes is wrestling with in this project. The second, which I shall return to presently, relates to the 'troubling structure' of auto/biographical temporality itself; the first is a more complex set of aesthetic and formal concerns related to how the particular patterns of this inherent time can be externalized and executed in writing – how, in Carrel's terms, we go about 'creating and fashioning things out of ourselves'.

Closely linked to memory but exceeding it in its incorporation of 'personality' and connections to 'physiological time', Carrel's 'psychological duration' proceeds through the same looping and doubling patterns described by Barnes in the letter, and formalized in the 'Beggars Comedy' drafts. Outlining the impression of duration on our physical being as recorded in our muscles and expressed through the degradation of our tissues, Carrel hypothesizes that:

> we realize that we change, that we are not identical with our former self. But that we are the same being. The distance from which we look back upon the small child, who was ourself, is precisely the dimension of our organism and of our consciousness which we compare to a spatial dimension. Of this aspect of inner time we know nothing, except that it is both dependent and independent of the rhythm of organic life, and moves more and more rapidly as we get older.[63]

Under the heading 'commenced 1932', Barnes's first 'Baroness Elsa' drafts move between the first and third person in order to capture the rhythms of this dynamic inner time unfolding in its own spatial dimension, erecting a textual architecture connecting the child with the present. Tellingly, in these early drafts Barnes places the action in a very specific time and place:

> "I am born at the East sea in my father's own house in Swinemünde" July twelfth, eighteen seventy four. So begins the story of Elsa, born Plötz, who was to become Baroness Elsa von Freytag-Lorighoven, who, for fifty four years was to be ridiculed, praised, loved, brutalised, being passionate, ridiculous, splendid and "impossible".

Apparently unsatisfied with this more chronological approach, Barnes begins to experiment with Elsa's material, an early 'Beggars Comedy' draft recording her attempts to convey something of the temporality of 'Old Europe' through rich description of its gabled houses, uneven cobbled streets, carvings and herring 'strung through the thin hard sills and dried to the colour of yellowing vellum', the fabric of a small town in which 'one lived in the core, and not on the surface of the earth'. In this context 'Madame Schmidt's' (Ida-Marie) derangement is patterned in the fabric of the town itself, like the passage of time that shows through the 'decaying walls of its cathedral', the 'slow decay of the mind [...] was something essential to the town's tradition'.

Like the Patchin Place poetry cycles, rather than trying to read these multiple drafts, notes and fragments as a teleological account of the development, and thus 'failure', of the 'Baroness Elsa' project, it might be more useful to think of them as an open system of migrating phrases, images and motifs that work out how to pry open narrative time in a manner recognized by Joesph Frank's early study of 'spatial form'. With reference to Proust, Eliot and Joyce, Frank's 1945 study identified a tendency in modernist aesthetics that he suggested reached its most extreme expression in *Nightwood*, whereby the reader was led to 'apprehend their work spatially, in a moment in time, rather than as a sequence' (225).[64] Certainly[65] *Nightwood* frustrates narrative linearity in favour of modes of simultaneity emphasized by Frank; however, I would suggest that a consideration for Carrel's model of inner time pushes this reading of *Nightwood* away from what we might call Joycean simultaneity (i.e. things occurring at the same time, in different places represented as a serious of juxtapositions and recurrences within the durational experience of reading), into the territory of pure spatiality – which is to say a place where characters are modelled not in relation to narrative time, but to their own, expansive, contradictory rhythms in relation to one another.

Elsa's distinctive tendency to 'fashion things out of herself' was of course particularly pronounced, and had already intrigued Barnes from afar. Embedded within an early journalistic piece mapping contemporary Greenwich Village pre-dating the period of their close confidence, Barnes provides a dazzling description of the strange simultaneity of the Baroness's extreme modernity and crumbling antiquity.[66] Absolutely woven into the fabric of the metropolis we see her:

> Leap lightly from one of those new white taxis with seventy black and purple anklets clanking about her secular feet, a foreign postage stamp – cancelled – perched upon her cheek; a wig of purple and gold caught roguishly up with strands of a cable once used to more importations from far Cathay; red trousers – and catch the subtle dusty perfume blown back from her – an ancient human notebook on which has been written all the follies of a past generation.[67]

Reiterating the eccentric and eclectic costumes and 'subtle dusty perfume' by now familiar from contemporary accounts of the Baroness's urban promenades, what is striking about Barnes's description here is her early appreciation of the Baroness's embodied aesthetics, the manner in which she not only applied paint, postage stamps and trash items directly to her skin, but of the way in which the reconfiguration of her body as open and unbound externalizes the passage of time on the surface of her body. As an 'ancient human notebook' the record of time's passing is made legible as a script *on* her body and cast *off* it in a manner that conceptually connects the labours of the silkworm that figures so prominently in Barnes's Patchin Place production with the 'subtle dusty perfume thrown back' from the Baroness.

While I absolutely agree with Taylor's reading of affective memory in Barnes, as a mode of writing where 'memory and emotion do not come from cognition', but powerfully reside within the body, I think Barnes's aestheticization of inner time somewhat complicates the rootedness of Taylor's account, and in the structural and spatial patterns that Barnes establishes we can trace the emanations of memory as something that moves out from the body, while never quite detaching from it.[68]

In a fragment related to the 'Baroness Elsa' project, we can clearly identify the blend of Elsa's own distinctive rhythms of recurrence with Carell's proposition that the apprehension of this inner time occurs in a spatial dimension:

> I think there is a difference in time according to the 'shape' of things, say the raised acanthus designs on a pillar, the art of engraving, the round, the flat, have something to do with the concept of time, so according to our own build, skeliton [sic], shape, form, angles, roundness, each of us must participate in a difference in time, lace must suffer a different time than that of satin, a cave from that of a well.

Disrupting the 'time-flow' of the narrative, as Frank's spatial theory implies, it is through the juxtapositions and interactions of these objects in space that we are made aware of the individual patterns of inner time shaping Barnes's objects and characters, an expression that can be made legible through careful attention to the 'shape' that these things take.[69]

A third set of variants (although not necessarily to be understood in such strictly chronological or classifiable terms) focus more squarely on the question of inner time, and how best to represent its emanation, or, as Barnes described it, the 'boundaries beyond the figure'.[70] As the heavily reworked opening in these pages repeats, 'the structure of the body can be studied without scalpel, without science; under hazard every part gives up its history'. Through close attention to the patterns and spatial form of this inner time, Barnes executes a detailed portrait of 'the little old lady, the Parisienne' as a creature shaped by and through time:

> An object in her own life that she has forgotten to dust, rendered down by a time which is too slow; the withered shoulders under the waist-length cape, the rustier skirts, less faded at the joint, where the cape has, for unrecorded years, made her its own [...] The small high bonnet holding her head up as if brought up on a scavengers spade, the lace still erect in the dignity of its decay crumbling away from the wires spread like an insects wing or an autumn leaf which is a tracery of summer.

Taking care to note the particular modes and qualities of decay inherent to the different materials of lace, velvet bands and heavier fabrics, Barnes creates a strikingly tangible sense of the simultaneous expressions of differently registered inner time. Within this sculptural image, Barnes records an inverse momentum; as the small withered frame of the woman recedes, she is covered and exceeded by the accretions of these patterns. Resonating with what Brian Glavey has more recently described as the moments of 'queer ekphrasis' in Barnes's work we can certainly identify the ways in which Barnes's overt stylization works here to 'dazzle one's estrangement – at once make it a thing and to make it beautiful through illumination'.[71]

While Glavey's discussion only lights on the trapeze artist Frau Mann as she, in turn, recalls to Doctor O'Conner's mind the body of the black circus performer, Nikka as something 'forgotten but comparable', her costuming is not only directly based on the Baroness, as has been well established, but vividly recreates the Baroness's quality – to paraphrase Carell – of fashioning things out of herself:

> Her trade – the trapeze – seemed to have preserved her. It gave her, in a way, a certain charm. Her legs had the specialised tension common to aerial workers; something of the bar was in her wrists, the tan bark in her walk, [...] She seemed to have a skin that was the pattern of her costume: a bodice of lozenges, red and yellow, low in the back and ruffled over and under the arms, faded with the reek of her three-a-day control, red tights, laced boots – one somehow felt they ran through her as the design runs through hard boiled candies, and the bulge in the groin where she took the bar, one foot caught in the flex of the calf, was as solid, specialised and as polished as oak. The stuff of the tights was no longer a covering, it was herself; the span of the tightly stitched crotch was so much her own flesh that she was unsexed as a doll. The needle that had made one the property of the child made the other the property of no man. (*N*: 12)

In Frau Mann's 'bodice of lozenges' we find a kaleidoscopic series of colliding associations; the Baroness's costuming practices and tendency to paint directly onto the surface of her skin in lurid colours; the swirling patches of paint and intersecting tin foil and pastel lozenges in her *Portrait of Berenice Abbot*; the dynamic activity of the circus performer held up against Williams's torpid modernism; the 'faded reek' that prominently recurs in descriptions of her; Barnes's own, evocative description of the Baroness as a human notebook; the reworked passages of the old Parisienne across the 'Beggars Comedy' drafts; the biography's detailing of the 'Living Statues'; Ida-Marie's 'strange handiwork' and the labours of the silkworm. Here the 'shape' of Frau Mann – her legs, wrists, skin and the 'bulge of her groin' – moulded by her years as a trapeze artist externalizes and expresses her personal history. Woven into the fabric of the 'stuff of the tights […] the tightly stitched crotch', her inner rhythm comes forward in her until in a literalization of Carrel; she has stitched past and present together and fashioned a carapace *out* of herself – her own 'shroud to metamorphose in'.

Glavey's description of Barnes's 'moments of ekphrastic interruption' is particularly compelling in this respect, the 'rhetoric of still movement' animating these passages that appears to 'hold narrative time in stasis […] freeze time into space' working not only at the level of narrative time, but as a means of recording and crafting this inner rhythm within dazzling passages of textual description.[72] More than this, the momentum that Glavey presents as characteristic of these ekphrastic descriptions according to which a figure is 'caught' in a 'falling arc' between 'expect[ation]' and 'execution' lends itself to a model of auto/biographic production, that is, how to render verbally the pattern and movement of time through a static image.

Returning to Barnes's letter to Coleman from September 1935 we can see the ways in which Barnes aligned her reading of Carrel and Proust with the deepening understanding of the nature of her own embodied autobiographic poetics in an attempt to move forward with the 'Baroness Elsa' project by 'mak[ing] her part of myself', and of making her *apart from* herself. Detailing a rather disastrous lunch hosted by Eustace Seligman which ended in a verbal altercation between the guest and her host, Barnes attempts to explain her horrified reaction at being brought out to look at the old and ailing police dog hiding amongst the expensive stables and horses and waiting to die. Claiming that the 'poor demented dog' understood the shame of his own 'disqualification' Barnes invokes the memory of the Baroness and 'that look [she] gave me long ago, just before she said "shall I trust you"'.

> As Proust has pointed out, two horrors joined suddenly, give you the significance of the one – I never before could quite describe what that look of Elsa's was, now here it is. Possibly none of the events of our life are real until the second event (like the meeting of sperm and ova) gives them body.[73]

Under this formulation it is the second event, the *re-vision*, that bestows significance and meaning to the first and by mediating and reconstructing the memory of Elsa through the encounter with the beleaguered dog, it is Barnes who gives 'body' and meaning both to Elsa's 'look' and the recurrence of Elsa herself through her own 'thinking heart'. While she directly invokes Proust in the sensation of these 'two horrors joined suddenly' giving significance to the one, the embodied qualities of memory and recurrence that she outlines here are also clearly informed by her reading of Carrel, and the patterns of her thinking in the 'Baroness Elsa' drafts. In a fashion following the Baroness's own collage aesthetics, the production of meaning here is forged through the shock of juxtaposition and in its ability to briefly illuminate something beyond immediate comprehension, a 'troubling structure' that also has an important antecedent in the correspondence related to the collaborative auto/biographic project.

As Cheryl Plumb has highlighted in her introductory notes to the annotated edition of *Nightwood*, Barnes's specific use of 'disqualified' in uniting the image of Elsa with that of the dog binds this letter (and, I would add, the 'Baroness Elsa' project she is discussing) to her own writing, in particular to *Nightwood*. Looking across the Barnes-Coleman correspondence from the period, Plumb highlights Barnes's justification for the 'unstructured' quality of her manuscript and her refusal to limit her narrative focus to the Robin-Nora relationship on the grounds that their story had to be mediated through the 'disqualification' surrounding them. With close reference to the letters, Plumb goes on to suggest that the disqualification invoked in relation to both the Baroness and the conceptual background of *Nightwood* referred explicitly to 'an awareness of a sense of shame, a suggestion that individuals who incurred public dismissal or scrutiny because of what happened to them or what they were, that is, Jewish, homosexual, or alienated from the values of a dominant culture'.[74]

Elsa's 'disqualification', one that Barnes had been able to give body and meaning to through the image of the dog, not only reappears in Barnes's repeated revisions of the 'Baroness Elsa' project (most notably in 'The Beggar's Comedy' drafts) but is (re)made as Barnes's own and endowed with 'significance' as it is incorporated by the 'thinking heart' behind *Nightwood*. Indeed, we can trace the ways in which the narratological emphasis on this mode of casting-out throughout the novel is carefully mediated and focused through the figure of the Baroness. Unable to move past the early childhood chapters in her reworking of the 'Baroness Elsa' manuscript, Barnes nevertheless incorporated and integrated Elsa into fabric of her novel through the processes of re-embodiment laid out in her letter to Coleman and structurally enabled by her reading of Carrel and Proust. Lynn DeVore's 1983 study usefully illuminated the extent to which Elsa's autobiography re-surfaced in *Nightwood*, and in particular in the character of Robin Vote. Problematically overlooking the significance of Barnes's own turbulent relationship with the silver-point artist Thelma Wood in the rendering of Robin, DeVore's study nevertheless has provided valuable ground for a consideration of the processes and broader significance of the auto/biographic interplay at work in this narrative incorporation of the Baroness.

Significant phrases and recurrent images from the various 'Baroness Elsa' drafts are clearly re-worked into the fabric of *Nightwood*, notably the description of the elegant but unknowable Polish-born 'Frau Schenk' across the 'The Beggar's Comedy' variants as a 'contemporary antiquity', the recurrent figuration of 'bowing down' or turning inward across the pages and the description of Elsa herself as 'death in reverse' or as 'a Roman fragment looking back into itself' on unrelated pages.[75] The famous passage in which Robin first appears in the novel discussed at the opening of this book clearly owes its debt to the Baroness, from the reconfiguration of the musky scent of her body as 'that earth-flesh, fungi, which smells of captured dampness and yet is so dry' to the effulgent emanations visually rendered by Theresa Bernstein and grasped in the Baroness's own sense of the transformative potential of her embodied art practices. Centrally though, it is the 'troubling structure of the born somnambule, who lives in two worlds – meet of child and desperado' that bears the imprint of the baroness, and of Barnes's ambitious vision for the auto/biographic project.

Clearly linked to the doubled structures of physiological and psychological time proposed by Carrel and explored in a spatial rather than purely durational dimension across the 'Beggars Comedy' drafts, the coming forward of the life within her in 'ungainly luminous deteriorations' is intimately bound up with the Baroness's own embodied self-representational practices, and with the doubled patterns of recurrence and *re-vision* activated in the auto/biographic project.[76] As Barnes writes:

> Such a woman is the infected carrier of them past – before her the structure of our head and jaws ache – we feel that we could eat her, she who is eaten death returning, for only then do we put our face close to the blood on the lips of our forefathers.

Indeed, the figure of the 'Somnambule' came directly from the Baroness herself, appearing in the dramatic fragment 'Chimera' and the advertisement for the Croquis Class, and prominently in the autobiography and in the desperate letters sent to Barnes during her time in Germany in which she declared 'My art has deserted me … it turns to dust in my hands … I am indifferent to it – I despise it. I am afraid of it. I am somnambule – in thrall, …. awakened before abyss of absolute icy nonsense'.[77] Strong archival evidence also supports the claim that Barnes's Baron Felix Volkbein is derived (in name if nothing further) from one of Felix Paul Greve's alter-egos, used when travelling through Europe.

One textual fragment now arranged alongside Barnes's notes on Elsa's time with Greve in Palermo reads: 'She was Gothic and interminably old – Felix Volkbein had been in Düsseldprf [sic], had wandered from there down to Palermo.'[78]

Rather than simply re-tracing possible biographic sources for Barnes's composite characters, I hope to have highlighted the extent to which the Baroness and her autobiography were of central importance in developing the complex structures of *Nightwood* and of Barnes's mature autobiographic poetics more broadly. Indeed, contrary to her own claims that 'I can't, I have never been able to plot or plan a book or give it, apparently any structure, I don't really think I know what a structure is, in the accepted sense', Barnes's application of her reading of Carrel and Proust in her treatment of the Baroness's manuscript not only directly informs the 'troubling structure' of the somnambule, but testifies to the depth of Barnes's thinking regarding the structural representation of the 'troubling' patterns of repetition, return and re-vision that we can trace throughout her work.[79]

Reaching maturity with Barnes's later work, these patterns are used to particular effect in *The Antiphon*. As Taylor has detailed, the act of *re-vison* described by Barnes in her letter to Coleman is absolutely central to the late play's examination of the '*performative* structure of trauma', but I also want to suggest other acts of 're-vision' at work here. While Taylor is right to point out Barnes's courting of an 'initiated' reader 'who might serve as witness and co-producer of her testimony', it is important to acknowledge Barnes's own, troubled understanding of the burden borne by the witness, and their role in co-producing meaning.[80]

The extent to which Elsa's recurrence in Barnes's writing and the central importance falls into a 'breach of faith' is interestingly framed in an unceremonious aside from Eliot, who, trying to get Barnes motivated with her new project insisted that:

> the chief use of the Baroness is to start you off, and if the result shows very little of the Baroness and mostly yourself well that's what we shall like best. So don't have any scruples about historical accuracy etc. but just make use of her.[81]

With this in mind, a consideration of the extent to which this *re-vision* percolated through Barnes's writing after the 1930s and the part it played in informing the structural patterns of her mature autobiographic poetics becomes increasingly compelling. Continuing to work on the manuscript in the years following *Nightwood's* publication, Barnes experimented with more elaborate treatments of the material, re-working and blending Elsa's manuscript with more recognizably

Barnsean prose patterns and imagery. Nevertheless, persistent scenes, phrases and images remain, resonating across the variants and out into Barnes's later writing as an internal refrain. Significant in this respect is the special emphasis placed by both Elsa and Barnes on the latter's traumatic childhood memories, particularly of her mother's depression, suicide attempts and eventual death, and the tyrannical force of her 'Teuton' father.

In what could be read as a reflection on her own autobiographic practices, Barnes draws attention to the great significance placed upon the memory of childhood to the adult artist Elsa, a testament to the 'great appreciation of what she herself signified'. As recorded in one of the prefaces, that 'she kept the memory clean and exact proves that childhood was of value [...] yet the return to childhood is a very difficult thing for anyone to accomplish, when they have surrounded that nucleus with the enormous vagaries that its being entails'.[82]

Echoing Carrel's interlocking concepts of physiological and psychological duration, Barnes structures this simultaneous accretion of time and unspooling of memory through an important intertextual shadow connecting the generative making and unmaking of Ida-Marie's 'strange handiwork' and the externalized products of the silkworm's labour:

> The child in Elsa sat enthroned amid a vast ramification of mature beauty and childish obscenity, [...] she spun about herself, the original child, born 'equal' the most devious and unequal cocoon, which was germain [sic] to the flesh. She was born it would seem that this bale of destiny should have for its pains, an enclosed eye to lament the spinning, and an intelligence to suffer the weave.[83]

iv. Denying the called response: Mothers, daughters and *The Antiphon*

> The ballerina on perfected toe
> Spins to the axis of a fortitude
> That is the sum of all her yesterdays
>
> *Djuna Barnes*, The Antiphon

Returning to *The Antiphon*, we can clearly identify the ways in which the messy materiality and densely woven intertextual reverberations familiar to Barnes's 'wounded' poetics are arranged in her late verse tragedy according to these 'troubling structures'. Concerned less with the memory of one traumatic event than with the processes of memory and remembering itself, it is certainly possible to read the various stylistic difficulties frequently attributed to the 'most impossible cabinet drama of the century' accordingly.[84] Standing as her most developed and intimate expression of trans-generational familial dynamics, inherited trauma and patterns of patriarchal violence, Barnes's text nevertheless absolutely resists the confessional and clarifying pressures of the 'biographic impulse' outlined above. In this late play, the messy materiality of Barnes's writing practices and the complex spatial patterns of 'inner time' and recurrence activated in the 'Baroness Elsa' project and structuring her autobiographic poetics work together to 'keep the wound open'.

As the title itself testifies to, the play cannot be sealed as a single, final or authoritative account, but is itself compositionally organized according to the 'antiphonal' structures of call and response.[85] While the counterpointed narratives of the living members of the Hobbs family are certainly arranged in an antagonistically antiphonal relationship to one another, more striking is the 'troubling structure' of the interruption of their reunion in the present with the echoes of dead voices and repressed memories of times long past. The keystone text of Barnes's mature autobiographic poetics, these antiphonal arrangements are essential both in her articulation of a surface 'family pattern' and in allowing her to develop a structural model through which to explore her own sense of the interplay between the past and the present, the timeless and the temporal, physical and psychological time.[86] In this respect the elaborate formal structures of the play are absolutely and intimately related to its dramatic and narrative content, enabling Barnes to explore the perpetual recurrence of a collective family history of trans-generational trauma and violence in the present without 'telling on the innermost secret'. Like the simultaneous unspooling of time and accretion of memory presented by the silkworm's embodied labours, or the generative making and unmaking activated in Ida-Marie's un-seaming and re-stitching of scraps and waste material, *The Antiphon* employs recurrence, repetition and return in order to 'baste a shroud/to metamorphose in', one that disrupts notions of time and narrative as linear sequence and refuses attempts to seal off the past as 'long dead'.

Establishing the circularity of this 'signifying if dizzyingly complex construction' in the opening lines of the play,[87] Miranda introduces the themes of return and remembering as a form of rupture which drives and dominates the dramatic action:

Here's a rip in nature; here's gross quiet,
Here's cloistered waste;
Here's rudeness once was home. (I, 8)

The insistence on immediacy in these opening lines with the throbbing repetition of 'here's' (at once place, moment in time, and playful homonym of 'hears') is counterpointed with a comparison to what was, establishing a tension between now and then which ruptures the supposedly stable ordering frameworks of 'nature', 'time' and 'history', as identified in relation to the treatment of spatialized natural history and the 'fossil's eye' within the Patchin Place cycles. The ancestral home bears the mark of the overlaying of multiple, conflicting histories as a 'haunt of time'. Once a college of chantry priests and now, after the Burley family's financial ruin at the hands of Titus and Victoria, given over to a shadowy group of 'travellers', the house is the site of original rupture in the Burley family chronicle. Stepping back into this world Miranda strikes the key note for what follows: 'the world is cracked – but in the breach my fathers mew' (I, 10).

In contrapuntal dialogue Jack and Miranda begin to expose the unhappy history of the family for whom 'everything is a little out of context', one that seems rooted in the ill-fated marriage of Augusta who 'so leaned on royalty and legend/ She replaced herself as her own adversary' (I, 12) to the coarser Titus Hobbs. In the first of a series of digressions and temporal shifts, Miranda interrupts these skirting reflections of her mother's past and returns her mind to the present, to the possible consequences of 'this afternoon'. Interrupted and counterpointed by Jack's sudden, short exclamations, the sense of 'dislocated time' (I, 13) at work across the play is introduced here in the abrupt shift between reported memory and an immediate, imagined future.

Disrupting the broadly symmetrical metre established between the two characters at the opening, Jack's lines introduce an asymmetrical element. Setting Jack's truncated responses against the pattern retained by Miranda's lines, Barnes develops the play's 'troubling structure' through the introduction of counterpointed time frames, achieved through the interplay of two levels of motion, a faster and a slower. Thus established, this polyrhythm continues to work throughout the play, gradually moving closer to the foreground as the layering of different rhythms (i.e. different sequences in time repeated) articulates the shifts between past and present, or re-imagined past as present. Prompted by Jack, Miranda returns her mind to the past. However, rather than reporting these events, she re-imagines Augusta in girlhood 'Boating the hedges with her open hand', graphically recreating Augusta's submission to Titus in the present tense and recasting the moment she lay 'Performing the tragic ballet on her back' as the origins of her unhappy marriage and this legacy of 'truncated grief' (I, 14–15).

The unstable temporal framework that supports a play published in 1958, set 'during the war of 1939' and that proceeds through the ornate patterns of approximated Jacobean verse is further complicated and compounded by the play's incorporation of a staggering range of literary, biblical, musical, historical and proverbial allusions. While Kannestein was quite correct to suggest that *The Antiphon* re-staged 'forms of Greek tragedy and early closet drama, and most directly revises the tone and grandeur of Elizabethan drama with a nod at the Jacobean tradition as well',[88] the scope of Barnes's scavenging is considerably broader, including references to nursery rhymes, Shakespeare, John Ball, the Metaphysical poets, Baroque composers, the Roman Catholic liturgical mass, Blake, Wordsworth, P.B. Shelly, nineteenth-century bestiaries, Dickens and her own contemporaries, as more recent scholarship has demonstrated.[89] This elaborate lattice work of textual and temporal reverberation is further convoluted by the recurrence of themes, motifs and narrative material from Barnes's own writing, including *Ryder*, several of the early one-acts and short stories, and the 'Baroness Elsa' manuscript.

Rather than stabilizing the Barnes oeuvre in an impersonal relation to an ordered and literary history, her recuperation and reanimation of frequently misquoted or altered snatches and fragments from a broad range of other texts render this recurrence uncanny and unsettling. As Taylor has highlighted in relation to Barnes's aping of the forms and diction of Jacobean tragedy, this self-conscious anachronism and insistence in re-animating dated forms produce a 'repetition with a difference', one which challenges both the formal unities and expectations of the revenge tragedy genre and of the concept of revenge itself.[90]

As we have seen, while Eliot had advocated an attuned sensitivity to the 'presence of the past' Barnes's disruptive and interruptive repetitions position her oeuvre in a troubling proximity to the organizing categories of tradition promoted by the poet. Moreover, in conflating the estranged return of these truncated or misquoted literary fragments with the recurrence of personal history and traumatic memory, Barnes fundamentally refuses the stabilizing framework of 'poetic impersonality' proposed by Eliot's essay. Neither making it new nor advocating a nostalgic return to tradition or the 'primitive', Barnes positions herself and her work in a fraught relation to the temporal dynamics typically associated with literary modernism and, perhaps more radically, challenges Eliot's retrospective re-shaping and re-structuring of the past according to the 'explanatory logic of narrative'.[91] Instead of situating her texts in the coherent and ordering frameworks of history and literary tradition, Barnes's citations and dizzying intertextual references work through *re-vision* to generate this disruptive repetition with a difference.

As Barnes's reading of Proust suggests, this *re-vison* is most powerfully generated in the sensation of 'two horrors joined suddenly', deployed by Barnes to great effect in the Patchin Place cycles with the 'troubling structures' of such arresting images as the recurrence of breastmilk in the lamentation. In a fashion following the Baroness's own collage aesthetics, the production of meaning between speaker and witness across the letters and drafts related to the 'Baroness Elsa' project is similarly forged through the jarring moment of two disparate images brought together and their illumination of a third, unseen thing. While the correspondence is not short of such moments, one in particular stands out in its relevance to the politics of witnessing, re-vison and illumination so central to *The Antiphon*.

Given the tendency of dreams to cut across seemingly fixed geographic and temporal points, and to distil and compress several narrative threads into composite images, it seems appropriate that in criss-crossing the pattern of her life and drawing out certain images for Barnes in her letters, the Baroness would turn to her own dreams. Recalled from some twenty years previously, one fascinating dream sequence returns to the scene of the mother's death, staging it, and its recurrence, as a particularly grotesque performance:

> Suddenly I saw before me a huge round building with dark entrance door – there I slipped in – and found myself in arena very much like that of colloseum [sic] in Rome – Amphitheatre – not quite that large – I went into first tier of seats – went – went – until I came to 8 metal statues – stiff erect – iron – I think. What was most stiffly erect – were their penises – for they were nude – I felt some apprehension – shudder – yet I had to pass them – to do so – I had to walk front – or – back wise – the passage being too narrow by their prescence – I passed them backwise – each of their penises touching my behind with mixed shudder of my body-soul – after passing – there – before me on the balustrade in the arena – stood coffin with woman corpse in it whose abdomen was worm pit – squirming! I looked at it – conscious of being apprehensive about the three iron statues – not daring to pass them again. That dream was in Palermo – 20 years ago.[92]

The shocking image of putrefaction clearly returns to the mother's death sequence in more lurid detail than the letter's more conventional communicative modes of reportage can accommodate. The priapic iron statues condense both the cast-iron rule of the tyrant patriarch, and the hard, insulated bodies of classical ideal form and Theweleit's 'soldier-male' discussed in earlier chapters, and the shock of the scene's juxtaposition between erect armoured male and the grotesquely open, rotting flesh of the woman's womb vividly draws the blurring between sex, death and gendered violence bound up with Elsa's connection between her mother's contracted syphilis and her uterine cancer.

In the overt staging of the scene in an 'arena very much like that of colloseum [sic] in Rome' the Baroness returns us once more to her preferred site of dynamic exchange – although the performative space of the circus-arena is here traded for the more dramatic/combative zone of the Roman amphitheatre. In the *re-vision* of her mother's grotesquely open corpse, the Baroness gives body to her own grotesque performance of femininity, the unavoidable image of the squirming 'worm pit' of the woman's womb pulling this scene closer to a kind of abject parturition.

In illuminating the violence done to her mother, Elsa's *re-vision* of Ida-Marie refuses the various silences imposed on her illness and death, and the censorship of her acts of gender disobedience. Further than an act of recovery and restitution however, the model of grotesque femininity displayed in the dream signals the recurrence of the daughter *in* the image of her mother. A dream from her Palermo days and her teasing out of a more concrete 'artist identity', it announces the beginnings of her experimentation with more radical and challenging modes of self-display, and both mother and daughter are here in a sense born again through the squirming worm/womb pit.

In recovering this dream sequence from twenty years previously, a period that covers Elsa's arrival in New York, her 'art dazzle' days and her own sense of dereliction in Weimar Germany, she also enlists Barnes in the act of its *re-vision*, recovering her mother and her own performance of grotesque femininity and entrusting them to Barnes.[93] In this respect, the arrangement of mother/daughter dynamics in *The Antiphon* takes on another aspect; while clearly staging elements of Barnes's own experiences with maternal ambivalence, the repeated requests of Augusta to have her daughter '*make me something*' (A: 186) carry with them their own uncanny resonances of Elsa's *re-vision* of her own mother and her 'strange handiwork' in her letters to Barnes, and of Barnes's failure to *make something* of the 'Baroness Elsa' material.

Once a car in a merry-go-round, the reuniting of the divided gryphon is particularly significant in this respect, not only in visually compounding the circularity of time and memory explored throughout the play that comes to particular prominence in the meta-theatricality of the third act, but metonymically representative of the unsettling return of the outmoded, anachronistic and estranged in the Barnes oeuvre. A merry-go-round presumably has no place in the grand ancestral home, its appearance there, along with the costumes, dressmaker's dummy and 'battered gilt mardi-gras' crown not only emphasizing the overt and self-conscious metatheatricality of the text, but visually reinforcing the mode of estrangement figured through Barnes's practices of return and retrieval. As the discarded objects of amusement parks and vaudeville shows, these objects also work to visually confirm the dense intertextuality of the Barnes corpus; visually referencing scenes from the early New York journalism and the Baroque interiors familiar to *Nightwood*, the disparate objects – once brought together – re-embody and re-animate these earlier texts in the play's present. As the stage for the final attempt at this *re-vsion* between mother and daughter, it also loops us back in an intertextual echo to the sublimated but central drama of the mother-daughter relationship in the 'Baroness Elsa' project.

Divided by Titus, the gryphon is brought back together by Miranda at the close of the second act in order to 'make of this divided beast/an undivided bed' (II: 155). However, the coming together of mother and daughter in the Chimeric combination of lion and eagle is not reparative but annihilating, as Mirada presages in her lines to Burley:

> Abjure it, you sit between two beasts in chancery
> Who fight, head down, between them for a grave
> That neither of them has a conduct for. (II: 154)

As Bonnie Kime Scott observed, the reassembled gryphon sets the stage for the mother and daughters struggle with the 'ways that they, like the gryphon, are split or united, and borne by one another'.[94] To this I would add that in doing so it also stages the (con)fusions activated in the processes of recovery and recurrence that structure the play and Barnes's autobiographic poetics more broadly.

While obviously at work throughout the play from Jack and Miranda's opening contrapuntal dialogue which moves between past and present tenses in recreating Augusta's unhappy history and consequences of her marriage to Titus (a theme picked up and re-worked by the other characters as they appear), to Augusta's attempts to have herself re-born through her daughter in the final act, the collapse of past and present in a compound image articulated by Barnes in 1935 is most effectively deployed in the pivotal Dolls House scene. In presenting Augusta with the miniature and attendant marionettes Jack encourages her to generate the 'second event' that will 'give body' to the first through repetition, as Taylor has discussed in light of the structures of repetition and witnessing that constitute the trauma response. Recognizing the likeness between the 'seven straightened mistresses', the miniature Titus and their historical counterparts, Augusta first confronts the abuses committed against her. With Titus reduced to 'A chip, a doll, a toy, a pawn' (II, 145) Augusta is able to 'thaw from history' and to challenge the authority of the patriarch, understanding, finally 'What apes our eyes are/Saw him great because he said so' (II, 148).

Having initiated this re-staging of the family's past, Jack invites her to 'Put your wink against this window pane, what do you see?' While looking through the window of the doll's house would be a rather unremarkable event in itself, the porous boundaries between the past and the present are here concentrated in the image of the transparent window which, while initially distinct and separate from the looking eye, is substituted for it as the scene progresses. The metaphorical substitution of window with eye emphasizes a shift from outside to inside, to the past as a stable and separate memory to its intrusion and disruption of the present as the shifts from past to present tense in Miranda's dialogue emphasize:

Do you remember what the cock-loft saw?
For that window is become your eye.
What do you see? (II, 148)

Augusta can turn away from the window; she cannot escape from the *re-vision* of the rape of her daughter and of her own complicity in the event as it recurs in her own seeing 'eye'. Echoing Barnes's detailing of this antiphonal structure outlined in her letter to Coleman, even while the 'first event' might lay dormant as seemingly insignificant for years, 'the crystal like a pregnant girl has hour/When it delivers up its oracle' (II, 151) and its *re-vision* in the 'second event' give body to its horror. Echoing the recurrent images of circularity common across the Patchin Place variants, Jack condemns Augusta to her memories and her culpability, prophesying that 'The eye-baby now you're pregnant with/You'll carry to your grave' (II, 151).

This conflation of death and birth and its frustration of narrative time moves increasingly to the foreground throughout the third act as Miranda, re-imagining her own conception and birth as the moment 'time commenced' (III, 161) is counterpointed by Augusta's repeated attempts to recast her own history and recreate a fantastical present where she is returned through Miranda's narrative re-telling to an idealized girlhood – to have Miranda refashion her own history and present it to her as something external and comprehensible. Resisting Miranda's attempts to return to 'a time when we were not related/[…] Before the tree was in the cross, the cradle, and the coffin', a time before conception 'When yet the salt unspilt, the bread unbroken/The milk unquested, uncried and unsprung' (III, 160–1), Augusta recreates an alternative fantasy where they can 'Jump the Day of Wrath', pretend 'The play is over' and 'play at being Miranda and Augusta' (III, 165). Moving breathlessly through the imagined backdrops of 'Osted, Monte Carlo, Brighton;/The Lido, Palm Beach, Breisgau, Carcassonne' Augusta gradually removes her daughter's shoes and accessories, arranging herself to play the parts of Empress Josephine, Lily Langtry and Helen of Troy upon the now 'undivided' gryphon car which she re-imagines as 'an excellent stage, fit for a play' (III, 158). Refusing her mother's repeated request to 'Come, play me daughter', or to divulge the details of her own history for the older woman's vicarious titillation, Miranda's abrupt interruptions cut across these gaudy scenes insisting 'there's no more time. All's done' (III, 169).

In terms of setting up the final violent exchange between mother and daughter, the costuming that Barnes describes here is significant in articulating the complex exchanges between mother and daughter and, again, is interestingly illuminated with reference to the 'Baroness Elsa' manuscript. Detailing the sequence where Elsa confronts her own tyrannical father, Barnes has her dress in her mother's clothes in a way that brings her own 'wounded' poetics into a direct relationship with the Baroness's costuming practices:

> She packed all her belongings in a small bag, her ribbons of velvet, and her one silk gown and her woolen dresses, she out on her hip lace boots and her cap with the velvet bows over the ears, then she changed her mind and putting on one of her mothers dresses, with lace cuffs that were too long for her, and a train which always looks ridiculous on a child who wears any length for the first time, came downstairs, rested her bag on the bottom step, and faced her father […] she said without deliberation, and apparently without interest 'so you cover my mother over like a cut, with that woman'. [Emphasis mine]

While the father's hastily arranged second marriage seals up the wound done to the bourgeois family with the death of the mother, and, of course, covering the father's own culpability in this respect, in making the mother uncannily recur through the daughter's appropriation of her wardrobe, Barnes's rewriting of this episode stages the moment of *re-vision* as a means of keeping the wound open. Removing her daughter's clothes and replacing them with her own Augusta similarly tries to move her daughter towards an act of mutually transformative *re-vision*, imploring the younger woman to 'Take mercy on my prentice cries, Miranda,/Leave me not so sharp, unsung, and shrill' (III, 171).

Just as mother and daughter are revealed as a tragic Chimera – tangled one inside the other but subject to a fatal estrangement that falls short of the illuminating and reparative work of *re-vision* – present and past are collapsed and confused as the seemingly submerged, linear substructures of time and history are disrupted, rearranged and foregrounded as various metrical and grammatical distortions move overworked patterns of return and refrain to the surface of the text. Augusta's demands to have her memories remade for her, culminating in her desire to see herself 'recalled' in and by her daughter, generate a perceptual and structural blurring, one foreshadowed in Burley's drowsily intoned recognition of the counterpointed movement between fast and slow, past and present that determines and drives the dialogue and dramatic exposition of the first two acts: 'One two, one two-/Compound motion' (II, 83). The specific use of 'compound motion', the trick of the eye whereby two separate lines of motion, horizontal and vertical, are blurred and combined when followed simultaneously, is especially revealing in reading the stylistic difficulties of *The Antiphon*. This tension between the horizontal and the vertical, between linear time experienced as duration and the excavations of history and memory are internally registered is precisely the fault line that *The Antiphon* emerges from, as a piece staging the truncated attempts of a family to explore, re-remember and undo the pattern of their individual and combined histories in a form that proceeds in time.

Despite Miranda's refusal to draw 'from out her poke so brave a silk/Could card a pigeon' (III, 187), the musical and spatial patterns rupturing the time-flow of the narrative nevertheless excavate the rhythms and traumas of the Burley family and works to fashion material out of itself in a way that recalls both Carell's spatial metaphors and the silkworms labours; while the task is beyond Miranda, *The Antiphon* invests in the (unfinished) work of spinning 'a shroud to reconsider in'.

Proceeding through an ornately stylized and self-conscious anachronism and dismantling and reorganizing literary genealogies, personal histories, prosodic structures and temporal sequence, *The Antiphon* can certainly be treated as illuminatingly representative of the patterns and practices developed in Barnes's mature autobiographic poetics. Central to the politics and poetics of autobiography explored through a play which is unravelled as a series of repetitions, revisions and variations, the 'troubling' relational tensions established between temporal sequence and the overworked patterns of recurrence that refuse to be organized into narrative coherence are also in turn highly revealing as to the role of waste and its recurrence in shaping the Barnes's corpus, its treatment of history and its fraught positioning in relation to literary modernism.

Deploying patterns of recurrence, repetition and variation, the 'failed' 'Baroness Elsa' manuscripts and the formal and thematic concerns of *The Antiphon* are deeply preoccupied with the generative and unsettling potential of waste in both its material and conceptual forms. Rupturing 'official' narratives just as Barnes cut into Thurn's 'sealed' account of Barnes's play as a spiteful raking over of things 'long-dead', these texts powerfully engage with strategies of recovery and re-use as a means of staging the 'unseaming' of official or dominant accounts, of revealing and re-making 'a history that runs against – and is in "deep conflict" with – the "official interpretative devices of [our] culture".[95] These texts not only frustrate the pressures of the 'biographic impulse' and the demands of facticity, coherence and clarity familiar to its promotion of a 'realist fallacy' through a process of constant revision and variation, but develop a set of *embodied* writing practices which work with this messy materiality to 'keep the wound open'. Structurally sustained by the 'troubling' patterns which reverberate across the corpus in antiphonal echoes, Barnes's treatment of waste in its unsettling mobility and disruptive capability is the privileged sign of the 'second event': as her texts demonstrate, it is only through the unsettling return of the past that the present is given body and significance.

Coda: Modernism recovered

> It will take him, as it will take the others, all his life to unravel the tangle of his upbringing
>
> *Djuna Barnes,* Ryder

Whether manifested in the surging, heterogenous and consumer-driven crowds of the modern metropolis, the un-corseted sexuality, volubility and unsettling visibility of the New Woman, or the excessive, ornamental or 'flabby' text, 'waste' emerged over the early decades of the twentieth century as an increasingly important conceptual category for identifying, separating and regulating the destabilizing effects of machine-age modernity. Intimately bound to the production of a twentieth-century consumerist and commodity-based modernity, as Rachele Dini has recently outlined, conceptions of waste nevertheless remain tied to their messy corporeal beginnings.[1] Figured through images of excessive, leaky bodies, sticky fluids, excremental products and a language of the unclean, the contaminating and polluting, these wastes articulated the threats to notions of the coherent and contained body and models of subjectivity central to Western culture, and were policed, regulated and excluded accordingly. Nevertheless, relying heavily on the gendered body for its metaphors, the language of waste and the scope of its concerns went considerably further than anxieties over corporeal integrity alone, leaking across a range of cultural, socio-political, psychological and aesthetic discourses throughout the period.

Just as a Progressive-era emphasis on industrial efficiency and economy relied on the effective elimination of waste for its success, exclusion of waste in its more abstract forms emerged as central to the definition and regulation of the system that produced it, whether in the contexts of the gridded and rationalized city, the coherent modern body or the ordered and 'clean' modernist text. When effectively managed, regulated and contained, waste manifested the smooth functioning of these systems, testifying 'in its very dereliction to the power which cast it down and out'.² Exclusion thus emerged as a powerful tool in defining, regulating and enshrining certain principles relating to modernity and the modern(ist) subject as such jettisoned material was reconfigured as the 'wastes [that] drop so that I might live'.³ In this respect, the anxious gendering of waste during this period as an engulfing and distinctly *feminine* threat telescoped into female bodies and replicated through a rhetoric of disintegration, disease and dissolution highlights the special role played by waste in the structuring and regulation of modern masculine subjectivity – and of a resolutely masculinist axis of modernist poetics and early twentieth-century avant-garde practices.

Whilst decades of feminist criticism have – alongside an expansion of other critical approaches and methodological tools – significantly redrawn the modernist map and expanded the terms upon which we define the practices and aesthetics of the historical avant-garde, attention to contemporary negotiations with waste enables a confrontation with the conceptual categories structuring modernist thought directly. Benstock's assertion that a Poundian/Eliotian axis of high modernism 'constructed itself on a political agenda of exclusion – the exclusion of the Other' takes on renewed significance in light of this project's delineation of the structural functioning of waste and its bearing on the historical marginalization of female writers and artists.⁴ If high modernism defines itself through a process of exclusion, the alignment of women with these jettisoned wastes thus appears central in the construction and definition of a strain of modernist thought and aesthetics invested in a rhetoric of purity, progress and the 'novelty of the new', one that seeks to purge itself of the ornamental excesses of the past while purifying and retaining the ordering structures of tradition and myth that such histories confer.

However, while the efficient elimination of waste might have proved more successful in the theoretical spaces of the industrialized factory, the clean and gridded metropolis, or the re-imagined schema of the inviolate, hard and contained (implicitly masculine) body, the reality of excessive production necessarily associated with an emergent commodity culture emphasized that such wastes can never be satisfactorily eliminated, only excluded or cast out once a commodity has exhausted its usefulness and diminished its value. Our late twentieth- and twenty-first century attitude towards consumption and disposability certainly speaks to the systems of economic value that promote strictly regulated divisions between commodities and cast-offs, while our confrontation with the synthetic and human-made wastes that are returned to us in our clogged oceans and overflowing landfills also underscores an anxiety with the persistence of waste, of our inability to eliminate it effectively that of course also has far-reaching environmental consequences.

Similarly unable to repudiate these symbolic wastes completely, the modernist and avant-garde practices we have traced instead attempted to contain, regulate and effectively manage these threats, of which the sublimation and 'calculated containment' of Elsa's excessive, messy and waste-based body-work within the margins of modernist histories have proven to be particularly revealing of. Deeply unsettling, the persistence of such objects, bodies or matter from beyond these margins nevertheless continues to challenge the operating structures which cast them out in the first instance, exposing the mechanisms of the system under which they were produced and the anxieties that regulate its functioning.

In this respect, waste not only provides a usefully illuminating framework for addressing the methods and motivations for the containment and regulation of certain bodies, texts and practices, but allows us to consider the extent to which certain practices might operate across these boundaries, developing a generative set of waste-based practices that intersect with the masculinist principles evident in early formulations of high modernist projects in revealing ways. Orchestrating the *return* of material and metaphorical wastes in these experimental texts and self-representational poses, the corporeal, autobiographic and performative practices developed by Barnes and the Baroness directly challenged the masculinist, rational discourses central to definitions of modernity and early formulations of modernist projects, and to the retrospective construction of neatly organized critical histories of both literary modernism and the historical avant-garde. Indeed, while Benstock presented a compelling case for the emergence of early twentieth-century avant-garde practices as high modernism's 'excluded other', under closer scrutiny it becomes apparent that such avant-garde pronouncements and aesthetics in fact frequently reinforced and replicated the principles and anxieties at the heart of high modernist poetics.

The Baroness's public performances placed the body – and its ability to scandalize – centre stage. The source of her livelihood as a showgirl, *tableaux vivant* and artist's model, her body was also the blank canvas upon which she executed and animated her own lived-Dada expressions, and throughout her career she would vehemently defend her notion of 'posing' – in all its guises – as art. Through her sexually explicit, linguistically challenging corporeal poetry, her flamboyant *couture d'ordures* and her provocative public displays, the Baroness consistently re-worked, challenged and extended the boundaries of this gendered, sexualized, nationalized and historicized body. Returning the used and worn-out utilitarian objects and commodities jettisoned as waste and applying them directly to her grotesquely excessive body in these performances, the Baroness not only challenged the visual thematics and masculinist bias of

New York Dada and the rationalizing tendencies of subsequent critical histories, but reclaimed the female nude as an autobiographic, performative and messy medium through which to explore modes of embodied female self-expression. As the anxious attempts to re-contain her within modernist marginalia attests to, this body was conceived of as dangerously disintegrative, her contravention of the 'forms, conventions and poses of art [that] have worked metaphorically to shore up the female body – to seal orifices and to prevent marginal matter from transgressing the boundary dividing the inside of body and the outside, the self from the space of the other' posing a direct threat to notions of modernist masculinity and aesthetics as contained, coherent and inviolate.[5]

Staging these corporeal performances as interventions in the private and public spaces of the First World War-era New York, the Baroness destabilized not only constructions of the body, but of the rational, ordered modern city. Collecting and reanimating the used material gleaned from her perambulations, the Baroness's urban performances expose the tensions between competing forces of rationalism and pluralism in shaping the modern metropolis and regulating the spatial and bodily practices within it. If New York was the new capital of modernity as Picabia and others so enthusiastically intoned, then the Baroness's collecting and costuming practices (and the ambivalent responses to them) illuminate the processes through which such formations are constructed, defined and maintained, and signal her broader challenge to the capitalist hegemonic order.

Similarly, through familiar tropes of detached objectivity, 'impersonal' poetics and a preference for the clean, contained and un-ornamented text, this Poundian/Eliotian axis of high modernist practices developed its own aesthetic systems for carefully mediating and regulating the potentially destabilizing or disintegrative threats of modernity. Significantly, these early modernist and avant-garde formations were shaped in illuminating ways through a negotiation with the past and history. While the Italian Futurists and early Vorticist pronouncements of Wyndham Lewis aggressively rejected the past in all its forms, the more self-consciously 'modernist' formations spearheaded by Eliot and Pound during this period took a more nuanced approach. Torn between the conflicting impulses towards a potentially fragmentary and disorientating 'newness' and the stabilizing structures of lineage and literary tradition, this strain of modernist thought re-imagined the past as a vital force by purging its wastes and retaining the purified ordering structures of tradition, classicism and linearity, developing a fragmentary but fundamentally ordered poetics appropriate for a 'culturally fragmented age'.[6]

Whether conceived of as the disruptive recurrence of memory, messy textual revisions or of the estranged return of literary history or discarded, outdated objects, the Barnes corpus instead stages its relation to history as one of recurrence, repetition and variation. Contrary to the paradoxically coherent logic of traditionalism and novelty infusing and informing literary modernism, Barnes's texts do not re-assimilate and recycle these fragments into organized and impersonal frameworks in order to re-affirm and re-imagine tradition, but demonstrate 'a form of collusion with the past which, far from nostalgically pure, is tainting and compromising'.[7] The contaminating effects of Barnes's texts, I have suggested, can be identified in their proximity to and treatment of waste which we can trace in their excessive *over*-production and messy materiality, the visceral and corporeal properties of Barnes's 'wounded' writing practices, the patterns of recurrence structuring her mature autobiographic poetics and their refusal to assimilate and re-integrate literary (or personal) history in an efficient and carefully managed system. In this respect, they 'collude' with the past in orchestrating the return of the used and worn-out, the wastes of history, complicating the stabilizing frameworks of tradition, genealogy and linearity framing modernist experiment.

In their incessant production of waste, excessive intertextuality and insistence on an interruptive and disruptive mode of repetition and recurrence, Barnes and the Baroness's texts are not simply antagonistically regressive, but in their autobiographic and anachronistic patterns '[indicate] that the project of modernity is indeed an unfinished history'.[8] In their proximity to these modes, they challenge the terms upon which the impersonal and the objective were deployed to stabilize the fraught negotiations between modernist tradition and the novelty of the new, unpicking the edges of this pattern and laying down their own subversive stiches.

The movement of Barnes from the cult-status of the outsider to an increasingly centralized position in academic discussions of literary modernism is indicative of the ways in which Barnes scholarship and the field of modernist studies have been mutually transformative in recent years. As the recent edited scholarly collection *Shattered Objects: Djuna Barnes's Modernism* attests to, while new critical and analytical approaches within modernist studies have generated a rich and textured body of scholarship on Barnes, we find ourselves turning increasingly to Barnes as a means of exploring the complexities and contradictions within modernist studies itself. Similarly, we turn increasingly to the Baroness as a way of challenging and extending our systematic approaches to modernism and the historical avant-garde. As with the resurgence of popular and critical interest in the subversive and counter-culture figure of the witch in recent years, the Baroness presents us with a set of practices that significantly expand our thinking about the historical avant-garde, modernity and literary modernism, and of the terms of our own critical approaches, embodying the 'strange holiness of being alive in a world of living things, the infinite possibilities for becoming, change, transformation and connection that the world offers'.[9]

Subject to historically and critically determined regulatory practices, the 'contaminative' qualities of this work are most forcefully expressed in the extent of its identification as waste and various attempts to cast it out beyond the boundary line of legitimized modernist modes. And yet if, as Benstock has suggested, 'fear of contamination is the founding premise of modernism',[10] we can see that from these marginalized zones waste – and the bodies, texts and practices identified as such – is indeed central to the definition and regulation of canonical modernist and early twentieth-century avant-garde thematics, giving new weight to the anonymous journalist's 1917 musing that 'women are the cause of modernism – whatever that is'.[11] Far from consigning them to the margins, Barnes and the Baroness open up a discussion of modernist wastes as radically transformative, stitched together in the richly textured patterns of a modernism recovered and remade.

Notes

Introduction

1   Djuna Barnes, fragment from amongst the 'Beggars Comedy' drafts, 'Elsa – Notes' Elsa von Freytag-Loringhoven Papers, Special Collections, University of Maryland Libraries. Series I, Box 1, Folder 3. Further references to the EvFL Papers are to the same collection unless stated otherwise.

2   In looking to this material more recently, Scott Herring has advanced a claim for the Patchin Place production as evidence of a 'geriatric avant-garde', pointing to the processes of composition detailed by O'Neal as evidence of a long-term art project in which the grocery lists themselves are subjected to the same compositional and revisionary processes as the poetry. While there is certainly overlap between mine and Herring's thinking here, I disagree that these modes of recovery and re-use are specific to the period of her Patchin Place residency, as my later chapters will discuss. Scott Herring, 'Djuna Barnes and the Geriatric Avant-Garde', *PMLA* 130.1 (2015), 69–91.

3   T.S. Eliot to Djuna Barnes, 10 August 1956. Djuna Barnes Papers, Special Collections, University of Maryland Libraries. Series II, Box 5, Folder 2. Further references are to the same collection unless stated otherwise.

4   Occupying over one hundred linear feet, the archive brings together drafted and reworked manuscripts, published works, correspondence, artworks and personal ephemera.

5   See J. Matthew Huculak, 'What Is a Modernist Archive?' *Modernism/Modernity*, Vol. 3, Cycle 1, March 2018. With a special emphasis on primary documentary sources of letters, archived notes, drafts and diaries in the analysis of late nineteenth- and twentieth-century literatures, the *Historicizing Modernism* series of which this book is included within of course testifies to the renewed scholarly energy and interest in the messy possibilities of the modernist archive, and of material that might previously have been overlooked as modernist waste. Sandeep Parmar's *Reading Mina Loy's Autobiographies: Myth of the Modern Woman* (London: Bloomsbury, 2013) is of particular interest to this project in this respect. In terms of Barnes scholarship, Cheryl Plumb's 1990 'restored' edition of *Nightwood* with its inclusion of excised drafts and extensive annotation highlighted the fertile lines of inquiry for a gendered analysis of the text's editorial history, which has

subsequently been developed by Monika Faltejskova's monograph *Djuna Barnes, T.S. Eliot and the Gender Dynamics of Modernism* (2010) and informed the detailed textual analysis underpinning Lynda Curry's timely re-assessment of *The Antiphon* as a 'violated' text. Julie Taylor's *Djuna Barnes and Affective Modernism* (2012) demonstrates a deep involvement with the Barnes archive, most compellingly in her careful reading of the various drafts relating to *The Antiphon*. Most prominently, Daniela Caselli's 2009 monograph is grounded in the careful focus afforded by almost exhaustive archival examination. More recently still, Scott Herring has proposed a model of 'late late modernism' for approaching Barnes's mature work, contextualizing the messy materiality of the Patchin Place work described by O'Neal as a 'geriatric avant-garde'. Herring, 'Djuna Barnes and the Geriatric Avant-Garde' (2015).

6   The expansive three volumes of *The Oxford Critical History of Modernist Magazines* edited by Perter Brooker and Andrew Thacker certainly speak to this, as do the various digital resources including The Modernist Journal Project and The Modernist Magazines Project. See Andrew Thacker, 'Modernism and the Periodical Scene in 1915 and Today', *Pessoa Plural* 11 (2017), 66–86.

7   Djuna Barnes to Emily Coleman, 30 November, 1937, cited in Daniela Caselli, *Improper Modernism: Djuna Barnes's Bewildering Corpus* (Surrey: Ashgate, 2009), p. 195.

8   Julie Taylor, *Djuna Barnes and Affective Modernism* (Edinburgh: Edinburgh University Press, 2012), p. 74; Caselli, *Improper Modernism*, p. 197.

9   In her letters to Eliot, Coleman described the *Nightwood* manuscript as a 'hodge-podge' and the Barnes-Coleman friendship was irrevocably damaged by the latter's reaction to disorderly *Antiphon* manuscript in 1958. Coleman to Barnes, 31 October 1935. DB Papers, Series II, Box 3, Folder 8; Barnes to Coleman, 23 August 1958. DB Papers, Series II, Box 3, Folder 20. Eliot gently chastised her writing practice as follows: 'I picture you searching for odd pages under the bed, under the carpet, behind the pictures etc. and then looking at them and wondering where they fit in. But I hope the chaos is not so bad as that'. Eliot to Barnes, 13 December 1953. Series II, Box 4, Folder 1.

10 Emily Coleman to Djuna Barnes, 1935. DB Papers, Series II, Box 3, Folder 7.

11 Barnes's own letters support the exasperated claims made by Eliot, O'Neal and others regarding the messy materiality of her writing practice which involved extensive revisions of single poems and whole manuscripts. In one particularly illuminating letter to Coleman, Barnes details the chaotic drawing together of the *Nightwood* manuscript: 'the whole damned floor is a mess of it no table big enough to spread it all out on, so I crawl about on the floor – last time I did that I was laid up, unable to walk, for three days.' Barnes to Coleman, 5 May 1935. DB Papers, Series II, Box 3, Folder 7.

12 Barnes writes: 'I think more effort has gone into it than anything I have done. [...] I do not know what else I can do. I apologize for the state of the manuscript. I've re-written it at least ten times. A stenographer twice. Still you see what shape it gets into the moment I get it under pen. The spelling is probably bad, the punctuation I know is ghastly.' Barnes to Eliot, 15 July 1953. DB Papers, Series II, Box 4, Folder 62.

13 Barnes to Natalie Clifford Barney, 31 May 1963. DB Papers, Series II, Box I, Folder 45.

14 See Elizabeth Pender and Cathryn setz, eds., *Shattered Objects: Djuna Barnes's Modernism* (Pennsylvania: Pennsylvania University Press, 2019). The introductory essay provides a useful overview of Barnes's critical reception from publication to contemporary expansions in the field of modernist studies, and of Barnes's vital role in navigating these shifting topographies.

15 See B.J. Elliott and Jo-Ann Wallace, *Women Artists and Writers: Modernist (Im) Positionings* (London: Routledge, 1994).

16 It should be emphasized that my positioning of Barnes and the Baroness here as 'marginal' is a result of my examination of their critical treatment in that latter half of the twentieth century, and an acknowledgement of the corrective focus of revisionist histories that I engage with. Certainly, considerable work has been done in recent decades to bring the full range and complexity of the Barnes corpus to light, as a continually expanding field of scholarship attests. However, as Caselli asserts in the opening of her comprehensive monograph, in the context of Anglo-American literary modernism, Barnes is still a relatively minor figure. Similarly, while it has been rewarding to chart the publication of a small but steady stream of scholarship focused on the Baroness that has emerged during my compilation of this thesis, she nevertheless remains on the margins of the already-marginalized New York Dada movement and is rarely discussed outside of these contexts. Caselli, *Improper Modernism*.

17 Djuna Barnes, *Collected Poems with Notes towards a Memoir*, ed. by Phillip Herring and Osías Stutman (Madison: The University of Wisconsin Press, 2005), p. 254.

18 As Caselli notes, the 'difficulty' that Barnes assigns to the Baroness mirrors the opacity of Barnes's own writing and, we could add, the somewhat taciturn reputation that she would grow into. See Caselli, *Improper Modernism*, p. 67.

19 Richard Cavell, 'Baroness Elsa and the Aesthetics of Empathy: A Mystery and a Speculation', in *The Politics of Cultural Mediation: Baroness Elsa von Freytag-Loringhoven and Felix Paul Greve*, ed. by Paul Hjartson and Tracy Kulba (Edmonton: University of Alberta Press, 2003), pp. 25–40 (p. 25). Also see Irene Gammel, *Baroness Elsa: Gender, Dada, and Everyday Modernity, a Cultural Biography* (Cambridge, MA: MIT Press, 2002); *Body Sweats: The Uncensored Writings of Elsa von Freytag-Loringhoven*, ed. by Irene Gammel and Suzanne Zelazo

(Cambridge, MA: MIT Press, 2011), hereafter referred to as *BS*; Amelia Jones, *Irrational Modernism: A Neurasthenic History of New York Dada* (Cambridge, MA: MIT Press, 2004).

20 Barnes, *Nightwood* [1936] (London: Faber and Faber, 1985). Hereafter referenced parenthetically as *N* followed by the page number.

21 Becci Carver, *Granular Modernism* (Oxford: Oxford University Press, 2014), p. 14.

22 Although modernism's rejection of its immediate literary past has proven to be more complex than initial pronouncements would suggest. Michael Levenson provides a useful account of the gendered terms of repudiation upon which such notions of historical discontinuity were founded: 'Victorian poetry has been soft; modern poetry will be hard (Pound's terms). Humanist art has been vital; the coming geometric art will be inorganic (Hulme's terms). Romanticism was immature; the new classicism will be adult (Eliot's terms)', Levenson, *A Genealogy of Modernism: A Study of English Literary Doctrine 1908–1922* (Cambridge: Cambridge University Press, 1984), p. ix. See also Hugh Kenner, *The Pound Era* (Berkley, CA: University of California Press, 1971); Stan Smith, *The Origins of Modernism: Eliot, Pound, Yeats and the Rhetorics of Renewal* (Hemel Hempstead: Harvester Wheatsheaf, 1994).

23 The passage cited by Duchamp is as follows: 'The more perfect the artist, the more completely separate in him will be the man who suffers and the mind which creates; the more perfectly will the mind digest and transmute the passions which are its material.'

24 For a succinct overview of the critical debate surrounding the 'gendering' of modernism, see Deborah Longworth, 'Gendering the Modernist Text', in *The Oxford Handbook of Modernisms*, ed. by Peter Brooker, Andrzej Gasiorek and Deborah Longworth (Oxford: Oxford University Press, 2010), pp. 156–77. Also see Sandra Gilbert and Susan Gubar, 'No Mans Land', in *The Place of the Woman Writer in the Twentieth Century*, 3 vols (New Haven, CT: Yale University Press, 1988–94); *The Gender of Modernism: A Critical Anthology*, ed. by Bonnie Kime Scott (Bloomington, IN: Indiana University Press, 1990); *Women in Dada: Essays on Sex, Gender, and Identity*, ed. by Naomi Sawelson-Gorse (Cambridge, MA: MIT Press, 1998).

25 Rita Felski, 'Modernism and Modernity: Engendering Literary History', in *Re-Reading Modernism: New Directions in Feminist Studies*, ed. by Lisa Rado (London: Routledge, 1994), pp. 160–91.

26 Bonnie Kime Scott and Mary Lynn Broe, eds., *The Gender of Modernism: A Critical Anthology* (Bloomington, IN: Indiana University Press), p. 2.

27 The shifting and expanding terrain of modernist studies is of particular importance to a discussion of Barnes and the Baroness, of their positioning as 'marginal' or 'forgotten' figures' and their progress from the peripheries towards the centre

as they reformulate the terms of such discussions. Barnes's critical reputation in particular has been shaped – and instrumental in shaping – this shifting critical landscape, as the new edited collection *Shattered Objects: Djuna Barnes's Modernism* emphasizes.

28 Following Andreas Huyssen, Tim Armstrong addresses the gendered associations between women and modernity directly: 'it is often suggested that modernism is founded on the confluence of two associated hate objects: women, and the sentimental mass culture they are said to passively consume'. Identifying the pervasive doctrine of 'paedomorphism' that manifests in the work of Williams and Pound as the equation of artistic activity with masculine sexual energy, Armstrong nevertheless takes a more nuanced approach to modernism as an inherently misogynistic movement utterly opposed to mass culture. Tim Armstrong, *Modernism: A Cultural History* (Cambridge: Polity, 2005), pp. 41–2.

29 Andreas Huyssen, 'Mass Culture as Woman', in *After the Great Divide: Modernism, Mass Culture, Postmodernism* (Bloomington, IN: Indiana University Press, 1986), p. 47.

30 Pound to Eliot, January 1937, *Letters of Ezra Pound 1907–1941*, ed. by D.D. Paige (London: Faber & Faber, 1951), p. 377.

31 Armstrong, *Modernism, Technology and the Body: A Cultural Study* (Cambridge: Cambridge University Press, 1998), pp. 42–74. See also Melissa Bradshaw, *Amy Lowell: Diva Poet* (Surrey: Ashgate, 2011).

32 Melissa Bradshaw, *Amy Lowell: Diva Poet* (London: Routledge, 2011), pp. 32, 71.

33 Ibid., pp. 32–5.

34 Jessica Feldman, *Victorian Modernism: Pragmatism and the Varieties of Aesthetic Experience* (Cambridge: Cambridge University Press, 2002), p. 6.

35 William Cohen, 'Locating Filth', in *Filth: Dirt, Disgust, and Modern Life*, ed. by Cohen (Minneapolis: University of Minnesota Press, 2005), pp. vii–xxxvii (p. ix).

36 Suzanne Raitt, 'The Rhetoric of Efficiency in Early Modernism', *Modernism/Modernity* 13.1 (January 2006), 835–51 (p. 849). For discussions of the gendering of waste, see Klaus Theweleit, *Male Fantasies, Volume I: Women, Floods, Bodies, History*, trans. by Stephan Conway (Cambridge: Polity Press, 1987); William Ian Miller, *The Anatomy of Disgust* (Cambridge, MA: Harvard University Press, 1997).

37 Ibid., p. 20.

38 Mary Douglas, *Purity and Danger: An Analysis of Concepts of Pollution and Taboo* (London: Taylor & Francis, 2003 [1966]).

39 Ibid., p. 44.

40 Cohen, 'Locating Filth', p. xi.

41 Michael Thompson, *Rubbish Theory: The Creation and Destruction of Value* (Oxford: Oxford University Press, 1979), p. 9.

42 David Trotter, *Cooking with Mud: The Idea of Mess in Nineteenth-Century Art and Fiction* (Oxford: Oxford University Press, 2000), 20.
43 See Dominique Laporte, *The History of Shit*, trans. by Nadia Benabid and Rodolphe el-Khoury (Cambridge, MA: MIT Press, 2000).
44 Trotter, *Cooking with Mud*, p. 20.
45 Miller, *The Anatomy of Disgust*, p. 58.
46 Mikhail Bakhtin, *Rabelais and His World*, trans. by Helene Iswolsky (Bloomington, IN: Indiana University Press, 1984).
47 Miller, *The Anatomy of Disgust*, p. 59. As Miller states: 'Disgust helps define boundaries between us and them and me and you [...] Disgust, along with desire, locates the bounds of the other either as something to be avoided, repelled, or attacked, or, in other settings, as something to be emulated, imitated, or married', p. 50.
48 As Cohen summarizes: 'In part because of the equation between woman and sex that is axiomatic to a male-dominated heterosexual order, female sexuality (and femininity itself) have a particular connection to filth. The filthiness ascribed to women, which is hardly confined to Leviticus, belongs to an age-old tradition of misogyny that, as feminist theorists such as Mary Russo have argued, reveres virginity and reproduction while condemning women for their supposedly un-contained, excessive bodies', William Cohen, *Filth: Dirt, Disgust, and Modern Life* (Minneapolis, MN: University of Minnesota Press, 2005).
49 Constructions of the female body as leaky, unstable, un-contained and excessive have subsequently received particular critical attention from feminist theorists in a variety of disciplines, including psychoanalysis, literary and cultural theory, and visual cultures. See Elizabeth Grosz, *Volatile Bodies: Towards a Corporeal Feminism* (Bloomington, IN: Indiana University Press, 1994); Julia Kristeva, *The Powers of Horror: An Essay on Abjection*, trans. by Leon S. Roudiez (New York: Columbia University Press, 1982); Mary J. Russo, *The Female Grotesque: Risk, Excess, and Modernity* (London: Routledge, 1994).
50 Grosz, *Volatile Bodies*, p. 203.
51 Gustave Le Bon, *The Crowd: A Study of the Popular Mind* (1895) (New Brunswick, NJ: Transaction, 2009); Georg Simmel, *On Individuality and Social Forms*, ed. by Donald N. Levine (Chicago, IL: The University of Chicago Press, 1971); Weber, *Economy and Society* (1922), chapter xvi, 'The City (Non-Legitimate Domination)'.
52 Elizabeth Wilson, *The Sphinx in the City: Urban Life, the Control of Disorder, and Women* (London: Virago, 1991), p. 6.
53 Marshal Berman, *All That Is Solid Melts into Air: The Experience of Modernity* (London: Verso, 1983), p. 132.
54 Simmel, 'The Metropolis and Mental Life', in *On Individuality and Social Forms*, ed. by Levine, (Chicago: University of Chicago Press, 1971) pp. 324–40 (p. 324).
55 Ibid., p. 325; p. 326.

56 See Dorothy Rowe, *Representing Berlin: Sexuality and the City in Imperial and Weimar Germany* (Surrey: Ashgate, 2003); Deborah L. Parsons, *Streetwalking the Metropolis: Women, the City and Modernity* (Oxford: Oxford University Press, 2003).
57 Simmel, 'The Metropolis and Mental Life', p. 326.
58 Simmel, *The Philosophy of Money*, ed. by David Frisby, trans. by Tom Bottomore and David Frisby, 3rd edn (London: Routledge, 2004), p. 71.
59 Rowe, *Representing Berlin*, p. 7.
60 *Sexuality and Space*, ed. by Beatriz Colomina (New York: Princeton Architectural Press, 1992), p. 2.
61 See Shari Benstock, *Women of the Left Bank: Paris 1900–1940* (Austin, TX: University of Texas Press, 1986); Parsons, *Streetwalking the Metropolis;* Cristanne Miller, *Cultures of Modernism: Marianne Moore, Mina Loy, and Else Lasker-Schüler* (Ann Arbor, MI: University of Michigan Press, 2005).
62 Wilson, *The Sphinx in the City*, p. 7.
63 Dana Brand, cited in Rebecca Loncraine, 'Voix-de-Ville: Djuna Barnes's Stunt Journalism, Harry Houdini and the Birth of Cinema', *Women: A Cultural Review* 19.2 (2008), pp. 156–71.
64 Until relatively recently, discussions of 'waste' as I shall be examining it over the course of this project have been limited to economic, anthropological and psychological discussions. A central, if sublimated concern for early formulations of psychoanalysis, material and figurative forms of waste were treated directly in later psychoanalytic frameworks, notably in Julia Kristeva's work on the abject and through the corporeal feminisms developed by Judith Butler and Elizabeth Grosz. In the field of comparative anthropology, Mary Douglas's seminal *Purity and Danger* (1966) provided the first properly *structural* account of waste as an ordering system. With the rise of ecocriticism in recent decades, an interest in consumption, production and waste has generated productive lines of inquiry as to the role of waste in contemporary consumer society, explored in various social and cultural histories of filth, garbage and waste: see Martin Melosi, *Garbage in the Cities: Refuse, Reform, and the Environment, 1880–1980* (Chicago, IL: Chicago University Press, 1981); Greg Kennedy, *An Ontology of Trash: The Disposable and Its Problematic Nature* (Albany, NY: State of New York Press, 2007). More recently, literary and historical analysis has been brought to bear on significance of waste in its nineteenth- and twentieth-century (cultural) contexts and a broad critical foundation is developing for addressing waste as something of a preoccupation for twentieth-century writers and artists: see Sara Crangle, 'Woolf's Cesspoolage: On Waste and Resignation', *Cambridge Quarterly* 40.1 (2011) 1–20.; Kevin Trumpeter, 'Furnishing Modernist Fiction: The Aesthetics of Refuse', *Modernism/Modernity*, 20.2 (2013), 307–26.
65 Cohen, 'Locating Filth', p. viii.

66 'I expel myself, I spit myself out, I abject myself within the same motion through which "I" claim to establish myself.' Kriteva, *The Powers of Horror*, p. 3.
67 Laporte, *The History of Shit*.
68 See Miller, *The Anatomy of Disgust*, pp. 42–59.
69 Susan Strasser, *Waste and Want: A Social History of Trash* (New York: Metropolitan Books, 1999), p. 12.
70 See Trotter, *Cooking with Mud*; Armstrong, *Modernism, Technology and the Body*.
71 In her study of 'Irrational Modernism', Amelia Jones convincingly presents a compelling model of the historical avant-garde's equivocal responses to the rationalizing forces of modernity that this project identifies with and considers in light of questions relating to gender, canonicity and certain textual strategies activated in Barnes and the Baroness's autobiographic poetics.
72 Jones, *Irrational Modernism*, p. 14.
73 See Donald J. Childs, *Modernism and Eugenics: Woolf, Eliot, Yeats and the Culture of Degeneration* (Cambridge, Cambridge University Press, 2007); Armstrong, *Modernism: A Cultural History* (Cambridge: Polity Press, 2005), pp. 64–89.
74 James C. Scott, *Seeing Like a State: How Certain Schemes to Improve the Human Condition Have Failed* (New Haven, CT: Yale University Press, 1998), p. 92.
75 Shari Benstock, 'Expatriate Sapphic Modernism: Entering Literary History', in *Lesbian Texts and Contexts: Radical Revisions*, ed. by Karla Jay and Joanne Glasgow (New York: New York University Press, 1990), pp. 183–203 (p. 186).
76 See Tryus Miller, *Late Modernism: Politics, Fiction, and Arts between the Wars* (Berkley, CA: University of California Press, 1999).
77 Barnes to Coleman, 20 September 1935. Series II, Box 3, Folder 7.
78 Levenson, *The Genealogy of Modernism*, pp. vii–ix.
79 Barnes, 'How the Villagers Amuse Themselves', *New York Morning Telegraph Sunday Magazine* (26 November 1917), in *New York Djuna Barnes*, ed. by Alice Barry (Los Angeles: Sun & Moon Press, 1989), pp. 246–53. This collection is hereafter referenced parenthetically as *NY* followed by the page number.

Chapter 1

1 Lewis Mumford, 'Toward a Rational Modernism', *New Republic*, 25 April 1928, pp. 297–8.
2 Ibid., p. 297.
3 Ibid.
4 Armstrong, *Modernism, Technology, and the Body*, p. 2.
5 George Hugnet, 'The Dada Spirit in Painting (1932 and 1934)', in *The Dada Painters and Poets: An Anthology*, ed. by Robert Motherwell, 2nd edn (Cambridge, MA: Harvard University Press, 1989), pp. 123–98, pp. 185–6.

6   John Unterecker records how Crane, 'roaring with laughter would pantomime in extraordinary detail all the Baroness's gestures and imitate broadly her heavy, strong, insistent speech' John Unterecker, *Voyager: A Life of Hart Crane* (New York: Farrar, Strauss & Giroux, 1969), p. 135.
7   George Biddle, *An American Artist's Story* (Boston: Little, Brown and Company, 1939), p. 137.
8   Ibid., p. 137.
9   See Dieter Miendl, *American Fiction and the Metaphysics of the Grotesque* (Columbia, MO: University of Missouri Press, 1996), p. 16.
10 Bakhtin, *Rabelais and His World*, p. 26.
11 As I will go on to highlight, Biddle describes the Baroness's sexual advances as a sensorialy overwhelming, vertiginous encounter. In relation to Bakhtinian notions of the transgressive principle of growth attached to the grotesque body, it is interesting to note that many of the popular contemporary accounts of the Baroness employ images of eating, copulation and expulsion in their narratives. William Carlos Williams emphasizes that, upon arranging her release from the 'Tombs', they went straight to breakfast and describes her elsewhere as a 'volcano'. Barnes's archived 'Baroness Elsa' notes recollect various excremental narratives including her delight in defecating on Margaret Anderson's doorstep and smearing excrement on a hotel window sill in recognition for poor service.
12 Bakhtin, *Rabelais and His World*, p. 320.
13 Meindl, *Metaphysics of the Grotesque*, p. 15.
14 Mary Butts, 'The Master's Last Dancing: A Wild Party in Paris, Inspired by One of Ford Maddox Ford's', *The New Yorker* (30 March 1998), pp. 110–13; Ben Hecht, 'The Yellow Goat', *The Little Review* 5.8 (December 1918), 28–40; William Carlos Williams, 'Sample Prose Piece: The Three Letters', *Contact*, 4 (1921); Williams, *The Autobiography of William Carlos Williams* (New York: New Directions, 1967).
15 Charles S. Brooks, *Hints to Pilgrims* (New Haven, CT: Yale University Press, 1921), pp. 93–95.
16 Gammel, *Baroness Elsa*, p. 4.
17 Armstrong, *Modernism, Technology, and the Body*, p. 6.
18 Naomi Sawelson-Gorse, ed., *Women in Dada* (Cambridge, MA: MIT, 1998), p. xii.
19 Susan Suleiman, *Subversive Intent: Gender, Politics and the Avant-Garde* (Cambridge, MA: Harvard University Press, 1990), pp. 11–28.
20 Jones, *Irrational Modernism*, p. 10.
21 See Sawelson-Gorse, *Women in Dada*.
22 Jones, *Irrational Modernism*, p. 10. Also see Sawelson-Gorse, *Women in Dada*.
23 Mary Douglas, *Purity and Danger* (London: Routledge, 1966), p. 121.
24 See Pierre Cabanne, *Dialogues with Marcel Duchamp*, trans. by Ron Padgett. See also Jennifer Mundy, ed., *Duchamp, Man Ray, Picabia* (London: Tate Publishing, 2008).

25 RoseLee Goldberg, *Performance Art: From Futurism to the Present*, 3rd edn (London: Thames and Hudson, 2011), p. 7.
26 See *Not the Other Avant-Garde: The Transnational Foundations of Avant-Garde Performance*, ed. by James M. Harding and John Rouse (Ann Arbor, MI: University of Michigan Press, 2006).
27 Ibid., p. 2.
28 Harding, *Cutting Performances: Collage Events, Feminist Artists, and the American Avant-Garde* (Ann Arbor, MI: University of Michigan Press, 2010), p. 6.
29 The case for this has been made explicitly in the realms of performance by theorist Jill Dolan who has insisted on a reading of feminist performance art as 'a resistant site of production', cited in Harding, *Cutting Performances*, p. 3.
30 See Gammel, *Baroness Elsa*.
31 EvFL, *BE*, 45.
32 James Harding presents the Baroness's syphilis as visceral metaphor for theatrical radically, read as a feminist alternative to Anontin Artaud's celebrated notion of theatre as a plague first presented in *The Theatre and Its Double* (1938). See Harding, *Cutting Performances*.
33 Claude McKay, *A Long Way from Home*, cited in Gammel, *Baroness Elsa*, pp. 321–3.
34 EvFL, 'Body Sweats' (*c*. 1924–5), reprinted in Irene Gammel and Suzanne Zelazo, *Body Sweats: The Uncensored Writings of Elsa von Freytag-Loringhoven*, ed. by Irene Gammel (Cambridge, MA: MIT Press, 2011).
35 EvFL, 'Standpoint' (*c*. 1925), reprinted in *Body Sweats*, p. 223.
36 EvFL, 'Purgatory Lilt' (*c*. 1924–7), reprinted in *Body Sweats*, p. 223.
37 EVFL Papers, Series II, Box 1, Folder 3 (*c*. 1924–7). EvFL to DB, 'Djuna Sweet' These letters are also discussed in the context of the Baroness's Berlin 'exile' in Gammel, *Baroness Elsa*, pp. 339–56.
38 See Gammel, *Baroness Elsa*, pp. 375–89.
39 In the notes towards her memoirs, Barnes details the Baroness's death and tragically under-attended funeral in Mont Joli cemetery. Describing the 'ancient gas stove' that she had bought against all advice because 'it looked like a coffee pot', Barnes determines that her death was an accident. See Barnes, 'Farewell Paris', p. 254.
40 EVFL to Jane Heap, *c*. 1922–3, cited in Gammel, *Baroness Elsa*, p. 304.
41 Gammel, *Baroness Elsa*, p. 290.
42 See Ibid., pp. 273–82.
43 Jane Heap, 'Dada', *The Little Review* 8.2 (Spring 1922), 46.
44 For information relating to the history of the Baroness's papers, see the introductory essay to the *Body Sweats* collection.
45 For a discussion of the performative modes of Elsa's Dada practice, see Jones, *Irrational Modernism*, Harding, *Cutting Performances*, and Gammel, 'Limbswishing Dada in New York: Baroness Elsa's Gender Performance', in *The Politics of Cultural*

Mediation: Baroness Elsa von Freytag-Loringhoven and Felix Paul Greve, ed. by Hjartson and Kulba, pp. 3–24.

46 Louis Bouché, 'Autobiographical Notes', cited in Gammel, *Baroness Elsa*. Elsa published over twenty poems with *The Little Review*, who also printed photographic reproductions of her sculptural pieces. Her controversial and stylistically innovative poetry instigated the 'art and madness' debate conducted within *The Little Review* from December 1919 between Evelyn Scott, Jane Heap and Elsa herself. Further than lambasting or defending an individual artist, this debate called into question definitions of Dada as an international art movement, and of modern art more generally. Importantly, she also featured prominently in the single issue of the avant-garde journal *New York Dada* produced by Marcel Duchamp and Man Ray in April 1921.

47 *The Dada Painters and Poets*, ed. by Motherwell; Arturo Schwartz, *New York Dada: Duchamp, Man Ray, Picabia*, ed. by Armin Zweite and others (Munich: Prestel, 1973); Francis Naumann, *New York Dada, 1915–1923* (New York: Abrams, 1994). It should be noted that Naumann significantly expanded the triumvirate of Duchamp, Man Ray and Picabia, to include patron Walter Arensberg amongst others. The categorization of Elsa as 'Other' here is defended by the view that she could not be properly included in either French or American categories, and was not a major contributor to Dada aesthetics.

48 Williams, 'Sample Prose Piece', p. 11.

49 Following Douglas's structural treatment of the relationships established between order and disorder, purification and contamination, we can see how the margins emerge as powerful sites indeed. Marking a boundary these outlines 'contain power to reward conformity and repulse attack'; they are at once the sign of order and the space of that order's transgression. Douglas, *Purity and Danger*, p. 141.

50 Douglas, *Purity and Danger*, p. 120.

51 Biddle, *An American Artist's Story*, p. 140.

52 Harding, *Cutting Performances*, pp. 50–3.

53 EVFL, 'The Modest Woman', *The Little Review*, 7.2 (July–August 1920), 37–40, reprinted in *Body Sweats*, pp. 286–9, p. 286.

54 Ibid., p. 287.

55 EvFL, 'A Dozen Cocktails Please', reprinted in *Body Sweats*, 48–50, p. 49.

56 EvFL, 'Spring in the Middle', c. 1924, reprinted in *Body Sweats,* p. 93.

57 EvFL Papers, Series I, Box I, folder 3, Djuna Barnes, 'Elsa Notes' 1933. References to this collection.

58 See David Ward and Oliver Zunz, eds., *The Landscape of Modernity: New York City, 1900–1940* (Baltimore, MD: Johns Hopkins University Press, 1992).

59 See Daniel Bluestone, 'The Pushcart Evil', in *The Landscape of Modernity*, ed. by Ward and Zunz, pp. 285–314 (Baltimore: John Hopkins University Press, 1992).

60 See Armstrong, *Modernism, Technology and the Body*.
61 Jones, *Irrational Modernism*, p. 14; see also Terry Smith, *Making the Modern: Industry, Art, and Design in America* (Chicago, IL: University of Chicago Press, 1993).
62 le Bon, *The Crowd: A Study of the Popular Mind* (1895); Simmel, 'The Metropolis and Mental Life' (1903).
63 See Sigmund Freud, 'Beyond the Pleasure Principle', in *The Standard Edition of the Complete Psychological Works of Sigmund Freud, Vol. XVIII (1920–1922)*, trans. by James Strachey (London: Vintage, 2001), pp. 7–64; Freud, 'The Ego and the Id' (1923) in *The Standard Edition of the Complete Psychological Works of Sigmund Freud*, trans. by James Strachey (London: Vintage, 2001), pp. 12–66.
64 Freud, *Civilization and Its Discontents* (1929), trans. by David McLintock (London: Penguin Books, 2002).
65 Trotter, *Cooking with Mud*, p. 20.
66 As Trotter proposes, literary modernism is 'at once compelled and repelled by symptomatic excesses and deteriorations', *Cooking with Mud*, p. 23. See also Trumpeter, 'Furnishing Modernist Fiction'; Raitt, 'The Rhetoric of Efficiency in Early Modernism'.
67 Cited in Francis Nauman, *The Recurrent, Haunting Ghost: Essays on the Art, Life and Legacy of Marcel Duchamp* (New York: Readymade Press, 2012), p. 72.
68 Marcel Duchamp, from a 1963 interview with Francis Roberts, quoted in Naumann, *The Recurrent, Haunting Ghost*, p. 175.
69 See Naumann, *Marcel Duchamp: The Art of Making in the Age of Mechanical Reproduction* (Ghent: Ludion Press, 1999), p. 68.
70 For Wood's commentary on the affair see Beatrice Wood, *I Shock Myself: The Autobiography of Beatrice Wood* (San Francisco: Chronicle Books, 2006).
71 See André Breton, 'La Phare de la mariée', *Minotaure* 2.6 (1935), 445–9 and his influential definition of the Readymade in *Dictionanaire abrégé du Surréalisme* as 'an ordinary object elevated to the dignity of a work by the mere choice of an artist'. cited in William Jeffett, 'Readymades, Sculptures, Objects: "A Happy Blaspheny"', in *Dali/Duchamp*, ed. by Dawn Ades and William Jeffett (London: RA, 2017), pp. 26–33, p. 32.
72 Marcel Duchamp to Suzanne Duchamp, 11 April 1917. Duchamp writes: 'Raconte ce detail à la famile: les Indépendents sont ouverts ici avec gros succès. Une de mes amies sous un pseudonyme masculin, Richard Mutt, avait envoyé une pissotière en porcelaine comme sculpture; ce n'était pas du tout indécent aucune raison pour la refuser. Le comité a décidé de refuser d'exposer cette chose. J'ai donné ma démission et c'est un potin qui aura valeur dans New York'. Cited in William Camfield, 'Marcel Duchamp's *Fountain:* It's History and Aesthetics in the Context of 1917', in *Marcel Duchamp: Artist of the Century*, ed. by Rudolf E. Kuenzli and Francis M. Naumann (Cambridge, MA: MIT Press, 1990), pp. 64–95, pp. 71–2.

73 For a full discussion see Gammel, *Baroness Elsa*, pp. 220–30; EvFL, 'The Modest Woman', 37–40.
74 Williams, *Autobiography*, p. 134.
75 Barnes, *Collected Poems with Notes towards a Memoir*, 254.
76 This is a case made most forcefully by Glyn Thompson, notably in a 2014 article published by *The Art Newspaper* co-authored by Julian Spalding entitled 'Did Marcel Duchamp Steal Elsa's Urinal?'
77 In a letter to *The Little Review* editors, she writes: 'And m'ars came to *this country* – protected – carried by fame – to use his plumbing fixtures – mechanical comforts'. EvFL to *LR*, c. 1922, cited in Gammel, *Baroness Elsa*, p. 228).
78 Wood, *I Shock Myself*, p. 30.
79 EvFL papers, Series II, Box 1, Folder 4 'Dearest Djuna'.
80 EvFL to Jane Heap, c. 1922, cited in Jones, *Irrational Modernism*, p. 142.
81 See Camfield, 'Marcel Duchamp's *Fountain*', p. 72.
82 Williams, 'The Sample Prose Piece', p. 11; see Gammel, *Baroness Elsa*, p. 171.
83 Michel Sanouillet and Elmer Peterson, eds., *The Essential Writings of Marcel Duchamp: Marchand du Sel, Salt Seller* (London: Thames & Hudson, 1975), p. 37.
84 Duchamp in interview with Otto Hahn, 'Marcel Duchamp', *L'Express* [Paris, 23 July 1964]. Quoted in Arturo Schwarz, *The Complete Works of Marcel Duchamp* (New York: Abrams, 1970), p. 466.
85 Robert Reiss, 'My Baroness: Elsa von Freytag-Loringhoven', in *New York Dada*, ed. by Rudolf E. Kuenzli (New York: Willis Locker & Owens, 21986), p. 82.
86 'The Choice of Readymades Is Always Based in Visual Indifference and, at the Same Time, on the Total Absence of Good or Bad Taste', in *Dialogues with Marcel Duchamp*, ed. by Cabanne, (London: De Cappo Press, 1971) p. 48.
87 See Jones, *Irrational Modernism*, p. 133.
88 DB, 'Elsa – Notes', 24 April 1933, cited in Naumann, *New York Dada 1915–23*, p. 173.
89 On castration anxiety and Dada see Jones, *Irrational Modernism*, p. 87.
90 Camfield quotes Ira Glackens, *William Glackens and the Ashcan Group* (New York: Crown Publishers Inc., 1957); Camfield, 'Marcel Duchamp's Fountain', p. 90.
91 Barbara Zabel, 'The Constructed Self: Gender and Portraiture in Machine-Age America', in *Women in Dada*, pp. 22–47 (Naomi Sawelson-Gorse ed., Cambridge, MA: MIT Press, 2001) (p. 22).
92 Huyssen, 'Mass Culture as Woman', p. 47.
93 Klaus Theweleit, *Male Fantasies, vol 1: Women, Floods, Bodies, History*, trans. by Stephen Conway (Cambridge: Polity Press, 1987), p. 385.
94 Jones, *Irrational Modernism*, p. 47.
95 Theweleit, *Male Fantasies, vol 1*, p. 409.
96 Miller, *The Anatomy of Disgust*, p. 43.
97 Theweleit, *Male Fantasies, vol 1*, p. 409.

98 Ibid., pp. 409–10.
99 Klaus Theweleit, *Male Fantasies, Vol 2, Male Bodies: Psychoanalyzing the White Terror*, trans. by Erica Carter and Chris Turner (Cambridge: Polity Press, 1989), p. 22.
100 Huyssen, 'Mass Culture as Woman', pp. 47, 52.
101 Mary Louise Roberts developed the French contexts of this reading in *Civilisation without Sexes: Reconstructing Gender in Postwar France, 1917–1927* (Chicago: University of Chicago Press, 1994). For a discussion of the New Woman in her American contexts see Estelle B. Freedman, 'The New Woman: Changing Views of Women in the 1920s', *Journal of American History* LXI. 2 (September 1974), 372–93; Carroll Smith-Rosenberg, ed., *Disorderly Conduct: Visions of Gender in Victorian America* (New York: Alfred A. Knopf, 1985); For an overview of these sources see Caroline A. Jones, 'The Sex of the Machine: Mecanomorphic Art, New Women, and Francis Picabia's Neurasthenic Cure', *Picturing Science, Producing Art*, ed. by Caroline A. Jones and Peter Galison (London: Routledge, 1998).
102 See Alex Goody on 'The Typist, who was imagined and represented within ongoing discourses about women's independence, their sexuality and their relationship to technology', Goody, *Modernist Articulations,* p. 110. See also Jones, 'The Sex of the Machine', p. 152.
103 Smith-Rosenberg, *Disorderly Conduct*, p. 246.
104 Winthrop Sargeant, 'Dada's Daddy, a New Tribute to Duchamp, Pioneer of Nonsense and Nihilism', *Life Magazine*, April 1952.
105 see George Baker, *The Artwork Caught by the Tail: Francis Picabia and Dada in Paris* (Cambridge, MA: MIT Press, 2010).
106 See 'Picabia, Art Rebel, Here to Teach a New Movement', in *New York Times*, 16 February 1913; 'French Artists Spur on American Art', in *New York Tribune*, Sunday 24 October 1915. In the latter Picabia is quoted as saying: 'Almost immediately upon coming to America it flashed on me that the genius of the modern world is machinery, and that through machinery art ought to find a most vivid expression […] The machine has become more than a mere adjunct of human life. It is really a part of human life – perhaps the very soul. In seeking forms through which to interpret ideas or by which to expose human characteristics I have come at length upon the form which appears most brilliantly plastic and fraught with symbolism. I have enlisted the machinery of the modern world, and introduced it into my studio'.
107 Francis Picabia, quoted in 'French Artists Spur on American Art', in *New York Tribune*, 24 October 1915.
108 M. De Zayas, Commentary, *291*, 5–6 (July–August 1915).
109 Lynda Nead, *The Female Nude: Art, Obscenity and Sexuality* (London: Routledge, 1992), p. 42.

110 Given my reading of *Fountain* as providing an insulated conduit to transfer the Baroness's Dada energies into more rational (and masculinist) forms, the status of the spark-plug as a device for *delivering* an electrical current rather than *producing* it is striking.
111 William Homer was the first to argue for Agnes Meyer as Picabia's Spark plug. See William Innes Homer, '*Picabia's Jeune Fille Américaine Dans L'état De Nudité* and Her Friends', *The Art Bulletin* 57.1 (1975), 110–15.
112 This work, and much of Meyer's poetry published in *291*, is focused squarely on modern female experience. 'Mental Reactions' follows the fragmented and posing thoughts of a woman torn between the emancipatory possibilities of extra-marital free-love, and the responsibilities that come with marriage and maternity. The word 'Flirt' features prominently at the top of the composition.
113 Carol Duncan, 'Virility and Domination in Early Twentieth-Century Vanguard Painting', in *Feminism and Art History: Questioning the Litany*, ed. by Norma Broude and Mary D. Garrard (New York: Routledge, 2018 [1982]), pp. 293–314, p. 306.
114 Paul Haviland, 'Statement', *291*, 7–8 (1915).
115 George Barker is clear on the question of influence here stating that 'Almost all of Picabia's mecanomorphs made reference to the thematics and forms of Duchamp's *Large Glass*'. Barker, *The Artwork Caught by the Tail*, p. 233.
116 Jennifer Mundy, 'The Art of Friendship', in *Duchamp, Man Ray, Picabia*, ed. by Jennifer Mundy (London: Tate Publishing, 2008), pp. 8–57, p. 23.
117 Jones, *Irrational Modernism*, p. 84.
118 Nead, *The Female Nude*, p. 57.
119 Sandeep Parmar has highlighted the subtle distinctions between contemporary accounts of the 'modern' and the 'new' woman. In the context of my discussion here I am using the term 'New Woman' as short hand to refer to the popularly circulated idea of the New Woman, as opposed to individual lives of modern women. See Parmar, *Reading Mina Loy's Autobiographies*, p. 31.
120 Goody, 'Cyborgs, Women, and New York Dada', *The Space Between: Literature and Culture 1915–1945* 3.1 (2007), 90.
121 See Dickran Tashjian, 'Authentic Spirit of Change: The Poetry of New York Dada', in *Making Mischief*, ed. by Francis M. Naumann with Beth Venn, (New York: Harry N. Abrams, Inc., New York), pp. 266–71; Willard Bohn, 'Visualizing Women in *291*', in *Women in Dada*, ed. by Naomi Sawelson-Gorse (Cambridge, MA: MIT Press, 2001) pp. 240–61; Goody, 'Cyborgs, Women, and New York Dada'.
122 Marius de Zayas, '291 – A New Publication', *Camera* Work 48 (October 1916), 62. Also see Bohn, 'Visualizing Women in 291', p. 241.
123 William A. Camfield, *Francis Picabia* (New York: Solomon R. Guggenheim Museum, 1970), p. 25.
124 Bohn, 'Visualizing Women in *291*', p. 241.

125 The framing of this double portrait within the September 1915 *291* number between a reproduction of an untitled still life by Braque on the front cover, and Picasso's *Violin* on the rear clearly announces the 'legitimacy' of these gendered thematics of New York Dada.
126 'Exhibitions in the Galleries', *Arts and Decoration*, 6.1 (November 1915), p. 35.
127 See Reiss, 'My Baroness', cited in Gammel, *Baroness Elsa*, p. 167.
128 Bohn, 'Visualizing Women in *291*', p. 244.
129 Ibid., p. 245.
130 Contrary to Gabrielle Buffet's recollection of Picabia's 1913 conception of artistic creation that 'Art is to create a painting without models'. See David Hopkins, *Marcel Duchamp and Max Ernst: The Bride Shared* (Oxford: Oxford University Press, 1998), p. 74.
131 Bakhtin, *Rabelais and His World*, p. 316.
132 Georges Bataille, 'L'informe', *Documents 1* (1929) reprinted in *Georges Bataille: Vision of Excess: Selected Writings, 1927–1939*, trans. by Allan Stoekl, Carl R. Lovitt and Donald M. Leslie Jr. (Minneapolis, MN: University of Minnesota Press), p. 31.
133 Williams, 'Sample Prose Piece', p. 11.
134 Kristeva, *The Powers of Horror*, p. 1.
135 Ibid., p. 2.
136 Ibid.
137 Ibid., p. 3.
138 Robyn Longhurst, *Bodies: Exploring Fluid Boundaries* (London: Routledge, 2001), p. 30.
139 Grosz, 'Julia Kristeva', in *Feminism and Psychoanalysis: A Critical Dictionary*, ed. by Elizabeth Wright (Oxford: Oxford University Press,1992), p. 198.
140 Kristeva, *Powers of Horror*, p. 3.
141 Laura Mulvey, 'Visual Pleasure and Narrative Cinema' (1975) in *Visual and Other Pleasures*, 2nd edn (Basingstoke: Palgrave Macmillan, 2009), pp. 14–30, p. 19.
142 Ibid., p. 15.
143 Kristeva, *The Powers of Horror*, p. 165.
144 Williams, *Autobiography*, p. 165; p. 169.
145 Ibid., pp. 164–5.
146 Ibid., p. 167.
147 Jacques Lacan, 'The Mirror Stage as Formative of the Function of the Id as Revealed in Psychoanalytic Experience', in *Écrits: The First Complete Edition in English*, trans. by Bruce Fink (New York: Norton, 2006), pp. 75–81.
148 Kristeva, *The Powers of Horror*, p. 10.
149 See Gail Weiss, 'The Abject Borders of the Body Image', in *Perspectives on Embodiment: The Intersections of Nature and Culture*, ed. by Gail Weiss and Honi Fern Haber (London: Routledge, 1999) pp. 41–60; Judith Butler, *Bodies That Matter: On the Discursive Limits of 'Sex'* (London: Routledge, 1993).
150 Ibid., p. 42.

151 Grosz, *Sexual Subversions: Three French Feminists* (St. Leonards, NSW: Allen & Unwin, 1989), p. 72.
152 EvFL, 'Thee I Call "Hamlet of the Wedding Ring": Criticism of William Carlos William's [sic] "Kora in Hell" and Why ...' Part I. *The Little Review* 7.4 (January-March 1921), 48-55, 58-60. Part 2. *The Little Review* 8.1 (Autumn 1921), 108-11, reprinted in *BS*, pp. 291-313.
153 Williams, 'Sample Prose Piece' pp. 10-13.
154 Ibid., p. 11.
155 Ibid.
156 Ibid., p. 11.
157 Brooks, *Hints to Pilgrims*, p. 93.
158 Williams, *Autobiography*, p. 168.
159 See Freud, *Civilization and Its Discontents*, pp. 41-3.
160 'The beginning of the fateful process of civilization, then, would have been marked by man's adopting of an erect posture. From then on the chain of events proceeded, by way of the devaluation of the olfactory stimuli [...] to the preponderance of the visibility of the genitals, then to the continuity of sexual excitation and the founding of the family, and so to the threshold of human civilization. [...] with man's adoption of an upright posture and the devaluation of his sense of smell, the whole of his sexuality – not just his anal eroticism – was in danger of becoming subject to organic repression, so that the sexual function has since been accompanied by an unaccountable repugnance, which prevents total satisfaction and deflects it from the sexual aim towards sublimations and displacements of the libido.' Freud, *Civilization and Its Discontents*, pp. 41-3.
161 Trotter, 'The New Historicism and the Psychopathology of Everyday Modern Life', in *Filth*, ed. by Cohen (Minneapolis: University of Minnesotsa Press, 2005), pp. 30-48 (p. 39).
162 Biddle describes the scene when, having returned from the war, he visited Elsa's apartment: 'As I stood there, partly in admiration yet cold with horror, she stepped close to me so that I smelt her filthy body. An expression of cruelty, yet of fear, spread over her tortured face. [...] Enveloping me slowly, as a snake would its prey, she glued her wet lips on mine. I was shaking all over when I left the dark stairway and came out on 14th Street.' Biddle, *An American Artist's Story*, p. 140.
163 Hecht, 'The Yellow Goat', p. 36. Hereafter referred to parenthetically as (*YG*).
164 Miller, *The Anatomy of Disgust*, p. 43.
165 Kristeva, *The Powers of Horror*, p. 85.
166 Ibid., p. 3.
167 Weiss, 'The Abject Borders of the Body Image', p. 44.
168 Grosz, 'The Body of Signification', in *Abjection, Melancholia and Love: The Work of Julia Kristeva*, ed. by John Fletcher and Andrew Benjamin (London: Routledge, 1990), pp. 80-103 (p. 89).

Chapter 2

1. While this 1996 exhibition certainly marked a resurgence of critical and scholarly interest in the Baroness, it should be noted that Robert Reiss's 1986 article '"My Baroness": Elsa von Freytag-Loringhoven', in *New York Dada* was, as Amelia Jones has emphasized, the first to focus on the Baroness in the context of New York Dada.
2. Schneeman at least was aware of the Baroness as an influential predecessor to the feminist performance art of the 1970s and beyond, even ventriloquizing the Baroness in a performance in 1997. See Harding, *Cutting Performances*, p. 22.
3. EvFL papers, 'Autobiography', Typescript. Series 1, Box 1, Folder 6.
4. Richard Cavell, 'Baroness Elsa and the Aesthetics of Empathy', in *The Politics of Cultural Mediation*, ed. by Hjartson and Kulba (Alberta: University of Alberta), p. 28.
5. Heap, 'Dada', 46. (*BS*: 331).
6. See Gammel, 'Limbswishing Dada in New York', pp. 3–24.
7. EvFL Papers, Barnes, 'Elsa – Notes', 1933: 'She made a great plaster-cast of a penis once, & showed it to all the "old maids" she came in contact with.'
8. See Gammel, *Baroness Elsa*, p. 213; Biddle, *An American Artist's Story*, p. 138; Anderson, *My Thirty Years War*, p. 179. The close connections that Anderson draws here between the Baroness's modelling, costuming practices and disorderly behaviour echo the framing of my inquiry here.
9. 'She Wore Men's Clothes', *New York Times*, 17 September 1910.
10. In Jack Halberstam's terms, rather than an imitation of maleness, Elsa's performance of a 'female masculinity' here 'actually affords us a glimpse of how masculinity is constructed as masculinity', Jack Halberstam, *Female Masculinity* (Durham, NC: Duke University Press, 1998), p. 1. For a more detailed discussion of the Baroness's performative Dada modes, particularly in the context of performance and gender theory see Jones, *Irrational Modernism* and Harding, *Cutting Performances*.
11. Biddle, *An American Artist's Story*, p. 189.
12. Goody, *Modernist Articulations*, p. 115.
13. See Sawelson-Gorse, *Women in Dada*; Harding, *Cutting Performances*.
14. Paul B. Franklin, 'Beatrice Wood, Her Dada … and Her Mamma', in *Women in Dada*, ed. by Naomi Sawelson-Gorse (Cambridge, MA: MIT Press, 2001), pp. 104–41 (p. 105).
15. Eliza Jane Reilly, 'Elsa von Freytag-Loringhoven', *Women's Art Journal* 18.1 (Spring Summer 1997), 26–33, 26–7; Alan Moore, 'Dada Invades New York at the Whitney Museum', *Artnet*, 12 September 1996
16. *Making Mischief: Dada Invades New York*, ed. by Naumann and Beth Venn (New York: Whitney Museum of American Art, 1996), p. 17.
17. Reilly, 'Elsa von Freytag-Loringhoven', p. 30.
18. Rozsika Parker, *The Subversive Stitch: Embroidery and the Making of the Feminine* (London: I.B. Tauris, 2010).

19 Marjorie Perloff, 'Poetics of Collage', in *Collage*, ed. by Jeanine Parisier Plottel (New York: New York Literary Forum, 1983), p. 10.
20 Christine Poggi, *In Defiance of Painting: Cubism, Futurism and the Invention of Collage* (New Haven: Yale University Press, 1992), p. 1.
21 Baker, *The Artwork Caught by the Tail*, p. 82.
22 See Rosalind Krauss (collection of her writings), 'In the Name of Picasso', in *The Originality of the Avant-Garde and Other Modernist Myths* (Cambridge, MA: MIT Press, 1986), pp. 23–41.
23 Ibid., p. 34.
24 Baker, *Caught by the Tail*, p. 77.
25 The Violence of this mode of collage is developed in Duchamp's *Three Standard Stoppages* (1913–14) in which the cutting action is performed with a saw.
26 Miriam Schapiro and Melissa Meyer, 'Waste Not Want Not: An Inquiry into What Women Saved and Assembled – FEMMAGE', *Heresies I* 4 (Winter 1977–8), 66–9.
27 The portrait was initially made for Abbott and given to her as a gift, rather than made for sale, or display in a gallery. It remained in Abbott's possession until the two women fell out in the 1920s, and the Baroness broke into Abbott's apartment and retrieved the picture. In a later letter to Abbot the Baroness writes: 'That you did [appreciate me] was proven by your accepting my picture – and valuing it much more at that time – than I did! In fact – it was a treasure to you! Such things give obligations – but you do not know of them – you are devoid of all sense of measure – out of proportion – you are soulmonster', EvFL to Berenice Abbot, undated. EvFL Papers, Series II, Box 1, Folder 1.
28 Schapiro and Meyer, 'FEMMAGE', p. 68.
29 Krauss, 'In the Name of Picasso', p. 39.
30 Anderson, *My Thirty Years War*, pp. 179–80.
31 EvFL to Berenice Abbott, undated. EvFL papers, Series II, Box 1, Folder 1.
32 Gammel, *Baroness Elsa*, p. 339.
33 Ina Loewenberg, 'Reflections on Self-Portraiture in Photography', *Feminist Studies* 25. 2 (1999), 399–408 (p. 399). See also Chadwick, 'How Do I Look?' in *Mirror Mirror: Self-Portraits by Women Artists*, ed. by Liz Reidel (New York: Watson Guptill, 2002), pp. 8–21.
34 Jones, *Irrational Modernism*, p. 21.
35 Zabel, 'The Constructed Self', p. 36.
36 Ibid., p. 36.
37 Reilly, 'Elsa von Freytag-Loringhoven', p. 26.
38 Barbara Zabel, *Assembling Art: The Machine and the American Avant-Garde* (Jackson: University Press of Mississippi, 2004), p. xiv.
39 See Kuenzli, 'Baroness Elsa von Freytag-Loringhoven and New York Dada', p. 448; Zabel, 'The Constructed Self', p. 36.

40 *Salt Seller* ['Cast Shadows'], p. 72.
41 Rather than reading the shadows as straightforward signs of absence as Amelia Jones has suggested, I would align Duchamp's invocation of the shadow here to earlier modernist experiments. In what could be read as a coda to Georges Braque's inclusion of the shadow of a nail represented in a traditional, illusionistic style within a series of increasingly Cubist violin and palette still lives from 1909, Duchamp aligns himself with the modernist master and goes a step further in removing the painted object altogether. While Braque's nail ironically invokes the traditional painterly techniques of representing 'reality' achieved by the illusionistic rendering of depth and solidity through perspective and the internal play of light and shadow, Duchamp extends this ironic gesture, prioritizing the shadow itself as the sign of representation. The shadow no longer stands in a secondary relationship to a painted object, employed to visually confirm its 'reality', but is prioritized as the primary signifier of the act of representation – of the activities of painting – itself. As Jean Clair has suggested, it is this dismantling of painterly modes of representation that inaugurates the Readymade: 'Where painting vanishes, the readymade makes its appearance'. Cited in Janine Mileaf, *Please Touch: Dada and Surrealist Objects after the Readymade* (Lebanon, NH: Dartmouth College Press, 2010), p. 51.
42 *Salt Seller* [*The Green Box*], p. 33.
43 See Eleanor S. Apter, 'Regimes of Coincidence: Katherine S. Dreier, Marcel Duchamp, and Dada', in *Women in Dada*, ed. by Naomi Sawelson-Gorse (Cambridge, MA: MIT Press, 2001), pp. 362–413 (p. 375).
44 Rosalind E. Krauss, *The Originality of the Avant-Garde and Other Modernist Myths* (Cambridge, MA: MIT Press, 1999), p. 198.
45 *Salt Seller* [*The Green Box*], p. 32.
46 Krauss, *The Originality of the Avant-Garde and Other Modernist Myths*, p. 206.
47 Dubbing herself 'M'Ars Teutonic', Elsa's letters and writings from this period highlight her belief in their intellectual symbiosis, and her frustration with his refusal to celebrate this cerebral union in a more physical relationship.
48 See Harding, *Cutting Performances*, p. 60. Harding goes on to critique Duchamp's 'safe' performance of Rrose Sélavy with the Baroness's more dangerous public and pointed gender critiques.
49 Dennis Hollier, cited in Dawn Ades, 'Camera Creation', in *Duchamp, Man Ray, Picabia*, ed. by Jennifer Mundy (London: Tate Publishing, 2008), pp. 88–113 (p. 95).
50 See Gammel, *Baroness Elsa* for a more detailed account of their relationship.
51 Biddle, *An American Artist's Story*, p. 138.
52 Gammel, *Baroness Elsa*, p. 178.
53 Ibid., p. 179.
54 Bakhtin, *Rabelais and His World*, p. 26.
55 Meindl, *American Fiction and the Metaphysics of the Grotesque*, p. 17.
56 Bakhtin, *Rabelais and His World*, p. 317.

57 With the visible inclusion of small metal finger cymbals or 'zills', the *Portrait of Marcel Duchamp* also connects itself to the Baroness's 1918 poem 'Meek Maru Mustir Daas', which invokes Duchamp in the 'silly little bells of perfect tune / Ring in thine throat' (*BS*: 237).
58 Kuenzli, 'Baroness Elsa von Freytag-Loringhoven and New York Dada', p. 449.
59 Ibid., p. 449.
60 See Barbara Zabel, 'The Constructed Self', in *Mirror Images: Women, Surrealism, and Self-Representation*, ed. by Whitney Chadwick (Cambridge, MA: MIT Press, 1998).
61 *Freud's 'On Narcissism: An Introduction'*, ed. by Peter Fongagy, Ethel Spector Person and Joseph Sandler (London: Karnac Books, 2012), p. x; pp. 73–4.
62 Ibid., p. xv.
63 See Lacan, *Feminine Sexuality: Jacques Lacan and the école freudienne*, ed. by Juliet Mitchell and Jacqueline Rose, trans. by Jacqueline Rose (New York: Norton, 1985); Jacqueline Rose, *Sexuality in the Field of Vision* (London: Verso, 2005).
64 Whitney Chadwick, 'An Infinite Play of Empty Mirrors: Women, Surrealism, and Self-Representation', in *Mirror Images*, ed. by Chadwick (Cambridge, MA: MIT Press, 1998) pp. 2–35 (p. 8).
65 Rose, *Sexuality in the Field of Vision*, p. 53.
66 Ibid., p. 53.
67 Frances Borzello, *Seeing Ourselves, Women's Self-Portraits* (New York: Harry N. Abrams, 1998), p. 167.
68 Chadwick, 'An Infinite Play of Empty Mirrors', p. 11.
69 See Jack Halberstam, *Female Masculinity* (Durham: Duke University Press, 2018 [1998]), p. 5.
70 Chadwick, *Women, Art, and Society*, p. 279.
71 Richard Sieburth, cited by Gammel, 'Limbswishing Dada in New York', p. 6.
72 Frances Borzello, *Seeing Ourselves: Women's Self Portraits* (London: Thames & Hudson, 1998), p. 19.
73 EvFL Papers, Series II, Box 1, Folder 15 'I succeeded! I regained my figure – craft – (I pose better than ever before!) I have confidence – conviction in that chance [...] this ploddingly plucky stubborn application – to *the one thing I know how to do – that I had known – discovered again'.
74 EvFL to Sarah Freedman, undated. EvFL Papers, Series II, Box 1, Folder 15.
75 See Laura Winkiel, 'Circuses and Spectacles: Public Culture in *Nightwood*', *Journal of Modern Literature* 21.1 (Summer 1997), 7–28; Goody, *Modernist Articulations*; Diane Warren *Consuming Fictions*; Jane Marcus, 'Laughing at Leviticus: *Nightwood* as Woman's Circus Epic', in *Silence and Power*, ed. by Broe (Carbondale: Southern Illinois University Press, 1991), pp. 195–205; Sheryl Stevenson, 'Writing the Grotesque Body: Djuna Barnes's Carnival Parody', in *Silence and Power*, ed. by Broe (Carbondale: Southern Illinois University Press, 1991), pp. 81–92.

76 See Gammel, 'Strip/Teasing the Bride of New York', in *Baroness Elsa*, (CAmbridge, MA: MIT Press, 2005) pp. 160–81. In detailing her reception as a model Gammel quotes Louis Boché: 'She posed for me and my pets, Alex Brook, Donald Greason and Carlson in our Miller Building Studio […] Her figure was good, but her face was far from beautiful, and she was past her youth.'

77 Citing an interview conducted with Theresa Bernstein by Francis Naumann, Gammel notes that the Baroness was known to have kept parrots (amongst dogs, mice and a host of other animals).

78 Russo, *The Female Grotesque*.

79 Carolyn Burke, *Becoming Modern: The Life of Mina Loy* (New York: Farrar, Straus and Giroux, 1996), p. 9.

80 Butler, *Bodies That Matter*, p. 1.

81 David Graver, 'Antonin Artaud and the Authority of Text, Spectacle, and Performance', in *Contours of the Theatrical Avant-Garde: Performance and Textuality*, ed. by James M. Harding (Cambridge, MA: MIT Press, 2000), pp. 43–58 (p. 53).

82 Gammel, *Sexualizing Power in Naturalism: Theodore Dreiser and Frederick Philip Grove* (Calgary: University of Calgary Press, 1994), p. 122.

83 EvFL, *Baroness Elsa*, p. 46.

84 Chadwick, *Women, Art, and Society*, pp. 281–2.

85 E. Gordon Craig, 'The Actor and the Übermarionette' (1907) cited in Graver, 'Antonin Artaud', p. 47.

86 Tracy C. Davis, *Actresses as Working Women: Their Social Identity in Victorian Culture* (London: Routledge, 2002), p. 125.

87 Graver, 'Antoni Artaud', p. 47.

88 Ibid.

89 See Barry J. Faulk, *Music Hall and Modernity: The Late-Victorian Discovery of Popular Culture* (Athens, OH: Ohio University Press, 2004), p. 147, and Stallybrass and White's discussion of disgust, sexuality and the working class, *The Politics and Poetics of Transgression*.

90 EvFL, *Baroness Elsa*, ed. by Paul Hjartarson and Douglas Spettigue (Ottowa: Oberon Press, 1992), pp. 44–5.

91 cf. Gammel, *Baroness Elsa*, p. 62.

92 EvFL, *BE*, p. 123.

93 Butler, *Gender Trouble: Feminism and the Subversion of Identity* (London: Routledge, 2006), p. 12.

94 Bakhtin, *Rabelais and His World*, p. 7.

95 Ibid., p. 40.

96 See Sarah Carpenter, 'Women and Carnival Masking', *Records of Early English Drama* 21 (1996), 9–16.

97 Làszló Kürt, 'Eroticism, Sexuality, and Gender Reversal in Hungarian Culture', in *Gender Reversals and Gender Cultures: Anthropological and Historical*

Perspectives, ed. by Sabrina Petra Ramet (London: Routledge, 1996), pp. 148–63 (p. 150).
98 Russo, *The Female Grotesque*, p. 61.
99 Butler, 'Performative Acts and Gender Constitution: An Essay in Phenomenology and Feminist Theory', *Theatre Journal* 40.4 (1988), 519–31 (p. 531).
100 Ibid., p. 519.
101 John Burger, *Ways of Seeing* (London: Penguin, 1972), p. 49.
102 EvFL Papers, Box 1, Folder 2, 'Written on a Sheet of Butcher Paper in the Subway'.
103 Mulvey, 'Visual Pleasure and Narrative Cinema', p. 19.
104 Chadwick, 'An Infinite Play of Empty Mirrors', p. 11.
105 Nead, *The Female Nude*, p. 1.
106 Anderson, *My Thirty Years War*, pp. 193–5.
107 For a discussion of the Diva personality see Bradshaw, *Amy Lowell*.
108 Graver, 'Antonin Artaud', p. 49.
109 Ibid., p. 51.
110 Artaud, cited in ibid.
111 Graver, 'Antonin Artaud', p. 51.
112 See Jones, Irrational *Modernism*; Jones, *The En-Gendering of Marcel Duchamp*.

Chapter 3

1 Thurn Budington to Barnes, 2 April 1958. Djuna Barnes Papers, Series I, Box 6, Folder 8.
2 Sidonie Smith, *A Poetics of Women's Autobiography: Marginality and the Fiction of Self-Representation* (Bloomington: Indiana University Press, 1987), p. 5.
3 Nathalie Cook, '"Mi-Rage": The Confessional Politics of Canadian Survivor Poetry', in *Confessional Politics: Women's Sexual Self-Representations in Life Writing and Popular Media*, ed. by Gammel (Carbondale, IL: Southern Illinois University Press, 1999), pp. 65–80 (p. 70). The second quotation is taken from Cook's citation of Linda Alcoft and Laura Gray, 'Survivor Discourse: Transgression or Recuperation?' *SIGNS* 18.2 (1993), 260–90 (p. 272).
4 Alongside repeated references in the Barnes-Coleman correspondence to the project throughout the 1930s including Coleman's lukewarm response to a chapter draft completed in 1939, Barnes also discussed the project with her friend and editor and Faber & Faber T.S. Eliot who advised Barnes to 'stop worrying about the Baroness […] just make use of her', Eliot to Barnes, 28 January 1938 Series II, Box 4, Folder 60.
5 In my definition of this project as a mode of auto/biographic writing I am employing critic Liz Stanley's useful term 'Auto/Biography' as a way of highlighting

my critical engagement with feminist treatments of the forms, theories and practices of life-writing that have developed in recent decades. I am also suggesting that this collaborative project, which rejects 'conventional generic distinctions' and blurs lines between authenticity and fiction, one life and another, can be usefully illuminated through such critical analysis. See Liz Stanley, *The Auto/Biographical 'I': The Theory and Practice of Feminist Auto/biography* (Manchester: Manchester University Press, 1992), p. 3.

6 Coleman writes to Barnes, 'This is the book of a deadly introvert. Such introversion as this is almost pathological [...] One of the reasons you have such great trouble with conversation is that you have never communicated yourself – and so cannot do people communicating. Your people speak to themselves.'

7 Barnes to Coleman, 20 September 1935, Series II, Box 2, folder 7.

8 Caselli, *Improper Modernism*, p. 258.

9 Alexis Carrel, *L'Homme cet inconnu* (*Man, the Unknown*) (New York: Harper & Brothers, 1935). Carell's text and particularly his theories of memory and inner time represent a strikingly under-researched aspect of Barnes's critical thinking in the 1930s. Later discredited for his Nazi sympathies and collaborationist tendencies, Barnes read his work and discoursed enthusiastically about some of his central ideas, as her correspondence from the late 1930s testifies.

10 Barnes, *The Antiphon* (1958) (Los Angeles, CA: Green Integer, 2000). Act and page number hereafter referenced parenthetically.

11 Growing up in a small log cabin in Cornwall-on-Hudson, Barnes's childhood was certainly unconventional. Like the children populating *Ryder*, the Barnes offspring had little formal schooling and were tutored instead by their journalist grandmother and one-time literary salon hostess Zadel Barnes and amateur musician father, Wald. After meeting Barnes's mother Elizabeth Chappell in England (re-imagined as the fictional town of Beewick in *The Antiphon*), Barnes's biographer Philip Herring details a courtship and marriage overseen by the charismatic Zadel and closely observed by both *Ryder* and *The Antiphon*. Returning to America, Wald began to put his philosophies of free love into practice, eventually moving his mistress Fanny Clarke into the marital home. The children were raised side by side until poverty forced Wald to make a decision between his wife and mistress and Elizabeth was made to leave along with her children in 1912. See Philip Herring, *Djuna: The Life and Work of Djuna Barnes* (New York: Viking, 1996).

12 Andrew Field, *Djuna: The Life and Times of Djuna Barnes* (New York: Putman, 1983), p. 185.

13 Barnes to Coleman, 14 December 1935. DB Papers, Series II, Box 3, Folder 8.

14 Barnes to Peggy Guggenheim, 15 April 1978. Series II, Box 8, Folder 31 (Caselli has as 15 April 1979. Series II, Box 3, Folder 30) and 22 March 1978. (Series II, Box 3, Folder 30).

15 Originally printed in the *Little Review* the original questionnaire and Barnes's response are reprinted in *Silence and Power*, ed. by Mary Lynn Broe, p. 66.
16 Barnes to Guggenheim, 15 April 1978. DB Papers, Series II, Box 3, Folder 30.
17 Barnes to Guggenheim, undated. DB Papers, Series II, Box 3, Folder 30.
18 Fastidious regarding the correction of erroneous statements regarding her life or work Barnes wrote to the W.H. Scarborough after the publication of his review of *The Selected Works of Djuna Barnes* in 1962. Among her various corrections she offers praise for the review's astute observation that '"To discuss substance, or to catch the spirit of the book on the wing is fruitless; it is to be experienced rather than read or discussed," and there I think you have put your finger on the whole disturbance regarding my work, particularly The Antiphon'. Barnes to W.H. Scarborough, 27 November 1962. DB Papers, Series II, Box II, Folder 51.
19 T.S. Eliot, 'Tradition and the Individual Talent', in *The Sacred Wood: Essays on Poetry and Criticism* (London: Methuen, 1969), pp. 47–60 (p. 53).
20 Ibid., p. 50. With reference to Barnes's own annotated copy of Eliot's essays, Julie Taylor has highlighted that Barnes places a question mark next to Eliot's claims of art as continual self-sacrifice. See Taylor, *Affective Modernism*, p. 6.
21 As Tyrus Miller has suggested, this perhaps goes some way to explaining the rather 'positionless' quality of the Barnes corpus in relation to modernist histories. See Miller, *Late Modernism*, p. 124.
22 Ibid., p. 125.
23 See Laura Marcus, *Auto/Biographical Discourses* (Manchester: Manchester University Press, 1994), p. 3.
24 Roy Pascal, *Design and Truth in Autobiography* (Cambridge, MA: Harvard University Press, 1960), p. 5.
25 Richard D. Altick, *Lives and Letters: A History of Literary Biography in England and America* (New York: Alfred A. Knopf, 1969), p. 289.
26 Stanley, *The Auto/biographical 'I'*, p. 8.
27 Monika Kaup, 'The Neobaroque in Djuna Barnes', *Modernism/Modernity* 12.1 (2005), 85–110 (p. 85).
28 Herring, *Djuna*, p, xx.
29 Ibid., p. xv.
30 Phillipe Lejeune, *On Autobiography*, trans. by Katherine M. Leary (Minneapolis, MN: University of Minnesota Press, 1989), p. 19.
31 Taylor, 'Revising *The Antiphon*, Restaging Trauma: or, Where Textual Politics Meet Sexual History'. *Modernism/Modernity* 18.1 (2011), 125–47 (p. 125).
32 While the polygamous household of Barnes's childhood is widely accepted as the model for the domestic dynamics of both *Ryder* and *The Antiphon*, Barnes's letters and fictional reworkings of these childhood experiences repeatedly reference Wald's violence and a pointed sense of dereliction of duty on the part of her mother, Elizabeth (see Herring, *Djuna*, 50, 52, 280). The question of a directly or

indirectly incestuous sexual violation is also raised across Barnes's correspondence and has certainly informed readings of the autobiographic nature of the both *Ryder* and *The Antiphon*. As Herring highlights in his biography, Barnes was generally consistent in her account of her first sexual encounter as a rape arranged by her father and an older neighbour, although in one account she does suggest that the rape was in fact performed by her father himself (Herring, *Djuna*, 53, 268)

33 Field, *Djuna*, p. 98.
34 See Louis F. Kannestein *The Art of Djuna Barnes: Duality and Damnation* (New York: New York University Press, 1977).
35 Field, *The Formidable Miss Barnes*, quoted in *Silence and Power*, ed. by Broe, p. 20.
36 See Broe, 'My Art Belongs to Daddy: Incest as Exile – The Textual Economics of Hayford Hall', in *Women's Writing in Exile*, ed. by Broe and Angela Ingram (Chapel Hill, NC: University of North Carolina Press, 1989), pp. 41–86. Broe directly correlates the roles played by abusive father and Eliot's editorial practices: 'by the authority of his pen, Eliot reproduces the incestuous desires of the violating father by his intrusion in the daughter's script' (p. 53). Also see Julie Taylor, *Affective Modernism*, p. 42.
37 See Lynda Curry, '"Tom, Take Mercy": Djuna Barnes's Drafts of The Antiphon', in *Silence and Power*, ed. by Broe (Carbon), pp. 286–99 (p. 290).
38 Using trauma theory as a way of approaching the contradictions and complexities in Barnes's texts and treatment of her narrative material, Julie Taylor's more recent study of *Affective Modernism* addresses this earlier critical work and offers a sophisticated reading of the autobiographic in Barnes.
39 Louise DeSalvo, '"To Make Her Mutton at Sixteen": Rape, Incest, and Child Abuse in *The Antiphon*', in *Silence and Power*, ed. by Broe, (Carbondale: Southern Illinois University Press, 1991), pp. 300–39 (p. 301).
40 Caselli, *Improper Modernism*, p. 194.
41 Thurn Budington to Barnes, 2 April 1958. DB Papers, Series I, Box 6, Folder 8.
42 See Janice Haaken, *Pillar of Salt: Gender, Memory, and the Perils of Looking Back* (New Brunswick, NJ: Rutgers University Press, 1998), p. 14. Also see Taylor, *Affective Modernism*, p. 50.
43 Barnes to Coleman, 30 November 1937. Series I, Box 3, Folder 10.
44 Taylor, *Affective Modernism*, p. 8.
45 Caselli, *Improper Modernism*, p. 196.
46 'I believe Freud, Jung and the rest are of little importance, because they now have a canned and labelled precept for every action, having, as it were commercialized the findings of the intuitive artists, like Dostoevsky'. Barnes to Coleman, 10 January 1936. DB Papers, Series II, Box 3, Folder 14.
47 See *Women, Autobiography, Theory: A Reader*, ed. by Sidonie Smith and Julie Watson (London: University of Wisconsin Press, 1998).
48 Ibid., pp. 3–4.

49 Georg Gusdorf, 'Conditions and Limits of Autobiography', in *Autobiography: Essays Theoretical and Critical*, ed. by James Olney (Princeton, NJ: Princeton University Press, 1980), p. 35.
50 Olney, *Metaphors of Self: The Meaning of Autobiography* (Princeton, NJ: Princeton University Press, 1972), p. 3. Also see Linda Anderson, *Autobiography: The New Critical Idiom* (London: Routledge, 2001).
51 Casseli, *Improper Modernism*, p. 194.
52 Ibid., p. 196.
53 Stanley, *The Auto/Biographical 'I'*, p. 14.
54 Carolyn Steedman, 'Culture, Cultural Studies, and the Historians', in *Cultural Studies*, ed. by Lawrence Grosssberg, Cary Nelson, Paula Treicher (New York: Routledge, 1992), p. 614.
55 Stanley, *The Auto/Biographical 'I'*, pp. 12–13. Also see Pauline Polkey, ed., *Women's Lives into Print: The Theory, Practice and Writing of Feminist Auto/Biography* (Basingstoke: Macmillan, 1999).
56 O'Neal, 'The Barnes Diaries', 27 November 1978, The Frances McCallough Papers, Special Collections, University of Maryland Libraries. Box I.
57 In connecting the messy intertextuality of the Barnes corpus and the compulsive revisions characterizing her writing practice with the functioning of her autobiographic poetics, Linda Anderson's conception of autobiographic modes as confounding the 'notion that there is one definitive or fixed version' through 'the writing and rewriting of the self over a period of time, through constant revisions or serial modes' proves particularly useful. Anderson, *Autobiography*, p. 9.
58 Caselli, *Improper Modernism*, p. 2.
59 Anderson, *Autobiography*, p. 5.
60 See Terry Threadgold, *Feminist Poetics: Poiesis, Performance, Histories* (London: Routledge, 1997).
61 Freud, cited in Taylor, *Affective Modernism*, p. 2.
62 As Anderson highlights in her discussion of the intersection of past and present in Freud's model of the return of the repressed, positioned outside of the normal processes of history and temporality, the past – and its return as a form of bleated knowledge – can only enter the present 'as repetition or intrusive memory, disrupting linearity and giving rise to a more complex temporality'. Anderson, *Autobiography*, p. 61.
63 O'Neal, 'The Barnes Diaries', 19 September 1978.
64 See Barnes to Zendon Barnes, 4 August 1975. DB Papers, Series I, Box 14. This letter details her various health concerns including a bad heart, varicose veins, painful arthritis and the removal of her gall bladder.
65 O'Neal 'The Barnes Diaries', 23 September 1978.
66 O'Neal's diaries, cited in Broe, *Silence and Power*, p. 356.
67 The papers relating to the notes towards the memoirs are described as 'diverse drafts written at various times and that at the time of her death bore at least four

different titles. Pages are missing, and narratives end abruptly [...] earlier texts went into the files to coexist with revisions, rather than into the trash bin' (*CP*: 3).
68. See Nancy J. Levine, 'Works in Progress: The Uncollected Poetry of Barnes's Patchin Place Period', *Review of Contemporary Fiction* 13.3 (1993), 186–200.
69. Barnes, 'Interviewing Arthur Voegtlin Is Something Like Having a Nightmare', in *I Could Never Be Lonely without a Husband: Interviews by Djuna Barnes*, ed. by Alyce Barry (New York: Sun & Moon Press, 1985), p. 81.
70. Laura Winkiel, 'Circuses and Spectacles: Public Culture in Nightwood'. *Journal of Modern Literature* 1 (Summer 1997), 9.
71. Ibid., p. 28. Also see Goody, 'Spectacle, Technology and Performing Bodies'.
72. Sigfried Kracauer, *The Mass Ornament: Weimar Essays*, trans. by Thomas Y. Levin (Cambridge, MA: Harvard University Press, 1995), pp. 75–88 (p. 76).
73. Winkiel, 'Circuses and Spectacles', p. 8.
74. Levine, 'Works in Progress', p. 186.
75. Ibid.
76. Ibid., p. 187.
77. Unlike Phillip Herring's interpretative mode of refinement, Scott Herring's shift from the published poems to the 'late life work in toto' parallels my own interpretive approach to this body of work. However, while Herring contextualizes this production as a 'senile sublime' or 'geriatric avant-garde' that he connects with core modernist projects of textual difficulty, novelty and stylistic or formal experimentalism, I look to it, rather, as an intensification of structural patterns of return, repletion and frame that we can trace across Barnes's work.
78. Levine, 'Works in Progress', p. 189.
79. Caselli, *Improper Modernism*, p. 85.
80. Levine highlights that regeneration and resurrection form the thematic focus of many of these cycles. In highlighting Barnes's messy writing practices as contributing to a poetics of waste I am suggesting that regeneration is also a central formal aspect of Barnes's poetics during this period.
81. For a discussion of the musical patterns of composition at work in Barnes's autobiographic poetics, see my chapter '"All that Tutti and Continuo": Musicality and Temporality' in Djuna Barnes's *The Antiphon*' in *Musical Modernism: Essays on Language and Music in Modernist Literature*, ed. by Katie Brown and Katherine O'Callaghan (Surrey: Ashgate, 2014).
82. Also, see Caselli, *Improper Modernism*, p. 103.
83. The thematic emphasis on circularity accompanying the story of the martyrdom of St Catherine executed on the spiked wheel is reinforced here by Barnes's invocation of the complex and ornate designs of the Rose window popular in Gothic construction.
84. Melissa Jane Hardie, 'Repulsive Modernism: Djuna Barnes's *The Book of Repulsive Women*', *Journal of Modern Literature* 29.1 (2005), 118–32, p. 123.
85. Ibid.

86 Ibid., p. 122.
87 Interestingly, sharing the same root with the Latin *vertere* (to turn), both 'verse' and 'worms' are homonymous in French – *vers*.
88 *The Works of Joseph Addison, Complete in Three Volumes*, Vol. I (New York: Harper & Brothers, 1837), p. 177.
89 Ibid.
90 'Card' in this sense does not refer to its more common usage as a noun but to an antiquated method of preparing untreated wool for spinning in which the raw material was first cleaned and separated with a sharp-toothed comb.
91 Thomas Middleton/Cyril Tourneur, *The Revenger's Tragedy* (1607), ed. by R. A. Foakes (Manchester: Manchester University Press, 1996), III, V, 72–5 (p. 89).
92 As Caselli points out, as well as marking this passage in her own copy of Webster and Tourneur, Barnes would also have been familiar with Eliot's citing of these lines in his 1919 essay 'Tradition and the Individual Talent'. See Caselli, *Improper Modernism*, p. 106. However, in an interesting echo of Barnes's own processes of retrieval, substitution and variation, it might be valuable to note that, in quoting this passage, Eliot replaced the original 'bewitching' with 'bewildering' (a change retained in Caselli's discussion). If, as Frank Kermode has elaborated upon in his identification of Eliot's textual 'improvement' here, the only textual support for this change was 'supplied by John Payne Collier, the Victorian scholar and forger, we can even say that Eliot chose a reading he knew to be fraudulent just because he liked it better'. Frank Kermode, 'Eliot and the Shudder', *London Review of Books* 32.9 (13 May 2010), 13–16 (p. 14).
93 Sidonie Smith, 'Bodies of Evidence: Jenny Saville, Faith Ringgold, and Janine Antoni Weigh In', in *Interfaces* ed. by Sidonie Smith (Ann Arbor, MI: University of Michigan Press, 2002), pp. 132–59 (p. 145).
94 Henri Bergson, *An Introduction to Metaphysics* (1903), trans. by T.E. Hulme (New York and London: G.P. Putnam's Sons, 1912.)
95 Ibid., p. 11.
96 Ibid., pp. 11–12.
97 Ibid., p. 14.

Chapter 4

1 EvFL Papers, Djuna Barnes Notes, 1924 and undated. Series I, Box 1, Folder 2
2 Building on Tyrus Miller's argument for a 'late modernism' and Daniella Casselli's notion of Barnes's anachronistic untimeliness, Scott Herring has characterized Barnes's Patchin Place Production as 'late late modernism'.
3 Hank O'Neal, '*Life Is Painful, Nasty and Short ... in My Case It Has Only Been Painful and Nasty*': *Djuna Barnes 1978–1981* (New York: Paragon, 1990), p. 149.

4   Asradur Eysteinsson, *The Concept of Modernism* (Ithaca: Cornell University Press, 1990).
5   EvFL Papers, Djuna Barnes, Notes, 1924 and undated, Series I, Box 1, Folder 2. (*does she publish this ..?*)
6   EvFL Papers, Djuna Barnes notes, 1924 and undated, Series I, Box I, Folder 2.
7   Could quote NW/Ant here?
8   As she writes to Barnes 'My book of poetry ... Oh! What may be – it would *do* for me to keep me – at least – floating – if I could see it *soon*! Djuna – it is *desperately* necessary for me'. Gammel's biography describes this period of the Baroness's life in detail. As she explains, much of the writing of this fascinating document was completed between the Bodelschwingh Home for women and a psychiatric asylum just outside of Berlin, written against her poverty and deep depression. See Gammel, *Baroness Elsa*, pp. 348–61
9   EvFL, 'Selections from the Letters of Elsa von Freytag-Loringhoven', *Transition* 11 (1928), 26.
10 Lynn DeVore, 'The Backgrounds of *Nightwood*: Robin, Felix, and Nora', *Journal of Modern Literature* 10.1 (1983), 26.
11 Something about DeVore identifying manuscript and Hjartson confirming Elsa as model behind Greve/Grove's novels.
12 See Hjartarson and Kulba, eds., *The Politics of Cultural Mediation: Baroness Elsa von Freytga-Lorighoven and Felix Paul Greve* and Irene Gammel, *Sexualising Power in Naturalism: Theodre Drreiser and Frederick Paul Grove* (Calgary: University of Calgary Press, 1994); 'Breaking the Bonds of Discretion'; 'Baroness Elsa's Intimate Biography', p. 445.
13 Emphasizing her drive towards sexual fulfilment, Elsa positions herself as taking on the dominant (traditionally coded masculine) role in initiating their affair. Echoing the later accounts of Williams and Biddle when faced with her destabilizing erotic energy, Elsa records that she 'felt his whole frame tremble' as she kissed him.
14 See Gammel, 'Breaking the Bonds of Discretion'.
15 Gammel, *Sexualizing Power in Naturalism*, p. 120.
16 EvFL Papers, Djuna Barnes Typescript, undated. Series I, Box 1, Folder 4. Ellipses that do not appear in square brackets belong to Barnes's typescript of the Baroness's holograph.
17 Gammel, '"No Woman Lover": Baroness Elsa's Intimate Biography'. *Canadian Review of Comparative Literature* 20.3–4 (1993), 451–67 (p. 455).
18 Benstock, 'Expatriate Sapphic Modernism', p. 191.
19 Ibid., p. 187.
20 The editors write: 'In part through her use of the dash and the portmanteau, the Baroness's poems mirror her own body. They are sinewy and muscular – flexing against the page, against syntax, and against language itself, creating an embodied, performative poetics'. *Body Sweats*, p. 13.

21 EvFL to DB, 'Dearest Djuna', undated. EvFL Papers, Series II, Box 1, Folder 3.
22 EvFL Papers, Series I, Box I, Folder 3.
23 Giving us an insight into her own compositional practices, and underscoring the amount of textual excess that this project produced the Baroness explains to Barnes: 'I know this is rather mixed up – but – maybe – it does not hurt the interest? Let me know. This is even a copy! I had to copy the whole thing – for the difficulty to express myself. It seems to become more and more difficult'. EVFL Papers, Series II, folder 3.
24 EvFl, autobiography. EvFL Papers, Series I, Box 1, Folder 4.
25 As is reiterated in Elsa's account, Berthe becomes increasingly detached from her family, retreating more and more into her own rooms, even declaring her intention to make 'myself an alter and a crucifix for my bedroom' (MM, p. 141). Given Elsa's repeated statements with regards to her father's atheism, this would certainly have been interpreted as a veiled attack on the authority of Ida-Marie's husband.
26 Although including a scene where the two girls wait up all night for their missing mother, imagining the horrific possibilities of their mother drowning or getting lost in the snow which Elsa recounts in an almost identical fashion, the shock of the mother's attempted suicide is undercut by the frozen river that she lands on, unscathed. By contrast Elsa's narrative includes a harrowing scene when her mother returns 'dripping wet', telling her children indifferently '"that she had tried to drown herself in the East Sea – had gone up to the breast in water – then courage had left her"', EvFL to Djuna Barnes, 'Djuna Sweeet', EvFL Papers, Series II, Box 1, Folder 3.
27 EvFL to Djuna Barnes, 'Djuna Sweet', undated. EvFL Papers, Series II, Box 1, Folder 3.
28 EvFl autobiography. EvFL Papers, Series I, Box I, Folder 4.
29 EvFl Papers, Series III, Box 1, Folder 20.
30 Kristeva, *The Powers of Horror*, p. 109.
31 'Djuna she never had for one minute been 'insane' but sane! Honest-!
32 EvFL to DB, 'Djuna Sweet'. EvFL Papers, Series II, Box 1, Folder 3.
33 EvFL Papers, Djuna Barnes Notes, 1933 and undated. Series I, Box I, Folder 3.
34 'EVFL to DB, 'Djuna Sweet', EvFL Papers, Series II, Box 1, Folder 3.
35 Rozsika Parker *The Subversive Stitch: Embroidery and the Making of the Feminine* (London: I.B. Tauris, 2010), p. xix.
36 Ibid., p. 75.
37 Parker, *Subversive Stitch*, p. 138.
38 J. Gorovoy and P. Tabatabai, *Louise Bourgeois Blue Days and Pink Days*, exhibition catalogue (Fondazione Prada: Milan, 1997) cited in Parker, *Subversive Stich*.
39 See Melanie Klein, *Love, Guilt and Reparation and Other Works: 1921–1945* (New York: The Free Press, 1975). Klein first develops the idea in 1929 in 'Infantile anxiety-situations reflected in a work of art and in the creative impulse'.

40 Elizabeth Bott Spillius, Jane Milton, Penelope Garvey, Cyril Couve and Deborah Steiner, *New Dictionary of Kleinian Thought* (London: Routledge, 2011), p. 470.

41 Stanley, 'How Do We Know about Past Lives? Methodological and Epistemological Matters Involving Prince Phillip, the Russian Revolution, Emily Wilding Davison, My Mum and the Absent Sue', in *Women's Lives into Print*, ed. by Polkey, (London: Palgrave Macmillan, 1999) pp. 3–21 (pp. 12–13). The marked shifts between third and first person narration, Barnes's present and Elsa's past across these manuscripts are particularly striking in this respect.

42 Benstock, 'Expatriate Sapphic Modernism', p. 191.

43 Ibid., p. 192.

44 'I can't say enough about the artistry of Proust, I've been raving about him for years'. Barnes to Coleman, 5 January 1939, Philip Herring Papers. For a discussion of Bergson's influence on Proust, and an assessment of his broader impact on modernist aesthetics, see Pete A.Y. Gunter, 'Bergson and Proust: A Question of Influence', in *Understanding Bergson, Understanding Modernism*, ed. by Paul Ardoin (London: Bloomsbury Academic, 2013), pp. 157–76.

45 T.S. Eliot, Ezra Pound and James Joyce are amongst those within Barnes's circle who were exposed to Bergson's writing and lectures, although their responses to his thinking are complex. See Paul Douglas, *Bergson, Eliot, and American Literature* (Kentucky: University Press of Kentucky, 1986). See also Mary Ann Gillies, *Henri Bergson and British Modernism* (Montreal & Kingston: McGill-Queens University Press, 1996).

46 Joseph Frank advanced his influential theory of modernism's 'spatial form' in a series of essay in 1945. Distinguishing between the temporal qualities of narrative and the spatial qualities of the plastic arts, Frank suggested that a central tenant of modern(ist) experimentation was its break with traditional narrative plotting in order to create narrative structures apprehended spatially in a *moment* in time, rather than unfolding sequentially. Significantly, Frank held Barnes's *Nightwood* as a preeminent example of this tendency, and Barnes herself was very impressed by Frank's reading of her novel. Joseph Frank, 'Spatial Form in Modern Literature', *Sewanee Review* 53.1 (1945), 433–56; 53.4 (1945), pp. 433–56; (1945), pp. 643–53.

47 Alexis Carrel, *Man, the Unknown* (1935) (London: Penguin, 1948), p. 85.

48 Ibid., p. 163.

49 Ibid., p. 165.

50 Julie L. Abraham, 'Woman, Remember You', *Silence and Power*, pp. 252–70.

51 See Herring 'Djuna Barnes and the Geriatric Avant-Garde'.

52 In 'Tradition and the Individual Talent' Eliot writes: 'The existing monuments form an ideal order among themselves, which is modified by the introduction of the new (the really new) work of art among them. The existing order is complete before the new work arrives.'

53 See Maud Ellman, *Poetics of Impersonality: T.S. Eliot and Ezra Pound* (Cambridge, MA: Harvard University Press, 1987); Eugenia M. Gunner, *T. S. Eliot's Romantic Dilemma: Tradition's Anti-Traditional Elements* (London: Routledge, 2015).
54 Carrel, *Man, the Unknown*, p. 166.
55 Julie Taylor discusses the question of poetic impersonality in light of Barnes's own equivocal relationship to autobiographic modes and disclosure in a manner that parallels my own treatment of these structural patterns of recurrence at work across the Barnes *oeuvre*. Highlighting that in Barnes's own copy of Eliot's essays Barnes included a question mark in the margin next to Eliot's statement that 'The progress of an artist is a continual self-sacrifice, a continual extinction of personality'. Taylor compellingly suggests that the addition here 'figures as a metonym for Barnes's ongoing interrogation of exactly how the personal should relate to fiction'; however, I would add that this mark also includes the question of what to do with the personality she had been entrusted with as much as her own.
56 Miller, *Late Modernism*, pp. 124, 125.
57 In her reading of *Ryder* Taylor emphasizes Barnes's recovery of the denigrated nineteenth-century sentimental tradition, while Caselli describes these aerchasisms as producing a 'language which is worn out, used, and never innocent', Caselli, *Improper Modernism*, p. 3.
58 Abraham suggests something similar in her discussion of Barnesean 'memory' as subsuming 'both history and literature, becoming the material of history and the means of writing', Abraham, '"Woman," Remember You', p. 261. Pointedly, in looking at Barnes's relationship to history, Julie Abraham makes a case for Barnes's 'turning towards women' in her construction of an expanded historical sense, including those marginalized and excluded from official histories.
59 Hardie, 'Repulsive Modernism', p. 122.
60 Ibid.
61 Barnes to Coleman, 20 September 1935. Series II, Box 2, folder 7.
62 Kristin M. Langellier, 'Personal Narrative, Performance, Performativity: Two or Three Things I Know for Sure', *Text and Performance Quarterly* 19 (1999), 125–44, 139.
63 Carrel, *Man, the Unknown*, p. 93.
64 Frank, 'Spatial Form in Modern Literature', 53.1 (1945), 433–56; 53.4 (1945), 433–56; (1945), 643–53.
65 Ibid.
66 Elsewhere Barnes aptly describes her as 'a contemporary antiquity'. comp too description of Robi as 'newly ancient' (*N: 40*). In looking at this early Barnes article Alex Goody describes the 'merging of ancient female embodiment and cutting-edge technology in her arrested moment' Goody, *Modernist Articulations*, p. 93.
67 Barnes, 'How the Villagers Amuse Themselves', pp. 246–52 (p. 249). The distinctive sense and she frequently returns to the compellingly strange simultaneity of the

older woman's ultra-modernity and crumbling antiquity evident in the repeated descriptions of her as possessing 'the head of a discarded Roman Emperor, green – inward and piercing eyes, a hoarse authentic voice'.
68 Taylor, *Affective Modernism*, p. 16
69 Frank, 'Spatial Form in Modern Literature: An Essay in Three Parts', *The Sewanee Review* 53.2 (Spring 1945), 221–40 (p. 231).
70 Barnes, 'Baroness Elsa' drafts. EvFL Papers, Series I, Box 2.
71 Brain Glavey 'Dazzling Estrangement: Modernism, Queer Ekphrasis, and the Spatial Form of *Nightwood*', PMLA 124.3 (2009), 749–63 (p. 752).
72 Ibid., p. 754
73 Barnes to Coleman, 20 September 1935. DB Papers, Series II, Box 2, folder 7.
74 Plumb, 'Introduction', *Nightwood: The Original Version and Related Drafts*, p. xviii.
75 The influence of Carrel in the distillation of Elsa into the *Nightwood* manuscript becomes particularly apparent through her re-working of the Elsa material after 1933. Barnes's treatment of Ida's turn to religion bears a striking resemblance to the repetition of bowed and kneeling figures occurring throughout *Nightwood*: 'One feels, when in the presence of any kneeling figure, an inturning of bodily forces; for every soul that prays for some boon, temporal or heavenly is at that moment not in space or time but has seized both, compressing them into the picture of the thing desired'.
76 In the vignette of 'disqualification' re-worked across 'The Beggars Comedy' fragments the description of the Parisienne as one '"at home" in a perpetual derangement of the visible world, akin to that nebulous moss-like growth that hangs on the side of dream, that portion of sleep that the cornea cannot gather' bears a striking resemblance to Robin Vote here.
77 EvFL Papers, Djuna Barnes Notes, 1924 and undated. Series I, Box I, Folder 2. Also, Loringhoven, *transition*, p. 23.
78 EvFL Papers, Djuna Barnes Notes, 1933 and undated. Series I, Box I, Folder 3.
79 Barnes to Coleman, 20 September 1935, Series II, Box 2, folder 7.
80 Taylor, *Affective Modernism*, p. 37.
81 Eliot to Barnes, 28 January 1938, Series 2, Box 4, Folder 60.
82 EvFL Papers, Djuna Barnes, Notes, 1933 and undated. Series I, Box I, Folder 3.
83 EvFL Papers, Djuna Barnes Notes, 1933 and undated. Series I, Box I, Folder 3.
84 Barnes to Janet Flanner, undated. Series II, Box 6, Folder 9.
85 Responding to Guggenheim's request for a definition of the unfamiliar term, Barnes sends her to the dictionary: 'Antiphon, n. Versicle, sentence, sung by one choir in response to another; prose or verse composition consisting of such passages'. Barnes to Guggenheim, 18 March 1958. Series II, Box 8, Folder 28.
86 'They are like a damned tapestry, all their threads and all mine intermingle in the family pattern [...] There is that inexorable design'. Barnes to Coleman, 23 March 1936. Series II, Box 3, Folder 9.

87 Richard Epsley, 'Djuna Barnes's *The Antiphon*: "Tedious … Because They Will Not Understand It"', *Women: A Cultural Review* 17.2 (2006), 188–201 (p. 189).
88 Kannestein, *Duality and Damnation*, p. 151.
89 See Caselli, *Improper Modernism* and Cathryn Setz, '"Trees of Heaven": Djuna Barnes's Late Metaphysical Verse', *Shattered Objects*, pp. 130–46.
90 Taylor, *Affective Modernism*, p. 40.
91 Felski, *The Gender of Modernity*, p. 1.
92 EvFL to DB, undated. EvFL Papers, Series II, Box 1, Folder 3.
93 In one of the long letters the Baroness wrote to Barnes detailing the mother's biography she writes: 'I give her to you here – to do her honour – because I respect you and love you – and want to make you present'. EvFL to DB, undated, 'Djuna Sweet', EvFL Papers, Series II, Box 1, Folder 3.
94 Bonie Kime Scott, *Refiguring Modernism*, Vol. 2, Postmodern Feminist Readings of Woolf, West and Barnes (Bloomington: Indiana University Press, 1995), p. 173.
95 Polkey, 'Introduction', *Women's Lives into Print*, p. xvii. Polkey cites Julie Hallam's essay, 'Self Image and Occupational Identity: Barbadian Nurses in Post-War Britain', pp. 123–36.

Coda: Modernism

1 See Rachele Dini, *Consumerism, Waste, and Re-Use in Twentieth-Century Fiction: Legacies of the Avant-Garde* (New York: Palgrave Macmillan, 2016).
2 Trotter, *Cooking with Mud*, p. 20.
3 Kristeva, *Powers of Horror*, p. 3.
4 Benstock, 'Sapphic Modernism', p. 186.
5 Nead, *The Female Nude*, p. 6.
6 Herbert N. Schneidau, *Walking Giants: The Presence of the Past in Modernism* (Oxford: Oxford University Press, 1991), p. 227.
7 Caselli, *Improper Modernism*, p. 197.
8 Rita Felski, *Beyond Feminist Aesthetics: Feminist Literature and Social Change* (Cambridge, MA: Harvard University Press, 1989), p. 169.
9 Rebecca Tamás, 'The Songs of Hecate: Poetry and the Language of the Occult', *The White Review* 24 (March 2019).
10 Benstock, 'Sapphic Modernism', pp. 186–7.
11 'Do You Strive to Capture the Symbols of Your Reactions? If Not You Are Quite Old Fashioned', *New York Evening Sun*, 13 February 1917.

Bibliography

Works by Djuna Barnes:

The Antiphon (Los Angeles, CA: Green Integer, 2000 [1958]).
A Book of Repulsive Women: 8 Rhythms and 5 Drawings (Los Angeles, CA: Sun and Moon Press, 1994 [1915]).
Collected Poems with Notes towards a Memoir, ed. by Philip Herring and Osías Stutman (Madison, WI: The University of Wisconsin Press, 2005).
I Could Never Be Lonely without a Husband: Interviews by Djuna Barnes, ed. by Alyce Barry (New York: Sun and Moon Press, 1985).
New York, ed. by Alyce Barry (Los Angeles, CA: Sun and Moon Press, 1989).
Nightwood (London: Faber & Faber, 1985 [1936]).
Nightwood: The Original Version and Related Drafts, ed. by Cheryl J. Plumb (Normal, IL: The Dalkey Archive Press, 1995).
Ryder (Normal, IL: The Dalkey Archive Press, 1995 [1928]).

Works by Elsa von Freytag-Loringhoven:

Baroness Elsa, ed. by Paul Hjartarson and Douglas Spettigue (Ottowa: Oberon Press, 1992).
Body Sweats: The Uncensored Writings of Elsa von Freytag-Loringhoven, ed. by Irene Gammel and Suzanne Zelazlo (Cambridge, MA: MIT Press, 2011).

Works Cited:

Abraham, Julie L., "'Woman, Remember You': Djuna Barnes and History', in Broe ed., *Silence and Power: A Reevaluation of Djuna Barnes* (Carbondale, IL: Southern Illinois University Press, 1991), pp. 252–68.
Addison, Joseph, *The Works Joseph Addison, Complete in Three Volumes*, Vol. I (New York: Harper & Brothers, 1837).
Altick, Richard D., *Lives and Letters: A History of Literary Biography in England and America* (New York: Alfred A. Knopf, 1969).
Anderson, Linda, *Autobiography: The New Critical Idiom* (London: Routledge, 2001).

Anderson, Margaret, *My Thirty Years War: The Autobiography, Beginnings, and Battles to 1930* (New York: New Horizon, 1969).
Apter, Eleanor S., 'Regimes of Coincidence: Katherine S. Dreier, Marcel Duchamp, and Dada', in Sawelson-Gorse ed., *Women in Dada* (Cambridge, MA: MIT Press, 1998), pp. 362–413.
Armstrong, Tim, *Modernism, Technology and the Body: A Cultural Study* (Cambridge: Cambridge University Press, 1998).
Armstrong, Tim, *Modernism: A Cultural History* (Cambridge: Polity Press, 2005).
Baker, George, *The Artwork Caught by the Tail: Francis Picabia and Dada in Paris* (Cambridge, MA: MIT Press, 2010).
Bakhtin, Mikhail, *Rabelais and His World*, trans. by Helene Iswolsky (Bloomington, IN: Indiana University Press, 1984).
Bataille, Georges, *Vision of Excess: Selected Writings, 1927–1939*, trans. by Allan Stoekl, Carl R. Lovitt and Donald M. Leslie Jr. (Minneapolis, MN: University of Minnesota Press, 1985).
Benstock, Shari, *Women of the Left Bank: Paris 1900–1940* (Austin, TX: University of Texas Press, 1986).
Benstock, Shari, 'Expatriate Sapphic Modernism: Entering Literary History', in Karla Jay and Joanne Glasgow eds., *Lesbian Texts and Contexts: Radical Revisions* (New York: New York University Press, 1990), pp. 183–203.
Bergson, Henri, *An Introduction to Metaphysics* (1903), trans. by T.E. Hulme (New York and London: G.P. Putnam's Sons, 1912).
Berman, Marshal, *All That Is Solid Melts into Air: The Experience of Modernity* (London: Verso, 1983).
Biddle, George, *An American Artist's Story* (Boston, MA: Little, Brown and Company, 1939).
Bluestone, Daniel, '"The Pushcart Evil"', in Ward and Zunz eds., *The Landscape of Modernity: New York City 1900–1940* (Baltimore, MD: Johns Hopkins University Press, 1992), pp. 285–314.
Bohn, Willard, 'Visualizing Women in 291', in Sawelson-Gorse ed., *Women in Dada* (Cambridge, MA: MIT Press, 1998), pp. 240–61.
Borzello, Frances, *Seeing Ourselves, Women's Self-Portraits* (New York: Harry N. Abrams, 1998).
Bradshaw, Melissa, *Amy Lowell: Diva Poet* (Surrey: Ashgate, 2011).
Brilliant, Richard, *Portraiture* (London: Reaktion Books, 2002).
Broe, Mary Lynn, 'My Art Belongs to Daddy: Incest as Exile – The Textual Economics of Hayford Hall', in Broe and Angela Ingram eds., *Women's Writing in Exile* (Chapel Hill, NC: University of North Carolina Press, 1989), pp. 41–86.
Broe, Mary Lynn, ed., *Silence and Power: A Reevaluation of Djuna Barnes* (Carbondale, IL: Southern Illinois University Press, 1991).
Brooks, Charles. S., *Hints to Pilgrims* (New Haven, CT: Yale University Press, 1921).
Burger, John, *Ways of Seeing* (London: Penguin, 1972).

Burke, Carolyn, *Becoming Modern: The Life of Mina Loy* (New York: Ferrar, Straus and Giroux, 1996).

Butler, Judith, 'Performative Acts and Gender Constitution: An Essay in Phenomenology and Feminist Theory', *Theatre Journal*, 40.4 (1988), 519–31.

Butler, Judith, *Bodies That Matter: On the Discursive Limits of 'Sex'* (London: Routledge, 1993).

Butler, Judith, *Gender Trouble: Feminism and the Subversion of Identity* (London: Routledge, 2006).

Butts, Mary, 'The Master's Last Dancing: A Wild Party in Paris, Inspired by One of Ford Maddox Ford's', *The New Yorker* (30 March 1998), 110–13.

Cabanne, Pierre, *Dialogues with Marcel Duchamp*, trans. by Ron Padgett (London: Thames and Hudson, 1971).

Camfield, William A., *Francis Picabia* (New York: Solomon R. Guggenheim Museum, 1970).

Camfield, William A., 'Marcel Duchamp's Fountain: It's History and Aesthetics in the Context of 1917', in Rudolf E. Kuenzli and Francis M. Naumann eds., *Marcel Duchamp: Artist of the Century* (Cambridge, MA: MIT Press, 1990), pp. 64–94.

Carpenter, Sarah, 'Women and Carnival Masking', *Records of Early English Drama*, 21 (1996), 9–16.

Carrel, Alexis, *Man, the Unknown* (1935) (London: Penguin, 1948).

Carver, Becci, *Granular Modernism* (Oxford: Oxford University Press, 2014).

Caselli, Daniela, *Improper Modernism: Djuna Barnes's Bewildering Corpus* (Surrey: Ashgate, 2009).

Cavell, Richard, 'Baroness Elsa and the Aesthetics of Empathy: A Mystery and a Speculation', in Hjartson and Kulba eds., *The Politics of Cultural Mediation* (Edmonton: University of Alberta Press, 2003), pp. 25–40.

Chadwick, Whitney, ed., *Mirror Images: Women, Surrealism, and Self-Representation* (Cambridge, MA: MIT Press, 1998).

Chadwick, Whitney, 'How Do I Look?', in Liz Rideal ed., *Mirror Mirror: Self-Portraits by Women Artists* (New York: Watson Guptill, 2002), pp. 8–21.

Chadwick, Whitney Women, *Art, and Society*, 4th edn (London: Thames and Hudson, 2007).

Childs, Donald J., *Modernism and Eugenics: Woolf, Eliot, Yeats and the Culture of Degeneration* (Cambridge: Cambridge University Press, 2007).

Cohen, William, ed., *Filth: Dirt, Disgust, and Modern Life* (Minneapolis: University of Minnesota Press, 2005).

Colomina, Beatriz, ed., *Sexuality and Space* (New York: Princeton Architectural Press, 1992).

Cook, Nathalie, '"Mi-Rage": The Confessional Politics of Canadian Survivor Poetry', in Gammel ed., *Confessional Politics: Women's Sexual Self-Representations in Life Writing and Popular Media* (Carbondale, IL: Southern Illinois University Press, 1999).

Crangle, Sara, 'Woolf's Cesspoolage: On Waste and Resignation', *Cambridge Quarterly*, 40.1 (2011), 1–20.
Curry, Linda, '"Tom, Take Mercy": Djuna Barnes's Drafts of The Antiphon', in Broe ed., *Silence and Power* (Carbondale, IL: Southern Illinois University Press, 1991), pp. 286–99.
Davis, Tracy C., *Actresses as Working Women: Their Social Identity in Victorian Culture* (London: Routledge, 2002).
DeSalvo, Louise, '"To Make Her Mutton at Sixteen": Rape, Incest, and Child Abuse in The Antiphon', in Broe ed., *Silence and Power* (Carbondale, IL: Southern Illinois University Press, 1991), pp. 300–39.
DeVore, Lynn, 'The Backgrounds of Nightwood: Robin, Felix, and Nora', *Journal of Modern Literature*, 10.1 (1983), 71–90.
Dini, Rachele, *Consumerism, Waste, and Re-Use in Twentieth-Century Fiction: Legacies of the Avant-Garde* (New York: Palgrave Macmillan, 2016).
Douglas, Mary, *Purity and Danger: An Analysis of Concepts of Pollution and Taboo* (London: Routledge Classics, 2003).
Duncan, Carol, 'Domination and Virility in Early Twentieth Century Vanguard Painting', *Artforum* (1973), 30–9, reprinted (revised) in *Feminism and Art History: Questioning the Litany*, ed. by Norma Broude and Mary D. Garrard (Boulder, CO: Westview Press, 1982).
Edwards, Erin, *The Modernist Corpse: Posthumanism and the Posthumous* (Minneapolis: University of Minnesota Press, 2018).
Eliot, T.S., *The Sacred Wood: Essays on Poetry and Criticism* (London: Methuen & Co LTD, 1969).
Elliott, B.J., and Jo Anne Wallace, *Women Artists and Writers: Modernist (Im)Positionings* (London: Routledge, 1994).
Ellman, Maud, *Poetics of Impersonality: T.S. Eliot and Ezra Pound* (Cambridge, MA: Harvard University Press, 1987).
Epsley, Richard, 'Djuna Barnes's The Antiphon: "Tedious … Because They Will Not Understand It"', *Women: A Cultural Review*, 17.2 (2006), 188–201.
Faulk, Barry J., *Music Hall and Modernity: The Late-Victorian Discovery of Popular Culture* (Athens, OH: Ohio University Press, 2004).
Feldman, Jessica, *Victorian Modernism: Pragmatism and the Varieties of Aesthetic Experience* (Cambridge: Cambridge University Press, 2002).
Felski, Rita, *Beyond Feminist Aesthetics: Feminist Literature and Social Change* (Cambridge, MA: Harvard University Press, 1989).
Felski, Rita, 'Modernism and Modernity: Engendering Literary History', in Lisa Rado ed., *Re-Reading Modernism: New Directions in Feminist Studies* (London: Routledge, 1994), pp. 191–208.
Felski, Rita, *The Gender of Modernity* (Cambridge, MA: Harvard University Press, 2009).
Field, Andrew, *Djuna: The Life and Times of Djuna Barnes* (New York: Putman, 1983).

Frank, Joseph, 'Spatial Form in Modern Literature', *Sewanee Review*, 53.1 (1945), 433–56; 53.4 (1945): 433–56; (1945): 643–53.

Franklin, Paul B., 'Beatrice Wood, Her Dada … and Her Mamma', in Sawelson-Gorse ed., *Women in Dada* (Cambridge, MA: MIT Press, 1998), pp. 104–41.

Freedman, Estelle B., 'The New Woman: Changing Views of Women in the 1920s', *Journal of American History*, LXI.2 (September 1974), 372–93.

Freud, Sigmund, 'Beyond the Pleasure Principle', in James Strachey, trans., *The Standard Edition of the Complete Psychological Works of Sigmund Freud*, Vol. XVIII (1920–1922) (London: Vintage, 2001), pp. 7–64.

Freud, Sigmund, 'The Ego and the Id' (1923), in James Strachey, trans., The Standard Edition of the Complete Psychological Works of Sigmund Freud, Vol. XIX (1923–1925) (London: Vintage, 2001), pp. 12–66.

Freud, Sigmund, *Civilization and Its Discontents*, trans. by David McLintock (London: Penguin Books, 2002 [1929]).

Gammel, Irene, '"No Woman Lover": Baroness Elsa's Intimate Biography', *Canadian Review of Comparative Literature* 20.3–4 (September 1993), 451–67.

Gammel, Irene, *Sexualizing Power in Naturalism: Theodore Dreiser and Frederick Philip Grove* (Calgary: University of Calgary Press, 1994).

Gammel, Irene, 'Breaking the Bonds of Discretion: Baroness Elsa and the Female Sexual Confession', *Tulsa Studies in Women's Literature* 14.1 (Spring 1995), 149–66.

Gammel, Irene, *Baroness Elsa: Gender, Dada, and Everyday Modernity, a Cultural Biography* (Cambridge, MA: MIT Press, 2002).

Gammel, Irene, 'Limbswishing Dada in New York: Baroness Elsa's Gender Performance', in Hjartson and Kulba, eds., *The Politics of Cultural Mediation: Baroness Elsa von Freytag-Loringhoven and Felix Paul Greve* (Edmonton: University of Alberta Press, 2003), pp. 3–24.

Gilbert, Sandra and Susan Gubar, *'No Man's Land' The Place of the Woman Writer in the Twentieth Century*, 3 vols (New Haven, CT: Yale University Press, 1988–94).

Goldberg, Rosa-Lee, *Performance Art: From Futurism to the Present*, 3rd edn (London: Thames and Hudson, 2011).

Goody, Alex, 'Cyborgs, Women and New York Dada', *The Space Between: Literature and Culture 1915–1945*, 3.1 (2007), 79–100.

Goody, Alex, *Modernist Articulations: A Cultural Study of Djuna Barnes, Mina Loy, and Gertrude Stein* (Hampshire: Palgrave Macmillan, 2007).

Graver, David, 'Antonin Artaud and the Authority of Text, Spectacle, and Performance', in Harding ed., *Contours of the Theatrical Avant-Garde: Performance and Textuality* (Ann Arbor, MI: University of Michigan Press, 2000), pp. 43–58.

Grosz, Elizabeth, *Sexual Subversions: Three French Feminists* (St. Leonards, NSW: Allen & Unwin, 1989).

Grosz, Elizabeth, 'The Body of Signification', in John Fletcher and Andrew Benjamin eds., *Abjection, Melancholia and Love: The Work of Julia Kristeva* (London: Routledge, 1990), pp. 80–103.

Grosz, Elizabeth, 'Julia Kristeva', in Elizabeth Wright ed., *Feminism and Psychoanalysis: A Critical Dictionary* (Oxford: Oxford University Press, 1992), pp. 194–200.
Grosz, Elizabeth, *Volatile Bodies: Towards a Corporeal Feminism* (Bloomington, IN: Indiana University Press, 1994).
Grove, Frederick Philip [Greve, Felix Paul], 'The Master Mason's House [*Maurermeister Ihles Haus*]', in Janice Haaken, trans., *Pillar of Salt: Gender, Memory, and the Perils of Looking Back* (New Brunswick, NJ: Rutgers University Press, 1998).
Halberstam, Jack, *Female Masculinity* (Durham, NC: Duke University Press, 1998).
Hardie, Melissa Jane, 'Repulsive Modernism: Djuna Barnes's The Book of Repulsive Women', *Journal of Modern Literature*, 29.1 (2005), 118–32.
Harding, James M., ed., *Contours of the Theatrical Avant-Garde: Performance and Textuality* (Cambridge, MA: MIT Press, 2000).
Harding, James M. and John Rouse, eds., *Not the Other Avant-Garde: The Transnational Foundations of Avant-Garde Performance* (Ann Arbor, MI: University of Michigan Press, 2006).
Harding, James. M., *Cutting Performances: Collage Events, Feminist Artists, and the American Avant-Garde* (Ann Arbor, MI: University of Michigan Press, 2010).
Hecht, Ben, 'The Yellow Goat', *The Little Review*, 5.8 (December 1918), 28–40.
Herring, Phillip, *Djuna: The Life and Work of Djuna Barnes* (New York: Viking, 1996).
Herring, Scott, 'Djuna Barnes and the Geriatric Avant-Garde', *PMLA*, 130.1 (2015), 69–91.
Hjartson, Paul and Tracy Kulba, eds., *The Politics of Cultural Mediation: Baroness Elsa von Freytag-Loringhoven and Felix Paul Greve* (Edmonton: University of Alberta Press, 2003).
Homer, William Innes, 'Picabia's *Jeune Fille Américaine Dans L'état De Nudité* and Her Friends', *The Art Bulletin*, 57.1 (1975), 110–15.
Hopkins, David, *Marcel Duchamp and Max Ernst: The Bride Shared* (Oxford: Oxford University Press, 1998).
Huculak, J. Matthew, 'What Is a Modernist Archive?' *Modernism/Modernity*, 3.1 (March 2018).
Hugnet, George, 'The Dada Spirit in Painting' (1932 and 1934)', rpt. in Robert Motherwell ed., *The Dada Painters and Poets: An Anthology*, 2nd edn (Cambridge, MA: Harvard University Press, 1989).
Huyssen, Andreas (collection of his writings), 'Mass Culture as Woman: Modernism's Other', in *After the Great Divide: Modernism, Mass Culture, Postmodernism* (Bloomington, IN: Indiana University Press, 1986), pp. 44–64.
Jones, Amelia, *Postmodernism and the En-Gendering of Marcel Duchamp* (Cambridge: Cambridge University Press, 1994).
Jones, Amelia, '"Women" in Dada: Elsa, Rrose, and Charlie', in Sawelson-Gorse ed., *Women in Dada* (Cambridge, MA: MIT Press, 1998), pp. 142–72.
Jones, Amelia, *Irrational Modernism: A Neurasthenic History of New York Dada* (Cambridge, MA: MIT Press, 2004).

Jones, Caroline A., 'The Sex of the Machine: Mechanomorphic Art, New Women, and Francis Picabia's Neurasthenic Cure', in Caroline A. Jones and Peter Galison, eds., *Picturing Science Producing Art* (Oxford: Routledge, 1998), pp. 145–80.

Jeffett, William, 'Readymades, Sculptures, Objects: "A Happy Blasphemy"', in Dawn Ades and William Jeffett, eds., *Dali/Duchamp* (London: RA, 2017), pp. 26–33.

Kannestein, Louis, *The Art of Djuna Barnes: Duality and Damnation* (New York: New York University Press, 1977).

Kaup, Monika, 'The Neobaroque in Djuna Barnes', *Modernism/Modernity*, 12.1 (2005), 85–110.

Kenner, Hugh, *The Pound Era* (Berkley: University of California Press, 1971).

Kermode, Frank, 'Eliot and the Shudder', *London Review of Books*, 32.9 (13 May 2010), 13–16.

Kracauer, Siegfried, *The Mass Ornament: Weimar Essays*, trans. by Thomas Y. Levin (Cambridge, MA: Harvard University Press, 1995).

Krauss, Rosalind E., *The Originality of the Avant-Garde and Other Modernist Myths* (Cambridge, MA: MIT Press, 1986).

Kristeva, Julia, *The Powers of Horror: An Essay on Abjection*, trans. by Leon S. Roudiez (New York: Columbia University Press, 1982).

Kuenzli, Rudolf E., ed., *New York Dada* (New York: Willis Locker and Owens, 1986).

Kuenzli, Rudolf E., 'Baroness Elsa von Freytag-Loringhoven and New York Dada', in Sawelson-Gorse ed., *Women in Dada* (Cambridge, MA: MIT Press, 1998), pp. 442–75.

Lacan, Jacques, *Feminine Sexuality: Jacques Lacan and the école freudienne*, ed. by Juliet Mitchell and Jacqueline Rose, trans. by Jacqueline Rose (New York: Norton, 1985).

Lacan, Jacques, 'The Mirror Stage as Formative of the Function of the Id as Revealed in Psychoanalytic Experience' (1949), in *Écrits: The First Complete Edition in English*, trans. by Bruce Fink (New York: Norton, 2006).

Langellier, Kristin M., 'Personal Narrative, Performance, Performativity: Two or Three Things I Know for Sure', *Text and Performance Quarterly*, 19 (1999), 125–44.

Laporte, Dominique, *History of Shit*, trans. by Nadia Benabid and Rodolphe el-Khoury (Cambridge, MA: MIT Press, 2000).

Le Bon, Gustave, *The Crowd: A Study of the Popular Mind* (1895) (New Brunswick: NJ, Transaction, 2009).

Lejeune, Phillipe, *On Autobiography*, trans. by Katherine M. Leary (Minneapolis, MN: University of Minnesota Press, 1989).

Levenson, Michael, *A Genealogy of Modernism: A Study of English Literary Doctrine 1908–1922* (Cambridge: Cambridge University Press, 1984).

Levine, Nancy J., 'Works in Progress: The Uncollected Poetry of Barnes's Patchin Place Period', *Review of Contemporary Fiction*, 13.3 (1993), 186–200.

Loewenberg, Ina, 'Reflections on Self-Portraiture in Photography', *Feminist Studies*, 25.2 (1999), 399–408.

Longhurst, Robyn, *Bodies: Exploring Fluid Boundaries* (London: Routledge, 2001).

Longworth, Deborah, 'Gendering the Modernist Text', in Peter Brooker, Andrzej Gasiorek, and Deborah Longworth, eds., *The Oxford Handbook of Modernisms* (Oxford: Oxford University Press, 2010), pp. 156–177.
Lynch, Kevin, *Wasting Away: An Exploration of Waste* (New York: Random House, 1991).
Marcus, Jane, 'Laughing at Leviticus: *Nightwood* as Women's Circus Epic, in Broe ed., *Silence and Power: A Reevaluation of Djuna Barnes* (Carbondale, IL: Southern Illinois University Press, 1991), pp. 221–50.
Marcus, Laura, *Auto/Biographical Discourses* (Manchester: Manchester University Press, 1994).
Middleton, Thomas/Cyril Tourneur, *The Revenger's Tragedy* (1607), ed. by R. A. Foakes (Manchester: Manchester University Press, 1996).
Miendl, Dieter, *America Fiction and the Metaphysics of the Grotesque* (Columbia, MA: University of Missouri, 1996).
Mileaf, Janine, *Please Touch: Dada and Surrealist Objects after the Readymade* (Lebanon, NH: Dartmouth College Press, 2010).
Miller, Tyrus, *Late Modernism: Politics, Fiction, and Arts between the Wars* (Berkley, CA: University of California Press, 1999).
Miller, William Ian, *The Anatomy of Disgust* (Cambridge, MA: Harvard University Press, 1997).
Morgan, Margaret M., 'A Box, A Pipe, and a Piece of Plumbing', in Sawelson-Gorse ed., *Women in Dada* (Cambridge, MA: MIT Press, 1998), pp. 48–102.
Motherwell, Robert, ed., *The Dada Painters and Poets: An Anthology*, 2nd edn (Cambridge, MA: Harvard University Press, 1989).
Mulvey, Laura, 'Visual Pleasure and Narrative Cinema' (1975), in *Visual and Other Pleasures*, 2nd edn (Basingstoke: Palgrave Macmillan, 2009), pp. 14–30.
Mundy, Jennifer, 'The Art of Friendship', in *Duchamp, Man Ray, Picabia*, ed. by Jennifer Mundy (London: Tate Publishing, 2008), pp. 8–57.
Mundy, Jennifer, ed., *Duchamp, Man Ray, Picabia* (London: Tate Publishing, 2008).
Naumann, Francis M., *New York Dada, 1915–1923* (New York: Abrams, 1994).
Naumann, Francis M. and Beth Venn, *Making Mischief: Dada Invades New York* (New York: Whitney Museum of American Art, 1996).
Naumann, Francis M., *Marcel Duchamp: The Art of Making in the Age of Mechanical Reproduction* (Ghent: Ludion Press, 1999).
Naumann, Francis M., *The Recurrent, Haunting Ghost: Essays on the Art, Life and Legacy of Marcel Duchamp* (New York: Readymade Press, 2012).
Nead, Lynda, *The Female Nude: Art, Obscenity, and Sexuality* (London: Routledge, 1992).
Olney, James, *Metaphors of Self: The Meaning of Autobiography* (Princeton, NJ: Princeton University Press, 1972).
Olney, James, ed., *Autobiography: Essays Theoretical and Critical* (Princeton, NJ: Princeton University Press, 1980).

Paige, D.D., ed., *Letters of Ezra Pound 1907–1941* (London: Faber & Faber, 1951).

Parker, Rozsika, *The Subversive Stitch: Embroidery and the Making of the Feminine* (London: I.B. Tauris, 2010).

Parmar, Sandeep, *Reading Mina Loy's Autobiographies: Myth of the Modern Woman* (London: Bloomsbury Academic, 2013).

Parsons, Deborah L., *Streetwalking the Metropolis: Women, the City and Modernity* (Oxford: Oxford University Press, 2003).

Pascal, Roy, *Design and Truth in Autobiography* (Cambridge, MA: Harvard University Press, 1960).

Pender, Liz and Cathryn Setz, eds., *Shattered Objects: Djuna Barnes's Modernism* (Pennsylvania: Pennsylvania University Press, 2019).

Perloff, Marjorie, 'The Invention of Collage', in Jeanine Parisier Plottel ed., *Collage* (New York: New York Literary Forum, 1983), p. 5.

Plumb, Cheryl, *Fancy's Craft: Art and Identity in the Early Works of Djuna Barnes* (New Jersey: Associated University Presses, 1986).

Poggi, Christine, *In Defiance of Painting: Cubism, Futurism and the Invention of Collage* (New Haven: Yale University Press, 1992).

Polkey, Pauline, ed., *Women's Lives into Print: The Theory, Practice and Writing of Feminist Auto/Biography* (Basingstoke: Macmillan, 1999).

Raitt, Suzanne, 'The Rhetoric of Efficiency in Early Modernism', *Modernism/Modernity*, 13.1 (January 2006), 835–51

Ray, Man, *Portraits, Paris – Hollywood – Paris*, éd. by Clément Chéroux (Paris: Centre Pompidou, 2010).

Reilly, Eliza Jane, 'Elsa von Freytag-Loringhoven', *Women's Art Journal*, 18.1 (Spring Summer 1997), 26–33.

Reiss, Robert, '"My Baroness": Elsa von Freytag-Loringhoven', in Kuenzli ed., *New York Dada* (New York: Willis Locker and Owens, 1996), pp. 81–101.

Roberts, Mary Louise, *Civilisation without Sexes: Reconstructing Gender in Postwar France, 1917–1927* (Chicago: University of Chicago Press, 1994).

Rose, Jacqueline, *Sexuality in the Field of Vision* (London: Verso, 2005).

Russo, Mary J., *The Female Grotesque: Risk, Excess, and Modernity* (London: Routledge, 1994).

Sanouillet, Michel and Elmer Peterson, eds., *The Essential Writings of Marcel Duchamp*, Marchand du Sel, Salt Seller (London: Thames & Hudson, 1975).

Sawelson-Gorse, Naomi, ed., *Women in Dada: Essays on Sex, Gender, and Identity* (Cambridge, MA: MIT Press, 2001).

Schapiro, Miriam and Melissa Meyer, 'Waste Not Want Not: An Inquiry into What Women Saved and Assembled – FEMMAGE', *Heresies I*, 4 (Winter 1977–8), 66–69.

Schneidau, Herbert. N., *Walking Giants: The Presence of the Past in Modernism* (Oxford: Oxford University Press, 1991).

Scott, Bonnie Kime and Mary Lynn Broe, eds., *The Gender of Modernism: A Critical Anthology* (Bloomington, IN: Indiana University Press, 1990).

Scott, James C., *Seeing Like a State: How Certain Schemes to Improve the Human Condition Have Failed* (New Haven, CT: Yale University Press, 1998).

Schwarz, Arturo, *New York Dada: Duchamp, Man Ray, Picabia*, ed. by Armin Zweite and others (Munich: Prestel, 1973).

Scott, Bonnie Kime, *Refiguring Modernism*, Vol. 2, Postmodern Feminist Readings of Woolf, West and Barnes (Bloomington, IN: Indiana University Press, 1995).

Shapiro, Meyer, *Modern Art, 19th and 20th Centuries: Selected Papers* (New York: George Braziller, 1978).

Simmel, Georg, *On Individuality and Social Forms*, ed. by Donald N. Levine (Chicago, IL: The University of Chicago Press, 1971).

Simmel, Georg, *The Philosophy of Money*, ed. by David Frisby, trans. by Tom Bottomore and David Frisby, 3rd edn (London: Routledge, 2004).

Smith, Sidonie, *A Poetics of Women's Autobiography: Marginality and the Fiction of Self-Representation* (Bloomington, IN: Indiana University Press, 1987).

Smith, Sidonie, 'Bodies of Evidence: Jenny Saville, Faith Ringgold, and Janine Antoni Weigh In', in Smith and Watson eds., *Interfaces* (Ann Arbor, MI: University of Michigan Press, 2002), pp. 132–59.

Smith, Sidonie and Julie Watson, eds., *Women, Autobiography, Theory: A Reader* (London: University of Wisconsin Press, 1998).

Smith, Sidonie and Julie Watson, eds., *Interfaces: Women, Autobiography, Image, Performance* (Ann Arbor, MI: University of Michigan Press, 2002).

Smith, Stan, *The Origins of Modernism; Eliot, Pound, Yeats and the Rhetorics of Renewal* (Hemel Hempstead: Harvester Wheatsheaf, 1994).

Smith, Terry, *Making the Modern: Industry, Art, and Design in America* (Chicago, IL: University of Chicago Press, 1993).

Smith-Rosenberg, Carroll, ed., *Disorderly Conduct: Visions of Gender in Victorian America* (New York: Alfred A. Knopf, 1985).

Stallybrass, Peter and Allon White, *The Politics and Poetics of Transgression* (London: Routledge, 1986).

Stanley, Liz, *The Auto/biographical I: The Theory and Practice of Feminist Auto/biography* (Manchester: Manchester University Press, 1995).

Stanley, Liz, 'How Do We Know about Past Lives? Methodological and Epistemological Matters Involving Prince Phillip, the Russian Revolution, Emily Wilding Davison, My Mum and the Absent Sue', in Polkey ed., *Women's Lives into Print* (Basingstoke: Macmillan, 1999), pp. 3–21.

Steedman, Carolyn, 'Culture, Cultural Studies, and the Historians', in Lawrence Grosssberg, Cary Nelson and Paula Treicher eds., *Cultural Studies* (New York: Routledge, 1992), p. 46.

Strasser, Susan, *Waste and Want: A Social History of Trash* (New York: Metropolitan Books, 1999).

Suleiman, Susan R., *Subversive Intent: Gender, Politics, and the Avant-Garde* (Cambridge, MA: Harvard University Press, 1990).

Tamás, Rebecca, 'The Songs of Hecate: Poetry and the Language of the Occult', *The White Review*, 24 (March 2019), 11–25, 24.

Taylor, Julie, 'Revising The Antiphon, Restaging Trauma: or, Where Textual Politics Meet Sexual History', *Modernism/Modernity*, 18.1 (2011), 125–47.

Taylor, Julie, *Djuna Barnes and Affective Modernism* (Edinburgh: Edinburgh University Press, 2012).

Tashjian, Dickran, 'Authentic Spirit of Change: The Poetry of New York Dada', in Naumann and Venn eds., *Making Mischief: Dada Invades New York* (New York: Whitney Museum of American Art, 1996), pp. 261–77.

Thacker, Andrew, 'Modernism and the Periodical Scene in 1915 and Today', *Pessoa Plural*, 11 (2017), 66–86.

Theweleit, Klaus, *Male Fantasies, Vol I: Women, Floods, Bodies, History*, trans. by Stephan Conway (Cambridge: Polity Press, 1987).

Theweleit, Klaus, *Male Fantasies, Vol 2: Male Bodies: Psychoanalyzing the White Terror*, trans. by Erica Carter and Chris Turner (Cambridge: Polity Press, 1989).

Thompson, Michael, *Rubbish Theory: The Creation and Destruction of Value* (Oxford: Oxford University Press, 1979).

Threadgold, Terry, *Feminist Poetics: Poiesis, Performance, Histories* (London: Routledge, 1997).

Trotter, David, *Cooking with Mud: The Idea of Mess in Nineteenth-Century Art and Fiction* (Oxford: Oxford University Press, 2000).

Trotter, David, 'The New Historicism and the Psychopathology of Everyday Modern Life', in Cohen ed., *Filth* (Minneapolis, MN: University of Minnesota Press, 2005), pp. 30–48

Trumpeter, Kevin, 'Furnishing Modernist Fiction: The Aesthetics of Refuse', *Modernism/Modernity*, 20.2 (2013), 307–26

Ward, David and Oliver Zunz, eds., *The Landscape of Modernity: New York City 1900–1940* (Baltimore, MD: Johns Hopkins University Press, 1992).

Weiss, Gail, 'The Abject Borders of the Body Image', in Gail Weiss and Honi Fern Haber eds., *Perspectives on Embodiment: The Intersections of Nature and Culture* (London: Routledge, 1999), pp. 41–60.

Williams, William Carlos, 'Sample Prose Piece: The Three Letters', *Contact*, 4 (1921), 10–13.

Williams, William Carlos, *The Autobiography of William Carlos Williams* (New York: New Directions, 1967).

Wilson, Elizabeth., *The Sphinx in the City: Urban Life, the Control of Disorder, and Women* (London: Virago, 1991).

Winkiel, Laura, 'Circuses and Spectacles: Public Culture in Nightwood', *Journal of Modern Literature* 1 (Summer 1997).

Wood, Beatrice, *I Shock Myself: The Autobiography of Beatrice Wood* (San Francisco: Chronicle Books, 2006).

Zabel, Barbara, 'The Constructed Self: Gender and Portraiture in Machine-Age America', in Sawelson-Gorse ed., *Women in Dada* (Cambridge, MA: MIT Press, 1998), pp. 22–47

Zabel, Barbara, *Assembling Art: The Machine and the American Avant-Garde* (Jackson: University Press of Mississippi, 2004).

Articles:

Dennis, Helen Bishop, 'The Modest Woman', *The Little Review* 7.1 (May–June 1920).

'Do You Strive to Capture the Symbols of Your Reactions? If Not You Are Quite Old Fashioned', *New York Evening Sun*, 13 February 1917.

'Exhibitions in the Galleries', *Arts and Decoration*, 6.1 (November 1915).

Freytag-Loringhiven, Elsa von, 'The Modest Woman', *The Little Review* 7.2 (July–August 1920).

Heap, Jane, 'Dada', in *The Little Review* 8.2 (Spring 1922).

Moore, Alan, 'Dada Invades New York at the Whitney Museum', *Artnet*, 12 September 1996.

Mumford, Lewis, 'Toward a Rational Modernism', *New Republic*, 25 April 1928.

Picabia, Francis, 'How New York Looks to Me', *New York American*, 30 March 1913.

Picabia, Francis, 'French Artists Spur on American Art', in *New York Tribune*, Sunday 24 October 1915.

'Refugee Baroness Poses as a Model', *New York Times*, 5 December 1915.

'She Wore Men's Clothes', *New York Times*, 17 September 1910.

291, Nos. 5–6, July–August 1915.

Index

Abraham, Julie L. 215, 277 n.58
Addison 188–9
Anatomy of Disgust (Miller) 19
Anderson, Margaret 2, 46, 103, 112, 155
Arensberg, Walter 54–5, 59, 63, 106, 255 n.47
Armstrong, Tim 14, 37, 52
avant-garde practices 8, 11–12, 16, 22, 26–8, 37–40, 53, 59–61, 89, 101, 133, 146, 156
    early twentieth-century 27, 132, 240–1
    historic 3, 5, 12, 27, 37, 39–40, 57, 59, 75, 105, 112, 197, 240–4

Baker, George 110, 258 n.105
Bakhtin, Mikhail 150–1, 250 n.46
Barnes, Djuna
    abandoned drafts and manuscripts 213
    "Anatomy of Night" 163
    The Antiphon 3–4, 7, 10–11, 15, 28, 157–8, 160–2, 167–8, 171, 173, 175, 186, 188–90, 198, 215, 227–9, 231–3, 235, 237–8
    autobiographic poetics 5–6, 9, 11, 15–16, 26–9, 157–60, 162–75, 177, 179, 185, 190, 192
    'Baroness Elsa' project 28, 112, 156, 160, 163, 175, 195, 197–8, 205, 213–14, 218–20, 222, 224–6, 229, 231–4, 236, 238
    Book of Repulsive Women, The 186
    Collected Poems with Notes towards a Memoir 172, 180, 247 n.17
    corpus 160, 162, 167, 172–5, 180, 185–6, 193
    correspondence with Baroness 3, 195–6, 211–13
    Creatures in an Alphabet series 3–4, 175
    deployment of tradition 213–28
    'estranged' position 7–8, 173, 198, 231, 234, 242–3
    formal and thematic concerns 78, 218, 238
    Greenwich Village series 23
    I Could Never Be Lonely without a Husband: Interviews by Djuna Barnes 272 n.69
    intertextual references 11–12, 159, 161, 171, 180, 185, 189, 193, 212–13, 228, 232, 234
    journalistic practices 23–4, 29, 178, 234, 244
    Ladies Almanack 162
    messy textuality 5–6, 9, 11, 28, 159–61, 167, 172–80, 185–6, 189–90, 192, 195–7, 206, 210, 215, 228–9, 238–9
    on mother and daughter relationship 205–13, 236
    Nightwood 2–4, 6–7, 9–11, 13, 28, 139, 160, 162, 166, 198, 205, 210, 213–16, 218–19, 221, 225–7, 234
    Patchin Place poetry 4, 11, 28, 159–60, 172, 175–7, 179–80, 185, 192, 196, 212, 214–15, 218, 220–1, 230, 232, 235
    'Rite of Spring' 157, 182, 184, 187, 189
    Ryder 11, 15, 162–3, 167, 171, 188, 212, 231, 239, 268 n.11, 269–70 n.32, 277 n.57
    silkworm image 184, 187–92, 218, 221, 223, 229
    spatial conventions 214, 220–2, 226, 229, 237
    structural patterns 10–11, 15, 28, 47, 112, 172–9, 186, 227
    'Work in Progress: Rite of Spring.' Typescript 181–4, 187, 189
    writing practice 3, 5–7, 9, 27–8, 158–9, 167–8, 171–2, 174–5, 177, 179, 181, 185–7, 192–3, 195–7, 205, 219, 229, 238, 243
Baroness, Freytag-Loringhoven, Elsa von. *See also* New York Dada

Abbott's friendship 65
abject aesthetics 60, 128–32, 152–3
autobiographic writing 195–7, 199, 202–6, 210, 212–13, 216, 219, 224–8
Body Sweats;The Uncensored Writings of Elsa von Freytag-Loringhoven 42, 99, 102, 202
body-work 27–8, 33–4, 85–6, 89, 92, 97–8, 101–2, 104, 131–45, 154, 241
Chimera 131–45
collage aesthetics 102, 111–12, 225, 232
costuming and posing 1–2, 83–4, 103–4, 116, 141, 143–4, 150–2, 223, 236, 242
couture d'ordures 8, 27, 34, 47, 145, 156, 241
Earring-Object 118
exclusion history 37–49
feminist criticism 99, 109
Forgotten – Like This Parapluie Am I by You 65–6, 113
God 63–4
grotesque elements 33, 35–7, 44, 49, 84–6, 88–9, 92–4, 97, 101, 125–6, 139–40, 143, 146, 148, 150–2, 154, 204, 207, 214, 232–3, 241
interruptive poetics 196–205
'King Adam' 101
letters to Barnes 3, 195–6, 204, 211–13
letter to Sarah Freedman 137
Limbswish 102, 115, 118
'Love – Chemical Relationship' 124, 127, 132, 141–2
'Memory Stench', handwritten draft 194
modelling 82–3, 114, 138
Modest Woman, The 64
Portrait of Berenice Abbott 107–9, 111, 117
Portrait of Marcel Duchamp 8, 62, 116–19, 122–3, 127, 131–2, 265 n.57
Readymade objects 29, 32, 65
'Refugee Baroness Poses as a Model: Woman Who Puzzled New York Art Students Reveals Her Identity' 143, 145–6
self-representation strategies 99–156
Swabian Fasching practices 103, 151
toilet humour 48–9, 56, 60–1
writing practices 1–3, 33, 206
Benstock, Shari 202–3, 241, 244
Bergson, Henri 192, 213–16
  An Introduction to Metaphysics 191
  Creative Evolution 191, 215
  l'étendu and *durée réelle*, concepts 213–14
  Time and Free Will: An Essay on the Immediate Data of Consciousness 191
Bernstein, Theresa
  Elsa von Freytag-Loringhoven 142
  Woman with a Parrot 140
Biddle, George 33, 48, 58, 88–9, 96, 103–4, 123–4, 136, 141, 154
body
  classical conception 35, 125, 148
  fragmented 36, 178
  male 14, 76, 104
Bohn, Willard 82
Brook, Charles, *Hints to Pilgrims* 36, 94
Buddha in the Bathroom, The (Norton) 54
Budington, Thurn 157, 267 n.1
Burger, John 153
Burke, Carolyn 144
Butler, Judith 145
Butts, Mary 36, 84

Camfield, William A. 56, 59, 78–9
Carrel, Alexis 213–14, 216, 218–20, 224–7
  inner time, theory 160
  Man, the Unknown 29
Caselli, Daniela 6, 11, 15, 169, 171, 173, 174, 189, 217
Cavell, Richard 101, 247 n.19
Chadwick, Whitney 130, 265 n.64
Cohen, William 16, 249 n.35
Coleman, Emily Holmes 3, 5–6, 29, 159, 161–2, 169, 172, 210, 214, 218, 224–5, 227, 235
Colomina, Beatriz 23, 251 n.60
Craig, Gordon 145–8
  übermarionette 145–8, 178
Crane, Hart 31, 33, 94, 253 n.6
Cubistic collage 109–11
Curry, Linda 167

DeVore, Lynn 199, 274 nn.10–11
de Zayas, Marius 38, 67, 72, 74–6, 79–84, 106

ELLE 79–80, 82
nymphomaniac New Woman 84
Dini, Rachele 239, 279 n.1
disruptive body practices. *See also* urban rationalization
  modern design 31–2
  New York Dada, concepts 31–3, 38–9, 43–4, 47, 53, 57, 60, 67, 69–71, 74–5, 78–9, 99, 105–8, 116–18, 123, 127–8, 132, 156, 178, 242
Douglas, Mary 17, 47
Duchamp, Marcel 32, 38, 40, 44, 46–7, 62, 65, 70, 82, 106, 116–24, 127–8, 156
  In Advance of a Broken Arm 108
  Blind Man, The 53–5, 58
  Bride Stripped Bare by Her Bachelors Even, The 53, 78
  Fountain 38, 53–7, 59–65, 94
  Green Box, The 122
  Large Glass, The 122
  photographic technologies 59–60, 122–3
  Readymade objects 35, 38–9, 53–5, 57, 59–60, 62–3, 71, 102, 111–12, 116–17, 122, 128
  Rrose Sélavy 56, 119, 122–3, 156
  Three Standard Stoppages 64
  Tu'm 122
  urinal's inversion 53–4, 56–8, 60–5, 94

Eliot, T.S. 3–4, 7, 12–14, 165, 172, 197, 217, 221, 227, 231, 242
  'Tradition and the Individual Talent' 163–4
  The Waste Land, 14
Enlightenment, The 67, 165

Felski, Rita 12, 248 n.25
feminine 13–14, 64, 69, 99, 107, 112, 115–16, 144, 209, 217
Field, Andrew 167, 268 n.12
Fletcherism 26
Frank, Joseph 221, 276 n.46
Freud, Sigmund 95, 130, 167
  Beyond the Pleasure Principle 51
  Civilization and Its Discontents 95
  Ego and the Id, The 51
  'On Narcissism' 129

Gammel, Irene 36, 44, 46, 57, 82, 113, 124–5, 147, 154, 199–200
gender 5, 16, 23, 36, 105, 134–5, 152, 156, 182, 184
Goody, Alex 70, 104, 178
Graver, David 145, 148, 155
Greve, Felix Paul 41, 58, 103, 200, 202, 204–7, 212–13, 226–7
  Fanny Essler 147, 191, 199, 201
  Maurermeister Ihles Haus 197, 201
Grosz, Elizabeth 20, 92, 98
Guggenheim, Peggy 43, 99, 136, 163

Hardie, Melissa Jane 185–6, 217
Harding, James. M. 38, 40, 123, 156
Heap, Jane 37, 43–4, 101
Hecht, Ben 36, 96
  'The Yellow Goat', 96–7
Herring, Phillip 166, 177, 180–2, 187, 190
Huculak, J. Matthew 4
Hulme, T.E. 12, 14, 248 n.22
Huyssen, Andreas 69

identification 2, 5, 17, 20, 24, 52, 60, 82, 92, 109, 115, 127, 129–30, 244
impersonality 11, 29, 111–12, 118, 164, 216
  poetic 12, 165, 231
Irrational Modernism (Jones) 52

Jones, Amelia 38, 51–2, 57, 70, 74, 78, 154, 156
Jones, Caroline A. 70

Kannestein, Louis 231, 270 n.34
Klein, Melanie 129, 211, 275 n.39
Krauss, Rosalind E. 110, 122
Kristeva, Julia 24, 86–8, 91–2, 98
Kuenzli, Rudolf, E. 127–8

Lacan, Jacques 91, 93, 129–32
Laporte, Dominique 19, 250 n.43
Le Bon, Gustave 20, 51
Lejeune, Phillipe 166, 269 n.30
Levenson, Michael 29, 248 n.22
Levine, Nancy J. 177, 179–80, 182
literary modernism
  ambivalent responses 52
  criticism 101, 104, 124, 151–2, 156

definition 7
mass-culture and modernity 100
regulatory practices 244
self-representational strategies 112, 165, 195, 241, 243
temporal dynamics 231
thematic concerns 238
Loy, Mina 27, 144–5, 165

Making Mischief: Dada Invades New York (exhibition) 99
Marcus, Jane 202–3, 212
marginalization 9, 13, 15–16, 26, 40, 105, 133
masculine 11–12, 21, 69–70, 75, 78, 99, 115, 153, 170, 240
McKay, Claude 2
Melissa Meyer 75, 105, 111–12
Miller, William Ian 16, 19, 97, 216
modernism. *See also* literary modernism
  aesthetics 13, 20, 31, 113, 197, 214, 221
  Barnes's poetry and fiction 9–16
  definition 4
  dominant modes 12
  feminine 12–14, 16, 21, 64, 69, 99, 107, 112, 115–16, 143–4, 152, 208–9, 217
  gender dimensions 5, 7, 12–16, 20–3, 25, 69–70
  high 12, 14, 26, 202, 240–2
  histories 3, 9, 14, 33, 132, 241
  late 195
  masculinity 13–14, 20, 36, 64, 67, 70–1, 78, 81, 104–5, 132, 170
  'maximum efficiency', principle 13
  'period model' of design: 31
  Woman-as-Machine and the Machine-Woman 85
Müller technique 26
Mulvey, Laura 88
Mumford, Lewis 31–2, 34, 67, 72–3
  notions of modern design 31–2, 34–5

Naumann, Francis M. 55, 106, 107–8, 117–18, 142
Nead, Lynda 74, 154
New Criticism 12
New Women 67–84
  sexual liberation 13

New York Dada
  avant-garde production 105
  commercial failure 44
  disruptive body practices 31–3, 38–9, 43–4, 47, 53, 57, 60, 67, 69–71, 74–5, 78–9, 99, 105–8, 116–18, 123, 127–8, 132, 156, 178, 242
  feminist revisions 99, 106–8, 116–18, 132, 156, 242
  mecanamorphic portraits 67–84, 116, 178
  modernism's relationship 27
  networks 38–9
  visual thematics 32–3, 53, 57, 123, 127–8
nudity 34, 72, 74, 148

obscurity 46, 150, 166, 169, 176
O'Neal, Hank 3, 172, 175–7, 196
ornamental excesses 12, 35, 52, 240

Parker, Rozsika 109, 208, 210–11
Picabia, Francis 32, 38, 44, 46–7, 67, 70–7, 70–82, 84, 106, 156, 242, 255 n.47, 258 n.106
  mechanical portraits 71–3, 77, 106
Picasso 110
  Still Life with Chair Caning 109
Plötz, Ida-Marie 28, 205–9, 211, 220, 223, 228–9, 233
Plumb, Cheryl 225, 278 n.74
Poggi, Christine 109, 263 n.20

Ray, Man 32, 38, 43–5, 43–7, 47, 60, 70, 106, 119–20, 123–4, 255 n.47
  Belle Haleine, Eau de Violette 119
  letter to Tzara 44–5
  Marcel Duchamp 120
  Rrose Sélavy 56, 119, 122–3, 156
  sexed objects 71
Rose, Jacqueline 130, 191
Russo, Mary J. 143, 152

Sawelson-Gorse, Naomi 37–8, 132, 253 n.18
Schapiro, Miriam 105, 111–12
Scott, Bonnie Kime 234
sculpture 56, 64, 89, 109, 115, 127–8
sexuality 21, 23, 36, 64, 69, 75, 93, 117, 130, 134, 166, 200

Simmel, Georg 20–2, 51
society and space
  gendered subjectivity 19–24
  individual structures 21–2
Stanley, Liz 165, 172
Stieglitz, Alfred 54–5, 59, 72, 76, 106
  photograph 55
Strasser, Susan 25, 252 n.69
subjectivity 21, 23, 67, 74, 117, 129–30, 153, 170, 239
sublimation 22, 33, 50–1, 132, 241
submission 53–4, 57, 90, 182
Suleiman, Susan R. 37, 40, 44
Surrealism 11, 57

Taylor, Julie 6, 174, 227, 231, 234
  trauma theory 6
Theweleit, Klaus 13, 67–8, 70, 73, 232
Thompson, Michael 18, 249 n.41
Trotter, David 17–18, 95
Tzara, Tristan 43, 45, 132

urban rationalization 49–67
  historical contexts 50
  nineteenth and twentieth century modes 50–3, 67–8, 72–3
  role of waste 52
  structural distinctions 51, 61, 68, 85, 89

Venn, Beth 105, 262 n.16
violence 17, 64, 167, 169, 207, 229, 233
  patriarchal 168, 206–7, 229

Wartime Act 103
wastes. *See also* Baroness, Freytag-Loringhoven, Elsa von, body-work
  aesthetics 34, 98, 128
  art practice 2
  –based practices 11, 28, 39, 111, 115, 160, 241
  corporeality, notion of 19–21, 24, 28
  definition 24
  feminist scholars 5
  functions of 5–6, 15, 175
  industrial production 24–5
  literal and metaphorical conceptions 14, 19, 26, 86, 241
  material 111–12, 151, 229
  polluting forms 9, 27, 60
  structural patterns 10
  symbolic contexts 7, 18, 241
  urban consciousness 20–5
Weiss, Gail 92, 98
Williams, William Carlos 2, 36, 47–8, 57, 89–91, 94–6, 133–5, 141
  Kora in Hell 93, 133, 135, 139
  'Sample Prose Piece: The Three Letters' 89–90, 93, 96
Wilson, Elizabeth 23, 250 n.52
Winkiel, Laura 178, 265 n.75
Women. *See also* New Women
  as-art-object 143
  as-machine 64, 85
  as-spectacle 149
Wood, Beatrice 54, 57–8, 59, 61, 106, 162
  Madonna of the Bathroom, 61
Wood, Thelma 166, 225
World War, First 27, 42, 53, 69, 144

Zabel, Barbara 74, 117, 122

www.ingramcontent.com/pod-product-compliance
Lightning Source LLC
Chambersburg PA
CBHW072123290426
44111CB00012B/1757